It's England class Barnes

MALCOLM ALLISON HINTS AT A MOVE FOR ENGLAND

I'M STUNNED

INJURED BARNES

Peter Barnes says he's not a world-beater yet

Furious Barnes hits out after being dropped

I'M NO SUPERMAN

Fans ask too much of him

OLE! BARNES A REAL HIT

BARNES STAR IN A CLASSIC

Leeds nip in for Barnes!

United ace in derby' blow

A Red revolution from little boy Blue!

GREAT TO BE HOME

Barnes stocks up

Barnes sacked!

THE
PETER BARNES
AUTHORISED BIOGRAPHY

JAMES
WARD

First published by James Ward, PO Box 822, Halifax, HX1 9FX, West Yorkshire, 2021
For all orders please email: accounts@manchesterfootball.org
For all other correspondence please email: Info@manchesterfootball.org

Design by Trevor Hartley

A CIP catalogue record for this book is available from the British Library.
13-digit ISBN: 978-1-9168852-0-2

Printed in the UK by Mixam

AUTOGRAPHS

BY GARY JAMES

HISTORICAL/FACTUAL

From Maine Men To Banana Citizens (1989), Temple Press

The Pride of Manchester (with Steve Cawley, 1991), ACL & Polar

Manchester: The Greatest City (1997 & 2002), Polar Publishing

Farewell To Maine Road (2003), Polar Publishing

Manchester City Hall Of Fame (2005), Hamlyn

Manchester City The Complete Record (2006), Breedon Books

Manchester City: 125 Years Of Football (2006 & 2007), At Heart Publications

Manchester: A Football History (2008 & 2010), James Ward

The Big Book Of City (2009), James Ward

The Big Book of United (2011), James Ward

Manchester: The City Years (2012), James Ward

Manchester City Folklore (2018), Conker Editions

The Emergence of Footballing Cultures: Manchester 1840-1919 (2019), Manchester University Press

Manchester City Women: An Oral History (2019), James Ward

FICTION

Atkinson For England (with Mark Brown, 2001), Empire

BIOGRAPHY

Football With A Smile: The Authorised Biography of Joe Mercer, OBE (1993 & 1994), ACL & Polar

Joe Mercer, OBE: Football With A Smile (2010), James Ward

The Peter Barnes Authorised Biography (2021), James Ward

TELEVISION

The History Of Football (2007), Channel M

THE
PETER BARNES
AUTHORISED BIOGRAPHY

BY GARY JAMES

FOREWORD BY PETER BARNES

Contents

Foreword

Having a biography written about yourself is a strange experience. You find yourself being reminded of moments in your life that you'd long forgotten. Sometimes these are good memories that you enjoy reliving but at other times they can be painful experiences. I've relived both over the last couple of years as this book has taken shape.

I had been talking with friends and family for several years about having a biography written but I was never certain when the right time would be. I kept putting it off and then about two years ago I spoke with Gary James about it. We had discussed it a few times over the years but suddenly we both felt the time was right to start the process.

Early on Gary suggested that the book should be written as a biography and not an autobiography as this would allow other voices to be heard and stories to be accessed from different angles where necessary. I liked that idea as I didn't want a book written that was simply glorifying my career. I wanted the book to be honest and truthful.

By the opening months of 2020 Gary and I were meeting regularly to talk

through my life and career. It has been an enjoyable experience – even when we've talked about moments of difficulty – and I hope this comes across in the book.

Something else I hope comes across loud and clear is the significance of my family to me throughout my life. Sadly, both my parents, Jean and Ken, have died over the last decade or so but they remain major influences on my life today. My dad was a footballer himself. He was a great wing-half, playing in that brilliant Manchester City team that won the FA Cup in 1956. In later years he became the club's chief scout and

brought a whole host of players through. These included many players from my own early days at the club as well as others from later years such as Alex Williams, Ray Ranson, John Beresford, Tommy Caton, Gerry Taggart, Andy Hinchcliffe, Ian Brightwell, David Brightwell, Steve Redmond, David White, Clive Wilson, Earl Barrett, Paul Moulden, Paul Lake, Jamie Hoyland, Paul Simpson, Neil Lennon, Darren Beckford, Jason Beckford and Ian Scott. I think it is a remarkable record.

I would like to highlight the support of my daughters Eloise and Jessica, my sisters Susan and Diane and my brothers Keith and Michael. I am now a grandfather – a role I enjoy enormously (I hope they enjoy reading this biography when they are able to over the coming years).

I have been fortunate to have been involved with several major clubs. My first was of course Manchester City and I would have stayed at Maine Road forever if I'd been allowed to. Leaving City was one of the most painful experiences of my life and, like so many former players who were pushed out or allowed to leave in 1979, I remain convinced that had we been allowed to continue to develop as a team under Tony Book we would have found further major success. It is so frustrating what happened to our club.

After City I had a couple of seasons at West Bromwich Albion. The supporters at the Hawthorns were superb, as they were at Maine Road, and I enjoyed my time there under manager Ron Atkinson. Had it not been for a break-in and an overwhelming sense of homesickness I may well have stayed there for several years, like my good friend Gary Owen did.

I made a mistake joining Leeds United from West Brom – you can read all about that of course! But Leeds had always been a club that I was fond of. I almost joined them before City and I idolised Eddie Gray when I was a youngster.

As with my first two clubs, the supporters of Leeds were passionate about their club and I only wish the club's had been moving upwards instead of down during my time there. The fans, as always, deserved more.

Spells in Spain and Coventry followed before I played for Ron Atkinson again at Manchester United. Under 'Big Ron' as he now was we had a great start to the 1985-86 season and I was suddenly back in the reckoning for an England place. After that I had a spell back at City; another with Tampa Bay Rowdies and various other clubs. I love football and I wanted to play for as long as I could.

Looking back I am proud of the clubs I played with and feel honoured to have played for some of the biggest and most famous teams. Appearing in 22 England games means a great deal to me and was something I never took for granted. My father, despite his immense talent, was never given the opportunity of playing for his country. He should have been and whenever I wore the England shirt I thought about dad and the many other great players who had not been given that chance. It meant the world to me to play for my country.

I was delighted when Gary James agreed to research and write this book. I've known Gary for years and he has always been determined to uncover the facts and establish the truth about everything he researches and writes. That dedication has helped enormously and working together has been good for us both. Sadly, during the course of writing this book Gary's mother has died and so have so many others who we both know. Most readers will know of Colin Bell and Glyn Pardoe – two of my colleagues who were both great

players at Manchester City – but we have also lost Derek Partridge who was a key figure working with me in promoting and managing the City Veterans team. I miss all three men enormously and my thoughts remain with their families.

There has also been the Covid pandemic which has caused the world to lose so many. I caught the dreaded virus in April 2020 and was ill for some time. Thankfully, the support of my family and friends helped me through and I have made a full recovery.

The pandemic and the tragedies have made me more convinced than ever that writing my biography has been important as it has allowed me to consider my life, my family and my friends. They are all important to me and I hope that comes across in the book.

In terms of my own career I would like to thank everyone who has helped me along the way. So many people have influenced my career and life that it is impossible to acknowledge them all here, though many of these are featured in the book of course. I would particularly like to recognise Steve Fleet and Johnny Williamson. Steve and Johnny were important in my early career development and should be remembered for all they have achieved for Manchester City. I'd also like to acknowledge: Morten Andersen, Ron Atkinson, Tony Book, Tommy Booth, Joe Corrigan, Dave Ewing, Allan Grafton, Asa Hartford, Les Jones, Rodney Marsh, Gary Owen, Dave Sexton, Tor Sønsteby and Neil Swift.

I hope you enjoy my biography and I would like to thank you for taking the time to read it.

Best wishes,
Peter Barnes

Preface

"

If I were the manager, coaching supremo or
chairman of Manchester City – depending on who wields
the most power – one of the established players whose
future I would scrutinise closely would be Peter Barnes...
One of the most talented and exciting players to emerge in
the last decade... He is without doubt City's most
valuable asset.

"

Journalist **DEREK WALLIS** writing in the *Daily Mirror*, 24 March 1979

By January 1979 21 year old Peter Barnes was a regular England international and being hailed as the saviour of English football.[1] He had scored the opening goal in a major Wembley final and was idolised by the supporters of Manchester City – a club he had supported since boyhood. His future looked secure and he felt his career would develop and build with, hopefully, the experience of playing in the 1982 World Cup in Spain and the opportunity of helping his team find UEFA Cup success. Then the news was announced by Granada TV that former boss Malcolm Allison was returning to Manchester City.

In the period between 1965 and 1970 Allison had been assistant manager to Joe Mercer as the club enjoyed a truly successful period winning the Second Division followed by the League Championship, the FA Cup, the League Cup and then the European Cup Winners' Cup (UEFA's second major trophy at the time). Allison, renowned for his coaching abilities, would surely help the City of 1979 win the UEFA

Cup and possibly further glory? That was the feeling as Allison arrived in a fanfare of positivity. In 1992 Allison explained: 'There was a director there – Ian Niven. He's still there now. He used to run the Fletchers Arms in Denton when I was first at City and I know he wanted me back. I'd never really had much to do with Peter Swales but I know that Niven and some of the others discussed my return. City's my club. It has been since I listened to the 1933 FA Cup final when they lost to Everton. I picked the underdog and they were mine from that day on. We'd had all that success in the sixties and start of the seventies, so when I was asked I had to go back. The welcome was wonderful – as you'd expect.'[2]

By the summer of 1979 the positivity had faded as City's European ambitions failed in a quarterfinal against Borussia Mönchengladbach. Many – including several players - blamed Allison and further criticism was to come his way when several key members of the squad were sold in quick succession, including Peter

17

Malcolm Allison

Barnes. Ken Barnes, a key member of the Manchester City 1956 FA Cup winning team and Peter's dad was far from happy. Ken was never one to hold back but more importantly he knew these players from his time as a coach at Maine Road, City's home, and as the club's chief scout. Ken interrupted a meeting between Allison, director Ian Niven and manager Tony Book. He shouted at Allison: 'what, do you think you're doing selling Gary Owen and the others? These players have so much talent and love this club and you're ripping it apart.' Pointing at Niven: 'And you! You're oblivious to what's going on. You are backing this man without a care for the future. You're ruining this club!' [3]

Discussing this in October 2002 Ken added: 'I don't know what Malcolm thought he was doing but I do know he was ruining a great side that – and I do mean this – could have found success in Europe. His transfers out were one thing but then the players he signed…. You saw them… you know what they were like. They either weren't good enough or they were nowhere near worth what Allison paid for them. He had completely lost the plot and didn't care about the consequences to City… and his friends on the board supported him.'

'Ken was the only man who wasn't afraid to speak his mind at that time,' said Roger Reade, a member of City's office staff during the 1970s and a key figure behind the club's forward-looking Junior Blues organisation. [4] 'Ken often marched in to see Peter Swales, the chairman, to tell him what he thought of things and Swales, and the other directors, had to listen because Ken knew his stuff. Ken was a true football man.

'At this time City was changing and I was upset at seeing my mates disappear. Gary Owen and Peter Barnes were ordinary lads who would have lunch with the rest of the staff. They'd pop in to the office where me and Ian Niven Junior worked and they'd ask us what was going on or what we were doing. They were truly nice people but once Allison came back things started to change and when he sold Gary then Peter I thought "it's time to leave" and I decided to move on. Like Gary and Peter I loved the club, but it was changing' added Roger. Roger, an avid City fan as well

In 1983 the Times detailed the financial plight of City. Their feature included a breakdown of the players transferred in and out by Allison.

Comings and goings

ALLISON BUYS	£	SALES	£
Silkman	65,000	Kidd	150,000
Robinson	765,000	Watson	150,000
Shinton	300,000	Owen	450,000
Stepanovic	140,000	Hartford	450,000
MacKenzie	250,000	Barnes	748,000
Daley	1,437,000	Channon	200,000
Lee	80,000	Robinson	400,000
Reeves	1,000,000	Futcher	130,000
		Silkman	50,000
	4,037,500		2,728,000
BOND			
Hutchison			
MacDonald	47,500	Henry	125,000
Boyer	250,000	Gow	125,000
Gow	220,000	O'Neill	75,000
Bond	175,000	Hutchison	125,000
O'Neill	350,000	Daley	free transfer
Hartford	275,000	Palmer	450,000
Francis	350,000	Francis	70,000
Baker	1,200,000		1,000,000
Cross	225,000		

as an employee at the time, held similar views to most fans with the letters pages of the *Manchester Evening News Pink* full of fans voicing their dissatisfaction. Derek Ridgeley of Hyde prophetically wrote in May 1979: 'If Barnes and Hartford are also allowed to leave Maine Road then I don't think it will be a matter of whether City win any honours next season – it will be more a matter of First Division survival being at stake.'[5] John Toomey of Poynton tried to remind City of Peter's significance by recalling words the chairman Peter Swales had uttered in 1978: 'Last year Peter Swales was quoted as saying he would sell the North Stand before he would sell Peter Barnes. I would like to ask Swales, through your letters page, "How much does he want for the North Stand?"'.

For Peter these were difficult times: 'Once it was made clear I was not wanted I had no choice. I had to move on. It was put across at times that I wanted to move but I didn't. I had a couple of journalists ask me about staying and I told them that if the

club didn't want me then I had to move on for the sake of my career. I didn't want to leave but I had to and instead of spending a decade in the City first team and helping the club find sustained success I had to look for a club with similar ambition. If it had been my choice I would never have moved. City was – and still is – my team. It's as simple as that.'

In 1965 the arrival of Joe Mercer as manager and Malcolm Allison as coach had resurrected the club after a few years of struggle, but in 1979 the second coming of Malcolm Allison changed the entire direction of the club for the worst. Newspaper articles talked of 'Trouble-torn Manchester City' and 'another crisis-filled week' with players demanding clear the air meetings.[6] City began to lose pace. For the fans the departure of heroes like Asa Hartford, Brian Kidd, Dave Watson, Gary Owen and Peter Barnes was depressing. As a footballer Peter looked for the positives but his sporting life was never to be the same again.

[1] 'Barnes asks fans: Treat me gently', *Daily Mirror*, November 16, 1977, 32.
[2] Interview with Malcolm Allison by Gary James in 1992 at Malcolm's flat in Yarm. Unless otherwise stated all subsequent Allison quotes come from this interview.
[3] Interview with Ken Barnes by Gary James on 24 October 2002 in the Blue Room at Maine Road. Unless otherwise stated all subsequent Ken Barnes quotes come from this interview.
[4] Interview with Roger Reade by Gary James in February 2020. Unless otherwise stated all subsequent Reade quotes come from this interview.
[5] 'Pink Postbag', *Manchester Evening News Pink*, 5 May 1979, 7.
[6] For example 'Hartford Showdown', *Sunday Mirror*, March 25, 1979, 47; 'Axed England star's future in the balance', *Daily Mirror*, March 24, 1979, back page; 'City sensation', *Manchester Evening News*, undated cutting in Peter Barnes' collection assumed to be April 19, 1979.

Above: Peter, Keith, Michael and Diane on a family holiday in 1967.
Right: Peter on the beach at Blackpool.

Chapter One

BORN INTO FOOTBALL

> " Football is not a negative game. I remember listening to a coach one day telling young lads to stop the other side scoring that way you won't lose. I said, 'yeah, and you won't win either!' Football's about entertainment, excitement and goals. Every player should be encouraged to open up play, not kill it off. My philosophy is simple – you can do anything at all on a football field at a given moment, so try things out. If you have an idea, try it. Don't be afraid. Don't follow the rules of how not to concede a goal, follow the belief that you can do something exciting, or that you can help another player shine. "

KEN BARNES interviewed by Gary James for *In Search of the Blues*, Manchester City v Newcastle United match programme, 1 May 2004

Peter Barnes was born into a footballing family in June 1957. He was the third child of Ken and Jean Barnes and from the moment he was born football was of immense importance to the Barnes family. Peter's father Ken was a current member of the Manchester City team, having arrived at City in May 1950. He was often described as 'the best uncapped wing half' of all time. He was unfortunate not to play for England with some, including Ken himself, believing there was a FA bias towards certain clubs, predominantly in the south. This is a view that fellow professionals, including team mates Johnny Hart, Fionan Fagan, Bert Trautmann and Johnny Williamson have all expressed in interviews in the decades since Ken's playing days. [1] Overwhelmingly, playing colleagues of Ken's believed his non-selection was as a result of bias within the FA selection committee to players from their preferred clubs and it is clear that Ken was certainly equal if not better than many players featuring for England in his position during the fifties. Whatever the politics, Ken was a consistently great City player.

Ken's first appearance for City came in January 1952 but, surprisingly, he didn't get another chance to impress until the second match of the 1954-55 season. Manager Les McDowall was tinkering with his new deep-lying centre forward tactical innovation and coach Fred Tilson and centre-forward Don Revie felt Barnes would help to make it succeed. The plan – ultimately dubbed the Revie Plan - came into force on Saturday 21 August 1954 at Preston. City were thrashed 5-0 with goalkeeper Bert Trautmann playing brilliantly to keep the score down. The next game saw Sheffield United arrive at Maine Road hopeful of victory. They left smarting after a thrilling 5-2 City win. Johnny Williamson believed the difference was Ken: 'The Plan evolved really. It was developed in the reserves but it wasn't one of those ideas that can be pinpointed to one particular day. In the reserves it was working with me and Ken Barnes, but when it was tried in the first team with Don Revie we got beat 5-0 at Preston. Then they

played Ken in the first team with Don and it clicked. You see it needed the two players, and Ken was the difference. Then there was no stopping it.' [2]

Williamson was right. Ken had been unable to command a first team place since arriving in 1950, but had been selected by McDowall to play as an attacking wing-half. With Revie playing as a deep-lying centre-forward, Ken was used to attack, distribute, and link up with Revie. The two worked together perfectly. Ken explained in December 2004 that Les McDowall had actually come close to dropping the Plan: 'I remember him talking with Fred Tilson and he wasn't convinced it'd work. He tried it against Preston and City lost 5-0. It was almost scrapped but Don Revie, apparently, stressed to McDowall that it had worked so well in the reserves because of my part in it. He urged him to give me a go. I played against Sheffield United and the Plan worked like a dream. From then on I became a regular and we started to get noticed as a team – it was a true team effort. Other sides had no idea how to combat it. They tried to get their wing half to mark Don but it still seemed to leave a man spare somewhere else.'

The plan did not simply involve one or two players, it was a real team strategy. Even Bert Trautmann was expected to play his part by making long, accurate throws to Revie, who would quickly provide a short pass to Ken. Revie would move forward, with Ken holding on to the ball while his colleague moved into position, then Ken would push the ball forward down the touchline for Revie to latch onto. By this point the opposition would already be confused. With Revie unmarked, he would be able to head for goal in relative freedom. It sounds incredibly simple, yet it worked and completely bamboozled many of the club's opponents. Few knew how to handle it. Players would be told to mark by numbers, but with a deep number nine confusion reigned. Williamson: 'Other teams had no idea how to counteract the plan. It surprised everyone and some of the other teams just could not work it out. Don't forget though that the quality of the players had a lot to do with it. Don and Ken were two exceptional players. Everyone knew that.

'People used to go on about the 'Revie Plan' but Don used to tell them it wasn't 'his' it was the team's. In particularly he used to tell them how vital Ken was. It wouldn't have worked without Ken, and Don made sure they all knew that.'

In 1955 the Revie Plan helped City reach the FA Cup final, where Jimmy Meadows was injured causing the club to play most of the final with only ten men. The following year, a year before Peter's birth, City returned to Wembley again. This time they won the FA Cup in dramatic fashion. With Ken's help they defeated Birmingham City 3-1 in a final that became

Keith Barnes in 1956 playing with the FA Cup after dad had won it with Manchester City.

Manchester City training (left to right): Roy Clarke, Ken Barnes, Dave Ewing, Bobby Johnstone and Billy McAdams.

The wedding of Peter's parents Ken and Jean. The man on the right (above) is Ken's team-mate, Manchester City captain Roy Paul.

known as the Trautmann Final, following a horrific injury to the City 'keeper which became commonly recognised as a broken neck. Trautmann, despite significant pain, played on for the final seventeen minutes of the game.

The first season after Peter's birth, Ken appeared in 39 League games, scoring eleven as City finished fifth. Three of those goals came in an extraordinary game against Everton on 7 December 1957 when Ken became only the third person to successfully convert three penalties in a Division One game, as City defeated Everton 6-2. Albert Dunlop, who later became a City scout working for Barnes, was the Everton 'keeper that day and Barnes remembered facing Dunlop for each attempt: 'I stuck one to the left, one to the right and he was so confused by the time the third award arrived that I could have back-heeled it in!' The great mid-fifties team was breaking up by this time and Ken began to take on the role of the experienced older professional, ultimately becoming the club captain.

Peter was born into this footballing world: 'I suppose the first thing I can remember was living in a Manchester City club house in Burnage. I only remember odd bits about that house and that time because Dad got a transfer to Wrexham as player-manager in May 1961. but I do remember that I went to a nursery called Green End Nursery School. They had a fete one Easter and I ran off because I was so shy. I couldn't stand the people all looking at me. We were all dressed up and everybody

was looking and I couldn't cope with the attention, so I ran off.'

Ken and Jean, Peter's parents, met at the Parkside Hotel, close to City's Maine Road stadium: 'Mum was a singer and Dad back then was in digs with Dave Ewing, close to the ground. After games the players would go back to the Parkside for a drink and upstairs there used to be like a cabaret show. Mum was up there singing and dad, Dave Ewing and some of the others would have been in the audience. Dad somehow got chatting to mum and the rest is history.

'My mum's parents, Fred and Ethel, lived in Moss Side in a typical terraced house with an outside toilet. The house was

Right: Peter's Grandad Fred.

25

demolished as part of the slum clearance programme. They both grew up in Moss Side and Fred was a plumber and Ethel was a seamstress. She made table cloths, handkerchiefs and things like that. I have a memory of being dropped off at their house by dad and it seemed like row after row of terraced houses. All the women were out cleaning their steps with one of those donkey stones they used to use. All proud women, making sure their houses were spotless. All the doors were open and my Nana Ethel's mum, Nana Rose lived opposite and they'd say "go over and see Nana Rose, or Great Nana Rose." She seemed very old at the time. She always had a hair net on, like Ena Sharples in Coronation Street. Everyone seemed to know each other and were in and out of each other's houses.'

Peter's grandparents remained in Manchester living their lives while the Barnes family moved to Wrexham: 'I have an older sister Susan, who is five years older than me, then Keith who is two years older than me, then Michael, who is a couple of years younger and then Diane, about six years younger than me. She was born in Wrexham. Dad had about 5 years as manager and they were quite successful years, winning promotion. Living across from us in Wrexham was Cliff Lloyd, the Wrexham secretary who was also be the Professional Footballers' Association secretary, later Chief Executive before Gordon Taylor. John Lloyd, a referee, was another neighbour.'

Wrexham became the growing Barnes' family home for most of the 1960s as Ken's career at Wrexham developed. Football remained important. Peter: 'Football was everything to us. Me and my brothers played it all the time. One day though

Right: Dad Ken in the red of Wrexham.

I went missing. My mum had to call the police because I couldn't be found anywhere on the streets around where we lived. I was about four, so not long after we'd moved, and there was a night match that night at Wrexham. The Racecourse Ground was about 3 miles from where we lived but that's where I turned up. I'd walked all the way to the ground. I even asked someone where it was – and they told me! Instead of questioning why a four year old was toddling off towards a football ground, they pointed the direction to me.

'I arrived at the ground and the secretary came out: "Peter – you're four. What are you doing walking here?" my dad heard what was going on and rushed out, "what are you doing here? How did you get here?" I just told him that I'd walked. I just wanted to watch my dad play football in that brilliant red Wrexham kit of the time.

'I remember seeing my dad play in a couple of games when I was about four. I couldn't tell you much about how he played then but I do remember thinking he was a loud bugger! Always shouting for the ball. Always involved. Always wanting to wear the number four shirt with his bandy legs. He was a skinny bloke who wanted to have every ball. He shouted at every player throughout the game – "Man on; Hold it; Give it here; I'm free; I'll have it; One-two…." He ate, slept and breathed football. He's the only man I know – perhaps Pep Guardiola is similar – that football was everything and he lived every ball. If dad was alive now and met Pep I think they'd get on because they are both so enthusiastic about the game. Dad was so keen.'

Ken Barnes had assembled a good team at Wrexham and for Peter this footballing life appealed: 'My older brother Keith loved

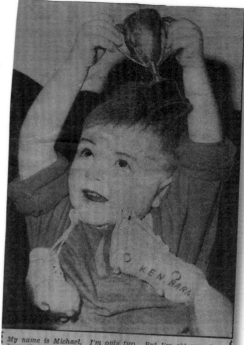

My name is Michael. I'm only two. But I'm old enough to know that Wrexham are the best football side in the world. I'm their No. 1 supporter and I should know. My dad is Ken Barnes, captain and manager of Wrexham. On Saturday they play Liverpool in the third round of the Cup – . . and I know we are going to win. Soon my dad will be doing just what I'm doing now (I hope). 'Cos Wrexham are "Up for the Cup."

playing and so me and then my younger brother Michael would get involved. Back then we all played in the streets without a care in the world. If we had a football great, but if not we'd get a tennis ball, or one of those plastic balls with holes in. We'd take them to school and be kicking them as we walked. We'd play every minute possible. Nothing would stop us. I was rubbish at cricket, although I got into the school team, and at rugby I'd try to avoid getting thumped, but football was my sport. It was everybody's back then.

'Everything had been going well for the family in Wrexham but then dad got the sack, as you do in football. He'd got them from the Third Division to the Second but sooner or later football managers know they're going to be sacked and that was it.'

Ken had brief spells at Bangor City and then Witton Albion: 'Dad's chairman was an insurance man. An older respectable guy. Distinguished - a bit like Albert and Eric Alexander at City – and I used to go with Dad sometimes. I'd hang around the dressing rooms and he had some good players. It was a decent standard and I remember matchdays you'd hear dad... The crowd won't have been too big and so dad's voice would boom out. He'd be on the pitch as a player manager and you'd hear that strong Brummy accent, littered with swear words. It was all passion. That's how it was. I remember seeing him in the dressing room at half-time, smoking a cigarette, reliving the match with each player. I'd have a cup of tea sat on the bench with my brother Keith and dad would be pacing up and down, telling the players what they had done right or what had gone wrong. He was backwards and forwards, showing them what to do. He never stopped talking and we sat there watching and listening. Dad would play every pass and every moment.

'Dad was full on. So passionate about football. At home it was different. He wasn't there that much because his life was football. He'd be off scouting if he had a free moment and he did what he wanted to do – football.'

Despite his passion for the game furthering his managerial career seemed unlikely for Ken and after Witton Ken had to look for other opportunities. The family moved back to Manchester and Ken performed a variety of administrative jobs outside of football: 'He was working for Jack Walker, the guy who eventually bankrolled Blackburn's Premier League success, in the steel industry and we moved to Chorlton. Our house backed on to my school – Chorlton High Upper School. It has since been demolished and replaced by houses, but that was my school. Nearby lived Joe

Mercer, Matt Busby, Denis Law, George Best…. Nowadays players live way out in the country but back then footballers lived in the suburbs, fairly close to the ground. Nice houses but still what you'd see as part of Manchester rather than leafy Cheshire. It was a good life for the players but nothing like the money they get today.

'Growing up in Chorlton was great for me. We were on a cul-de-sac and there weren't that many cars so we could play in the street. We lived in a moderate semi in a nice area of Manchester with a garden and so on. We could play football anywhere – the garden, the street, the school playing fields backing on to our house. If we played in the street we'd often get in trouble – I remember putting a window or two through with wayward shots. You'd quickly disappear when that happened! Our gateposts were usually the goals and our poor neighbour across the road had no choice and we used her posts as the other goals. We'd play three/four-a-side and it would last all day. Only ending when mum would call "your tea's ready" or "you've got school tomorrow and it's getting dark!" If someone's mum called them in for tea early you'd then be juggling the teams again to make them fair, or you'd be whinging at your mum telling her that the teams were now not balanced.

'I'd walk to school with my two brothers with my school blazer on and I'd have a tennis ball in my pocket and a green plastic ball at my feet, tapping it against the wall, playing one-twos when I was passing people. At school we'd all put our blazers down and start playing. Several games at the same time, crossing each other. It would be the same at every break and going home. Football all the time.'

At Chorlton High the school only played friendly games during Peter's time there but his previous school, Chorlton

Park Junior School did win football team competitions. He remembers being nervous: 'I was ten or eleven and was so shy. I had to get up in front of the whole school. The head used to make you get up and say the results. I hated being in front of the school. I used to go red and hated it. I never wanted to talk in front of a crowd. Nowadays I can cope but it was something that I struggled with for years.'

It is clear from a number of events in Peter's life, most notably the 1976 Professional Football Association player of the year awards, that he was an extremely shy and nervous person when asked to speak in public. Peter loved playing football but the social life of a professional footballer was difficult for him at times. At an early age Peter was relatively quiet and shy. He let his footballing feet do the talking: 'I really struggled to speak to people but on the football pitch I did alright. I could use both my right and left feet and so, being naturally left footed, I was able to go around players.

My brother Keith was a big influence on me then. He modelled himself on George Best and, although I was a Blue, I loved Best. We were all George Best fans, even if we supported City. Back then we didn't get many games on television so when we did see football we loved it, no matter who it was. Around the time of the 1966 World Cup for some reason I got myself an Everton kit. I've no idea why I got an Everton kit... maybe because of Alan Ball in the World Cup. I loved playing in that blue but I was never an Evertonian. I just loved the football kit and didn't think it was wrong or anything to wear another club's colours – I just loved football, as did my brothers. Dad was fantastic because he always kept my feet on the ground. I remember playing schoolboy football and scoring a hat trick. Afterwards Dad told me I did okay but didn't go overboard with praise. You often see young players drown in praise and it can set you off with false impressions. Dad never did that. He

Manchester Boys U15 in 1972. Back Row (left to right): R Botham, A Black, J Harding, T Dunne, D Ryan, P Selley, Peter, J Nixon, T Conway. Front: G Barret, C Coxen, G Coyne, P Bowles, L Worthington, M Buckle, P Sutcliffe.

Peter (right of trophy) as a Whitehill player.

encouraged my brothers and I and offered advice, but he didn't allow us to get carried away. When I played for Manchester Boys dad would occasionally come and watch.

'He couldn't always watch because he'd be away scouting but when he did come you knew he was there. You'd get a feeling. We used to get changed in a wooden shack… it was awful… splinters everywhere and then we'd walk out. Dad would be stood on the sidelines and I'd hear people saying "that Ken Barnes is here, y'know from City" and I'd hear all of this going on around me. It didn't make me nervous but I did think I'd have to do my best because he's watching. Every word he'd utter would be one of wisdom. You'd hear the voice "Pete, take them on more." Nothing else just that but I knew he was right. He'd seen something and I listened. I'd start challenging more…. Attacking more. It was encouragement but he'd do it for the others as well. There was no nepotism. Dad would encourage us all with his pearls of wisdom. As his son I had to stand on my own two feet. There was

never ever going to be an opportunity given to me because I was Ken's son. Absolutely no way. I think we all know of footballing fathers who have tried to help their sons but it doesn't work. In fact it can go against you. Better to be given opportunities because of what you can do, not what your father did.'

Throughout Peter's career people would often talk about Ken's contribution to City. Some would say Ken was a better footballer, some would say Peter, but it's not something that either man really wanted to discuss. Back in 2002 Ken was asked whether he was a better footballer than Peter: 'Well, that's a question! He was a different player to me. He played in a different position and he played in the seventies and eighties not the fifties and sixties. Peter played for England – I didn't. So if it's about playing for your country then Peter was a better player.'

Due to the footballing differences it will always be an impossible question to answer. Peter: 'It's impossible because we played in different positions and at different times. You can't compare. I always worry for players who are in the same positions as their fathers – the Schmeichels and Summerbees for example. No matter how great the son is they will always be compared to their fathers. Fortunately, those comparisons can't work with me and dad. I never saw dad play at the height of his career so I can't say. Some of his old mates used to say to me when I was playing "your dad was a better player, y' know." If dad was there he'd always jump in "no I wasn't. Peter's the better player." Personally I have no idea and we'll never know.'

Peter's dad was a major influence on his interest in football but it was his brothers that were more directly influential in Peter's early career: 'Keith is two years older than me and Michael is about three years younger than me. They were both unlucky when it came to football. Keith thought he was George Best and wanted to play like him. He imitated Best and was skinny – like dad. In fact both Keith and Michael looked like my dad while I looked more like my mum. Keith went on to play for several non-league clubs but he suffered from asthma and that affected him. I remember him going green and falling off a chair as a kid. He loved both football and music – a massive Rod Stewart and David Bowie fan. He could do anything with a football. He made the ball talk and he played right-wing or upfront as a striker. Socks rolled down… never wore shinpads… shirt out just like Best. When playing Keith would get the ball and then, imitating Best, would keep the ball and go on the attack. He'd pass two or three players, get in the six yard box and aim to tap it in. Always tried to walk it in. He had pure skill but I do remember my dad getting frustrated because he wouldn't pass. Dad was on the touchline once shouting "Keith, pass the BLOODY BALL!" He had a month's trial at United when Paddy Crerand was coaching. One day

Keith came home and told us that Paddy had laughed about his weight – he thought Keith was being starved at home because he was so skinny. Keith should've made it professionally though.

'Michael was even more unlucky than Keith. I played for Manchester Boys and so on but Michael played for England Boys with Clive Allen and Andy Ritchie. He was the third of Ken's boys to go down the footballing path but I think the pressure on him was great. Michael always suffered with nerves. I shared a bedroom with him and he had a number of issues. When he was about sixteen or so he was diagnosed with a mild case of schizophrenia.'

Peter loved playing football with both his brothers and, having an older brother keen to play attacking attractive football, the experience helped him develop. Keith was probably more of a direct footballing influence on Peter than his father, though Peter tended to follow his mother's approach to life more than perhaps his

Peter's older brother Keith on holiday.

brother and he was always determined to act and look professional. If he had a game, Peter would ensure his boots and kit were immaculate and ready in advance. He felt more disciplined in his outlook to the game than perhaps Keith: 'I was obsessed with it. I knew I wanted to be a player by the time I was twelve. From that age I tried to act like a model professional. It was my entire focus.'

Despite Peter's determination it was often difficult to get the support at school: 'Mr Crofts was the head at Chorlton High and he didn't like sports. He wanted us to be all academically gifted and he felt we wasted our time with sport. He used to say to me "go and do a degree, don't waste time on football" but then years later when

I got in to the England team he sent me a nice letter, as did my English teacher Mrs Collins. That was nice but it did seem odd that the head said things like "We are so proud of you. We always knew you had a talent." Even though he used to shout at me for playing!'

Peter simply wanted to play but school often got in the way. He gained recognition in the various age related Manchester Boys teams and went on to play seven times for the Manchester Boys Under-15s before he was dropped. The reason? He had failed to turn up for training: 'I couldn't make the session because I was on detention at school.' [3]

As far as Peter was concerned, school got in the way of football and he struggled to understand why teachers objected to some of his footballing activities: 'There used to be a hole through our garden fence straight into the school field. So if the ball

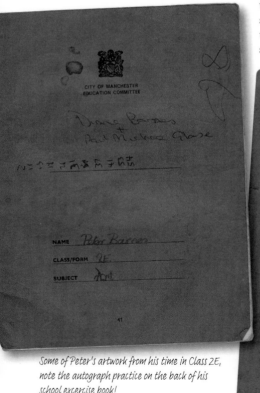

Some of Peter's artwork from his time in Class 2E, note the autograph practice on the back of his school exercise book!

GEMINI

FORD

WINSTON CHURCHILL

PETER BARNES

went over the school fence we'd use the hole to get through and go and get the ball instead of going around, out the school gates, down the street and so on. One day Mr Roberts, the deputy head, who was a large, round, really tough teacher saw me sneak through the hole to get the ball. I heard this loud shout "Barnes! Come here." I thought "Oh no, Pebble's after me!" We called him Pebble because we thought he was shaped like one.'

Peter apologised for using the hole in the fence then Pebble bawled at him, asking what the owner of the garden he had just traipsed through would think: 'I said, it's my garden sir!' Whether that enraged the teacher further or not isn't clear but Peter was sent to the head: 'I got there and Mr Crofts punished me with the strap six times for going in to my own garden. I kept trying to explain but he didn't care. Strapped for going in my own garden to get my own ball and when I got home I was in trouble again with mum and dad because I'd got the strap… for going in my own garden!'

The Barnes family garden was full of old balls and the children's love of football often meant they were in conflict with their dad. Even though Ken was a passionate football man he did not see his garden as a place to play the game, instead Ken wanted his garden to be immaculate. He loved gardening after spending various close seasons working for the parks department of Manchester City Council. The money footballers earned in the 1950s had to be supplemented in the summer months somehow and Ken enjoyed working in Ladybarn Park, tending to the flowers. That interest stayed with Ken throughout his adult life. Peter: 'We had a swing at the bottom which we used as a goalpost and then this lovely long lawn, with a border on the left with roses and other flowers that he had been tending to and nurturing.

He cherished his lawn and his flower beds. We'd be in there while he was at work and we'd be kicking the ball at the swing and it would be flying off hitting the roses, or we'd fire the ball against the fence and it would knock the heads off his flowers. We'd play one-touch. Keith would be at the swing and we'd do one-touch where you'd chip it or head it and aim to score. If Keith got in the way of the shot then you'd have a chance with the rebound. If you won you'd play Mike, then the winner of that would play Keith and so it would go on. Keith never liked losing and so if you did beat him it must have hurt because he was the oldest, so he'd charge after you and start wrestling you. I remember him jumping on my younger brother Michael and so then I jumped in to help our Mike to fight off Keith. That was a typical day for us in the garden.'

The high-spirits of the Barnes boys would soon end when they heard Ken's car coming home: 'We knew we'd messed his garden up. His geraniums were all bent and their heads were on the ground. We panicked. We started to hide. Mum was making tea and was unaware of what was happening but one of us would be on the garage roof, another down the side… anywhere we could go. Dad would get out of his car, greet my mum "hello Jean, how's it been? Where are the kids?" He'd look out of the window and see the bald patches on his lawn, the damaged flowers, heads on the floor and then we'd hear him…."Where are you?" The door would bang and he'd be shouting and swearing!

'One day he was at home and he saw us playing one-touch on his lawn. He loved that garden and it must have got to him. My sister was upstairs looking out of the window when she saw dad come marching out of the house with a knife in his hand. He picked up the ball we were playing with and

A Barnes holiday photo showing Peter (nearest camera) sunbathing.

burst it with the knife. He then booted what was left of the ball over the fence into the school field. He bawled at us "Go on play in the field; Go and play in the park; but don't play on my effing garden!" He loved football but he loved his garden too.'

Years later, as Peter's career developed Ken was asked about the footballing exploits of his boys: 'They were a bloody nuisance – football, football – morning, noon and night. It got so bad at one time I was sticking a knife in their footballs. But what happened? The next morning their mother would go out and buy them three more!' [4]

Ken added: 'It may sound strange coming from me, a professional who has lived his life in the game and loves it, but it reached a stage where I was sick to death of them and their football. I'm a keen gardener and crash would go the footballs over the flowers, ruining them, then at night, if I packed them off to bed, there they would be, thumping a ball about around the bedroom. They knocked over, broke, or

wrecked many of the more fragile trophies and mementos I'd picked up during a lifetime in the game.'

For Peter and his brothers, there seemed to be a determination to play no matter what Ken or anybody else would say, while Ken continued to try to focus on his garden whenever he was home. Peter: 'One of our neighbours used to work at Manchester Crematorium and would look after the flowers there. He used to arrange for my dad to get a lorry load of manure each year. Our front garden was just concrete and so once a year the lorry would tip the manure on to the concrete. Mum hated it! Can you imagine the neighbours or United fans talking: "I see Ken Barnes has a load of you-know-what on his drive again." We all had to walk past it every day to go to school or the shops. It stank.

'I was probably too young to understand this, but I think my dad was frustrated when he was out of the game. It must have got to him quite a bit. We lived about two miles from Maine Road where dad should've been working had things been different but instead he was trying to make a living in the steel industry. Him getting that job was fate. He bumped into a City fan called Norman Wilkinson who was the manager of Jack Walker's company. He asked dad what he was doing and dad told him that he hadn't managed to get any work and so Norman suggested he worked for them selling steel.

'Dad went on the road selling steel for Jack Walker, but you know what it's like. If you're a footballer, especially one of dad's experience you want to be in football nothing else will do.'

As well as working in steel Ken had a spell working for an insurance broker in central Manchester but his mind was clearly elsewhere throughout his time outside of the game. City supporter Paul James remembers a meeting with Ken during his time working in insurance: 'My car insurance had run out and I needed to get it sorted, so I called into my broker and was shocked to see Ken Barnes serving. He started to do my paperwork and we chatted about City, the 1956 final and about my hero Roy Paul. Ken came to life chatting with a passion about that time and about Roy. Eventually, I needed to get back to work and so I paid my premium and left with the documents. The next day I needed to sort out my car tax, so I took my log book, newly sorted insurance documents and renewal letter to the post office. When I got to the counter the cashier told me she couldn't give me my tax disc because the insurance policy was written for a Mr Roy Paul not Paul James!' [5]

Ken's abilities were certainly wasted in both the insurance business and steel industry. Fortunately it wasn't long before Ken returned to football. Joe Mercer had taken over as City boss in 1965 after the club had dropped to its lowest ever position up to that points. Peter: 'Joe bumped into dad at a function I think and he had a good chat with him. He said to dad "Ken, you've got to get back into football. You've a lot to offer." Joe offered him a job as Reserve Team Trainer and from that point on he was back and he was happy. In fact he never really left City after that. It must have been a wonderful time for him to be at City in the late 1960s. To be in that environment with some of his old mates like Johnny Hart and working for a man like Joe Mercer.... It must have been a great period for dad.'

Joe Mercer was a man who respected Ken and was always keen to ensure others recognised the former City star's attributes. In an interview in 2002 Ken remembered: 'Joe and I both played at wing-half and I was at a dinner once where Joe was speaking. He said: "There's a man in this room who has kept me going for another ten years. That man is Ken Barnes. Every time I read a match report about City it always says, Ken Barnes is another Joe Mercer." I suppose my name stuck in his mind because of the link, anyway, he asked me to come back to Maine Road as a coach and I enjoyed working with him, Mal, and the others. Football was my life and passion, so it was great to be back at a club I loved. I think Joe recognised that as well.' [6]

Mercer often talked of the entire backroom staff playing their part in the club's successes and he regularly discussed the work of Ken Barnes and Johnny Hart. The modern era has tended to forget their contribution during City's glory years of the late 1960s and early 1970s, focusing usually on Mercer and his assistant Malcolm Allison, but without Ken and the others the club may not have developed in the way it did during that time. Peter: 'Joe Mercer was a gentleman and I think my dad really appreciated the efforts Joe went to to bring him back to City. It gave his life purpose again.'

The Barnes household in 1975... Michael, Peter, Keith, Diane, dad Ken and mum Jean.

Ken took on various jobs at City, including assistant manager and chief scout: 'He loved the place. If you ever talk with any of his old mates they'll always tell you about his office. He'd always have a pot of tea on and would welcome some of his old friends or current players. I remember going in before I played for City and seeing Denis Law, Colin Bell, Dennis Viollet the ex-United star, Mike Summerbee, Bobby Johnstone and Johnny Williamson... it would be packed with big names. I remember popping in and seeing them all. Sometimes they'd be talking about the horses, but usually it would be football.'

For years Ken's office was an equivalent to the Anfield boot room where former stars, wise-old footballers, current internationals and so on would sit, chat and put the footballing world to rights. Over the years that followed Ken became a vital member of the backroom staff and during the 1980s he helped guide the careers of youngsters Paul Lake, David White, and Ian Brightwell. Ken's influence was felt right through to the mid 1990s at Maine Road.

[1] During 2002-03 Gary James interviewed these men for his book *Farewell to Maine Road* (published by Leicester based Polar Publishing in 2003) and interviewed them all again between 2003 and 2009 for a series called 'In Search of the Blues', published in the *Manchester City match programme*.

[2] Johnny Williamson interviewed by Gary James in December 2003. Unless otherwise stated all Johnny's quotes in this book are from interviews Gary James performed with him between 2002 and 2020.

[3] *Manchester City v Burnley match programme*, April 19, 1975, 12.

[4] 'Pop's so proud of his Barnestormer', *News of the World*, c.1976 Specific date unknown. From the Peter Barnes collection.

[5] Paul James interview with Gary James, June 20, 2019

[6] Ken Barnes interview with Gary James, October 24, 2002

Chapter Two

SKIES ARE TURNING TO BLUE

No one here can love and understand me
Oh, what hard luck stories they all hand me
Make my bed and light the light
I'll arrive late tonight
Blackbird, bye bye

A verse from *Bye Bye Blackbird* by Ray Henderson & Mort Dixon, published 1926

Once Peter's father Ken was back at Maine Road in a coaching capacity, Manchester City became even more important to the entire family than it had been previously. Peter's grandfather Fred was a frequent attendee at Maine Road and was actually the person who first took the young Peter there to watch a game: 'I remember being dropped off by dad there once. Just me and Fred was stood there in his braces – all the old men seemed to wear them back then with their trousers high up – and he said to me "Peter, you know that I'm a City fan don't you? Well I was thinking I'd take you to the match." Before I knew it I had a rattle and a knitted scarf on and we were walking towards Maine Road from his terraced house in Moss Side. It would have been about 1967 and I'd have been about ten.

PLEASE HAVE CORRECT MO

'We turned a corner and then he said "just hang on here a minute, Peter" and he went into the betting shop. He had his newspaper under his arm, walked into the Bookie's and I had to stand outside. He probably only put a few pence on the races but that was his thing. He came out, grabbed my hand and off we went to the old Scoreboard End at Maine Road – where the North Stand was later built. We queued up, went through the turnstiles and I loved every minute of it. The sounds, the smells… it was such an exciting place to be. Fred started to talk to me about the team, telling me how great they were… Harry Dowd,

Maine Road as it would have looked when Peter first attended a game, with his grandfather.

Above: The hut was City's first souvenir shop which stood in front of two club houses. Groundsman Stan gibson was living at 219 on the left.

Below: The turnstiles for the Scoreboard End of the ground.

Ken Barnes, Don Revie and Johnny Williamson during their days together as players at Manchester City.

Glyn Pardoe… He said "watch number ten. My favourite – Nelly Young." From that day there was only one team for me. People often think I was City because of dad but it was my mum's dad, Fred that took me and made me a Blue. I was hooked. I can't remember the game or the opponents but I do remember the general feelings and the excitement of it all.'

Football clubs find a way of getting inside individuals and often supporters become fans of a particular club because of the general feelings experienced rather than a specific goal or moment. Maine Road or the specific City colour of blue were both frequently highlighted by fans as the reason they became supporters of City and Peter fell in love with the club because of the sights and sounds experienced that day with his grandfather. [1] The bond between grandfather and grandson is different to a parent-child relationship and for young Peter his grandad Fred was influential: 'This was a special time for me. I think Grandad

was proud of that too. I think it was something he did; something he developed in me and that was special for us both.'

With Ken employed by the club and Peter attending games and supporting the Blues it was inevitable that as Peter's abilities at football became obvious then opportunities to establish a career at City would arise. All Ken's sons were keen to develop their own footballing careers with all three having spells at the club at some point. But City was not the first club to show interest in the young Peter: 'I used to play for Gatley Rangers, who played behind the Tatton Cinema. Mrs Welch and her husband used to run the team and I played there with our Keith when I was about thirteen. It was a great club. We played in blue and we'd play on a Sunday. Then afterwards we'd go back to Mrs Welch's garage and she'd give us all a bowl of soup. We'd all be piled in there having our soup and some bread. I loved playing for them. It was a great team to be a part of and it was wonderful. That was my first amateur team and by then City started to take notice of me. The Chief Scout Harry Godwin would be hearing about me with Manchester Boys.

'Leeds United was the first club to properly show interest though. Johnny Williamson, one of dad's old mates who had been with City in the fifties and was a good friend of Don Revie's, was aware of how I was doing. I knew Leeds had great wingers – my position – and other great players…. Eddie Gray, Peter Lorimer, Johnny Giles, Billy Bremner…. All great players. Leeds was a magnificent team and should have won more trophies. So when Johnny said to me "I've been chatting with Don Revie and he'd like you to go to Leeds with your brother Keith to see how things might work out." So, me and Keith went over there. Stayed in digs, went to the training ground. Got our expenses. It was wonderful and Leeds was a great club. We'd heard about how Don Revie looked after the staff – not just the first team but the entire staff at the club. It seemed to be a wonderful club and Revie was a great man. He looked after the staff and it was like a close-knit family. I think it was because it was so hard when Don and dad were players that some of them chose to do things differently when they became managers. They'd had it hard and I think Don knew that treating the entire club in a different way would encourage people. You'd get more out of everybody.

'Johnny Williamson took me and Keith over in his car. It was before the M62 was built and it took us a couple of hours to get to Leeds over the tops. As I was two years younger and I was a left winger I think they felt I had something to offer and so, as a left footed player, I was given more of a chance than Keith. I think Don thought "Ken's son and he's left-footed… We might be able to do something with this lad." I ended up having about seven trials and Leeds wanted to sign me on schoolboy forms but then Johnny Hart stepped in.'

Johnny Hart was another key member of Manchester City's 1950s team who was by this time a prominent member of Joe Mercer's backroom staff at Maine Road. Johnny: 'Ken was never one to show favouritism and I could see what was happening. I used to ask Ken how his lads were doing and then he said to me that

Ken Barnes at Maine Road.

Peter was about to sign schoolboy forms with Leeds. Well, I wasn't having that! I said "what do you mean signing schoolboy forms for Leeds? He should be here. He should be at City!" The lad was a City fan. His dad was a City cup winner. Blue blood running through the family and he was about to sign for Leeds! Well, I said to Ken to get him here.' [2]

The intervention by Johnny ensured Peter became a City player: 'It was thanks to Johnny that I came to City. Harry Godwin the chief scout spoke with me and I signed schoolboy forms. I remember being in Harry's office and him telling me he wanted me on schoolboy forms. He told me it wouldn't stop me from playing for Leeds when the time was right if I still wanted but it would mean I could live at home and train at City.'

Journalist Don Evans was aware of the Leeds connection. Writing in 1976 he commented: 'Don Revie wanted Peter so much when he was Leeds manager that they had him at Elland Road nine times, but in the end loyalty to Maine Road won his signature.' [3]

Once Peter had made his decision the big issue was that someone had to tell the Leeds manager. Fortunately, Johnny Williamson stepped in and made the call to Don Revie: 'Don, you won't believe this but Ken's lad Peter has decided to sign for City!' Don was not particularly pleased but never seemed to hold it against Peter or Ken when their paths crossed in future years: 'Dad was a mate of Don's but I didn't really know him, so I managed to avoid those awkward moments you'd have for some time. It wasn't really until my England youth career developed that I had to meet him – he was the England manager at the time and I think by then it was all irrelevant that I'd turned Leeds down a few years earlier.'

According to Don, the first time he was aware of Peter's development after his Leeds trials was at an England youth training session at Lilleshall: 'I was on the touchline with Les Cocker watching these teenagers moving around trying to catch the eye. Suddenly the kid exploded down the wing past three defenders and cracked a superb left foot shot against the bar. It had me blinking and I turned to Les and said: "Who is that?" He answered: "You should know. You played often enough with his father. That's Peter Barnes, Ken's son." And in that moment, I knew that here was another lad who was destined for a very bright future. Not because he was Ken Barnes's son, but because he had that extra little flourish that made him stand out.' [4]

Peter is not surprised that Don failed to recognise him initially at Lilleshall: 'He had never been a visitor to our house or anything but when I was with the England Youth team Dave Sexton was the under 21 manager; Ken Burton was the Youth manager and Don came to watch us in the Canary Islands.' That competition was the four team Atlantic International Tournament which occurred in January 1975 and Peter played for the England Youth team in all three matches against Poland, West Germany and Las Palmas. [5] Against Poland, England drew 1-1 with Peter praised in the press: 'Manchester City's Peter Barnes, whose juggling skills had the Canary Islanders raving, almost gave England a just result with a series of blistering late shots.' [6]

The match with West Germany ended in a 4-2 win to give England the trophy. In addition to Peter other players included: Alan Curbishley, John Sparrow, Bryan Robson, Steve Smith, and Andy Keeley. [7] After the West Germany game Peter remembers a strange situation with the England senior boss: 'Don came onto the coach to say "well done." He shook hands

THE JINX HITS ENGLAND AGAIN

Steve Curry LAS PALMAS Tuesday

England 1 Poland 1

THE POLISH plague that has left such significant scars on English football in the last two years almost struck again.

In a four-country international youth tournament Poland went ahead against England, raking up the nightmare memory of our World Cup elimination in 1973.

But Alan Curbishley, an elegant product of the West Ham academy, replied with a 30-yard shot.

And Manchester City's Peter Barnes, whose juggling skills had the Canary Islanders raving, almost gave England a just result with a series of blistering late shots.

Poland had clearly made their own interpretation of the UEFA ruling on the 18-year-old age

limit for these matches as East Europeans so often do.

They pushed on a mountainous centre half, Budka, who was more man than youth, born in the 'forties rather than the 'fifties.

It was quite evident, however, that Ken Burton has achieved a level of success in building an understanding with the short time he had to get these young players together.

Barnes is quite clearly a player of outstanding skill and once he learns to channel it effectively he will have a more positive impact than his famous clubmate Rodney Marsh.

Poland were effective on the counter-break and it was from such a move that Baran gave them the lead 18 minutes into the second half. It was a lead they held for only nine minutes.

intercepted 30 yards crossed for to Jim the ball close in. Bury were They had up front. ence tried

ed at their half. Bury of the term a stage in

ENGLAND YOUNGSTERS TRIUMPH

Don Revie's young masters won the four-team Atlantic International youth soccer tournament in the Canary Islands yesterday when they beat West Germany 4—2 in their final game.

England ended with five points from three names played, followed by a Las Palmas side with four, West Germany two and Poland one.

the Walker Cup match with Great Britain at St. Andrews in May. Also named are George Burns, Bill Campbell, Marvin Giles, John Grace, Jay Haas, Gary Koch, Dick Siderowf and Craig Stadler.

FRANK'S TITLE

Salford International Frank Bruno, 22, won his first East

BASTIAT OUT

Lock forward Jean-Pierre Bastiat has dropped out of France's RU team to meet England at Twickenham on Saturday because of a knee injury. Claude Spanghero replaces him.

SWISS WIN

FOR REVIE

England 4, West Germany 2

LAS PALMAS, Saturday.—Don Revie tonight watched the teenagers who will help to shape the future of English international football win a four-nation youth tournament here by beating West Germany in their final game.

And high on his list of successes will be Peter Barnes of Manchester City and Ian Smith of Spurs, who as a fullback has had a hand in most of the nine goals England have scored in matches here against Poland, Las Palmas and Germany.

England's opening 15 minute spell against Germany almost suggested a massacre. In the 11th minute the ball flowed from Mark Nightingale to Ian Smith, on the overlap, whose perfect centre was headed home forceably by Ipswich's Keith Bertschin.

Three minutes later the indefatigable Bertschin provided the cross for Chelsea's Tommy Langley to head number two.

But memories of Mexico, 1970, came flooding back in the 33rd minute when England's defence, suspect down the middle, left Bede unmarked to drive a fine shot past Birmingham's Steve Smith.

The German defence was just as static in failing to cover Langley who headed in from Ian Smith's free kick in the first minute of the second half.

Bertschin got England's fourth and Schmidt pulled one back for Germany.

Coventry 1, Arsenal

WHIZZKIDS UNITED!

Don's boy wonders conquer

RINGMASTER Don Revie paraded his pride of young lions yesterday.

The England soccer boss sent his youth team roaring into Europe at an international tournament in Las Palmas, in the Canary Islands.

Don's superkids slammed the West Germans and drew with Poland to win the four-nation competition.

Yesterday the boss joined his boys — back, left to right: Mark Nightingale (Bournemouth), Ken Burton (team manager), Peter Barnes (Manchester City), Andy Keeley (Spurs), Don Revie, Steve Smith (Birmingham), Brian Robson (West Brom.), Tom Langley (Chelsea).

Front: Ian Smith (Spurs), Rick Wilcox (Leicester), Keith Bertschin (Ipswich), John Sparrow (Chelsea), Alan Curbishley (West Ham).

England soccer boss Don Revie relaxes at the poolside with his triumphant youth squad after their cup-hunting plunge into Europe.   Picture: BRIAN ARIS.

43

with all the players and congratulated us. Then he got to the front of the coach and said "right lads, we're now going to do something important. Something I used to do at Leeds and I do it with the Seniors... I'm going to put on my favourite song now – "Bye Bye Black Bird". We all looked at each other, then Don got hold of the microphone and started singing! On and on he went: "No one here can love and understand me." We certainly didn't understand him! "Oh, what hard luck stories they all hand me; Make my bed and light the light; I'll arrive late tonight; Blackbird, bye bye." He's then waving his arms up and down "come on lads, join in." We all started to sing! All these England Youth players desperately trying to remember the words to a song that was out years before we were born: "Where somebody waits for me; Sugar's sweet, so is she; Bye bye blackbird." I remember thinking "if this is the Under 21s what would it be like in the full England squad?"

That day on that England Youth coach the shy, unassuming, Peter realised he had made the right decision to join City instead of Leeds as a boy if only for the fact that Peter's singing voice was not perhaps of the standard Don would have wanted: 'my old teammate Gary Owen would've done alright at Leeds. Gary's got a good singing voice! Joking aside, I think Don was a great figure for Leeds and he probably was respected as a father figure. I was disappointed not to join Leeds and it was a club I always had a lot of time for. They'd treated me well and players like Eddie Gray were superb and my heroes, but choosing City was the right thing to do then.'

The signing of thirteen year old Peter in 1971 was announced in the Manchester City match programme, which highlighted that he was the son of Ken. Chief Scout Harry Godwin was quoted as saying: 'Like all professionals, Ken has little or nothing to say about Peter's chances. I have yet to see the boy myself but other scouts speak highly of his promise – and that's good enough for me.' [8]

Peter's life soon revolved around City: 'I lived and breathed City. Every moment I thought of playing. I pushed myself. I cleaned my boots. I did everything I could to ensure I developed at City. I went down to Maine Road every Tuesday and Thursday night. We used to run along the back of the Kippax Stand or the Main Stand. Six times across the full length then we'd be inside playing skittleball. I couldn't wait to get to Maine Road on those days. It was all I wanted. All I dreamed of... and I didn't have to sing for the manager!'

Peter developed well within City's youth structure of the time and was asked by Harry Godwin to call into his office for a chat one day: 'He told me that I was progressing well and that as I was coming close to my fifteenth birthday then the time was right to discuss signing me as an apprentice professional. They always liked to sign you around your fifteenth birthday. I began playing for the B team and then I remember being signed as an apprentice professional on £6 50p a week. Handed to me in a brown wage packet. There'd be a wage slip inside and there'd be a couple of quid taken out for tax then I'd give my mum a couple of pounds. There'd be nothing left! There were some that thought I was only at Maine Road because of Dad, but I worked hard to prove them wrong.'

In addition to City's senior team, the club set up included a reserve team, an A team and a B team with the best players progressing through each level, though gifted players could progress into the reserves if they were ready. Youth team coach Steve Fleet tried to ensure everyone got their chance, and he was always supportive of Peter. He was keen to see Peter's career develop because of the player's willing approach to learn: 'Peter had the greatest skill and he was one of the nicest young players as well. He was always appreciative of the support given to him. He had lots of natural skill but was grateful for the advice given.' [9]

Peter was one of twenty-two amateurs on City's books at the start of the 1972-73 season and, as was custom at the time, they had a variety of jobs to fulfil on a

rota basis. They also would be expected to clean the boots of the senior professionals. Peter ended up responsible for the boots of 1960s and early 1970s City winger Mike Summerbee: 'The boot room was tiny at Maine Road and there wasn't much space in there at all. The big international stars had more boots than anybody else because they'd have boot deals or be given some to try. Adidas or Puma boots would arrive and I used to love the smell of the new boots and the aluminium studs. You'd pull out a new boot for Franny Lee, Colin Bell or Mike Summerbee and look at them. I remember some arriving made out of kangaroo skin from Adidas I think. The latest fashion. I went to Mike Summerbee and asked him if he wanted me to do anything with them and he said "don't clean them, just break them in for me." It was a wonderful feeling. We had a similar shoe size – if your shoe size was 8 you'd wear a 7 boot so that the leather would stretch. I used to take Mike's boots, sit in the bath for half an hour with them on and the leather would stretch. It would mould itself to my feet. I'd wear Mike's boots for a week, playing in them, cleaning them and so on. That way they'd stretch and so when he came to wear them on match

Peter (third from the left, front row) with the young England party and Don Revie (back row, dark suit, far right).

day they were perfect and wouldn't hurt him…. My feet would be agony with blisters and plasters everywhere but Mike's would be fine!

'I think Mike took a shine to me. He had a shop with George Best for a while and he used to have a shirt business too. Some days he'd arrive at the ground with a pile of shirts and hand them to me. They'd have his name embroidered in them. Some of them were in great condition but others would be frayed because he'd had them a long time I guess. It didn't bother me. I'd go home and say to my brother Keith that I'd got him some shirts. I'd hand him the frayed ones and I'd keep the others!

'I felt quite privileged. Sometimes there'd be jumpers too. I felt great and I'd show my mum what Mike had given me. Mike was great with me and was always trying to offer advice about crossing or kicking – and about kicking the opposition but I couldn't do that!'

The professionals would generally treat the young apprentices well but occasionally the older pros, especially those that had been part of the Maine Road furniture since their own apprenticeships, liked to play tricks. It was part of the traditional dressing room culture which tried to test the individuals. Whether it was right or not is another matter but the fact is that when Peter was taking his first steps as an apprentice some of the longstanding players were keen to test or tease him and his peers: 'Mike Doyle was a bugger! He'd make you feel so small. He treated apprentices as dirt. I remember him sending someone upstairs for a pot of tea: "Go on, we've had a hard training session and we want a pot of tea. Upstairs." We weren't supposed to go upstairs to the offices to make a pot of tea, so the apprentice was in trouble for doing that and then in trouble again when he didn't bring a full pot of tea. Then Mike

would be moaning about the apprentice: "In my day we did what the pros wanted, not like these apprentices today. They haven't a clue." It was all about serving your time. It had happened to them so it was going to happen to you. I hated that. We never knew where we stood with some of the players. It was hard being a youngster.

'There were lots of pranks too. Every day something would happen. There used to be a sauna near the bath – it was built like a giant fridge with a large door on it. We were allowed to use it but I hated it because I used to get claustrophobic and I was frightened someone would try and lock me in. There wasn't a lock on it but the fear was there. I remember sitting in there when I was a professional – these pranks happened to us all, even when we'd made it – and I was with Asa Hartford and a couple of others. Then we heard a noise. Someone was messing with the door. We tried to get out but it was Roy Bailey, the physio, having a laugh. Then we'd hear Joe Corrigan's voice – he was out there too. We had no chance of opening it with Big Joe out there but then the real prank happened… We heard Roy shout "right Joe, open the door." As the door opened we could see Roy holding a hosepipe and he was pointing it at us. He switched it on and we got drenched in freezing cold water!'

Former FA Cup winner Dave Ewing and the ex-first team goalkeeper Steve Fleet were responsible for the youth set up at Maine Road back in the early 1970s when Peter was there. Dave was a tough task master, while Steve was the type of man who would motivate by encouragement. Steve would treat young players respectfully and with a positive outlook while Dave was more of a traditional, forceful coach: 'Dave Ewing would scream at you and you had to do what he said. It was his style. He would take you into the dressing room, turn the lights out and boot balls at you in the dark! You had to dodge them but had no idea where they would hit.'

Peter's younger brother Michael was also on City's books as a youngster. 'I think he suffered a little under Dave Ewing. Michael, Nicky Reid and Kevin Glendon were all in the same class at school and all came to City. Nicky made it at City and I think he was more confident than our Michael. So when Big Dave's shouting at Nicky it's like water off a duck's back, but for Michael it was the wrong approach entirely. His health concerns affected him but that time under Dave must have impacted him.'

In the *News of the World* Michael was once described by journalist Don Evans as: 'likely to become one of the greatest wing-halves British football has seen for years'. [10] Evans added: 'Arsenal, Burnley, Derby County and Leeds have been leading the chase for Mike "but I've always been a City fan so it was always on, I suppose, that I'd end up there." Father Ken, who confirms that the signing of Mike "is imminent" admits his lad "is one of the best prospects I've seen." Others talk of his skill, courage, ability to read situations and power of distribution. A top scout admits: "His potential is frightening," the sort of comment made about elder brother Peter a couple of years back.'

Ken Barnes was often asked about his boys as their lives developed and, if he wasn't talking about their destruction of his flowers, he would give general comments on their footballing skills. He tried to avoid over-promoting any of them, preferring instead to let their feet do the talking but occasionally trusted journalists would manage to get Ken to open up. In 1976 Don Evans asked him about the footballing talents of his boys: 'You could spot the talent in all three at a very early age, though

I still feel that Mike, with all his skills, was around at the wrong time. Peter has arrived at the right age, with sanity at last coming back into the game.' Ken's comment on Peter referred to the use of wingers who had been out of favour at times during the sixties and early seventies. Ken went on: 'All I wanted for all my kids was for them to be happy and so, once I could see that there was nothing but football for Peter, then I gave him all the assistance I could. Of course, it's a great feeling, seeing him do well, and I still rate Keith as good as him and Mike will be.' [11]

Peter believes that Michael was a tricky, thoughtful player who could have succeeded but the professional football world of the 1970s was mainly the preserve of traditional footballing coaches who ruled, rather than the more thoughtful, individualistic coaching style of the modern era. Michael did go to Stockport County when Mike Summerbee was there as manager but Peter remains convinced that a different approach at City would have worked better for him: 'It was the style of

The sauna in use in 1968 by Francis Lee and Tony Book with then Chief Scout Harry Godwin (next to door) and Malcolm Allison outside.

Ken Barnes , Johnny Hart, Dave Ewing and Harry Godwin.

the period. I remember Dave bawling at me just because I was having a bit of an off-day. I heard his loud Scottish voice shouting "Peter! Pass the ball, don't lose it!" I think I was one of his favourite players but I still got the abuse. That's how it was. It was wrong and I wish we could go back and change that.

'Steve Fleet was different to Dave though. Steve fought my corner and I know he cared about the individuals not just the football. There was a contrast between the two. Steve had been understudy to Bert Trautmann for years and so I think he understood that the actual game of football was only really a part of it all. He used to arrive at the ground looking smart, looking professional. His coaching was excellent and he wanted people to play and enjoy it. He encouraged you to be confident on the ball and his approach was always positive. He used to tell us how much he believed in us and would make sure he had a quiet word with every player to encourage them. If you made a mistake you knew you'd made a mistake – no footballer needs telling. So what is important is how that manager or coach then gets you to move on from a mistake. Steve knew what to do.

He knew what each individual needed. He didn't have to shout at you and bawl about a mistake you'd made. He wouldn't shout. He'd make you feel good and I benefitted from that. Some players need an arm around the shoulder and Steve was good at that. He helped my career enormously.'

Another City youngster who remembers this time well is midfielder Gary Owen, who also has a lot of time for Steve Fleet's approach: 'He was the one for me. He was the one who got it going. He loved my enthusiasm and my personality. He once told me that it used to give him a boost when he saw me come in with my enthusiasm. He loved seeing me and Peter playing together. He was the first part of that set up and he is very good at judging someone's personality. I remember years later I was playing for the first team and the ball was knocked in front of the goal and someone slid in and blocked it, but the opposition got the loose ball and went upfield and had a shot which Joe Corrigan saved. As goalkeeper Joe went mad of course, but Steve said to me "never stop doing that. Okay, the attempt was blocked but if you see an opening go for it. You play what you see because others don't see that pass. They don't see what you see. Don't let anybody ever say not to do that. Has Joe Corrigan never fumbled one or come out too late? Of course he has. Don't you ever stop doing what you're good at." Steve Fleet was great with both me and Barnesy. He used to say to us "Go and play. Just play." He encouraged us enormously.'

Tony Book, who became City's manager in April 1974 after a spell as assistant, recognised Steve's skills: '[he] is very enthusiastic and has worked non-stop in whipping the youth policy into shape. The average fan would be amazed at the amount of hours he has employed on City's behalf, but because his contribution will only be seen in future years there is a danger that his part will not receive from everybody the acknowledgement it deserves.' [12]

Steve's advice worked wonders for Peter and throughout his playing career if the player was struggling on the pitch he'd think back to his time at Maine Road playing for Steve: 'His philosophy was simple but it worked. On tactics he used to say to me "there's three options. When you pick the ball up don't always take the man on. Look across the park and if you can hit a diagonal then do that…. If you can play a one-two then do that…. But, nine times out of ten, if you're around the penalty area just think of taking the full back on, getting to the by-line, getting the cross in or finishing with a shot. End product." He gave me confidence to play my own game and that stayed with me.'

Playing for Dave Ewing was somewhat different: 'His booming Scottish voice shouting at you. You could hear it miles away. He never talked quietly and if you were struggling he'd scream at you across the pitch.'

Peter's first Central League game came away at Burnley on 2 February 1974 at the age of 16 when City won 3-1. Peter was not on the scoresheet but he was mentioned in the club's match report: 'Peter Barnes, having his first outing in the reserves had a rasping shot just over the top.' [13] On 4 April Peter was recorded as the star man when City's A team drew 1-1 at Tranmere: 'A brilliant performance by Peter Barnes, looking every inch an exciting prospect for the future, was one of the many delights in the City A team best display of the season. Barnes was the scene-stealer and his outstanding play was crowned by the equalising goal, a 22 yard left-footed free kick.' [14]

By the end of the 1973-74 season Peter had started seven Central League games and scored a goal. That goal came in the final match of the season at home to Manchester United in front of a crowd of 2,191. Apart from the experienced Glyn Pardoe and goalkeeper Keith MacRae the team was predominantly young players such as Paul Power, Dennis Leman and Ged Keegan. That season Ron Saunders, who had only been appointed first team manager by new chairman Peter Swales in November 1973, was dismissed on 11 April 1974 after less than six months in charge and despite taking City to the League Cup final. There was some uncertainty throughout the club but former captain, and Saunders' assistant manager, Tony Book was given the managerial role. The idea was to steady the club.

Tony was keen to hear from the coaches about potential future stars and he called an update meeting after the last Central League game of the season – the derby match with United that Peter had scored in. Peter later found out how the meeting went: 'Steve Fleet, Dave Ewing and Tony Book met up to talk about prospects and Tony asked about me. I was already making my first steps in the Reserves by this time – I think I'd played three Central League games by the time Tony was appointed manager. They'd all come in the two months before Saunders was sacked. Tony looked at Dave and asked him his thoughts about me: "No, no, Peter Barnes lacks a bit of heart!" Steve interrupted and challenged him on it. He'd been at the game and he said he saw it differently: "Peter laid two on and scored one. What more do you want from a young lad? You're saying he's a bit chicken? That's not what I saw." Tony Book listened to them both and, well, that summer I became a professional. He must have listened to Steve.'

Steve had been quite enthusiastic about Peter for some time. Referring to the 1972-73 season a *Shoot* article commented: 'Three years ago when Barnes was only 15 a *Shoot* correspondent was standing with City's youth coach Steve Fleet on a windswept pitch near the Pennine foothills outside Oldham watching the club's "B" team and Fleet pointed at Barnes saying: "Everyone who sees that lad has no doubt within a few minutes of setting eyes on him that he'll play for England."' [15]

Peter was unaware of that at the time but he did recognise the support he received from Steve, whereas he did not always understand what Dave Ewing wanted from him: 'I think Dave wanted something else from me, but I wasn't the type of player that he hoped for. I was never going to be a Mike Summerbee. If he got kicked he'd give it back, but I wasn't like that. I always thought that if someone kicked me then I'd won and that was enough for me. Dave wanted me to be like Mike but I was a different type of winger. I couldn't be physical in that way. Steve knew that and Tony got it too. I'd rather make the defender look foolish. I loved going around them, nutmegging them, using my skills, and once I'd done that I'd look back at the player I'd just beaten and give them a look. On the

football pitch I could do that – off it I was so shy – but on it if I did something well I wanted to see the face of the opposing player.'

Another City youngster whose career would be linked to Peter's for much of the following decade was Gary Owen. Gary was a useful friend to have on the pitch as he was never afraid to jump in to protect Peter: 'Barnesy was not the type to retaliate. It wasn't him. I fought his battles often from when we first played together in the reserves through to our days at West Brom. There was a game at Carrow Road when we were in the City first team and I remember Kevin Bond, who was playing for Norwich then, carting him and I vividly remember going up to Kevin and saying "So, you've done him? Guess who is next? That's you! You're next!" He was a centre back and I'm relatively small compared to him I guess, but I meant it and I added: "Be ready, because I'm coming for you!" You could do that in those days. If one of their team got one of yours then you'd go to even it out. Peter was not the sort of player who would do that and he needed the protection instead. That's the way the game was. I loved it though. I liked confrontation. My dad was a rugby player and I was brought up to stand your corner no matter how small you were.

'I remember when I was sixteen playing against Macclesfield reserves and Steve Fleet had to take me off before I got sent off. I was going in hard and fighting with open age players – I was a kid! I knew I had to stand my corner.'

Gary and Peter would play together at various levels at City, England and West Bromwich Albion: 'I met Peter when I was fourteen and first went to City as a schoolboy. I was living at St Helen's and going to school in Warrington, so getting to Maine Road involved trains and buses.

Chief Scout Harry Godwin used to collect me from the station and we'd get the bus to Maine Road. He was a welcoming figure at Maine Road and as I'd never been to Manchester before it was great to have someone like him looking after you. At the ground you'd meet up with the other schoolboys and Barnsey was probably a first year apprentice and we would be training with his age group and the reserves. He was probably closer to my age than he was to some of the older ones but because he was so good he would play at a higher level. I knew him through training with him and he was a friendly face. The more you went to City in school holidays and so on, the more you'd get to know the other players and the greater the attraction to stay.

'When I reached the right age I signed apprentice forms and Peter would have been a first year professional. Very quickly I got into the reserves and played alongside Peter and some of the older players, like Mike Summerbee, who'd be coming back from injury perhaps. I remember we played against a player called Ken Knighton at Sheffield Wednesday. He was an old professional. Very experienced and an excellent player. We played against him in the reserves and he came to me after the game and told me that both me and Peter had a great future in the game: "Trust me, I know great players when I see them and I've been in the game a long time." I was sixteen and Barnesy was seventeen.

'We became good friends and occasionally I'd stay over at his house with his whole family and sometimes he'd come to St Helen's and stay with me and my family. That's how our friendship formed. As we came through the levels people started to say we had a telepathic understanding. I always seemed to know where he was and he knew where I was. I think that came from training together and

with our positions – he was a wide player and I was inside-forward. My strength was to pass the ball and his was his pace and also his dribbling skills. I eventually got to know when the ball came to me whether I would play it to his feet or if there was room to place it towards the full back because I knew his pace would get him there. Sometimes I knew I could play the ball to his feet even if he was being tightly marked because he had a great touch. I'd wrap it up to him at pace and, before the full back could get a challenge in, it'd be one touch and go and I could play inside the full back which would make me look like a world beating passer and made him look like he's got space all day long. So it worked really well.

'It worked wherever we were on the pitch. Even if I had my back to him – sometimes I'd drift inside a bit – I knew that wherever I was on that pitch I could turn and without even looking I could hit a ball knowing that he would be there. He was not looking to see where I was going to put it. He knew that when I got it where it would be if I was to pass to him or he'd see a space and we'd both know that's where it would be going. He was so fast that I knew that if I put it into a space he would skin the defenders and get it. If a full back had held back and given him space then I could pass to his feet and he could take the full back on.' [16]

Gary and Peter's telepathic approach was frequently commented on and, once Gary had done his job and passed the ball, Peter would head for goal. Gary jokes: 'He never passed back to me of course! Typical winger, wanting the glory for themselves. I'd go to support him but nothing came back. I used to tell him for years that his kit on the last day of the season was as clean and perfect as it had been on the first day whereas mine was covered from top to bottom! I had more yellow cards for protecting him than he had for protecting me!'

Once Peter was on the fringes of the first team squad the coaching styles of first team football and the reserves seemed at times to be at odds with each other. Unlike the Pep Guardiola years for City when the first team and all other teams at the club were expected to follow a similar style and pattern, back in 1974 the reserve manager, Dave Ewing, could play whatever style or system he wanted. Sometimes, as in the 1950s with the development of the deep-lying centre-forward tactic known as the Revie Plan, that freedom helped the club move forward but usually it was more likely to confuse players than enthuse them. Dave was his own boss and was keen to ensure that everybody, no matter whether they were on the fringe of the first team or years away from that, was treated in a tough, 'do as I say' manner. Peter: 'I'd gone from the youth team to the reserves at about 17. It was a good reserve team and Dave was shouting at us all for some reason. Remember back then reserve games could include international players who had been dropped or were fighting their way back from an injury. We played against some tough teams too – Marine, South Liverpool…. Not just professional players from the elite teams. You had to grow up quick.

'On this particular day we were playing a reserve game at Maine Road and I'd done something wrong. I'd lost the ball somehow. Something silly. I heard Dave shouting abuse then a great big scream – he'd jumped up so quickly to tell me off that he'd banged his head on the concrete ceiling of the dugout. He was screaming more than ever after that. "Pee-ter, Pee-ter, get hold of the f****ing ball" I don't know how it didn't knock my confidence, probably because I

could see him holding his head in pain as he's shouting! I was nervous about what he was going to say because, back then, if you were the winger who lost a ball you'd still be held responsible if the opposition scored five minutes later. They wouldn't think that after I'd lost it then suchabody had a chance to rectify the situation or that someone else had failed to do their job, it was always the fault of the attacking player who lost it.

'I was dreading half time. In the dressing room Dave screamed at me, telling me that I should have given the ball to someone else… on and on he went. I got slaughtered. In the second half I then played a good game. I put the ball in and set us up for a goal and then I heard "Brilliant Peter," in that strong Scottish accent. We ended up winning 2-1 so it had all changed around. He came up to me "Well done Peter. Brilliant game." That's how he was. Off the field a lovely, family man but when you were playing for him you had it tough at times. He was typical of that era but, no disrespect to Dave, he wouldn't stand a chance in the modern era, not as a coach. He wanted you to graft – like he had as a player. He did an excellent job as a stopper in that great 1950s City team.'

Gary Owen remembers Dave Ewing as more of a gentle giant: 'Dave loved the fire I had. He'd been an aggressive centre-half. I didn't mind being shouted at. You have to be told and it's all part of learning. You have to think how it's done of course, but Dave was great. He would shout but he'd also put his arm around you and say "great game today son. You've been fantastic. You'll be in the first team squad next week. He'd whisper in your ear and tell you the good stuff as well as give you a bollocking if you needed one. Peter was actually one of his favourites. When Barnsey wasn't around or was in the first team, he'd talk positively about him and use him as an example for us to follow. I've no doubts that he thought Peter was a great young player.'

During the 1974 close season, seventeen year old Peter was signed as a professional. One of twenty-eight on City's books at the start of the 1974-75 season: 'It was a difficult time for some of the apprentices when you were approaching the end of the season or your seventeenth birthday. There'd be quite a few of us hanging around together, doing all the jobs, helping the laundry women and so on…. It was like a family and you wouldn't want to lose anyone from that family. One by one you'd start to be told whether you were being signed as a professional. I was one of the lucky ones who got the good news but there were friends of mine who were told they were not being signed on. It broke their hearts. It was all we had ever dreamed of and then, can you imagine, someone telling you after you'd put everything in to it that you were being released? Heart breaking. I was lucky but it hurt me too. I'd feel a little guilty that I was signing pro and some of my friends were being released. Often there wasn't much in it but the club management

Peter signed professional forms for Manchester City in the summer of 1974.

had to decide. Before I was told I was so nervous. I worried that I'd be moved out and I had no idea what I would've done if I had. I never thought of doing anything but be a professional footballer. If I'd lost that at seventeen I really have no idea what would've happened. I had no other plan or interest.'

[1] In *Farewell to Maine Road* (Gary James published by Polar Publishing in Leicester, 2003) supporters often described how their love of City came from the stadium, colours, atmosphere and ambience surrounding match day.

[2] Johnny Hart interview by Gary James, December 2004.

[3] 'Another star from Barnes super stable', News of the World, c.1976, undated cutting from the Peter Barnes collection.

[4] 'Two England bankers', *Daily Express*, 19 February 1975.

[5] *Manchester City v Burnley match programme*, 19 April 1975, 13.

[6] 'The jinx hits England again', *Daily Express*, c. January 1975, undated cutting from the Peter Barnes collection.

[7] 'Whizzkids United!', *Daily Mirror*, 28 January 1975, 3.

[8] *Manchester City v Wolverhampton Wanderers match programme*, 6 March 1971, 3.

[9] Steve Fleet interview by Gary James, April 2004.

[10] Another star from Barnes super stable', *News of the World*, c.1976, undated cutting from the Peter Barnes collection.

[11] 'Pop's so proud of his Barnestormer', *News of the World*, c.1976, Specific date unknown.

[12] *Manchester City v Coventry City match programme*, March 22, 1975, 3.

[13] *Manchester City v Manchester United match programme*, March 13, 1974, 10.

[14] *Manchester City v Liverpool match programme*, April 12, 1974, 14.

[15] 'Peter Barnes – Crown Prince destined to be King of Maine Road', *Shoot/Goal Soccer Calendar 1976*.

[16] Interview with Gary Owen by Gary James, March 13, 2020.

Chapter Three

DEBUT

> **"**
> Barnes is quite clearly a player of outstanding skill and once he learns to channel it effectively, he will have a more positive impact than his famous clubmate Rodney Marsh. **"**

Journalist **STEVE CURRY** commenting on Peter after his performance against Poland for England Youth in January 1975

The 1974 close season was an important one in the development of seventeen year old Peter's career as he became a professional at Manchester City. As a left-footed player he felt he had a good opportunity to break into the first team at some point over the following couple of years but he assumed he would have to wait: 'I never expected to get into the team particularly early. I used to dream of getting my chance when I was about nineteen. I didn't have a career mapped out but I did think that if I could make my debut when I was nineteen then that would be about right. City's left-sided players started to disappear though and I was on the conveyor belt. When I was in the A team we'd be playing at Cheadle and then as soon as our game finished you'd be on the minibus heading back to Maine Road to catch the reserve game. I used to love watching the reserves then – we had George McBeth and Steve Carter on the wings and these were both tricky wingers. They dribbled well and would take people on – I wanted to be like them but knew they were ahead of me in the pecking order so I'd have to improve. I used to push and push myself. I'd watch them and others, like Mike Summerbee and Eddie Gray at Leeds, and that helped me work hard. The competition was good.

'I used to sit there and question how do I overtake George and Steve? So when I got my chance I was determined to make it my position. I couldn't mess up the chance when it came and I knew this. At school they'd tried to play me as an inside-forward but I was naturally a winger and that was

where I wanted to play. Players like Jimmy Johnstone for Celtic were incredible – I remember seeing him against Leeds at Elland Road when I was on trial there. He was magnificent and that made a big impression on me. When the chance came it was important I didn't mess it up. I wanted the challenge of being an attacking winger in a great team and it came sooner than I expected.'

Peter was a regular for the opening ten reserve team games in the Central League at the start of 1974-75 and was being noticed

by opponents, such as the Wolves star Derek Dougan. Dougan had played against Peter in a reserve game in September and was full of praise for him. Peter's exploits in the Central League brought him into contention for a place in the first team and on 9 October 1974 he made his debut as substitute in the League Cup against Second Division Manchester United: 'My job was made easy when I first broke into the first team – and for the next few years actually – because I was playing with good, strong seasoned pros who had won trophies and been around the club for some time. Men like Alan Oakes made my life easy and you'd learn off them. When I got into that first team at seventeen I just thought it was great. I couldn't wait for my moment and that moment came at Old Trafford against United. Arthur Albiston made his debut for United that night as well and I'd played against him at B team, A team and in the reserves.'

A crowd of 55,159 witnessed a tight game with United taking the lead with 15 minutes remaining. It was controversial, as it so often is in a derby, as the ball was adjudged to have hit the hand of City's Jeff Clarke just inside the penalty area. A penalty was given and was netted by Gerry Daly – his sixth successive penalty scored that season alone and it was only 9 October! Five minutes later Peter was brought on to replace defender Glyn Pardoe as Tony Book looked for an equaliser: 'It was a full house and I think there was at least 15,000 City fans packed in behind the goal. Rodney Marsh was captain and Mike Summerbee, Colin Bell, Dennis Tueart and Asa Hartford were all playing. When the ball hit Jeff Clarke's hand we knew a penalty was on its way and we knew Gerry Daly would score – he didn't miss many. Then Tony Book decided to bring me on. I started to think "making my debut at Old Trafford, in a derby, this is something special." The atmosphere was incredible as I started to warm up. The noise was deafening and I came on. I remember shouting for the ball and no one hearing me because of the intense atmosphere. I soon realised there was no point shouting. I knew I didn't have long but I remember being on the ball and I could see the City fans behind the goal that I was heading to. I beat a player and that gave me confidence and I kept going then I saw that Mike Summerbee was on, but I think it was Jim Holton who was nearby

and he looked like he would have a go and tackle Mike. I held off a second and then I put the ball through to Mike and he ran on to it and then smacked it from about twenty yards out. I watched the ball just sail above the crossbar. So close!

'Although we didn't score – and we lost the match – I did feel quite happy that I'd done okay. Doing something the first time you get the ball was important to me and I felt pleased with myself. I felt I'd delivered enough to justify being brought on as substitute. The mood wasn't great in the dressing room afterwards because of the penalty but a few of the team said nice things to me, so that pleased me a great deal.'

Peter was only on the pitch for the final ten minutes and, in the following match programme, manager Tony Book gave his view of the seventeen year old's debut: 'a contender for England Youth honours this season and a teenager who has grown in stature over the last few months. He didn't get much of a senior chance in the League Cup tie, being pitched into the fray for the last 10 minutes or so when I decided we needed to open up as many attacking options as possible to save the tie. The handful of things which Peter did were carried out properly and effectively. He's shaping in the right direction.

'I had a little bit of a go at Peter a short while back about his tendency to overdo his work on the ball. Now that's not a bad fault in a youngster – he's only 17 – and it would be negative to drive such individuality out of him, but we had to convince Peter that there needed to be an end product to his runs; that the ball needed putting in the danger zone when he created havoc. We have been working hard on him and he has responded – and let me add that he has an absolutely tremendous left foot, which will be worth many goals in seasons ahead.

'Like the rest, Peter is only going to come through effectively with experience under his belt. To give these young players the chance might affect results, which is something we cannot afford in our present competitive position.' [1]

Book's honest appraisal of Peter's abilities was refreshing, as were his words that City's League season could not be jeopardised simply to give a young player an opportunity. Presumably, these were similar concerns to those Pep Guardiola would have had in 2018-19 when considering the role of Phil Foden. Peter: 'It must be so exciting being Foden. Pep's been doing the right thing with him and being around so many successful international players will be doing him the world of good.'

Peter's full debut came at Burnley three days later when an injury to Rodney Marsh caused Tony Book to shuffle his team a little. Peter: 'It's odd what you remember… We wore the white shirts with the diagonals on them – a great shirt that one… The tunnel was in a strange place, behind the goals – it seemed so odd! They had a great team at the time and Keith Newton, an England international, was their right back. Before the game he came over to me and said "congratulations on being picked. I hope you have a long and successful career Peter, but don't play too well today!" It was nice that he said that and I appreciated it, coming from an elder statesman of the game. I had a decent game but it was a 2-1 defeat.'

Daily Mail, Monday, October 14, 1974

PAGE 3

FREAK OWN GOAL RUINED GREAT SHOW SAYS CITY BOSS

Unlucky Clarke can smile again after Book pep talk

JEFF CLARKE expected an angry ticking-off from Manchester City manager Tony Book when, for the second time in four days, his atrocious luck landed his side in trouble.

Instead, the unhappy 19-year-old was praised for a display with just one blemish—the freak own goal which gave Burnley a win they did not deserve.

'It's been my unlucky week,' said the young centre-half who gave away a decisive penalty in the League Cup derby against Manchester United last Wednesday.

'This time I should have left the ball well alone when Keith MacRae shouted to me. If something like this happens again I'll have had it.'

Lesson

But Book had no drastic measures in mind when he said: 'It was such a bad break for the lad that anybody who saw it could only feel sorry. He had given a tremendous performance and I was pleased by his reaction to this setback. Instead of flying into a panic, he fought even harder to make up for it.

Burnley had the strange experience of firing only one shot of note in 90 minutes and yet emerging with two goals. City challenged home keeper Stevenson 11 times and managed to score only once—and that from the penalty spot.

Burnley's goal, however, was something special—an object lesson in how to profit from a swift move without frills. Newton, Noble, and Hankin get the ball through at top ... to Paul Fletcher, who snapped

By RONALD CROWTHER

| Burnley | 2 |
| Manchester City | 1 |

up his one chance with a superb flourish.

Manager Jimmy Adamson was realistic enough to admit that his side, who have got their best results away from home this season, had not played well.

City, with Summerbee putting in a prodigious effort at centre forward and Oakes the outstanding player in the game, did play well. But at times Summerbee lacked close support and Stevenson was a discouraging influence with fine saves against Doyle and Tueart.

Talent

Burnley, though not as assertive as usual in midfield, again showed some of the riches from their treasury of young talent.

Brian Flynn, the exciting Welsh lightweight, gave a 19th birthday display that made it easy to understand why Adamson admits: 'There's nothing that I can teach this boy.'

And Ian Brennan showed the strength and assurance of a budding Emlyn Hughes.

Entertainment: 7-8.
Referee: R. Capey, T.

City's Peter Barnes shows his style by beating Collins

Bolton fall to Waggy power

By PETER JOHNSON

Hull City ....
Bolton Wanderers ....

IT WOULD have eased the consciences of a few Bolton players had they listened to Hull manager John Kaye after his team extended their unbeaten run to six games.

'Ken Wagstaff,' claimed, 'is playing better now than I've ever seen him. When he's in this mood there's hardly a defence in the Second Division capable of stopping him.'

Bolton need not then have been so guilty about being destroyed by a bulky and no less whiz, less than nimble year-old.

Admittedly, both his goals —the sixth and seventh of this his testimonial season were scored when Bolton were labouring under handicaps. Centre - half Paul Jones was having five stitches cut forehead when he got the first. Full-back Tony Dunne had already limped off with pulled muscle when Waggy ran through a porous defence for his second.

But Jones his head heavily swathed in bandages, had no excuses.

'Waggy apologised for causing the injury—I think it was with his elbow,' he said. 'But it was a pure accident and didn't affect me all that much. Anyway, we could have had enough big men left at the back to deny him any trouble.'

Entertainment: 8—
Referee: Terry Bos

Barnes in for injured Tueart

By PETER GARDNER

ROD GOES NEAR: BARNES SHINES

MANCHESTER CITY skipper Rodney Marsh was twice within inches of scoring in a dreary first half against Luton Town at Maine Road this afternoon.

First Marsh was off-side as he pushed a close-range shot over the line. Then a minute later he saw a second close-range shot go agonisinly wide.

The Blues were weakened by Asa Hartford's suspension and Dennis Tueart's ankle injury from Wednesday's 2-1 victory over Arsenal.

Peter Brnes, the 17-year-old left-winger had the crowd on its feet with some superb football.

Luton created a good opening in the first 10 seconds, when Alston, the Preston-born striker who made his name for Australia in the World Cup, escaped Clarke and half-hit a right-foot volley, which MacRae held diving to his left.

Bell put City in trouble with a pass back intercepted by Aston, who was promptly fouled by Hammond, for a free-kick near the touch-line. The former Manchester United winger, recalled to the Luton attack, took the free-kick himself and MacRae came out to foist the ball to safety.

MacRae was again in action when he had to come 15 yards from his line to beat Aston and Husband to Alston's headed-through ball. It was certainly a bright opening by Luton and an uneasy spell for City's defence.

Young Barnes, making his home League debut — 22 years after his father Ken played his first game at Maine Road — came into the picture with a beautifully flighted cross to the far post. Summerbee's header was blocked and Luton scrambled the ball clear.

Luton again opened City up with a fine run by Alston, who sent Aston away, and Clarke did well to cut out his centre and slam the ball to safety.

by Matt D'Arcy

Barnes earned himself a generous round of applause when he switched to the right and embarked on a superb run, which needed the combined attention of three defenders to bring to an end.

Barber did well to hold Summerbee's firm header as Bell and Marsh moved in.

Another back pass, this time from Oakes, had City in trouble as Hindson won possession, but the Luton winger lobbed the ball high over the bar.

Barnes was showing no signs of nerves and when after another exciting run Barber got the ball away, but Bell won a second corner off Aston and Hammond's header flew over the bar.

Luton, who had won only one League match this season, were quick to break and Husband went through, beating off Hammond's challenge. But MacRae came out quickly and bravely to block his shot.

FIERCE SHOT

Marsh made something out of nothing when he turned quickly in the Luton penalty area and drove in a fierce shot which Barber held under the bar. But soon after the City skipper was caught off-side trying to steal through on to a fine lob by Summerbee.

Litt stopped Marsh with a firm tackle on the edge of the Luton penalty area as

THE TEAMS

MANCHESTER CITY: MacRae; Hammond, Donachie; Doyle, Clarke, Oakes; Summerbee, Bell, Marsh, Henson, Barnes. Sub: Leman

LUTON TOWN: Barber; Shanks, Thomson; Chambers, Litt, Garner; Hindson, Husband, Alston, West, Aston. Sub: Fuccillo.

Ref: M Lowe (Sheffield).

City tried hard to get into the game. But again Luton looked quick and decisive on the break. Husband was unmarked beyond the far post, but his header gave MacRae no trouble.

Bell threw his arm up, demanding a greater challenge from his forwards, when, for the second time the match, Barber was able to come unhampered from his line to collect a long right-wing cross from Hammond, watched but not tackled by several City forwards.

Then came one superb move to highlight this dreary game when Marsh back-heeled a cute pass to Bell, whose drive struck a Luton defender on the back and curled over the bar.

City finally had the ball in the net five minutes before half-time. But Marsh was off-side as he pushed the ball over the line after Barber had failed to hold a fine drive by Doyle following good work by Bell.

Then a minute later Marsh was again unlucky when he moved on to a low, right-wing cross from Barnes, but his shot curled just past the post.

Half-time: Manchester City 0, Luton Town 0.

City put a lot of pressure on Luton ...

When Luton hit back MacRae had to come out of his area to kick clear from Chambers, who was put clear by Husband. Then Husband and MacRae both went full length to a wicked cross from Aston, but the ball ran loose to Alston, who was robbed by Doyle.

Barnes was quick to move on to a header by Doyle, but as he flicked his shot wide he was given off-side.

Clarke almost had MacRae in trouble with a casually-struck back pass — the third time in the match City players that had made such a mistake. But MacRae came out quickly to pluck the ball of Aston's toes.

After 58 minutes Barnes must have wished the earth could have opened and swallowed him up, for he missed one of the easiest chances possible — only five yards out and with the goalkeeper lying stranded on a corner of the six-yard box.

It followed a magnificent build-up by Marsh and Bell, with Barber failing to cut out Bells cross. Barnes ran in and called to Summerbee to leave the ball to him — then held his head in anguish as he scooped it high over the bar.

Although Barnes is a tremendously entertaining player, City missed the punch of Tueart up front.

But it all came out right after 67 minutes, when City took the lead after an untidy scrummage in the Luton goalmouth.

Marsh lobbed a cross from the left into the Luton six-yard box. Bell and Doyle and Marsh himself when he arrived on the scene — all had stabs at a shot before the ball broke to SUMMERBEE, unmarked five yards out, who had no trouble in pushing the ball over the line for his second League goal of the season.

(Continued on Page 1)

Peter plays this one for dad

YOUNG Peter Barnes, who makes his home debut for Manchester City today, said last night: "I hope I don't let anyone down—especially my dad."

Dad is Ken, former Manchester City captain, who made his debut at Maine Road 22 years ago.

Peter gets his chance against Luton because £240,000 Dennis Tueart hasn't recovered from an ankle injury sustained in the midweek win over Arsenal when he scored both City goals.

Ken, now City's chief scout, said: "I shall be away tomorrow and won't see Peter's first match in front of the City fans.

"But I've told him to play as he knows he can

By ALEC JOHNSON

play. I don't believe in being soft with players, and the same goes for Peter.

"He wanted to try to make it in big-time football. This is his chance. It's up to him to show everyone what he can do.

crowd. Maine Road fans are still the same as they were in my day.

"They give you a fair crack of the whip. If Peter makes good, he couldn't have a better audience rooting for him."

Penalty shocker

Swansea 3, Rochdale 3

AFTER leading 2—0 through Leo Skeete

the winner had come from Peter Barnes…
if only because his home debut provided
the only colour in the match. But he missed
what must have been the easiest chance of
the season so far, spooning a ball from Bell
over the top from less than six yards with
the entire goal gaping.' [5]

Mike Summerbee was the first to
console Peter when his shot ballooned over
the bar: 'I said, "Don't worry, it happens to
me in every game." At least he was in the
right position to have a go. He has a lot of
ability and is carrying on where his dad left
off. He takes on people because he can beat
them.' [6]

City beat Luton with a goal from
Summerbee and that evening the Blues
were second on goal average to Liverpool.
A couple of weeks later City were top of
the League and hoping for glory, meaning
that Peter had been introduced into a side
that not only contained quality but was
also hopeful of league success. The Blues,
who were beaten League Cup finalists the
previous season, felt that under Tony Book
they were ready to make a serious bid for
honours. Sadly that challenge faded over
the coming months with the belief being
that the club lacked a quality target man.
Book rectified that by signing Joe Royle,
who made his debut on Boxing Day 1974,
but by that time City had dropped and a
title challenge could not be sustained.

During this period Peter was back in
the reserves: 'When I went back into
the reserves I felt really confident.
I knew I'd played in the first team
and knew I'd get my chance again.
I was prepared to wait. Also, when
you returned to the reserves you
were treated a little bit differently.

A letter from a City fan following Peter's debut.

Ken, Keith, Michael and Peter Barnes in October 1974.

Now, you're a first team player who is here to deliver for the reserves. Dave Ewing started treating me differently and treated me like I was one of his prodigies. One of the ones he had got into the first team and that made him quite proud I think. He'd be telling players to be like me all of a sudden. I'd passed his test and now I'm helping the others.'

Talking in the City match programme shortly after Peter made his debut Dave Ewing explained how his role worked before commenting on the satisfaction he received from the job: 'As soon as they come into my squad I usually say to them "Glad to see you and I'll be glad to see the back of you – providing, of course, it's the right way." That's to the first team. And you get a great deal of satisfaction when a boy finally makes it. You've given him a helping hand as he's graduated. Our job is simply to

prepare the boys for the first team. I doubt if any club in the country gives them such a fair chance, but that's always been our policy.'

The entire approach seemed to be that players were pushed hard by coaches such as Dave with the likes of the more thoughtful, sensitive Steve Fleet in the minority. Manager Tony Book commented on the setup in 1975: 'A manager's success often depends on the men he has around him and in Ian [McFarlane, Book's assistant] and Dave [Ewing], as well as the control of the youth scheme by coach Steve Fleet, we have found a formula that is not only productive but is also a pleasure for the professional players at City to work under.

'The bullying and bawling which does go on might look frightening at first sight to the casual observer, but it is something that the players expect and need. What's more, they want it – because they realise that it is all done in their best interests.'

Talking specifically about Ewing, Book added: ' Dave has never needed to sell himself with City people. They've known his whole-hearted approach for decades, and he's carried it through to great effect with his handling of the Central League side. The youngsters respect him immensely... He shouts at them, rollicking stuff at times. But for him to get the return he does, is proof that there is a bond of trust and respect which will never be easily broken.' [7]

Ken Barnes at a game with Tony Book (right).

Peter: 'They did try and toughen you up and that worked with some players but not all. Football was a much more physical game than today. You'd be fouled four or five times before the referee would step in and even then it'd often be a word, nothing else.' Whether at youth, reserve or first team level, Peter was a target for opposing defenders and they'd often try to leave their mark: 'I knew it was coming. Every time I played I knew that the full back opposite me would have been told in the dressing room to kick me. Leave an impression. Their job was to get the ball but by kicking you or hurting you in some way they'd think they'd won the battle and you'd shrink. I'm sure it happened to me but I tried to win by using my skills to embarrass them. Mike Summerbee used to say to me when I was first making my way: "give them a kick first. Let them know you're there. If they kick you they've won." I couldn't do that. That wasn't me or my style. Instead I'd get out on to the pitch and, as early as possible, I'd try to drop my shoulder and jink around them or nutmeg them.... Anything I could that was about skill and not about force. If I'd have tried to be physical they'd have come back harder!"

Overall, Peter was satisfied with his first opportunities in the senior team and did

not expect to return again during 1974-75, though he was hopeful. Then in January his chance came again with a FA Cup tie with Newcastle. This was an unusual tie as City were actually drawn away to Newcastle but, due to crowd disturbance, St James's Park was to be closed and the team had to play their home tie on their opponents ground. Peter's chance came as new signing Joe Royle was cup-tied but the game ended in a 2-0 defeat away at Maine Road – itself

a strange experience! Two months later another first team opportunity appeared. It was to be a memorable one for the youngster as he scored his first League goal. City lost 2-1 to Carlisle United on Wednesday 19 March 1975. That night Peter played as an inside-left but had been forced to miss playing in the second leg of England's UEFA Youth Cup tie with Spain due to his appearance for City. [8] Peter had played in the first leg of the UEFA Youth Cup qualifying round against Spain in Bristol on 25 February 1975, which England drew 1-1. England's senior team manager Don Revie had already watched Peter playing for England Youth in the tournament in the Canary Islands in January 1975 and also at a series of England

SOCCER FOR THE 1980'S Steve Curry on the young creators

Two England bankers

At last, we've another Haynes

IT WAS in Vina Del Mar, Chile, on a clammy June day in 1982 that Johnny Haynes, deflated, defeated and dog-tired dragged an England shirt off his back for the last time.

West Ham's Alan Curbishley was just four-and-a-half years old, an East End toddler barely old enough to kick a ball.

For Haynes that was an international farewell—a bitter swansong to an exceptional international career. For that 3—1 defeat by Brazil put England out of the World Cup.

With his departure from the game's legendary passer of a ball—a man with an apparent built-in radar system who could dispatch a ball like a guided missile, certain the target would be found.

Down the intervening years Alf Ramsey, who took over international management the next season and adamantly refused to select Haynes, never found anyone adequately to replace him.

Don Revie, too, laments our inability consistently to pass the ball well. But he is luckier than Sir Alf. For now Alan Curbishley is 17 and on the Hammers' staff.

Glittering

And Revie has seen for himself that down at the Upton Park nursery Wally St. Pier, the most famous Soccer scout of them all, has dug up another gem to add to his glittering rou ... of successes.

Revie saw Curbishley twice in matches during last month's youth tournament in the Canary Islands, games in which he proved beyond question that he has special qualities that make him outstanding.

The England manager never afraid to back his judgment with open praise if he thinks it is merited, is reticent about over-stressing the merit of young players.

But he says of Curbishley: "I was very impressed from the moment I first saw him in the Youth trials at Lilleshall. I picked him out then as an absolute natural.

"He was very rare gifts for a boy of his age. His control, his balance and his reading of situations are brilliant for a boy of his age. These are qualities that are born in a player.

"You can work with players like him to produce these things, like stamina, his build; but you don't need to interfere with what he was born with.

"In the matches in the Canary Islands, where the teams were playing for something, his pass ing was superb. Boys like that

THOUSANDS of anonymous scouts, who weekly scour desolate parks watching kids put a ball around, will testify to the difficulty of isolating true Soccer talent.

The quest goes on endlessly in the remote hope that one day they will unearth a super-star. Occasionally they feel that surging excitement that is born of seeing a star in the making.

By the time teenagers find their way into League football—many are lost along the way—it is easier to assess their chances of making the grade.

What is more difficult to determine is the chance they will eventually have of playing for their country.

The World Cups of 1982 and 1986 seem a lifetime away. Yet some of the men who will play for England then are already in the game beginning the slow climb to success.

Some, like Kevin Beattie, have quickly established names, destined hopefully for long and loyal Soccer service to their country's cause. But who among them still to make a name will one day play for England.

Today, Steve Curry selects two exciting youngsters he believes will reach the top . . .

● Alan Curbishley

● Peter Barnes

Peter Barnes gives Revie a glimpse of the past and hope for the future

A CURSORY glance at the Charlton family lineage provides all the evidence needed on the part genetics can play in the production of sporting genius.

So Peter Barnes, Manchester City, had a good chance of making a Soccer star from the day he was born.

That was in June, 1957, just over 12 months after his father Ken had played in his second successive Wembley F.A. Cup final for Manchester City.

The man who paved centre-forward for City in both those Wembley matches the first leg 3—1 to Newcastle United, the second won by the same margin against Birmingham City, was ... Don Revie.

So there was a certain irony in the afternoon last autumn when Revie went to watch the England youth trials at Lilleshall.

The England manager takes up the story: "I was on the touchline with Les Cocker watching these teenagers mov ing around, trying to catch the eye. Suddenly this kid exploded down the wing past three defenders and cracked a goal-first foot shot against the bar.

"It had me blinking and I

turned to Les and said : 'Who is that ?' He answered : 'You should know that's your player ...' enough with his father. That's Peter Barnes, Ken's son.'

"And in that moment, I knew that here was another lad who was destined for a very bright future too because of the way Ken Barnes, because he had that extra little flourish that made him stand out.'

Revie met up with Peter Barnes again at the FA Cup final in May and he was as impressed with the precocious talent of the young son of a famous father.

"The usual pattern nowadays is for a winger to show the ball up to plenty — make them look naturally brave and brave enough to take anybody on.

"Peter is a compact little

player, short and not very broad of shoulder. But what shoulders he has he uses superbly, bending them in a way which takes him by people in the way the great wingers always did it.

"But he is never content simply to use his task as getting behind the defence and passing on a cross, though he can do it effectively.

"He knows that his left foot is just as important a part of his armoury as his intricate dribbling skills and uses it to prise explosive shots at goal.

"This talent has already won recognition—he scored in a week—and he is impressionably always ready to take his place in the spotlight of regular League Soccer.

"His father, the man who was just as responsible as the Don himself for the way the Manches ter City team made opera tional, is naturally his son's greatest critic.

He told me : "I would just say that I feel Peter has the ability to become a very good player and I am proud of the way he has proved myself.

"He has come about me. He knows that his left foot is what I first realised that he had this special bit of something

extra that could make him reach for the top.

"I felt then as I do now, that having the talent is one thing. Applying it is another and in this respect he has quite a lot of learning to do.

"So far in his career he has not had any set-backs. He's graduated through schoolboys, apprentice professional to pro status and it is all run smoothly. But this is only the start for him.

Promise

"What I will say is that Peter has terrific application and a great temperament—two things which I feel are important if he is to go all the way to the top.

Barnes has two other sons Barnes, the 19-year-old Keith and 14-year-old Michael; he says there are both useful players. Keith is an apprentice not playing in City's "A" team and Michael is playing for Manchester schoolboys at the moment and showing a lot of promise.

"But it is Peter, who I believe will go on to play for England one day.

"I have an idea that Peter Barnes is destined to achieve even greater fame than his determined father.

Natural

And he told me : "He has fantastic promise. To start with he has a natural left foot which is an extrovert skill is becoming very rare in football today. He is very quick and well balanced and what impresses me is that anything is the way he takes on defenders.

youth trials at Lilleshall. In February 1975 he commented on how impressed he was with Peter's wing play: 'He goes past them as if they were not there.' [9] Later in the season he told journalist Steve Curry why he believed Peter was a great talent: 'To start with he has a natural left foot which is an attribute that is becoming very rare in football today. He is very quick and well balanced and what impresses me as much as anything is the way he takes on defenders. The usual pattern nowadays is for a winger to draw his defender. This boy takes the ball up to them-makes them commit themselves and is brave enough to take anybody on.' [10]

Revie, possibly remembering how close Leeds had come to signing Peter during his time as manager often spoke positively of the young player.

At City, the Carlisle result was seen as a major blow to the club following the disappointment of being unable to continue their title challenge. Manager Book was under pressure during a period that was being described as 'the toughest phase in his career of walking the tightrope of soccer management. Carlisle, doomed by self-admission to make a quick return to the Second Division, last night became only the second team to smuggle two points

Peter's first goal in City's first team.

out of Maine Road. And Book admitted afterwards: "This is definitely the most important phase of the season." Now he has to balance the dwindling prospects of winning a place in Europe against the urge to transfuse new blood into an anaemic looking side.' [11]

Journalist Derek Potter's only positive comments regarding City in his match report of the game came when he discussed Peter and, fellow youngster, Ged Keegan: 'The advent of a new City was heralded by the arrival of England youth international Peter Barnes on the left and Gerry Keegan, who took over on the right as a 71st minute substitute for Mike Summerbee. These two young recruits will clearly play a big part in the new brigade manager Tony Book is re-forming.

'It was Barnes who crisply hit a knee high volley to score his first League goal in the 26th minute. Three minutes earlier Laidlaw had even more spectacularly volleyed Carlisle into the lead with the defensive marking adrift.'

By the end of that week the young winger was asked to take on an additional role. It was an unusual request from manager Tony Book and led to Peter acting as chaperone to a fifteen year old

Norwegian called Morten Andersen. Morten was a dedicated City fan: 'Most people in Norway support Liverpool or United but I didn't want to be a sheep. In the late sixties and early seventies City had been on TV in Norway with all their finals but I had never seen them play in the blue shirts, only the black and red. Then I saw them on TV in a League game wearing Sky Blue and that was the first time I knew they wore blue. I love that colour. It's a fantastic colour and I became a City supporter when I was about eleven. I started buying souvenirs from the City souvenir shop and I communicated with Mrs Yvette Price, the manager of the shop. I told her that I wanted to come to England in one of my letters.

'This was 1975 and Mrs Price went to see the manager Tony Book and told him "There's a crazy Norwegian who has been buying all my souvenirs. Everything. He wants to come to Manchester and I was wondering if we should invite him." Tony Book looked at her and then said "Yes, let's do that." So I received an invite and I stayed at Mrs Price's house in Cheadle.' [12]

At this time City was regarded by the media as a family club. One that would go above and beyond the call of duty to ensure fans and non-fans alike would be treated well. The idea of inviting a fifteen year old from Norway to come and stay is certainly somewhat different to how most clubs acted at this time but the Blues were to do even more. Morten was not invited to simply attend a game. In fact he was invited to spend almost every moment of his time in England with the club: 'They invited me to Maine Road every day and allowed me to sit in the dressing room. I was only fifteen – I think my parents would be arrested if that happened now! I came on my own by airplane and I had never been to England before.

'On my first day I met Tony Book and the director Ian Niven. They allowed me to be in the dressing room and most of the time I just sat there. Saying nothing. Just observing. Usually I was sat next to Big Joe Corrigan. Mike Summerbee made sure everything was okay and looked after me. He told me where to sit and took photos of me in the dressing room with the players. Tony Book decided that a young first team player should look after me and so Peter Barnes, who was two years older than me, was given that job. He had only made his debut earlier that season and had played only a few games. From that point on we became very good friends.'

The friendship between Morten and Peter continues to this day and they often meet. Back at Easter 1975 Peter acted as Morten's guide and chaperone: 'One Sunday Peter came with Tony Henry and Alan Godfrey to Mrs. Price's to see me…. That was the first time I ever tasted a beer! It was a remarkable experience giving so much access to the players and Maine Road. Mrs Price used to take me to Maine Road each day and I spent all day at the ground, seeing the players or just walking around the stadium. Mrs Price warned me not to wander – as a fifteen year old who had never been to Manchester I think she worried. She told me not to go to Moss Side, so what did I do? I went to Moss Side. It was different to what I was used to and I did worry once I was there but I was wearing a Norwegian jacket – my normal jacket. I looked crazy so everybody stayed away from me!'

Peter remembers the jacket: 'It had large seventies collars and I think it was velvet! Wearing the jacket with a pair of jeans. I've since been with Morten to see his mum in Norway and the house he was brought up in. It was a wooden house in the countryside really. Can you imagine coming

Morten Andersen with Peter during one of his later visits.

from there to a big industrial, working class city as Manchester was then, and wandering around on your own at fifteen?'

While he was here City made sure Morten saw a few games: 'I watched four games while I was here – Coventry, Middlesbrough at home and then Wolverhampton and Derby away. Franny Lee was playing for Derby and he was a good friend of Mrs. Price so we met him before the game. At that time he was also training at Maine Road on Mondays because of his business near Manchester. We became close friends.'

Looking back on that time Peter remembers: 'Morten was two years two days younger than me and I think I was the youngest in the first team squad. I'd just signed pro and made my debut and I'm told to look after this Norwegian guy who had just arrived. I remember asking where he was staying and someone told me he was staying at Mrs Price's. So here he was

a Norwegian, staying with the woman who ran the club shop and being chaperoned by a lad who had only just got into the first team squad. We seemed to spend more time talking about what we were to do with Morten than tactics!

'There was a party coming up at Mrs Price's for someone and so I was invited to that. We were all going around introducing Morten to each other: "He's from Norway. He's fifteen." It must have blown Morten's mind that suddenly he was with these First Division players in a city he'd never been to before… in a different country. It must have been a culture shock. I don't think I could have done that on my own at fifteen, but he did and it was a strange – but wonderful – experience for us all. He blames me for introducing him to beer – but we were hardly allowed to drink, so I think it would've been a half or something.

'At Maine Road Morten was everywhere we went. I think Tony Book felt sorry for him, coming all this way. He didn't want him to get bored and I remember him telling us to "Look after young Morten. He's on his own. He's Norwegian." Again "He's Norwegian" as if that meant something. I remember thinking "Should I take him home to meet my mum?" That didn't happen but I do remember wondering what I could do with him. I think we sent him to see Stan Gibson, the groundsman, thinking that'll keep him busy for a couple of hours. Can you imagine Stan: "Who are you?" "I'm Morten." "Oh, the Norwegian." He'd come back and we'd say "Have you been to the main office yet? Go and see Bernard Halford or Julia, Tony Book's secretary." He'd be off again. Can you imagine Bernard, the club secretary, trying to sort out the bills or something and there's a knock at the

door. Morten goes in: "Tony Book invited me over." Bernard thinks: "No one's told me we've signed a young Norwegian player!" After a few days everybody knew Morten was wandering around the place, even though some never actually met him.'

When City played Coventry at home on 22 March 1975, former City boss Joe Mercer was then a director of the visitors and when he heard about Morten's visit he decided to pop downstairs to see the youngster. Peter: 'Can you imagine Tony Book's having a chat with Joe upstairs and just happens to mention that there's a Norwegian lad visiting, so Joe says "I'd like to meet him" and he goes off to see him? It seems so strange now that this entire situation happened but back then footballers were just lads off the same streets as everybody

Yvette Price.

else. We lived amongst fans. We didn't see ourselves any different so, bizarre as it sounds, meeting a Norwegian who loves the club so much he's decided to come and stay with us would've intrigued us. Back then if Harry Todd on the door came in and said "There's someone to see you", you'd go out and see them. It was as simple as that. It could be anyone but that's how it was at City.'

Manchester City were a major club at this time, heading into the final weeks of the season and while Morten's stay at Maine Road may be somewhat unusual it does demonstrate that the club was a friendly, welcoming one and that those who worked there had empathy with their fans. No matter how successful City had become – make no mistake Manchester City were perceived as a footballing giant at this time – the club and those that were employed there displayed humility and a welcoming attitude.

City ended that season eighth, seven points behind champions Derby whose title-winning squad included former Maine Road great Francis Lee of course, who many felt could have made a difference had he not been transferred out of Maine Road the previous close season. Peter appeared in three top flight games, a FA Cup tie

and the League Cup game with United that season and, with appearances as part of England's youth set up, he began to be noticed by leading football managers and personalities of the day. They talked of him in positive terms. He was also suddenly aware that he was now a player who would be offered boots and other items of kit from suppliers: 'One of City's directors was John Humphreys who was also a director of the kit manufacturer Umbro. He popped down to see me one day and he invited me to the Umbro factory in Wilmslow. He gave me directions and I struggled to find it at first, then I spotted this alleyway that was all painted in City blue. I walked down it and that was Umbro. John Humphreys met me and took me on a guided tour. I was only 17 and I was thinking "he's a director of City and he's showing me around Umbro! I'm only a player, he's a director!" It shows you how football's changed.

'Mr Humphreys gave me a pair of boots and a pair of training shoes. It was great and I suddenly felt special. Instead of me having to wear Mike Summerbee's latest boots to get them match ready I now had to get my own provided boots sorted. It's difficult to explain how much of a moment that was for me.'

[1] Manchester City v Arsenal match programme, October 16, 1974, 3.
[2] 'Unlucky Clarke can smile again after Book pep talk', Daily Mail, October 14, 1974, 31.
[3] 'Barnes in for injured Tueart', Manchester Evening News, October 18, 1974, 20.
[4] 'Rod goes near: Barnes shines', Manchester Evening News Pink, October 19, 1974, 16.
[5] 'City Lack touch of champions' Sunday Express, October 20, 1974. Cutting in the Peter Barnes collection but page number unknown.
[6] 'It was hard to watch, too, Rodney', article by Bill Elliott in an unknown newspaper taken from collection of Peter Barnes. Believed to be the Daily Express.
[7] Manchester City v Coventry City match programme, March 22, 1975, 3.
[8] Manchester City v Burnley match programme, April 19, 1975, 13.
[9] Manchester City v Chelsea match programme, October 5, 1974, 8.
[10] 'Two England bankers', Daily Express, February 19, 1975.
[11] 'Tony on tightrope', Daily Express. Cutting in the Peter Barnes collection but specific date and page number unknown.
[12] Interview with Morten Andersen by Gary James, February 9, 2020

Chapter Four

PETER'S CHANCE

> Peter must be the trickiest winger in the Football League. His all-round agility and close ball-control make him one of the best players. I saw him against Leeds for the first time and his wing wizardry amazed me until he had to limp off. He does not have the best heading ability in the team, but he is the greatest on the ground. I was so impressed with Peter that after the match I went to buy a large photo of him..

Eleven year old fan **HOWARD JOHNSON** quoted in the
Manchester City v West Ham United match programme, January 17, 1976.

Manchester City's last senior game of the 1974-75 season came on 26 April but for Peter the weeks that followed were somewhat hectic. He had a driving test to prepare for but he had also been selected to play for England in the UEFA Youth Tournament, nowadays known as the UEFA Under 18s Championship, to be held in Switzerland during May. The competition is significant with all footballing nations competing for the highest continental prize available to them at this level. England had reached the finals after winning their qualification tie with Spain 2-1 on aggregate and were placed in a group with Northern Ireland, the Republic of Ireland and Switzerland.

Peter scored the only goal of England's opening match with the Irish Republic: '[England] scored their goal seven minutes from the end. Barnes finishing off a good move down the left.' [1] Relatively straightforward wins over the home nation Switzerland (4-0) and Northern Ireland (3-0) placed England top of their group and into the semi-finals. Peter didn't score in either of those games but he did hit the bar against Switzerland and had set up the second for Glen Hoddle against Ireland. According to reports: 'The skill of the England teenagers had the crowd gasping with admiration.' [2] England youth manager Ken Burton commented: 'I'm delighted with the performance of the whole team.

1975

SFV ASF

INTERNATIONALES JUNIORENTURNIER

TOURNOI INTERNATIONAL DES JUNIORS

TORNEO INTERNAZIONALE DEGLI JUNIORI

INTERNATIONAL YOUTH TOURNAMENT

ENGLAND
ANGLETERRE
INGHILTERRA
ENGLAND

Barnes, Peter Simon
Bertschin, Keith Ed.
Bielby, Paul Anthony
Curbishley, Llewelyn
Fisher, R.
Fox, Peter David
Hart, Peter Osborne
Hoddle, Glenn
Keeley, Andrew J.
Langley, Thomas W.
Middleton, John
Nightingale, Mark B.
Pimblett, Frank

Roberts, James Dale
Robinson, Neil
Robson, Bryan
Smith, Ian Ralph
Sparrow, John Paul
Sutcliffe, Peter David
Taylor, Richard
Trewick, John
Wicks, Steven John
Wilcox, Richard J.
Wilkins, Raymond C.
Willey, Alan

14

City boy gives England
a winning start

PETER BARNES of Manchester City gave England a winning start to the EUFA international youth soccer championship in Switzerland last night, but the 1-0 victory over the Irish Republic was not wholly convincing.

The British Isles' other two representatives, Northern Ireland and Wales, both drew.

Northern Ireland were held 1-1 by Switzerland in

Emmenbruecke and the Welsh played a goalless draw with Italy in Chiasso.

England, six times winners of the championship, scored their goal seven minutes from the end. Barnes finishing off a good move down the left.

But earlier the Irish had hit the post and the bar as

they exposed weaknesses in the English defence.

Switzerland scored first against Northern Ireland, Amacker firing into the net after taking a pass from an indirect free-kick.

Brotherston equalised in the 28th minute, hammering home a headed pass from McCreary.

PETER BARNES
... scored the only goal in England's win.

DAILY MIRROR, Wednesday, May 14, 1975   PAGE 27

From JACK STEGGLES
Kriens, Tuesday.

England 3, N. Ireland 0

ENGLAND took just nine minutes to clinch their place in the semi-finals of the Little World Cup in Switzerland tonight.

A devastating burst brought them two brilliant goals, and killed the game as a contest.

Ipswich striker Keith Bertschin headed the first in the 6th minute, after a great cross from Glenn Hoddle had left Irish keeper Peter Ritchie floundering.

Then three minutes later, skipper Butch Wilkins and Peter Barnes set up the second for Spurs starlet Hoddle.

England became complacent after that marvellous start and allowed the initiative to slip away.

The Irish, who could never hope to match England's skill, showed they were not

England blast a double clincher

tricky Tottenham winger, was the biggest danger to England as 'keeper John Middleton was given a lot of work to do for the remainder of the first half.

Middleton earned England's gratitude by producing brilliant saves from Manchester United's Dave McCreary. Brothers

BUTCH'S BITE STINGS SWISS

From JACK STEGGLES : England Youth 4, Switzerland Youth 0

BUOCHS, Sunday

ENGLAND destroyed Switzerland and almost certainly clinched a place in the semi-final of the Little World Cup here today.

The skill of the England teenagers had the crowd gasping with admiration.

a breathtaking display by firing two of the goals.

Wilkins strolled almost arrogantly as he master-minded operations from midfield.

"What an inspiration Butch was. He must have covered every blade of grass," enthused England manager Ken Burton.

"I'm delighted with the performance of the whole team. We showed these people what skill is all about."

Wilkins produced a glorious chip to make

We showed these people what skill is all about.'

In the semi-final England defeated Hungary 3-1. Peter: 'It was a tough competition and seems to be forgotten by the wider public these days but at the time it was a major tournament. We played Finland in the final at Bern and Ray Wilkins, who I shared a room with at various levels for England, scored the winning goal and we won 1-0. Ray was a great guy to share with and a lovely man.'

On his return to England that summer Peter finally passed his driving test: 'I failed my first driving test and then passed it second time. My first car was a second hand red Mini – how ridiculous for a City player to get a red car! It cost me £60 I think it was a 850cc engine. I bought a new wooden steering wheel and an eight track cassette player. I had speakers put in at the back and I listened to Rod Stewart and Elton John cassettes. Exciting times. When Gary Owen, who was my mucker then, started to drive he got a green Mini 1000 – it was newer than mine. He must have had more money than me! In those days we all had spaces on the Maine Road forecourt and I'd pull into my space in my Mini. There'd be Rodney Marsh's V-type Jaguar, Mike Summerbee's Jensen Interceptor… lots of flash cars. I used to get some stick from the others: "A red Mini! What are you thinking?" I decided that when I could afford it I'd get a better car.

'My next car was an 1100 Ford Popular, pale blue – City's colour of course! I had a black vinyl roof put on it and I thought it was flash. When I eventually made it as a regular in the team I got a Ford Capri. It was a navy blue and gold John Player Special Ford Capri, 2 litre engine. I bought it from a friend of my dad's who was a car dealer on Hyde Road. He ordered this car for me brand new. The Capri was the car to have and this was a special edition. I think I got that when I was about twenty and I remember going on tour with City. I was still living at home then and I shared a bedroom with my younger brother Mike. Keith, my elder brother, had his own room. Anyway, I'm coming back from the tour and I'm in a taxi on my way home when I saw a Capri that looked exactly like mine pass us. "No, it can't be" I'm muttering to myself. Then we caught up to it at the lights and I could see it had my number plate – TJA 818S - and sat in the driver's seat was Keith! Not only that but he was wearing some of my clothes!

'I said to the taxi driver "that's my car!" I don't think he believed me. He'd probably had other young blokes in his cab pointing at flash cars and saying they were there's, but this was mine. Somehow Keith had searched my bedroom and found my keys while I was away. He had been driving around in my John Player Special car, wearing my clothes. I was fuming when I got home and I went in to see my mum. She tried to calm me down, but it did end in a brotherly argument.'

From the moment Peter made his debut in 1974 fans started to notice him: 'Whenever I pulled up at Maine Road or came out of the ground to go to my car, there would be fans there. It didn't seem to matter when it was there'd always be someone. I was so shy back then that I didn't know how to handle it. There'd be autograph hunters and you'd sign for them. I tried never to let anyone down but I found it tough speaking and meeting fans because of my shyness. They'd ask you questions about the team and you'd try to answer without giving anything away. I didn't really get much attention until after my debut and then there was no hiding place. I loved the fans and always appreciated the support I got. Still do. But it was a shock at

Young autograph hunters await Peter as he pulls up in his John Player Special Ford Capri.

how quickly I'd gone from being just a boy playing in the B team to suddenly appearing for the first team in front of fifty-odd thousand.'

In the 1970s the idea of training footballers to speak with fans or the media was simply not considered. Clubs were able to train boys to play football and educate them with tactics but life skills and methods for handling the fame were not in place: 'It was challenging. City were at the forefront for fan-related activities. There were the annual pantomimes at the social club – I always tried to avoid that type of thing. It wasn't me. I know Rodney Marsh, Mike Summerbee and some of the others threw themselves into it but I couldn't do that. I was terrified of the attention. There was also the Junior Blues with Roger Reade and Richard Sutton back then... I'd go to meetings and I'd get involved. It was always packed with kids and their parents. I could cope with that and as I got older it became

natural to do that side of things, but initially I did find it tough.'

Manchester City were the first club to create a supporters organisation for young fans. The Junior Blues was a fantastic institution which created an affinity with the club that would last a lifetime. Often young families who could not afford the matchday experience would join the Junior Blues and feel close to the club, so meeting players like Peter was great for them but it also meant that the wider Manchester public, not just match going fans, could connect with the club and, when City hit periods of failure, the loyalty of those who first became interested in the club via the Junior Blues ensured City remained a popular club. For Peter, being thrust into this world was an education. His father was a more outspoken figure whereas Peter was introverted and uncomfortable in social situations: 'It helped me develop as a person and I had to get over my shyness. Nowadays

I love getting out there and meeting fans, but back then I worried about it. I always did it but it was painful at times. I didn't know what to say and I couldn't believe fans wanted to meet me either. Over the years I improved and I think because of the efforts made back then by the club with the Junior Blues it helped us players see this as the normal way to act. That's why so many of us continue to meet fans and attend supporter meetings now. We were thrust into that spotlight and were forced to talk – forty years on I've got better at it, but it did take a long time.'

A key figure behind the Junior Blues during this period was Roger Reade who, over the years fulfilled a variety of roles at Manchester City: 'I was a City fan who was working in his dream job at the time. Every day I was part of that set up at City and I loved every minute. I was aware of Peter from when he broke into the reserve team as an apprentice and then into the first team. It was a tough business back then for any kid to break into the first team. It was a much more physical game. That's why it was so amazing when he broke into the team at that age. Peter's about a year younger than me and Gary Owen is two years younger and so we got on quite well. We were the same age group and I admired them so much for getting into the first team. This was a time when City had older, seasoned professionals… it wasn't a time when the club was desperate and threw anybody in. They had to deliver and to achieve that at that age was remarkable. So Peter getting his chance in 1974-75 was really satisfying for me. I think we all hoped that 1975-76

would see him get many more chances. I think Peter was quite humble about what his achievements and so that added to it for me.' [3]

When the 1975-76 season commenced there were twenty-five professional players at City, including Gary Owen, but neither Peter nor Gary had featured in any of the preseason first team games, although Peter had appeared in a reserve team friendly at Blackpool. At the season's start manager Tony Book had said: 'No one gets a first team place on reputation alone and that is why we shall be encouraging these youngsters to keep pushing.' [4] Book wanted to bring more young players through the ranks and had released a few senior players, including Mike Summerbee and Mike Horswill, suggesting this would make it easier for those currently in City's A team to progress through the ranks. Neither player was to get their chance for some time with Peter's first senior start of the season being a League Cup tie at home to Nottingham Forest on 8 October 1975. Dennis Tueart had suffered a heel injury in a 3-2 victory at Arsenal the previous Saturday, giving Peter his opportunity.

Forest manager Brian Clough told the press: 'I was praying Manchester City would beat Norwich because I wanted to play the best. City are one of the most entertaining and talented sides in the First Division at home. We have no serious thoughts of shocking City but we hope to give a good account of ourselves against a side that is potentially one of the best in the land.

'When I last came to Maine Road it was with Leeds United and we lost 2-1. If we keep the score down to 2-1 tonight then I think we'll show the strides that Nottingham Forest have taken.' [5]

Clough predicted the score accurately with goals from Colin Bell and Joe Royle helping City achieve the 2-1 result. Peter retained his place for the home League game the following Saturday with Burnley, which ended goalless. It was the last City game for captain Rodney Marsh: 'We should have beaten them, since we completely played them off the park, but we drew 1-1. Ian MacFarlane, the assistant manager, and Tony Book were jumping up and down throughout the match. They were furious because we weren't scoring. After the game, we went back into the dressing room and Ian MacFarlane went absolutely ballistic at all the players' [6]

In his biography Marsh then describes MacFarlane punching Dennis Tueart after Tueart had disagreed with him about the performance and goes on to say that he had challenged Tony Book about it, asking what the City manager would do about it. There's a confused picture as Tueart did not play that day but Marsh is adamant this occurred. Peter: 'I can't remember Dennis being punched but the dressing room was quite a volatile place at times. I liked Ian MacFarlane and he often looked after the younger lads, but he was quite vocal too and I'm sure he clashed with Rodney at times. They just didn't get on. Ian knew Rodney was talented but he probably thought "Who is this flash guy who never wears socks? Who does he think he is?" They were always going to clash and never really saw eye to eye. He probably felt that same way about Dennis too, but I don't remember this happening that day. It might have done because the dressing room was quite volatile at times. I do think it was a make-or-break

moment for Tony Book though. Tony had known great success as a player and now he was our manager and there was a lot of expectation there.'

In the aftermath Marsh was put on the transfer list and never played for City gain. Roger Reade, who worked in the offices at Maine Road, remembers: 'Ian was a larger than life character. He was quite loud and you could hear him up the corridors at the ground. You'd be in the offices and you'd hear him booming out at reception "Hello, aye. How you doing?" in his Scottish accent. He was brilliant for morale for most of the team.'

The Marsh-MacFarlane saga rumbled on for weeks with many fans supporting Rodney Marsh, leading to Tony Book writing: 'The insoluble problems between Rodney and the club are difficult to explain in a few words. It is not my way to cause public offence, but I found that he had unusual ways about him – I always felt that he gave the impression to the management and coaches that they were mugs, that they were not meeting standards he wanted to set. Should the tail wag the dog?

'As his manager, he always gave me the impression that he believed I was not good enough for what he wanted: that he would only be happy working under one boss, Malcolm Allison, the man who originally brought him to Maine Road. And working under Terry Venables, his longstanding friend, who is now chief coach with Malcolm at Crystal Palace.... I feel that Rodney did not appreciate the lengths we went to in trying to make it work... I then had to make a positive move or permit the problem to fester, which could have been to the detriment of everyone, including Rodney.' [7]

According to Book: 'There have been slogans on the Maine Road walls, a non-stop battering from the mailman, small deputations of fans arriving at the ground attempting to find the thinking behind the decision.'

For Peter this was an odd re-introduction to the first team: 'It was difficult because I was still the new boy and didn't know what politics there were between some of the players and the management. It was a tough world in the dressing room at times but I tried to focus on my own arrival in the team. I couldn't really get involved too much because I was still more of a reserve player than a first teamer. I certainly wasn't a regular at this time. Mike Doyle was made captain and we all looked to him for leadership in the dressing room but Tony Book coped really well at this time. He had young players like me, Ged Keegan and Kenny Clements coming through and he backed us totally. It could have all backfired but Tony was keen to introduce us and revitalise the team. It was decisive time and us younger players had to stand up to the mark. We had to play well and do all we could to ensure we stayed in that team. Tony wanted us to stay in but we had to deliver… and if we didn't it'd be Tony getting it in the neck. Can you imagine the reaction if we'd have failed while Rodney was still on the books but not being played?'

New captain Mike Doyle was particularly outspoken at this time about Rodney Marsh and the situation at Maine Road, but he chose to act in a conciliatory manner in the weeks that followed, commenting: 'There is no ill-feeling among the City players about Rodney. There is a lot of regret that it has not worked out to the benefit of the club. Everybody on the staff hoped he gets fixed up with a club as soon as possible.' [8]

Doyle admitted: 'there is now a lot of pressure to live with at City. Particularly for the manager, who made the transfer-listing decision, and also for the players who have to produce results that will show they are not dependent on any individual. But it would be unfair of fans who rave about Rodney to sell short the volume of ability possessed by so many other players.'

Once Marsh was out of the City team Tony Book reshaped his team with several positional changes that ultimately benefitted Peter: 'Tony was honest with us and I knew I had to deliver. He put his faith in me and I'll always be grateful for that. If you think about Phil Foden in 2018 and 2019, Pep hasn't gambled with him. He's introduced him when it was safe to do so. He's not dropped a star, much loved international player like Tony did. Pep's approach is probably what most managers would like to do but that only adds to the view that Tony was exceptionally brave back in 1975. There was so much pressure to play Rodney with fans on his side, but Tony did what he believed was in the best interest of the team and the club. That's a brave manager.'

Asa Hartford, who had been appearing in the number seven shirt was moved to Marsh's number ten. Tueart returned to the left wing after his injury and Peter retained his place, moving to the right wing for the game with Tottenham on 18 October. As well as the changes brought on by Marsh's transfer-listing the team was ill-equipped for a potentially gruelling game with Spurs as there were a number of players struggling with their health at this time, including Peter who was showing signs of influenza. It was no surprise when City were losing early into the game. Doyle: 'We were two goals down in the early stages, winger Peter Barnes should really have been home in bed because he was running such a high temperature, Asa Hartford was still struggling with his shoulder injury, Colin Bell was on the brink of an outbreak of 'flu and Dave Watson was playing in the critical centre forward position.' Peter: 'The team needed me – or someone, it just happened to be me – and I desperately wanted to play. This was a chance for me and while I didn't want Rodney to be dropped I had to seize the chance to become established in the team.'

Dave Watson was City's regular centre-half but with Joe Royle out with injury and Rodney Marsh on the transfer list Tony Book felt he had no choice but to play Watson in the key attacking position, but the opening stages caused so much concern to the City boss that Watson was brought back into defence for a while. The Blues looked completely out of the game by half time but their fortunes changed in the second period when, according to journalist Mike Langley: 'a Tueart pass to Watson altered everything. For Watson crashed through a tackle by Young, who is either slow or overweight – or maybe both. Jennings plunged out. Watson shot. "He didn't hit it clean," said Jennings. So the ball bounced, and spun off the keeper's hand over the line.' [9]

The makeshift striker later commented that he preferred stopping goals than scoring them. Watson's goal gave City hope but with players showing signs of illness it was still tough going. Peter was certainly struggling on the wing with Book considering making a substitution, but suddenly Peter burst into life and saw an opening: 'Barnes, on the point of being withdrawn for illness, flung over a left-wing cross that hit McAllister just as Jennings advances. The deflection flew to Bell, who headed in off a post.'

The City fightback secured a 2-2 draw and for Peter a regular place in the first team now seemed a possibility: 'I never let it go to my head. I never thought I'd made

HOW THE BLUES EARNED THEIR SPURS!

THE Blues put up a terrific fight in the 2-2 draw at Tottenham last Saturday. And they really earned their spurs!

COLIN BELL beats Pat Jennings [right] to get the point and gets the congratulations of Dennis Tueart and Asa Hartford [below right]. Earlier it had been Dave Watson's turn to share the joy of scoring with Tueart and Bell [below]. You could say young Peter Barnes found it a hair-raising experience in his duel with Steve Perryman [below left].

twelve

it. I knew I could be out of that team quite quickly, so I continued to work hard and did all I could to ensure I was picked, but it was tough at times that season.'

Soon after the Spurs game a feature in *Shoot* magazine asked City captain Mike Doyle what he thought of Peter's ability. He responded with a couple of strong statements: 'Peter has more talent than Rodney Marsh, Asa Hartford and Colin Bell put together. I believe, and many people at Manchester United have said it as well, that he has more ability now than George Best had at the same age.' [10] Another man quoted in the magazine was City's assistant manager, Ian MacFarlane: 'Peter is the best prospect in British football. But when we've groomed him, he'll be a world-beater.' Despite this praise Peter remained level-headed and told the magazine: 'Sometimes

he could have helped City to real success. He was the sort of player you built a team around.' [11]

Peter is equally positive about Oakes: 'A magnificent player. Loyal club servant who is often overlooked when people talk about great English footballers of that period. Underrated. He never put a foot wrong. Always tackled at the right time; knew what to do; and had a great left foot. He used to be brilliant at hitting a ball to you over forty yards. I'd call him Mr Dependable. He did the simple things well and you needed players of his quality and ability in your side. He gave 100% every game and was wonderful for City. One silly thing that sticks in my memory is that Alan and some of his generation of players who had won everything at City always called you by your first name. It wasn't Barnes, Barnesy or "oi you", it was always Peter. It seems a small thing but it's not. I respected him a lot and couldn't believe that from the start he was polite, respectful and used my first name. I was just a kid and he was a stalwart of the dressing room but he didn't see it like that. That's a real gentleman. I learnt so much off him and Glyn Pardoe. They talked to you like they were your older brother. You'd be walking off the pitch and they'd come over to give you some advice – not to shout or anything like that. They just wanted to help and it was all done in a friendly, caring manner. Other players would shout and bawl, but not Alan and Glyn. I learnt so much from everyone in the dressing room but I felt so lucky listening to these two. I listened with respect to them and all the team. Imagine going in to that dressing room and seeing the experience… then being called Peter and welcomed in. Humble people.'

Peter's third League game of the season was a 1-1 Maine Road draw with Bobby Robson's Ipswich Town. One man who

I can't believe I am really playing alongside great players. That's why I was sometimes shattered when they bawled me out during games when things weren't going too well. But they are professionals and their attitude has helped me. I couldn't have a better opportunity to make it – being with a great club and great players.'

Another longstanding player appearing for City during 1975-76 Alan Oakes admitted that he loved this period of his career, especially playing with Peter: 'I enjoyed it all, and I remember playing a few games with Peter Barnes in front of me. I loved that. He was such a gifted player and it was great for me to play behind someone that exciting at that stage in my career and in his. I know this came a couple of years after I'd moved on, but it irritated me when Peter Barnes was sold because I believe watched both City and United around this time was broadcaster Terry Christian. He remembers this game for a great performance by Colin Bell: 'It was one of those games City struggled in but it was Bell that changed things. City looked like they would lose it but this was when Bell always added something else. He scored and it ended in a draw. He came in from the right hand side, took it in to the box and just slotted it in. It came from nowhere. It was like a one man army. It was as if he said "leave it to me. I can do this." That's what Bell added and he was great to watch.' [12]

For Peter, the Ipswich draw was followed by a strange trip to Sheffield United on 1 November. Book: 'It needed a lot of resilience to overcome the crop of problems we encountered on our visit to Sheffield United.' [13] As City were traveling over the Pennines their coach was involved in a crash. No player was seriously injured but several appeared to suffer whiplash injuries, including crucial defender Dave Watson, though manager Book was delighted that the player decided he could play on: 'He insisted on taking his place in the side despite the jolting he took. We took the immediate precaution of telephoning Maine Road and instructing Keith MacRae and Geoff Hammond to rush over to Sheffield, and it wasn't until the last minute that we had to decide that Joe [Corrigan] would be unable to keep his ever-present record in goal – so Keith stepped into the breach. Joe, who had complained of feeling unwell on the trip over, was confined to bed at the hotel headquarters which we used.'

For City the game with Sheffield suddenly appeared more difficult than it ought to have been because of the crash but Book's side did manage a 2-2 draw with Peter scoring his first goal of the season. Book was delighted: 'I was thrilled to see Peter Barnes, our exciting teenage

winger, scoring his first goal of the season, at Sheffield. I hope that results continue satisfactorily because in these circumstances I can give Peter the number of games he will require to settle in properly and display all the flair of which he is capable.

'I said at the outset that he would need one-dozen consecutive matches before we start to see the real talent shining through. Experience is all he requires: the boy is raw, but has a lot of skill and a tremendous amount of ability. We are working with him every day and I believe it is the spadework which my assistant, Ian MacFarlane, did with him in training which resulted in him being a marksman at Sheffield. Ian has been concentrating on getting Peter to react to situations developing across the opponents' playing area, and it was such an incident that he moved in at Bramall Lane and snatched a goal from virtually very little.'

Throughout the early and mid-1970s football seemed to be having a debate concerning the role of wingers. Manchester City, and United for that matter, preferred to have wide, attacking players but elsewhere teams were not so keen on wing play. Terry Christian, renowned for being a Manchester United fan, recognises that both Manchester clubs played with style down the wings: 'I grew up near Brooks Bar between Maine Road and Old Trafford and me and my mates used to go to the games at either ground. It wasn't an issue in those days. My mate David Lindsay was a City fan and so we used to go with him. We liked going to City because it was 5p more at United and that was the price of a Marvel comic or whatever. In fact it was 5p more at United to stand than it was to sit in the Platt Lane at City. I remember seeing Peter in his first few games, which were in 1974, and he did this spectacular shot which hit the crossbar in one of them.

'I always felt Peter was one of those

Peter in action against Sheffield United in November 1975.

players who wasn't looked after. It's a different era now but back then it was an era where if they had skill "kick 'em". He had lumps kicked out of him every game. That's what the defenders would do. They used to get away with tackles that were sending off type of tackles really. The pitches weren't great which didn't help either but Peter shone even considering all of that. Peter was part of a City team that was top four but looked as if they would win the League. Liverpool were too strong but they weren't particularly too good to watch.

'In 1975 Tueart and Barnes were quick but the problem earlier that season was that Marsh used to drag play back. He'd put his foot on the ball and slow everything down. The opportunity would be missed. He'd take too many touches on the ball. He

had one brilliant game for City and that was when they won 4-0 at Maine Road to Jack Charlton's Middlesbrough (13/09/76). Once Marsh had been dropped and Peter Barnes was playing City improved and Peter was outstanding that season of 1975-76. City had suddenly got rid of the shackles of Marsh – I think he was a liability.

'Football was the cheapest form of entertainment. Even going to the pictures was more expensive than football. You went to football with your mates and we'd have just enough money to get in. We couldn't even afford a programme. It was like a day out and you'd get to talk about the game all week. The only teams that seemed to play with wingers then were City and United. A lot of the football around this time was negative so City and United were the entertainers. The ones you wanted to watch. Most clubs would perhaps have one winger. Few had two but United and City did. Every team that won the League were quite defensive but United and City were different. It was fun watching City and I supported City whenever I went to see them – except when they played United of course!'

What Christian says about City's attacking style is true with newspapers frequently debating either the need for wingers or whether more emphasis should be placed on wing play. Ron Fenton, a former Burnley and West Bromwich Albion star, frequently used his column in the Nottingham Football Post to call for more attack-minded football. He eulogised about the efforts being made by Tony Book and his use of Peter and Tueart at City: 'Peter Barnes and Dennis Tueart have consistently destroyed defences this season with thrilling wing play. And their success with Manchester City promises to speed up the return of wingers in the League game.' Under the headline 'City lead the way in re-birth of wing play' Fenton added: 'Manchester City are today's classic example of a team who can produce a brand of football to delight the fans and do so successfully. If they go on to win the Championship with Barnes and Tueart as the inspiration then manager Tony Book will have done the game a big service it is sure to accelerate the re-birth of wingers.' [14] United's 18 year old fullback Jimmy Nicholl's comments about Peter and others was typical of the period: 'He was always a forceful player. He'll be one of the few all-out attacking wingers I've met.' [15]

The idea that City was spearheading a return of attacking flair down the wings was prevalent during this season. John Lucy was one journalist who thought that Peter, in particularly, was a breath of fresh air for modern football: 'Here is a youngster brimming over with talent, who kills stone dead the theory that the days of the winger are gone. Barnes has the ability to take on and beat the best of full-backs and then cross the ball to advantage. His exciting play has added a new dimension to the Manchester City attack, and I am sure it will not be very long before we see him in an England shirt.' [16] Another journalist, Neville Foulger, described him as 'a really exciting prospect with international potential', while the tough-tackling Liverpool defender Tommy Smith was quoted as saying Peter: 'has been showing such tremendous skill and directness this season and is being tipped as an England international of the future.' [17] Peter: 'It naturally meant a great deal when fellow professionals or former players mentioned me. I remember how I felt when the great Tom Finney started to suggest that I should play for England. It was a real honour and I didn't think he even knew who I was. It was all a dream for a young player to hear any other player, especially a respected English international, say something positive about you.'

After City's 2-0 victory over Birmingham City on 8 November 1975 journalist Paul Fitzpatrick's report of the game was predominantly an enthusiastic piece on Peter's performance: 'Barnes was a joy. He is playing with a refreshing innocence at present that seems too good to last. Hardened professionals are not going to take kindly to having the ball pushed impudently between their legs, and Barnes, as his reputation increases, could come in for some rough treatment. It is to be hoped that his talent will endure; that he can maintain the confidence which he possesses in abundance at present; that he will continue to believe in his own rich ability. But Barnes should survive. He is level headed, and physically has developed considerably since he made his first appearance a year ago. He looks a truly exciting prospect.' [18]

Fitzpatrick went on to claim that Dennis Tueart, recognised as a major star for City at this time, was: 'a little overshadowed by Barnes at present.' That was a significant statement as Tueart was, and still is, recognised as one of the club's biggest heroes in the 1970s and to be compared with him at so young an age was a major honour for Peter.

Peter was performing exceptionally well as City challenged in both the League and the League Cup. There was little separating the top eight sides with the Blues on 24 points in seventh place and QPR leading on 27 points, prior to facing Coventry on 13 December. Against Coventry Peter netted in a 4-2 victory: 'Tueart robbed Powell on the half way line and centred on to Royle's head and Barnes dummied the through ball past King for the goal of the afternoon.' [19] Peter was regarded as one of the stars of the game, along with Tueart: 'Neither Derby nor Leeds nor anyone else at the top of the League could have excelled City's showing… when the game was won and lost and all the extravagant skills of Tueart and Barnes, in evidence in vivid flashes throughout the 90 minutes, were revealed in their full glory.'

The victory over Coventry left City fifth after 21 games, the half way point of the season. There was high hope that Book's side would mount a title challenge in the second half of the campaign but, on Boxing Day, City faced Leeds United and a Maine Road crowd of 48,077 watched with immense disappointment as a run of fourteen League games without defeat came to an end. The visitors won 1-0 but this game also saw the end of Peter's own run of twelve consecutive League starts as the eighteen year old suffered a cracked collar bone in a collision. Looking back Peter remembers: 'That really did upset me at the time. The pitch was hard and frosty and I don't think the match would be played if it was now. As an attacking player you didn't mind those sort of conditions but defenders hated it because they couldn't keep their balance. In my mind I remember I was heading towards the Platt Lane Stand and I'd gone past Frank Gray. He then grabbed my shirt to try and hold me back but he then fell on top of me with his boot going into my collar bone. We were playing Liverpool next and I would have loved to have played in that game. That was the game back then – our biggest rivals at the time.'

Peter, as always, had suffered some rough play and commented at the time: 'Frank Gray seemed to be taking every opportunity he could to lunge at me. I managed to pass him a few times and that may have added to his frustration because the one that got me I really felt.' According to journalist Alan Dunn: 'A major factor was the departure with a cracked shoulder blade of City's talented winger, Barnes, following one of a number of odd looking tackles by Frank Gray in which he tended to run into the back of a player. Barnes's departure robbed City of the ability fully to use both flanks.' [20]

Initial reports suggested Peter would be out for a month. [21] His replacement was Paul Power for the clash with title contenders Liverpool the following day. That game ended in a 1-0 defeat. Games between City and Liverpool were often viewed as of immense significance in the 1970s with that game, played in front of an Anfield crowd of 53,386 – the Merseyside club's largest of the season to date and over four thousand more than the crowd Liverpool attracted for the visit of Manchester United earlier in the season.

The attendance was some thirteen thousand higher than Liverpool's average. Peter: 'I missed that game but every match with Liverpool back then was treated as a major event. The crowds were often bigger than those for Liverpool's games with United and the national media would see them as either title clashes or games between two of the biggest clubs in the country. It is quite annoying that the modern day media overlook this.'

Peter's views are correct and during the 1970s the clashes between Liverpool and City were often bigger games than others faced by either club. Inevitably, derby matches tended to get more attention for both clubs, but City-Liverpool clashes were often of more significance than those between United and Liverpool at this time. The rivalry between Liverpool and United developed later in the decade and was raised further when Alex Ferguson started finding success at Old Trafford. United fan Terry Christian: 'If you talk about grudge matches… As a kid I was never aware of any United rivalry with Liverpool. It only started when United were in Division Two (1974-75). The Scousers always hated the Manchester clubs but I think that was because no matter how many times they won trophies they never quite did it with the same style.

It was a weird time to watch football but City and United were the ones who played exciting, attacking football. Everton were bigger rivals to United back then and were seen as the more glamorous game for us all. Everton were a major club then and a scary team to face. I gave an example in a documentary I did on Liverpool in the FA Cup final in 1971 – we were all supporting Liverpool in our house because you all tended to support the northern club over the southern club.'

Peter missed games against Liverpool and Middlesbrough in the League and a 6-0 victory in the FA Cup over Hartlepool during late December and early January: 'I played a reserve game against Bolton on 10 January 1976 as I tried to get back to fitness. I was alongside Gary Owen who was named as substitute for the first team against Hartlepool in the Cup. I was really pleased about that because I wanted Gary to get his chance. I think he was ready for the first team but we'd been going well and he didn't get his chance. Then the injuries came and I missed three games in total.' Tony Book was also delighted with the development of Gary Owen but he was also desperate for Peter to return to the first team: '[Owen] is a prominent candidate for this season's England youth international team, and I would have no fears about bringing him in if my recognised squad was depleted or form lapses necessitated change…The absence of Peter Barnes, who went off injured in the first half of the match against Leeds, has been sorely felt.' [22]

At home to West Ham on 17 January 1976 Peter returned to first team action, but it was another game which saw him kicked and lunged at from the start: 'A fierce tackle, by Lampard on Barnes in the first minute suggested that West Ham might be the overall aggressors.' [23] Another foul came after a mazy run that ended in the penalty area when: 'Lock had unnecessarily kicked Barnes up in the air 12 minutes into the second half.' [24] The game was scintillating and ended in a 3-0 City win. Limited highlights were also shown on television, though journalist Paul Wilcox was far from happy with the BBC's judgement: 'So who decides which should be the No. 1 game for Match of the Day? Possibly the powers that be felt that Manchester should not hog the limelight for the second Saturday running. And, of course, Jimmy the beard had opted to go to Wolverhampton. But every one of the spectators at Maine Road must be left only with the thought that the man with the final say at the BBC is no judge of entertainment value at all.'

Coincidentally, that day's City match programme included a considerable number of letters from fans about the eighteen year old. The club was running a competition to find the most popular player discussed was Peter: 'Peter Barnes has captured the hearts of hundreds of young Blues. It's no disrespect to any other individual on the staff but no other individual nominated for this competition this season has received such a volume of tributes as our teenage winger…. It is clear that he is a definite NUMBER ONE with the City youth brigade.' [25] The comments came from a variety of fans, both male and

female, such as this from Paul Phoenix: 'The first time I saw Peter Barnes this season was against Nottingham Forest in the League Cup. He really impressed me with his great speed and passing power… I was also amazed at the pace he showed when he sped past a Norwich defender in a recent match. He's mustard. He really has a great future ahead of him and I can tell you he is a great favourite with the Kippax Streeters.'

Jane Leigh wrote: 'Peter is the weenyboppers favourite of Maine Road. He is young and has little experience, yet he plays like a veteran… Each week he grows in confidence and more skills just flow from those gifted feet. Peter has a lovable, cheeky grin and he always seems to enjoy his football. In fact, he is an ideal advert for football and an answer to its critics. How

Gary Owen, Mike Summerbee and Peter Barnes at a Junior Blues meeting.

can football finish within 10 years if players like Peter Barnes are still turning out.'

For club employee Roger Reade, who contributed to City's programme at this time, those fan letters were typical of the way everyone seemed to feel about Peter: 'There was an excitement about the place. Peter's arrival in the team as a regular boosted the mood around the place and he seemed to take it all in his stride. I was working in the offices then, along with Ian Niven Junior, and Peter and Gary [Owen] would pop in, come to your desk and have a chat with you. No airs and graces. No 'I'm a first teamer' from Peter or anything like that. That was great. The big named superstars of the club wouldn't do that. They wouldn't be comfortable walking into the office and saying "how are you doing?" but Peter did. He saw us all as equal. Maybe it was his dad's influence? The same was true for Gary too. They knocked about as mates and they'd often go to events together. You may not believe this but both of them actually offered to join the Junior Blues at that time. They wanted to promote it and they were 17 and 18 so they were still young enough to be members because back then the Junior Blues was a club for supporters aged zero to eighteen. They were fabulous. I know Peter was quite shy but he still volunteered to do Junior Blues events on a Sunday and the two of them would do anything to promote that and the wider football club. Their whole attitude was about them not being superstars. They just wanted to be and act like ordinary people. Even when Peter was picked for England a year or so later – which was fantastic for all of us – he never acted differently or saw himself as anything but the same lad who used to come to my desk just for a chat. That humble approach endeared a lot of people to Peter.

'Of course, Peter's brother Michael had been on City's books and he was another talented – but humble – player. He was grounded but really skilful. As an apprentice he was a popular lad but I always wondered whether having their father so closely involved in the club worked against both players. Ken was a great footballer himself and inevitably there'd be comparisons, but not only that Ken was a popular presence at Maine Road during the time they were apprentices and so on. I wonder if that pressure – not necessarily from Ken but from those around the club who may have talked about Ken's achievements perhaps – may have impacted on their careers. Especially Michael. Knowing Ken he would've only wanted the best for his lads and would've wanted them to express themselves how they wanted, not how he or anybody else may have wanted. I don't think he would have directly put any pressure on them at all. I think the only thing he would've wanted was for them to stay grounded and humble.'

Around this time Peter's father Ken was interviewed about his son's performances during the 1975-76: 'It's been a fairy tale for him. Everything went right for him when Rodney Marsh was dropped out of the team and he came in. But the danger is, as I keep telling him, that he could think it's going to be too easy. He's not had a setback yet and, although he has had a meteoric rise and publicity beyond all proportions, we won't really know his quality until he's met a few setbacks and encountered some of the downs of soccer as well as the ups.' [26]

'That was typical of dad,' says Peter. 'He was always trying to keep my feet on the ground. He knew the game could be cruel at times and didn't want me, or anyone else for that matter, to think "that's it, I've made it." I hadn't made it and I never assumed I had. I just wanted to play and continued to push myself, but even if I'd been a world-

Peter rounds David Lawson before having a shot in the 3-0 win over Everton on February 21, 1976.

beater or the greatest player ever, dad would still have down-played it all. He'd have kept me level-headed.'

Ken was asked in 1976 if Peter's skills had come from Ken's genes: 'It's no good saying it's hereditary. Otherwise all former soccer stars would have brilliant young soccer playing sons, but how many can you think of? Even the greatest of them all, Stanley Matthews, produced a son who played tennis, not soccer! Basically it's a question of environment and desire. I learnt all my football at an early age. The basics of control, passing, angles and imagination. All the great players have some special instinct in respect of imagination but how do you teach it? The answer is you can't. It is merely something you learn by experience on your way up.'

By 13 March it was still possible for Book's City to mount a serious challenge for the title as they lay in seventh place, eleven points behind leaders QPR with three games in hand, but they would have had to rely on a number of other powerful sides failing. In addition there were injuries to key players, such as Dave Watson, and significant changes behind the scenes with assistant manager Ian MacFarlane resigning leading to Tony Book advertising for a replacement: 'I have now finished sifting through the 20 serious applicants and have broken this down to a short list of five men.' [27] Ultimately, Bill Taylor would be appointed coach. Roger Reade: 'It took some time for this to be resolved and we weren't certain what Tony was going to do or who he would bring in. Then he brought in Bill Taylor – a lovely, lovely man. One of the nicest people you could meet. I used to babysit for Bill and he was a wonderful fella. He was a complete contrast to Ian MacFarlane. One was loud and the other was so quiet. Bill was never a shouter and his coaching was brilliant.'

During this period Peter was delighted

MANCHESTER CITY

PETER BARNES

and headed it just over the bar. We beat them 3-2 and it was a great start to the first team for me. Barnsey helped and we had that telepathy.'

Owen played four League games in the final weeks of the season with his chance coming because of injuries. This affected consistency with City ending the campaign eighth, seventeen points behind champions Liverpool. Of the final eleven League games City had won three, drawn one and lost the rest. Terry Christian: 'Liverpool were not a great side to watch. They wore you down. City and United played with flair and were attack minded but Liverpool just knew how to stop attractive sides from playing. They were a spiteful side. Everyone forgets what a spiteful side they were. They could play if they wanted to but there was a Mourinho-esque element to their play away from home, especially if they played a team that could attack them. Remember in those days they could pass back to the goalkeeper and they'd kill the game. Ray Clemence would roll it out and then Tommy Smith or another defender would tap it back. Endlessly. In fact it was against City when Liverpool were at their worst doing this.'

Terry was at the Maine Road meeting with Liverpool on 19 April 1976. It was a makeshift City team with Dave Watson out through injury and Colin Bell in the side despite not being fully fit. Peter: 'Colin seemed to be dragging his leg when he ran. I don't think he was ready to return but we all wanted him in the team of course, though you do wonder if they should have just waited until the following season. As a player you'd always want to get back into the team and because the squad wasn't particularly big there would be some pressure I suppose. We all wanted to see

when Gary Owen was given his debut against Wolverhampton Wanderers on 20 March. Gary remembers the game well: 'Peter played on the left and I remember Asa Hartford telling me to go into the centre for the kick off so that I could get a first touch of the ball. First ball saw Joe Royle get the ball out to me. I drift out left and gesture to Willie Donachie to come forward. I cut across Asa Hartford and moved towards Barnsey – we were like a magnet drawn to each other in games. Even though I was central I ended up going that way. I saw Mike Bailey, the old captain of Wolves, coming and I said to Willie: "come, come" and as Willie's moving I nutmegged Bailey… this was the first five seconds of my debut and I'd nipped it through his legs, then played inside the full back for Barnsey. Barnsey slammed it right across the goal and I think it was Joe Royle who went bang,

Colin back – fans, players, management and directors – and so we'd look forward to his return.'

Terry Christian remembers the negative approach exhibited by Liverpool that day: 'It was about Easter time and Liverpool started David Fairclough in the game which was unusual because he had that reputation of coming on and scoring as a substitute. There was all that Super Sub business. This day Liverpool beat City 3-0 and Fairclough scored a couple of late goals (88 and 89 minutes). They'd been at their negative worst and we sat there watching City try to play football but they kept killing it and then picked City off when they got their chance.'

Unlike Liverpool, City and United were perceived as the glamour teams as far as wing play was concerned for most in the media. According to the *Guardian*, it was Manchester's clubs that were transforming football from a dull defensive game into one that would, years later, be remembered as a glamour period for the game: 'The two Manchester clubs are protagonists in the resurgence of orthodox wingers.' [28]

Peter was heralded as contributing to this transformation in football style and he ended the 1975-76 season a regular, making 27 League starts and one appearance as substitute in the League, scoring three goals. But it was in the League Cup where City and Peter shone most this season.

[1] 'City boy gives England a winning start', *Manchester Evening News*, May 10, 1975.

[2] 'Butch's bite stings Swiss', *Daily Mirror*, May 12, 1975, 27.

[3] Roger Reade, interviewed by Gary James in January 2020. All subsequent Reade comments are from this interview unless otherwise stated.

[4] 'Likely Lads', *Manchester Evening News Soccer 75-76*, 7.

[5] Clough quoted in: Gary James, *Manchester The Greatest City* (Leicester: Polar Publishing, 1997), 303.

[6] Rodney Marsh with Brian Woolnough, *I was born a loose cannon* (Altrincham: Optimum Publishing Solutions, 2010), 79-80.

[7] *Manchester City V Ipswich Town match programme*, October 25, 1975, 2-3.

[8] Ibid., 10-11.

[9] 'Spurs give it a touch of horror', *The People*, October 19, 1975, 47.

[10] 'Peter Barnes – Crown Prince destined to be King of Maine Road', *Shoot/Goal Soccer Calendar 1976*, published 1975.

[11] Interview with Alan Oakes by Gary James, 2005.

[12] Interview with Terry Christian by Gary James, January 22, 2020. Subsequent Christian comments are from this interview.

[13] *Manchester City v Birmingham City match programme*, November 9, 1975, 2-3.

[14] 'City lead the way in re-birth of wing play', *Nottingham Football Post*, December 20, 1975, 6.

[15] *Manchester City v Manchester United match programme*, November 12, 1975, 21.

[16] 'Youth bursts through our soccer gloom', *Nottingham Football Post*, December 6, 1975, 6.

[17] 'City must not be put on spot again', *Coventry Evening Telegraph*, December 6, 1975, 41; 'The rivals', *Liverpool Echo*, December 20, 1975, 21.

[18] 'Bell strikes right tone', *Guardian*, November 10, 1975, 16.

[19] 'City quick to remedy problems', *Guardian*, December 15, 1975, 18.

[20] 'Injury to Barnes lames City', *Guardian*, December 27, 1975, 18.

[21] 'Angry Dave raps champs', *Daily Mirror*, December 27, 1975, 32.

[22] *Manchester City v West Ham United match programme*, January 17, 1976, 3.

[23] 'New faces win hands down', *Observer*, January 18, 1976, 23.

[24] 'City set the right mood for Wembley', *Guardian*, January 19, 1976, 16.

[25] *Manchester City v West Ham United match programme*, January 17, 1976, 11.

[26] 'Famous dad let's Peter make his own mind up', *Sports Echo*, February 7, 1976, 4.

[27] *Manchester City v Derby County match programme*, April 10, 1976, 2-3.

[28] 'Wingers work wonders', *Guardian*, December 8, 1975, 16.

Chapter Five

THE LEAGUE CUP

> City have a more open and adventurous style
> of play and more individuals capable of producing the
> unexpected. I am particularly referring to City's wingers,
> Dennis Tueart and Peter Barnes, who provide
> tremendous width and penetration to their team's
> attacking play.

England Manager **DON REVIE** providing his views prior to the
League Cup semi-final, *Sports Argus*, January 10, 1976

The 1975-76 League campaign saw Peter become an established member of the first team, though manager Tony Book was cautious when talking about the young player. Book frequently discussed having to protect Peter during his development. As with Phil Foden at Manchester City in 2019-2020 the media and wider public wanted to see more of the player and believed he was good enough to play at any level and in any competition, but his manager was keen to protect the player while ensuring first team fixtures were not compromised in any way.

For both City and Peter the 1975-76 League games would ultimately be overshadowed by events in the League Cup which, at that time was perceived as a glamorous money-spinning tournament for clubs with the prospect of European qualification being a major attraction.

MANCHESTER CITY F.C.
1975 ● 1976

v NORWICH CITY
WEDNESDAY, SEPTEMBER 17th 1975
LEAGUE CUP 2nd ROUND REPLAY

MATCH MAGAZINE

Price 10p

v NOTTS. FOREST
WEDNESDAY, OCTOBER 8th 1975
LEAGUE CUP 3rd ROUND

MATCH MAGAZINE

Price 10p

City had defeated John Bond's Norwich 6-1 at neutral Stamford Bridge in a second replay of their second round tie. Peter had played in the first replay, coming on as substitute for Joe Royle, which ended 2-2 at Maine Road. Then he started the third round 2-1 victory over Nottingham Forest. That win put City into the fourth round and set Manchester up for a League Cup derby match for the second successive year and brought a nice reminder of how far Peter's career had developed in only a year. At the time of the 1974 League Cup meeting he had yet to start a League game, now he was a regular and was a member of the England Under 23 squad after impressing at youth level: 'It was always a thrill to play against United. That first League Cup game, my debut, was at Old Trafford and a disappointment overall to the club as we'd lost, but for me I thought I had done okay. The 1975-76 League Cup meeting with United was different because I knew

I was part of a great team – it wasn't a one-off appearance – and I knew we were capable of beating any side. Second Division United had shocked City in 1974 but now it was two First Division teams at Maine Road and we were not going to be beaten again. We were going for this from the start.'

As Peter says, the Blues were determined to attack from the outset and by the end of the game United had been soundly thrashed. The contest was over inside the opening thirty minutes when the Blues ran United's defence ragged with some highly skilful and exciting football. As early as the first minute City took the lead. Peter was obstructed by United's Jimmy Nichol. Alan Oakes took the free kick, sending the ball into the penalty area. Denis Tueart pulled it down and comfortably drove the ball into the net. Peter: 'The early goal was important but we were never going to lose that night no matter what. The atmosphere was incredible and we went on to absolutely batter United.'

Five minutes after the goal Colin Bell stayed down following a tackle from United captain Martin Buchan. Colin Bell: 'I remember Dennis Tueart knocking me through on the inside-right position, and I had three options - the first I was going to have a shot if the ball would sit right, from about 25 to 30 yards out. Or I could even quicken up and go for goal first thing. The third option was to drag the ball inside a defender - and it was Martin Buchan as it happens. I was weight bearing on my right leg as I dragged the ball to let him go past at speed, and he caught my knee - bent the knee backwards, burst a couple of blood vessels, did the ligaments, did the cartilage, and off I went. That was the beginning of the end of my career.' [1]

Maine Road fans chanted 'Animal'

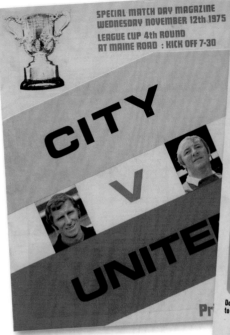

to Buchan as Bell was stretchered off, believing the injury was intentional, but Bell does not accept that view: 'People ask me if the tackle was done on purpose. I don't believe it was and don't believe things like that should happen in the game. No - it's a man's game, you take the knocks.' Peter expresses similar views: 'I like to think that no professional would try to harm another. The game was much more physical in the Seventies than it is in the 2020s and challenges were expected. I was kicked often. It was the way it was, but that night with Colin was awful to see. I think we all knew when we saw his face that this was significant. The challenge didn't look too bad initially but his face said it all.'

Dennis Tueart also felt the challenge did not appear too bad on the night: 'It didn't look anything at the time. It really didn't. I've seen it on tape many, many times. I've watched it in slow motion, slowed it right down still trying to see, and

it looks so innocuous. But you knew that when Colin went down there really was a big problem. At the time you had no idea of the extent of the damage. It also left a major hole in our side - a major hole! He would have been a major miss to any side, but ours in particular because we had such a balanced side. Such a settled team. He and I worked quite well together because I used to operate on the right a lot and he did as well. If I drifted off and left the position he would fill it. Then there was his phenomenal ability to get up and down the field. And of course his goalscoring as well. I don't think we were really as good after Colin's injury.' [2]

United fan, but regular attendee Terry Christian, believed that Colin Bell was a truly outstanding player at this time: 'Bell was just about finding himself for City and England when the injury struck. You can't help wondering whether an injury like that today would be nothing medically. I'm sure players have suffered worse but current treatment is so much better than then. I think a fit Bell would have helped England reach the 1978 World Cup and he'd have still been playing for England in that. He was improving game by game. He'd be contributing a few goals and he had that confidence. I think he may well have been a better player for England too than he was for City.'

The injury ultimately would end Bell's career, although he did return to action before the end of the season for four of the last six games. Christian: 'I remember them bringing him back and him wincing when he was in a 50-50 ball. It was sad to see. Before his injury he'd impact so many games. If City were struggling he'd do something to earn them a draw when they should've lost, or he'd turn a draw into a win.' Initial thoughts were that the player would only be missing for about a month: 'The price of success was a serious injury to England star Colin Bell. Bell was carried off after only three minutes with badly torn muscles in his right thigh and he will need a month to recover. This means he will miss England's vital match in Portugal next week.' [3]

Tommy Booth was brought on to replace Bell and the Blues dominated the match. Asa Hartford was the star man as he gave a tremendous display and after 28 minutes he netted from Joe Royle's knock-down. Tueart scored the third and for midfielder Asa Hartford, having Tueart on one wing and Peter on the other was perfect: 'In that United game we had Peter Barnes wide on the left and Dennis Tueart wide on the right. As a midfield player it was great for me – I always had options.' [4]

In the Second half Peter crossed for Royle to clip the ball into the North Stand

goal. It was a well-deserved 4-0 thrashing. Journalist Paul Fitzpatrick commented on the brilliance of City's team: 'City's performance, had Bell remained in their ranks, would have been commendable enough. Without him it was little short of miraculous, for City had to substitute a defender – Booth – although he played a big part in City's victory. Indeed, no one played below par, and even Corrigan, on the few times that he was tested, looked unbeatable. Bell's departure could have been calamitous. Instead it inspired City.' [5]

Talking specifically of the individuals Fitzpatrick added: 'It was difficult to fault a single City player. From Corrigan, who made one outstanding save from McIlroy in the second half, to the talented Barnes, City bristled with class and flair... Barnes is probably the most exciting young player to emerge since George Best.' He ended his piece with a word of support for the City boss: 'This was City's eleventh game without defeat, and without doubt provided vindication of the sacking by Tony Book of his wayward genius, Marsh. Who needs the unpredictable skills of Marsh when City can achieve heights like this without him?'

City manager Tony Book.

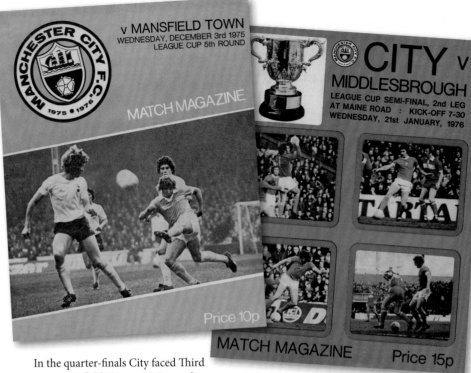

v MANSFIELD TOWN
WEDNESDAY, DECEMBER 3rd 1975
LEAGUE CUP 5th ROUND

MATCH MAGAZINE

Price 10p

CITY v
MIDDLESBROUGH
LEAGUE CUP SEMI-FINAL, 2nd LEG
AT MAINE ROAD : KICK-OFF 7-30
WEDNESDAY, 21st JANUARY, 1976

MATCH MAGAZINE   Price 15p

In the quarter-finals City faced Third Division Mansfield Town on 3 December at Maine Road. The game ended 4-2, but the match was not as comfortable as the scoreline suggests. The Blues went through to the two legged semi-final against Jack Charlton's Middlesbrough. A few weeks later journalist David Lacey analysed the club's development during 1975 believing that Tony Book's determination to play exciting, attack-minded football was paying dividends. He discussed the Blues' positivity and commented about their wing play: 'It is refreshing to see that Manchester City have Tueart running wide, ever ready to cut inside, accelerate and go for goal, while on the opposite flank peter Barnes has considerable potential. He is exceptionally fast; faster than Leighton James and possibly stronger. "We are trying to make him do the simple things in away matches," said Ian MacFarlane, City's assistant manager, on Saturday, "not to take too many people on and get caught." MacFarlane has a point. Talent like this is a rare commodity and needs careful preservation.' [6]

The first leg of the semi-final at Ayresome Park ended in a 1-0 defeat, but it was not a poor performance by the Blues. Peter had returned following his shoulder injury that had kept him out for almost three weeks but did little of note during the match. [7] Peter: 'They were a good side under Jack Charlton and I had a quiet game. I didn't see much of the ball. Souness was there spraying the ball around for them and they were on top. We had our chances but it was a difficult game. In a two-legged game 1-0 defeat away from home isn't a bad result, so we were feeling okay after that match.'

It had taken Middlesbrough almost 66 minutes to break the deadlock, thanks to City's excellent defence: '[City] must have been grateful for the inspiring qualities of Doyle, the tenacity of Barrett again preferred to Clements, and the experience of Booth, restored to his old centre half position in place of Watson, a late withdrawal with back injury. And, as ever this season, City were indebted to Corrigan, whose goalkeeping this term is beyond praise.' The majority of the game was played out in midfield with Oakes, Hartford, and the emerging Paul Power putting up a good fight on City's behalf. In attack Royle and Tueart's attempts were impressive, with Tueart doing all he could to silence the Middlesbrough fans who 'booed almost every time he touched the ball, and he did not endear himself to the home crowd with some over dramatised acting when brought down by Cooper and Boam.'

The second leg saw a youthful City side take Middlesbrough apart and prompted

the *Guardian* to report: 'There is little doubt that some of the best football in the land is being played in Manchester at present.' [8] In the fifth minute Peter rescued the ball at the dead ball line and then centred to twenty year old Ged Keegan, who proceeded to head home his first senior goal. Immediately the pressure of the first game was lifted and City were able to control the match: 'We were definitely up for it. The Kippax was loud and that goal settled things. We had no doubts before the game that we'd do it but you can never be too careful. If we'd have gone into the second half still losing 1-0 on aggregate then we may have lost our edge but we were up for this as soon as we came out and the goal helped us to control the leg.

'I used to love midweek games under the floodlights. The Maine Road changing room wasn't that large and we'd be all packed in there. The place would smell of liniment and our physios Freddie Griffiths and Roy Bailey would be doing their stuff, preparing us physically for the game.

Three of the goalscorers in the second leg against Middlesbrough – Alan Oakes, Joe Royle and Peter.

WHAT A WAY...

NUMBER ONE: Heading for Wembley via Gerard Keegan's first senior goal for City as he steers in a Peter Barnes cross. That 5th minute breakthrough was the dream start that eased the pressures and wiped out Boro's first-leg advantage.
Picture by courtesy of the Daily Mirror

Tetley Bittermen. You can't be

NUMBER TWO: The sweet smell of success is there—with only 11 minutes g time Alan Oakes unerringly fires in a lef-foot shot after Gerard Keegan had lai aside and City have taken the lead and the initiative.
Picture by courtesy of the De

CITY 4

(City win Leag

NUMBER THREE: More left foot power, this time from another youngster revelling in the big-match atmosphere. It proves the 'killer' punch from Peter Barnes scored within a minute of the second half resumption and giving City a 3-1 advantage on aggregate.
Picture by courtesy of JIM HUTCHISON OF THE Daily Mail

THUMBS UP: The strike force tha the dressing room afterwards an

twelve

That night we had a nervous excitement, knowing a good performance would take us to Wembley. We knew what we had to do and I remember walking down the Maine Road tunnel and hearing the atmosphere. You'd see the Kippax as you walked down and that moment when the realisation hit from the fans that we were almost out was always great. The roar would go up and then the club would play "The Boys in Blue" record and we'd be out ready.'

Six minutes later Keegan laid the ball off for the experienced Alan Oakes to fire a left-foot shot past the Middlesbrough 'keeper. City's dominance over Middlesbrough continued and a minute into the second half Peter scored to give City a 3-1 aggregate lead: 'Barnes in possession; Craggs missed his tackle and Barnes was able to run on and score a fine goal, beating Platt with an angled shot.' One minute from the end Joe Royle made it four, and kept his record of scoring in every round. Afterwards Tony Book expressed his delight: 'When you bring kids in like Ged Keegan, Paul Power and Peter Barnes and they play like this, it

NUMBER FOUR: No doubts by the 89th minute. But just to emphasise the point striker Joe Royle keeps up his record of having scored in every round by dashing in on a Boro 'passing mistake just over the half-way line and striding on to steer in the fourth. *Picture by courtesy of the Daily Express*

DDLESBROUGH 0

semi-final on 4 - 1 aggregate)

desbrough's League Cup dreams. Keegan, Oakes, Royle and Barnes relax in staking how they feel about the night's events.
Picture by courtesy of County Press, Wigan.

...TO GET THERE

thirteen

The following issue of the City programme celebrated the memorable semi-final success.

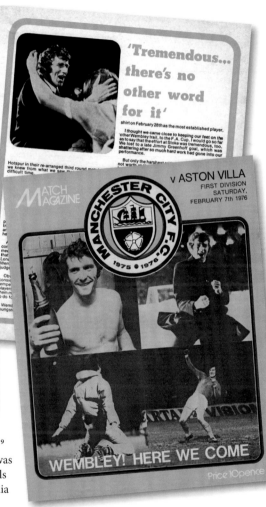

'Tremendous... there's no other word for it'

gives you a feeling you just can't express.' [9] Book's opposite number, Jack Charlton, was not so euphoric: 'Four shots and four goals – what a lesson in finishing.' Special media praise went to Peter with the *Guardian* highlighting the qualities of the ever-dependable Alan Oakes and committed striker Joe Royle before commenting: 'But these players will not mind taking second place to City's youngsters; to Barnes, in particular, who is gracing the game so long starved of genuine wingers.' [10]

City were back at Wembley, for their third League Cup Final: 'I couldn't wait! My old man had played there and won the FA Cup in 1956 and this was to be my chance. His team shocked others with their Revie Plan – even the Busby Babes couldn't cope with that as Dad's team baffled those stuck in the past with their tactics – and, while these were different times, I was proud of our attacking style. We were a team capable of beating any team and, while others may have won more trophies than us, we played with style and in an attack-minded way. Our plan wasn't to pass back to Joe Corrigan in nets and time waste… it was to go at the opposition whoever they were.

'The final was against Newcastle who had beaten Tottenham in the semi, but we didn't care who it was. We were ready.'

YOUNG PETER'S REALLY THE TOPS

IT MAY cause the young man to blush crimson, but the 'weeny-boppers' have a new idol—at least, they do at Maine Road. Fourteen-year-old **Jane Leigh**, of **Woking Road, Cheadle Hulme, Cheshire,** told us all about him, and the torrent of mail from City fans aged under-16 about this pop-favourite proved that she's not far off the mark.

Maybe he's not got a following of Osmonds proportions. But Peter Barnes has captured the hearts of hundreds of young Blues. It's no disrespect to any other player on the staff but no other individual nominated for this competition this season has received such a volume of tributes as our teenage winger.

In response to our recent appeal for letters telling us why Peter is such a big hit among the junior Blues the mailbag never stopped swelling and it is clear that he is a definite NUMBER ONE with the City youth brigade.

CONSIDERATION

It was no easy task to select three winners. But, as we have done in the past when requesting letters about other individuals in the first team squad, we took the age of each entrant into consideration and kept a close watch on the number of words in each letter. Remember, each entry has to contain **no less than 20 words and, if possible, no more than 100 words.**

The three winners will each receive two complimentary stand seats for the home League match against Everton on February 21st, and these will be forwarded in the near future. Congratulations to the winners—and now let's meet them and hear their views.

Ladies first, and Jane Leigh told us:

"Peter is the weenyboppers' favourite of Maine Road. He is young and has little experience, yet he plays like a veteran.

"Established in the first team and with England under-23 honours already within his grasp, Peter must be destined for higher honours. Each week he grows in confidence and more skills just flow from those gifted feet.

"Peter has a lovable, cheeky grin and he always seems to enjoy his football. In fact, he is an ideal advert for football and an answer to its critics.

"How can football finish within 10 years if players like Peter Barnes are still turning out."

Peter, who is not 19 until next June, may be blushing at the bouquets. But his followers believe they are well earned. Just like the second winner, **Paul Phoenix** of **Hope Road, Sale, Cheshire,** who was brief but quite passionate about the appeal generated by the young winger:

"The first time I saw Peter Barnes this season was against Nottingham Forest in the League Cup. He really impressed me with his great speed and passing power.

"He laid off some great balls against Manchester United in the League Cup and I was also amazed at the pace he showed when he sped past a Norwich defender in a recent match. He's mustard.

"He really has a great future ahead of him and I can tell you he is a great favourite with the Kippax Streeters."

But the youngest fan to pass on an accolade—and our third winner—is 11-year-old **Howard Johnson,** of **Briony Avenue, Hale, Altrincham, Cheshire,** and he penned the following tribute:

"Peter must be the trickiest winger in the Football League. His all-round agility and close ball-control make him one of City's best players.

"I saw him against Leeds for the first time and his wing wizardry amazed me until he had to limp off.

"He does not have the best heading ability in the team, but he is the greatest on the ground.

"I was so impressed with Peter that after the match I went to buy a large photo of him."

We did have one special request from 15-year-old **Stella Jones,** of **Silsden Walk, Kersal Vale, Salford,** on behalf of her 18-year-old friend Janice Cox, and while the over-age limit prevented us from giving the contribution the normal consideration, we present the poem which Stella submitted on Janice's behalf.

Never wishing to be ungallant, we fulfil the request:

"Peter Barnes plays on the wing,
Soon at City, he'll be King.
When he gets the ball, watch him turn and sway,
England 'caps' must soon flood his way.
To see him play is such a treat,
With his good looks and magic feet.
With lightning speed,
round defenders he'll dart
And it's clear to see,
he's won Jan's heart."

It's obvious to us that he's already captured many hearts, even though his first team career has only stretched to 20 senior games—and two of those as substitute in the League Cup.

Now we turn to another member of the City staff for whom we invite letters. This time we want to hear from all under-16's (girls and boys) about right back **Kenny Clements** —what qualities you like about this youngster who came into the first team last August.

You may wish to write about his qualities as a player, or tell us a story about a meeting you've had with him. Kenny doesn't necessarily have to be your biggest favourite on the staff—we'd be happy to know the reasons why you are delighted that he's a member of the senior squad.

There will be complimentary tickets for a forthcoming City home game to the winning entrants, and closing date for letters is first post on Saturday, January 24th. Send all entries to: **City Mailbag, Manchester City Football Club, Maine Road, Moss Side, Manchester.**

eleven

A page from the City match programme v West Ham, January 17, 1976

ALL IN THE FAMILY...

Dad, Ken Barnes, talks tactics via the chessboard with sons Peter (left) and Michael

ANOTHER STAR FROM BARNES SUPER STABLE

MANCHESTER CITY are about to scoop almost every top Soccer club in the country—by signing a 15-year-old kid already spoken of as likely to become one of the greatest wing-halves British football has seen for years !

He's Manchester schools Under-15 skipper Michael Barnes, in fact he held the job originally as a 14-year-old, and if the name's familiar, then it should be.

He's the son of City chief scout and former wing-half Ken Barnes, and younger brother of that other so-talented 18-year-old winger Peter Barnes, also of City.

City fan

Arsenal, Burnley, Derby County and Leeds have been leading the chase for Mike "but I've always been a City fan so it was always on,. I suppose, that I'd land up there."

Father Ken, who confirms that the signing of Mike by City "is imminent," admits his lad "is one of the best prospects I've seen." Others talk of his skill, courage, ability to read situations and power of distribution.

A top scout admits: "His potential is frightening," the sort of comment made about elder brother Peter a couple of years back.

Ken Barnes's old pal and team-mate Don Revie wanted Peter so much when he was Leeds manager that they had him at Elland Road nine times, but in the end loyalty to Maine Road won his signature.

Today winger Peter, who played such a vital part in taking City to the League Cup Final, is spoken of as "The Stan Matthews of the Seventies," and is a member of Revie's Under-23 England squad.

As a rival chief scout chuckles: "With that sort of talent in the family, Ken should concentrate on personal management."

DON EVANS

---

1 'Colin Bell interviewed by Gary James, *****CHECK DATE

2 Dennis Tueart interviewed by Gary James, *****CHECK DATE

3 'Wolves Shock', *Reading Evening Post*, November 13, 1975, 24.

4 Ian Penney, *Blue Heaven: Manchester City's Greatest Games* (Edinburgh: Mainstream, 1996), 133.

5 'City show no mercy', *Guardian*, November 13, 1975, 19.

6 'Book proves his point', *Guardian*, December 22, 1975, 16.

7 'Hickton's goal is decisive', *Guardian*, January 14, 1976, 20.

8 'City's final flourish', *Guardian*, January 22, 1976, 20.

9 'Boy, You're a hero!', unknown newspaper cutting from the collection of Peter Barnes, published January 22, 1976.

10 'City's final flourish', *Guardian*, January 22, 1976, 20.

Peter was hoping for a better outcome than his dad enjoyed in a Wembley final against Newcastle 21 years earlier.

Chapter Six

THE FINAL

> Peter Barnes, the sensitive boy who froze in front of the television cameras and stammered his acceptance of the Young Footballer of the Year trophy is ready to express himself in the way that suits him best. He has established himself again in spirit as Manchester City's extra dimension – a left winger – and awaits the word from manager Tony Book to join the club's pursuit of the League Championship and FA Cup.

Journalist **JOHN ROBERTS** commenting in the *Daily Express* during the 1976-77 season (undated cutting in Peter Barnes' collection).

ity's League Cup final opponents would be Newcastle United, and the race for Cup Final tickets was a tough one. In 1974 City were able to put some final tickets on open sale, but in 1976 a large increase in the number of season ticket holders, and a reduction in the amount of tickets available meant that City could not satisfy their average attendance. A large number of fans were disappointed, but City secretary Bernard Halford pointed out that he had even taken the unusual step of writing to all the other League clubs, apart from Newcastle, asking for any spare tickets from their allocations.

For Peter the build-up to the final was interesting: 'It was a great week prior to the final but City being City we didn't follow the usual cup final

THE EMPIRE STADIUM, WEMBLEY

THE FOOTBALL LEAGUE CUP FINAL

SAT., FEB. 28, 1976

KICK-OFF 3.30 p.m.
YOU ARE ADVISED TO TAKE UP YOUR POSITION BY 3 p.m.

TURNSTILES **D**
ENTRANCE **9**

EAST STANDING ENCLOSURE

CHAIRMAN: WEMBLEY STADIUM LTD

STANDING £1.50
TO BE RETAINED

SEE PLAN AND CONDITIONS ON BACK

February 1976

Dear Peter,

Wembley 1976 League Cup Final
Manchester City v. Newcastle United
─────────────────────────────

Please find enclosed:- (a) Room partners
                        (b) Menu
                        (c) Itinerary for the above mentioned

Freddie Griffiths and I made a preliminary investigation of "Champneys"
a few weeks ago and discussed our impending stay with the Management at
the establishment. It is one of Europes premier health resorts,
specifically directed towards physical well-being and anti-stress factors.

The following items ensued from our talks:-
1. We are confident that our stay will in no way interfere with their
other guests, in fact we are sure they will enjoy having us there.

2. Every effort will be made by the staff at Tring to make our stay
happy and successful.

3. Special diets have been carefully prepared to ensure you get the
correct amount of carbohydrates, fats and protein (copy attached).

4. All treatments available, apart from specialised physiotherapy,
facial massage and hair dressing, at no extra charge. An appointment
will be given you for your daily massage and you are requested to
adhere to this time to ensure its' continuity.

5. Golf, tennis, croquet, badminton and table tennis, and other indoor
games, will be available.

6. No smoking allowed.

7. Your dress throughout the stay will be casual and it is prudently
suggested that you include a dressing gown in your attire.

8. As mentioned the rooms are slightly smaller than desirable but each
contains a colour television, radio, telephone, toilet and shower
facilities.

cont/.................

Wembley 1976 League Cup Final
Manchester City v. Newcastle United
─────────────────────────────

R O O M I N G   L I S T
Doubles:-

    1. Barrett and Clements
    2. Power and Keegan
    3. Bell and Doyle
    4. Watson and Tueart
    5. Pardoe and Oakes
    6. Donachie and Hartford
    7. Corrigan and Booth
    8. Barnes and Royle
    9. Bailey and Humphries
    10. Griffiths and Caprio

Singles:-

    K. MacRae
    Mr A K Book
    Mr I MacFarlane
    Mr P Gardner

AKB/JMcC

routine. We spent the week at Champneys health farm at Tring in the Chilterns – unheard of at the time to stay somewhere like that – and I shared a wooden cabin in the grounds with Joe Royle. Every time Joe came in, the cabin would shake! When people got up in the morning you could hear them. You'd hear Joe Corrigan a few doors down open his door and he'd say hello to whoever was around. I think they decided they didn't want footballers in the main house and so they put us down the garden in these chalets. You can imagine someone thinking "we don't want the footballers in the main house, stick them down the garden where they'll not be heard." We trained in between oak trees down the bottom of the garden. It was a huge garden and we'd be down at the bottom for training with Tony Book and Ian MacFarlane. You'd hear one of them say "that oak tree there can be a goal post and we'll stick this here for the other post." It was like going back to football in your garden. Then we'd be training on the lawn and doctors in white coats would be cutting across, or watching us making notes! I remember thinking "we're playing in a cup final in a couple of days and we're using oak trees for goal posts." It was all a bit surreal. A bit comical.

'I think we all lost weight that week. There was virtually no food at the health farm. We went to the main house to eat in a private room there but we seemed to be on a strict diet. To me we just ate raw mushrooms and things! The lads were starving. We couldn't wait to get to London to get some food inside us. It was Colin Bell's birthday while we were sat on the patio and the chef brought out a large cake. We all sang happy birthday but I don't think they allowed us to eat it! The camaraderie was great that week. The humour of it all and just being together helped us prepare. We didn't see much of Asa Hartford though! He seemed to like the beauty treatments and he went to get a facial or to visit the spa every day!'

Wembley 1976 League Cup Final

PLAYERS' ITINERARY

Monday 23rd February:

          Training at Maine Road 10.15 a.m.

Tuesday 24th February:

          Training at Maine Road 10.30 a.m.
          Lunch at Maine Road
          Depart for Tring immediately after lunch
          Arrive Tring approx 5.00 p.m.
          Massage and sauna immediately after room
          allocation
          Dinner
          Free evening

Wednesday 25th February:

          Completely free day
          Golf has been arranged
          Treatments available
          Horse racing after lunch

Thursday 26th February:

          Training 10.15 a.m.
          Lunch and treatments
          Free afternoon

Friday 27th February:

          Training 10.15 a.m.
          Lunch
          Treatments
          Free afternoon – Apart from Press Reception 2.00 p.m.
          Visit to local cinema after dinner

Saturday 28th February:

          Breakfast to be served in your rooms by
          club officials
          Lunch 12.15 p.m.
          Team talk 12.45 p.m.
          Depart for Wembley 1.15 p.m.
          Arrive Wembley 2.00 p.m.

AKD/JMcC

N.B. the above is subject to slight alteration.

Colin Bell's birthday celebrations at Champneys.

'All week, while we were at the health farm, the media had been full of stories of how Malcolm Macdonald would tear us apart. He'd scored five goals against Cyprus for England and this was going to be his finest moment, but in the end he didn't get a look in. Mike Doyle and Dave Watson stopped him and I can't remember him getting a kick of the ball.'

The final was played on 28 February with City the favourites. Newcastle were suffering with injuries and 'flu symptoms. Every member of City's team had already played at Wembley except Peter and Ged Keegan, but they seemed confident in any case.

In preparation for the big game, captain Mike Doyle told the press that the Blues would do all they could to win the trophy.

During the interview reporter Alec Johnson suggested that Wembley newcomers Peter Barnes and Ged Keegan would be the ones likely to let City down. Doyle refused to accept that: 'Rubbish! Peter is not only a tremendously talented player - he's got his head screwed on the right way. He just isn't the sort to get all worked up. In fact, I'll bet that he could prove the biggest success of the whole match. He's a natural. He does things superbly without having to think or worry. Keegan is in the same mould. He'll feel at home, because he's already one of the City first team pool. If he wasn't something special he wouldn't be in it!'

Peter loved the journey to Wembley on League Cup final day: 'It was great seeing all the fans arriving. We travelled in the coach and you'd see cars, vans and coaches with

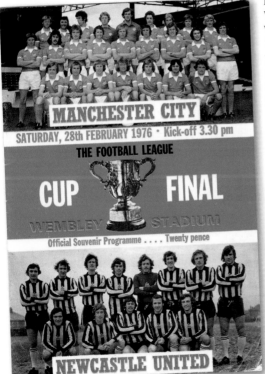

pale blue and white scarves out the windows. Every so often someone would use their horn or start waving through their own car windows to you. As you got closer you'd see more fans on the streets, heading to Wembley. Again there'd be fans in City scarves and hats or carrying banners they'd made. You don't see so many homemade banners at Wembley now – I suppose it's for safety or fire reasons – but back then it was all part of the Wembley spectacle. You'd get down to the big gate where the coaches would arrive at the stadium and there'd be fans all massing around that area waiting. They'd open the gates and the we'd go in. I remember Helen Turner with her bell being there, ringing it as we arrived.

'I remember walking to the dressing room and having butterflies in my stomach. I'd never played at Wembley before then but I had been to the stadium two years earlier to watch the final against Wolves. It was a magnificent feeling to walk into the dressing room, to see the communal bath, to walk down the tunnel on to that lush green pitch. At the time Wembley felt so special and you knew that your only chance of playing there would be to play for England or to get there in a final with your club.'

Peter was nervous but as they walked around Wembley trying to get their minds focused City's assistant manager seemed to be somewhat giddy. 'I have a strange memory of that day and it's of our coach Ian McFarlane,' remembers Peter. 'He was always wearing tartan and was a real larger than life character. A mad Scotsman really. We were out on the pitch before kick-off and he had the ball and was taking shots at Corrigan. You could tell he loved being on the pitch at Wembley and wasn't going to miss his chance to have a kickabout on the turf. We tried to get the ball off him but couldn't. He was like the teacher played by Brian Glover in the film Kes! This was his day and we weren't going to stop him. It was really funny.

'I was eager for the game to start. With football you need to get the game going and do something decent early on to settle – or at least I did. Our team had a good number of us who had come through the ranks – Joe Corrigan, Ged Keegan, Willie Donachie, Mike Doyle, Alan Oakes, Tommy Booth and me. In fact City had only paid a fee for Dennis Tueart, Asa Hartford, Dave Watson and Joe Royle. Predominantly homegrown lads who had come through their apprenticeship with dad, Steve Fleet, Dave Ewing, Harry Godwin, Johnny Hart and so on. We were a family club from people like Julia McCrindle in the office through to Bernard Halford and the players. Everybody had a smile on their faces and we were all in it together. That's how I remember it.

Lovely people and it extended beyond those connected with match activities at Maine Road. Don't forget we had Roy and Kath Clarke running the social club and Roy Little at the University grounds – beautiful people who had played for the club or lived a life with City for decades. I couldn't believe that I was playing alongside players like Alan Oakes and Mike Doyle... to me they were real legends of the club and here I was in 1976 playing alongside them at Wembley. I couldn't believe it.'

Peter enjoyed walking out on to the pitch with the rest of the team shortly before the game was due to start: 'The City fans had that end of the stadium, so as you walked up the tunnel you could hear a tremendous roar above and behind you. Knowing they were our fans was brilliant and I can't imagine how that would feel if you were the opposition.'

Once the final commenced both sides played open, attractive football, although Newcastle seemed to have the edge for a while. Joe Corrigan palmed a 25 yarder from Malcolm Macdonald round the post at one point, then a foul by Newcastle's Keeley on Royle brought an important free-kick: 'After 11 minutes Hartford's free-kick from the right found Keeley and Howard following Royle and Watson, but ignoring Doyle, who stole in behind them to head the ball back via Newcastle defenders, to Barnes. The bounce was awkward for the young forward and he did well to keep his shot down.' [1] Peter fired a half-volley into the net to give City the lead. He immediately ran off the pitch in celebration, while the City supporters on the East Terrace danced with delight: 'It was great for me to score the goal at the end where all the City fans were. I could see them all react as I ran towards them. We'd worked on the move a little in training and I remember looking for it. I think it was by chance really

Peter runs towards the City fans to celebrate his Wembley goal (above) where he is joined by Dennis Tueart and Joe Royle (right).

that it was headed down towards me and I came for it. It bounced nicely for me and I just hit it on the volley and thankfully it went in.'

Back in 1976 Tony Book explained how the goal came from a set piece developed in training: 'It was Asa Hartford's idea. He suggested that for a free kick from one of the flanks our three big men should run forward as the kick came over to leave Doyle free on the far post. He got the kick, Asa took it, and it happened exactly as we planned, with Doyle's header eventually reaching young Peter Barnes who scored a goal his performance deserved.' [2] City staff member and fan Roger Reade was delighted with that goal: 'It was brilliant for us all to see Peter score that. It was something they'd practiced on the training ground at Platt Lane. It came off superbly. That was fantastic. We all knew that Newcastle had been hit with some kind of 'flu virus that week and as time moved on you knew they

were going to struggle – and they did but not until after they'd stunned us with their goal.'

That equaliser came twenty four minutes after Peter's. Malcolm Macdonald sent in a low centre. Watson, Corrigan and Newcastle's Gowling all raced for the ball with the Newcastle man managing to get to it first and he stabbed it home. Peter: 'We were still the better team and we knew we'd do it. The adrenalin was going and we couldn't wait for the second half to put things right.'

As the players came out for the second half, all Blues hoped for an early goal to re-establish control of the game, but few

Dennis Tueart scores City's second against Newcastle.

expected it to arrive within a minute of the restart. Dennis Tueart remembers how the goal came about: 'Apart from the style of the finishing, it was a move we'd used an awful lot. When Colin Bell got injured we would try several different players to fit in there and we ended up with Tommy Booth playing right side midfield - Tommy was a centre half but he had a lovely touch, lovely player on the ball, that was the beauty of Manchester City we always had good ball players with ability, right from the back to the front. Tommy came in and did a job on the right side of midfield, and it was no good me going to the far post for crosses with Willie Donachie always marauding down that left side. Always coming out and getting down that left side. He always marauded, did it loads of times, and Willie's always either knocking them short or playing far post. Tommy would get the far post and, as I say, I would drift off and go into the middle to find any bits of spare balls dropping down. I'd try to get on the end of the knock downs not the first one.

'The goal itself, I've seen it on tape. Willie's going, I've gone to the far post, then come away from the far post because Tommy's gone there. But as I've checked back into the centre, I'd gone in too far, the ball's gone over to Tommy. Tommy's got half a head on it, and knocked it back. It just went a wee bit behind me. Well, I'd always been fairly good at volleying right from an early age, and I'd scored a goal, probably it was the first or second game of the season, against Norwich. Which I think was technically a better goal, it flew in the net, overhead kick. I'd scored overhead kicks at school, I'd side volleyed which is slightly different, but timing and volleying had always been a strength, and it just came. Speak to Denis Law and he'll tell you any balls that come to you as a forward, no matter which way they come to you, you just try and twist your body and get some kind of contact onto it. Because you know the general area where the goal is, and I connected pretty well, it went across and bounced in.

'It was important because they'd come back before half time and got the equaliser. We'd worked a good free kick for the first goal. Well worked. Marvellous when I see it on tape. Because we'd tried it on the training pitch, and it worked to perfection. So that gave us the lead. Then they got a good goal back, we'd been caught a little bit square at the back. Then it was important because it was the 46th minute, just after half time, when we got ourselves back in front. I've never known so many people have a go at me for scoring a goal too early, because they were still at the toilet or queuing for a cup of tea! They couldn't get back in time. It was an important goal though, because we'd dominated the majority of the first half. But we went in at 1-1. So, it was important to get quickly back in the lead again, and make them come out again. Which we did. 46th minute you can't have much before that in the Second Half!' [3]

It could have been Joe Royle who scored the winner, but an effort from him had been disallowed. Royle: 'It would have been nice. I'd scored in every round and that would have been the full set. The winning was more important though.' [4] Peter: 'Joe was unlucky with that. He deserved a goal for everything he'd done for us that season and in that cup run. He'd scored six goals in the League Cup that season and I don't think we'd have got to Wembley without him.'

Newcastle did have chances to level again later on but City remained the dominant side. The goal seemed to kill much of the fight that had pushed the 'flu stricken Newcastle side forward. Journalist David Lacey reported: 'Certainly they tired rapidly in the last half-hour and throughout the game Nattrass, damaged knee heavily strapped, was really in no fit state to encounter Barnes, Donachie, Hartford and

anyone else who cared to take advantage of the broad avenue of space available on the left wing.' [5]

At the final whistle Tueart swapped shirts with a Newcastle player and wore his home town colours for the Cup presentation, which led to him 'being exhorted by an official to go up and receive a loser's tankard.' Peter: 'It was a thrilling moment of course walking up those deep, high steps to collect our tankards, especially for those of us from Manchester. Playing for your home town team at Wembley and winning the trophy meant a lot. If I hadn't been playing I'd have been in the stands watching. It meant something as a player of course; and it meant something as a fan. I was also pleased that I'd got a bit of revenge over Newcastle for my dad I suppose. He was in that 1955 team that lost to Newcastle in the FA Cup final, so that was something else I remember feeling happy about.

'After collecting our tankards we went on our lap of honour. You did the full lap of Wembley back then, no cutting corners and only celebrating in front of your own fans. We headed around to the Newcastle end first and they all stayed and applauded us. They were wonderful and it irritates me enormously when the fans of a losing club don't bother to stay to watch even their own team collect their runners' up medals these days. No matter who wins, reaching a major final is an achievement and fans should stay and applaud both teams – but if they can't do that they should at least applaud and show their support for their team!'

As City walked around the stadium Dave Watson's City shirt was rapidly becoming blood stained. The big centre half, who had been doubtful for the game right up until three hours before kick-off due to problems with a slipped disc, collided with Alan Gowling when the Newcastle man attempted a glancing back header, and after the match television cameras filmed him having stitches in the dressing room.

Another moment caught by the cameras was the sight of the injured Colin Bell waiting for the winners in the dressing room. He was naturally delighted with City's success, but viewers realised that his loss had been a major one. Then, as the dressing room became livelier,

Dennis Tueart filled the League Cup with champagne and walked into the Newcastle dressing room to offer his opponents a drink. Malcolm Macdonald, who over the years has suffered a great deal at the hands of City - most notably when his Huddersfield side were defeated 10-1 in 1987 - was the first to drink.

Manager Book, who became the first

Peter, in between a bloodied Dave Watson and Joe Royle, on the lap of honour at Wembley.

man to win the trophy as a player and as
a manager, was delighted with the result:
'This was my greatest moment. It was a
tremendous final and Tueart's goal was
something special... quite out of this world.'
Over the years since 1976 Tueart's overhead
goal has naturally been remembered
and entered City folklore as a defining
moment, overshadowing perhaps Peter's
goal and the contribution of others. This is
inevitable; however it is worth reminding
ourselves of the contemporary media
coverage of the final to see what those
writing and reporting on the final thought.
Distinguished journalist Hugh McIlvanney
was full of praise for the performances of
Ged Keegan, Mike Doyle, Tueart, Donachie
but mostly for Peter's contribution, who
he described as an 'ebullient, highly skilled
newcomer to Wembley.' [6] He went on:
'Barnes, whose father was in the City team
that lost to Newcastle in the Cup Final of
1955, attacked with an eager confidence that
declared a firm intention of salvaging family
pride. His willingness to run at and beyond
Nattrass, or anyone else who showed in
front of him, was one of the most effective
contributions to the first half, and only the

PICTURES BY

At Wembley:
ERIC GRAHAM
IAN CURRIE
Homecoming:
JOHN HOLLAND

LIKE father like son . . .
proud dad Ken Barnes,
City's Chief Scout,
places the League Cup
on the head of son
Peter, the dazzling
young winger who set
the Blues on their way
with his 11th minute
goal . . . what a start
to his first game at
Wembley !

BO
CO
DO

BARNES, TUEART
CITY'S DAZZLERS

By PETER GARDNER

PETER BARNES and Dennis Tueart
set today's League Cup final alight
with glorious goals, to give Manchester City the edge over Newcastle
United at Wembley.

For Barnes it was a fairy-tale debut
with an 11th minute goal at the grey,

TWO

Hull 0
Att. 20,000
Blackpool .. 1
Att. 8,000
Blackburn .. 1
Att. 12,000
Sunderland. 0
Att. 11,000
Oldham 3
Att. 13,000
Fulham 0
Att. 12,000

LEAGUE CUP FINAL
MANCHESTER CITY.   2
NEWCASTLE UTD...   1
FINAL SCORE

most miserably unromantic spirits in the ground could fail to be thrilled when he scored after 11 minutes.'

Describing Peter's goal McIlvanney commented: 'Keeley and Kennedy rose in anxious collision to attempt a clearance, but the mis-hit header that resulted merely dropped the ball in front of Barnes. It bounced awkwardly, but he used his left foot to come down on it with killing economy, and it went swiftly inside the goalkeeper's left-hand post.'

The *Manchester Evening News'* Peter Gardner called it a 'glorious goal' while journalist Frank McGhee simply claimed that Peter's goal: 'added a "Roy of the Rovers" touch to the game.' [7] He added:

'The performance of this natural winger, always willing to take on opponents, beat them with pace and head for the line, must have delighted the watching England manager, Don Revie.' [8] According to McGhee, Peter's goal gave him 'a memory to warm him for the rest of his life.'

Reports were positive on the role of Peter; City's performance and on the final as a whole: 'Saturday's game at Wembley was a peacock compared to some recent cabbage whites, full of individual skills and achievements with both teams placing a heavy emphasis on attack but won, paradoxically, by the better-organised defence. Manchester City, a more profound side than Newcastle United, made greater use of Wembley's space and, apart from two short periods in the first half, always looked likely winners.' [9]

How City's programme from the following home game celebrated the League Cup triumph and Peter's PFA award.

Peter provided his thoughts on the final to Peter Gardner: 'I'm still trying to come down to earth after getting a goal after just 11 minutes of my first game at Wembley. It came from a set piece when the ball landed in front of me and bounced up I didn't think – I just whacked it in and what a feeling that was. I was nervous going out there, but once the whistle went I was able to relax a bit more and then the goal drove away all the tension. Although we let them back once, I felt when the second one went in we would be determined enough not to let them back a second time.' [10]

After the success City held a celebratory banquet: 'My mum had come down to Wembley and came to the banquet, so that added to it. She didn't often see me play – I think she came to about three of my games. She was always nervous that I'd get injured. So it was great that she was there that day. The whole night was special and the trophy was on the top table with Tony Book, the chairman Peter Swales and the other directors.' For Peter Swales, two years and four months into his reign as City chairman, it was a great celebration and expected to be the first of many: 'As Chairman, the 1976 League Cup was my first trophy, and I certainly didn't think it would be my last! It was great to win it, but the League Cup wasn't the highlight it should have been because, obviously, I thought it was the first of many. I probably felt like Johnson did when Everton won the F.A. Cup in '95. He would certainly have thought "this is the first of plenty".'

Roger Reade remembers the celebrations in 1976: 'I was only about nineteen and that was a great night. Trophies were so much harder to win in those days and so the celebrations were something special. The League Cup had a significant status too and it got you a

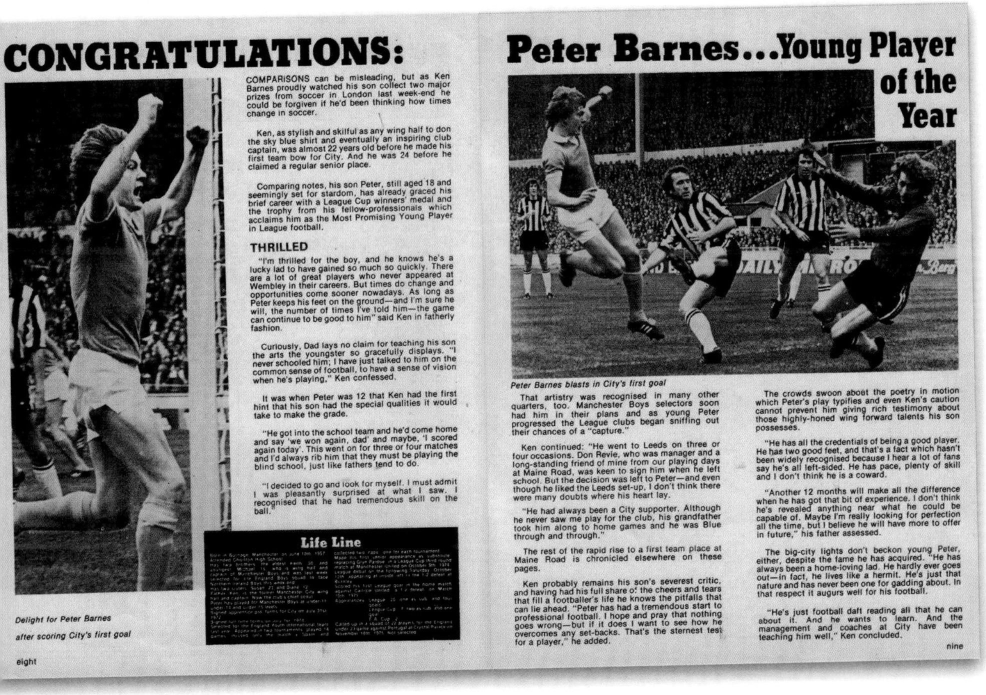

CONGRATULATIONS:

COMPARISONS can be misleading, but as Ken Barnes proudly watched his son collect two major prizes from soccer in London last week-end he could be forgiven if he'd been thinking how times change in soccer.

Ken, as stylish and skilful as any wing half to don the sky blue shirt and eventually an inspiring club captain, was almost 22 years old before he made his first team bow for City. And he was 24 before he claimed a regular senior place.

Comparing notes, his son Peter, still aged 18 and seemingly set for stardom, has already graced his brief career with a League Cup winners' medal and the trophy from his fellow-professionals which acclaims him as the Most Promising Young Player in League football.

THRILLED

"I'm thrilled for the boy, and he knows he's a lucky lad to have gained so much so quickly. There are a lot of great players who never appeared at Wembley in their careers. But times do change and opportunities come sooner nowadays. As long as Peter keeps his feet on the ground—and I'm sure he will, the number of times I've told him—the game can continue to be good to him" said Ken in fatherly fashion.

Curiously, Dad lays no claim for teaching his son the arts the youngster so gracefully displays. "I never schooled him; I have just talked to him on the common sense of football, to have a sense of vision when he's playing," Ken confessed.

It was when Peter was 12 that Ken had the first hint that his son had the special qualities it would take to make the grade.

"He got into the school team and he'd come home and say 'we won again, dad' and maybe, 'I scored again today'. This went on for three or four matches and I'd always rib him that they must be playing the blind school, just like fathers tend to do.

"I decided to go and look for myself. I must admit I was pleasantly surprised at what I saw. I recognised that he had tremendous skill on the ball."

Life Line

Delight for Peter Barnes after scoring City's first goal

eight

Peter Barnes...Young Player of the Year

Peter Barnes blasts in City's first goal

That artistry was recognised in many other quarters, too. Manchester Boys selectors soon had him in their plans and as young Peter progressed the League clubs began sniffing out their chances of a "capture."

Ken continued: "He went to Leeds on three or four occasions. Don Revie, who was manager and a long-standing friend of mine from our playing days at Maine Road, was keen to sign him when he left school. But the decision was left to Peter—and even though he liked the Leeds set-up, I don't think there were many doubts where his heart lay.

"He had always been a City supporter. Although he never saw me play for the club, his grandfather took him along to home games and he was Blue through and through."

The rest of the rapid rise to a first team place at Maine Road is chronicled elsewhere on these pages.

Ken probably remains his son's severest critic, and having had his full share of the cheers and tears that fill a footballer's life he knows the pitfalls that can lie ahead. "Peter has had a tremendous start to professional football. I hope and pray that nothing goes wrong—but if it does I want to see how he overcomes any set-backs. That's the sternest test for a player," he added.

The crowds swoon about the poetry in motion which Peter's play typifies and even Ken's caution cannot prevent him giving rich testimony about those highly-honed wing forward talents his son possesses.

"He has all the credentials of being a good player. He has two good feet, and that's a fact which hasn't been widely recognised because I hear a lot of fans say he's all left-sided. He has pace, plenty of skill and I don't think he is a coward.

"Another 12 months will make all the difference when he has got that bit of experience. I don't think he's revealed anything near what he could be capable of. Maybe I'm really looking for perfection all the time, but I believe he will have more to offer in future," his father assessed.

The big-city lights don't beckon young Peter, either, despite the fame he has acquired. "He has always been a home-loving lad. He hardly ever goes out—in fact, he lives like a hermit. He's just that nature and has never been one for gadding about. In that respect it augurs well for his football.

"He's just football daft reading all that he can about it. And he wants to learn. And the management and coaches at City have been teaching him well," Ken concluded.

nine

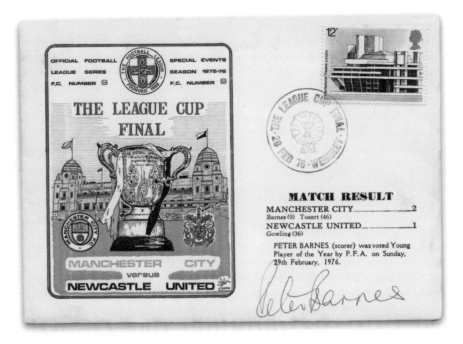

12°

MATCH RESULT

MANCHESTER CITY.............................2
Barnes (9)   Tueart (46)
NEWCASTLE UNITED..................1
Gowling (36)

PETER BARNES (scorer) was voted Young
Player of the Year by P.F.A. on Sunday,
29th February, 1976.

guaranteed European place.' For Peter's
father Ken the banquet was a special
occasion: 'When it's your playing success
you can't always take it in. You live
through the drama and excitement of it
all as a player, but you don't savour it. It's
impossible to enjoy it in the way supporters
can – you can watch it, enjoy it, suffer with
it in some ways as well, but for players
you're working and can't pause to think of
it as a significant historical moment. But,
in 1976 when my son Peter was playing for
City against Newcastle in the League Cup
final, I was able to enjoy it as a supporter.
I was nervous because it was my son, but
I was able to savour that occasion and
look around at the packed stadium, but I
never had the opportunity with my own
key games. When it came to the banquet I
could enjoy it and reflect on what Peter had
achieved that day.'

The day after winning the League Cup
the media called on Peter early: 'They

wanted a photograph of me and Dennis
Tueart as we'd both scored. They decided
to do this in my bathroom – I'm in the
bath and Dennis Tueart's pouring water
out of the cup over me! The things they get
you to do.' Both Peter and Tueart stayed in
London that Sunday for the Professional
Footballers' Association (PFA) awards.
Peter had been shortlisted for the young
player award while Tueart was to be named
in the First Division team of the year. The
award, held at the London Hilton Hotel, had
been decided by votes from all professional
footballers over the weeks before the final,
so Peter's performance at Wembley played
no part in the decision process. Peter was
up against Manchester United's Gordon
Hill and Steve Coppell, Liverpool's Jimmy
Case, Burnley's Brian Flynn and Liam
Brady from Arsenal.

On the night a nervous Peter was
sat in his dinner suit waiting for the
announcement: 'I can laugh about this

now but at the time it was painful. At the awards I was sat with Dennis Tueart but we were the only City people there because of the homecoming. We also shared a table with a few United men. The guys on our table were telling me I had a good chance of winning and I remember Tueart saying that I had to thank so and so – the list kept growing. When it was announced that I'd won I got up, still with the lads telling me to say this and say that, and as I collected the award from Gordon Banks I looked around the room. It was packed with over 700 players. Dickie Davies from ITV was the host and he stood a little behind me. I was still worrying about what to say when I started my speech: "My Lords, Ladies, and Gentlemen…" I looked around the room and saw there were no ladies. Great start! Then I said: 'I'd like to ah… ah… ah…' I froze!

'Funnily enough the Liverpool players were just in front of me and I remember Kevin Keegan urging me to just say anything. I could hear Dickie Davies behind me whispering "say something… anything!" I eventually thanked someone – the players I think – and then I went back to my seat. It was the most frightening experience of my life at the time!'

Peter won the award with a huge majority while goalkeeper Pat Jennings took the senior award. [11] Back at home in Manchester Peter's mum Jean was watching: 'The programme was live on ITV that night and I mum was sat there watching with Michael. I got up to speak, she heard the applause and then when I started I froze. Mum's sat there saying: "Michael, the sound's gone on the telly. I can't hear what Peter's saying!" She couldn't believe it was silent.'

Roger Reade: 'That was Peter's shyness. That was a reminder that he was still that same lad. He froze and I remember

shouting at the telly "Peter, say something!" It was just because he was such a shy guy. So humble. He was stuck in that room with a thousand of long established players, all looking at him. Major stars that he himself would've idolised all watching and waiting for this young boy to speak. Terrifying for him. In some ways it provides a lovely summary of Peter. He was shy and humble and probably saw himself out of place in that environment. He was a superstar and a truly great footballer and deserved his place there but, knowing Peter, he would never have thought that.'

The following week's *News of the World* columnist Patrick Collins discussed Peter and the awards. Their analysis was spot on:

PFA Young Player of the Year.

'He looks even younger in a dinner jacket than he does in a sky-blue shirt. A slim, floppy-haired lad, blinking in the harsh television lights as he tries to find the words to thank his fellows for electing him the best young footballer of the year.

'There are 18-year-olds who would make more confident speeches than Peter Barnes. There is none who plays football better or more attractively than the gauche, skinny kid who beguiled both Wembley Stadium and the Hilton Hotel last weekend. "That Hilton thing was terrible, really terrible," he says. "I'd been practising all day what I was going to say, then when it came to it, I was stood there searching for words. I could feel everyone in the place trying to prompt me. Terrible, wasn't it? Dead nerve-wracking."

'And the day before? The day he scored a goal for Manchester City after a 12-minute acquaintance with Wembley and provoked a host of comparisons with a litany of wingers bearing names like Matthews, Best and Finney, and persuaded the uncommitted that here, indeed, was one of the great players. What about the day? "Well that was just a game, wasn't it? I mean nerves don't come into it really. You go out and play and you've got good players round you and it all works out. I mean compared to speaking to a big crowd of people, that's easy."

'There is something marvellously

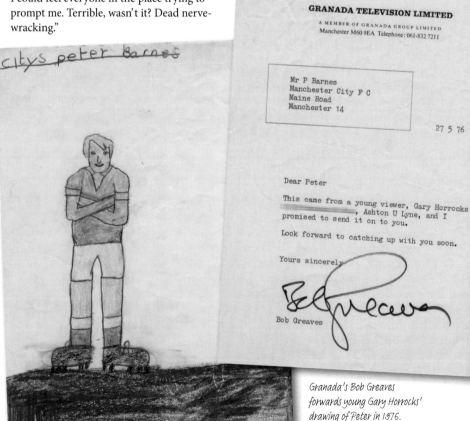

Granada's Bob Greaves forwards young Gary Horrocks' drawing of Peter in 1976.

Peter and the Manchester City squad with the League Cup in 1976.

refreshing about Peter Barnes, something which makes you hope and pray that his talent will take root and flourish.' [12]

Collins continued: 'He gives every indication of being both ordinary and unspoiled, and at a time when the game is increasingly falling victim to the excesses of its young superstars.'

There was something endearing about Peter that seemed at odds to the general views of pampered, prima donna players that were often portrayed during this era. Peter appeared to have his feet on the ground which was a remarkable feat considering he had only made his debut the previous season, that he only became a regular after Rodney Marsh was dropped from the team earlier in the season and his age. So much positivity, success and adulation had arrived so quickly that it's a wonder he managed to remain level-headed. He explained to Collins how he saw the coming months: 'They tell me next year will be the real test. Like this year I've played and it's gone well and everyone's surprised. Next year they'll be looking for me, trying to find out if I really am a player.'

It was this approach that was helping to keep Peter focused, although it was difficult. The amount of fan mail increased significantly throughout the 1975-76 season but after the PFA awards the volume increased again, though those writing the letters were older than his regular fans: 'I got more fan mail that week than at any other time, but it was all from mothers. They all wanted to give motherly advice!'

The increased attention from mothers Peter received was welcome but he also began receiving increased attention from rival fans. On the last day of the 1975-76 season he was in the City side that faced Manchester United at Old Trafford. It was Peter's first game there after the PFA awards and he received considerable abuse from the home fans, this included broadcaster Terry Christian: 'I'll never forget that. "I'd like to errr, errr. I'd like to say err, errr".

We all started singing it at Old Trafford. There was the "Barnsey, Barnsey give us a speech" and then every time his name would be announced we'd go "I'd like to say err, err, err." Cruel!' It was an achievement winning that award and we all knew that. He deserved it but you know what football fans are like. It had to be done.' Gary Owen remembers the abuse: 'It was all part of the derby day routine: "Barnsey, Barnsey, give us a speech" then City fans would chant an abusive song about Tommy Docherty.'

The banter was an everyday part of Manchester football at the time. Peter: 'United's full back was Alex Forsyth for this game. We used to call him Bruce of course. Whenever we played United you'd go past him muttering 'Nice to see you, Brucie. Nice!" Every time I passed him! After the PFA awards I did get abuse at Old Trafford and I suppose I was an easy target. I remember going to take a corner at the Stretford End and the United fans all doing that 'I'd like to errr, errr' chant. I found it funny eventually but that time I think it was the first time I'd heard it and I completely messed up the corner – which added to the abuse of course!'

Christian: 'I don't remember it getting to Peter on the pitch but if it did then you've got to question the way football clubs looked after their players back then. There's the whole psychology of it all. Footballers were going to get abuse for stuff like that, so clubs should have helped them prepare for it. He'd had the accolades and was a talented player and maybe he needed more from the club. He was a shy player and never cocky, so maybe there was a confidence issue.' Media training for footballers was unheard of at the time. Gary Owen: 'Peter was a kid and none of us were tutored in how to talk with the media or how to handle the crowds. We just had to get on with it.'

Peter's memories of that time also show the great rivalry that existed between Blues and Reds and the other teams in the region. The banter from the Stretford End and from the Kippax at Maine Road livened up games and, although sometimes it overstepped the mark, it was always typical of Manchester and Mancunian life at the time.

[1] 'City's conquest of Wembley's space', *Guardian*, March 1, 1976, 22.
[2] 'All good pals and jolly good company', *Observer*, February 29, 1976, 20.
[3] Dennis Tueart interviewed by Gary James, 1996.
[4] Joe Royle interviewed by Gary James, March 2010.
[5] 'City's conquest of Wembley's space', *Guardian*, March 1, 1976, 22.
[6] 'Football League Cup Final', *Observer*, February 29, 1976, 20.
[7] 'Sky's the limit', *Manchester Evening News Wembley Picture Special*, March 1, 1976, 11; 'Mac's wall of tears', *Daily Mirror*, March 1, 1976, 23.
[8] 'Mac's wall of tears', *Daily Mirror*, March 1, 1976, 23.
[9] 'City's conquest of Wembley's space', *Guardian*, March 1, 1976, 22.
[10] Sky's the limit', *Manchester Evening News Wembley Picture Special*, March 1, 1976, 12.
[11] 'Barnes top young player', *Daily Mail*, March 1, 1976.
[12] 'You don't need words, Barnes!', *News of the World*, March 7, 1976, 19.

Chapter Seven

CHALLENGING LIVERPOOL

> Last season City unearthed the Young Footballer of the Year in Peter Barnes, a player of such heightened skills that his wing displays inevitably had people recalling the days of Matthews and Finney... The biggest disappointment for City followers perhaps is the continued absence of Peter Barnes. The career of this talented youngster will not reach maturity in the Central League or on the substitute's bench, although Book will not now want to disrupt a side unbeaten in the League since they were at Ipswich on October 23. Barnes' footballing ability is unquestioned. His appetite for hard, physical conflict has yet to be proved but there are many who feel that the best of Royle and Kidd would be seen if Barnes were plying them with a winger's service from the left.'

Journalist **PAUL FITZPATRICK** assessing the role of Peter Barnes in the *Guardian*, January 21, 1977, 18.

Two weeks after their last League game of the 1975-76 season Manchester City were in Japan for their first tour of the Far East. Games with a Japanese XI and a South Korean XI were scheduled across both countries and this was perceived at the time as a ground breaking initiative for the club at a time when few European clubs toured those countries. Peter was a member of the tour party and started four

of the seven games played. The Blues won all games apart from a 4-2 defeat to South Korea's B team at Seoul on 30 May 1976, which manager Tony Book was reported as saying: 'his team, including many reserves, were tired after four matches in Japan, all of which they won without conceding a goal. He said errors caused three of the four goals.' [1]

For the PFA Young Player of the Year,

the 1976-77 season was expected to see him develop further with the added challenge of European football coming via the UEFA Cup, however player changes were to affect Peter's opportunities for the opening of the new season. Experience was something manager Tony Book felt was lacking in his team, especially as Colin Bell's injury was actually more serious than initially thought when the player was brought back into the team for four of the final six games of the previous season. It would ultimately be a long fight to return to fitness for the talented international. To fill the gap and meet what Book saw as the challenge of Europe he brought in 29 year old Fulham and Ireland international midfielder Jimmy Conway: 'I need a right-sided midfield player as insurance for Colin Bell. Colin has not fully recovered from his injuries, but I expect him to be all right by mid-September. However, with European commitments in the EUFA (sic) Cup it is important to cover every position and I am now delighted to include Jim Conway in my plans.' [2] Book also brought in the former Manchester United European Cup winner Brian Kidd who City had first been interested in signing in December 1969 when his future at United seemed in doubt: 'I recall City's reported interest and it flattered me. I wouldn't have hesitated about moving, but the trouble blew over.' [3]

Peter saw the arrival of Conway as part of new coach Bill Taylor's plans: 'Bill had arrived that summer as coach, replacing Ian MacFarlane, and that's where we signed Jimmy Conway from. Bill was a lovely man, polite and loved his football, but it was defence first. He was a cautious coach. The type who preferred not to concede. I know dad chatted to him often and challenged him the then modern view that

P/FL

An Agreement made the TWELFTH

day of JULY 1976 between J.D. HALFORD of Maine Road, Manchester, 14 in the County of Lancashire the Secretary of and acting pursuant to Resolution and Authority for and on behalf of the MANCHESTER CITY FOOTBALL CLUB of Maine Road, Manchester (hereinafter referred to as the Club) of the one part and

PETER SIMON BARNES

of 4 Clovelly Road, Chorlton-cum-Hardy, Manchester in the County of Lancashire

(hereinafter referred to as the Player) of the other part **Whereby** it is agreed as follows:—

1. The Player hereby agrees to play in an efficient manner and to the best of his ability for the Club for the period of two (years/years) (hereinafter called "the initial period of employment") from the Twelfth day of July 1976 to the 30th day of June 1978 Unless the initial period of employment shall either be (a) previously determined in accordance with the provisions of one or other of Clauses 10, 11 or 12 hereof or (b) terminated, extended or renewed as provided by Clauses 17 and 18 of this Agreement.

2. The Player shall attend the Club's ground or any other place decided upon by the Club for the purposes of or in connection with his training as a Player pursuant to the instructions of the Secretary, Manager, or Trainer of the Club, or of such other person, or persons as the Club may appoint.

3. The Player shall do everything necessary to get and keep himself in the best possible condition so as to render the most efficient service to the Club, and will carry out all the training and other instructions of the Club through its representative officials.

4. The Player shall observe and be subject to all the Rules, Regulations and Bye-Laws of The Football Association, and any other Association, League, or Combination of which the Club shall be a member. And this Agreement shall be subject to any action which shall be taken by The Football Association under their Rules for the suspension or termination of the Football Season, and if any such suspension or termination shall be decided upon the payment of wages shall likewise be suspended or terminated, as the case may be and in any proceedings by the Player against the Club it shall be a sufficient and complete defence and answer by and on the part of the Club that such suspension or termination hereof is due to the action of The Football Association, or any Sub-Committee thereof to whom the power may be delegated.

5. The Player shall not engage in any business or live in any place which the Directors (or Committee) of the Club may deem unsuitable.

6. Unless this Agreement has previously been determined by any one of Clauses 10, 11 or 12 hereof as hereinafter provided, the Player shall not before the last day of the playing season next preceding the expiration of any further or additional further period for which this Agreement shall have been renewed in accordance with the provisions of Clauses 17 or 18 hereof or before the last day of the playing

13. The following special provisions laid down [unclear] the Player will compete are accepted by and will be observed by the [unclear]

(a) It is hereby agreed by the Player that if he shall at any time be absent from his duties by reason of sickness or injury he shall, during such absence, be entitled to receive only the difference between the weekly wage he was receiving at the time of his sickness or injury and the amount he receives as benefit under the National Insurance Act, 1946, or The National Insurance (Industrial Injuries) Act, 1946, and for the purpose of this Clause his wages shall be deemed to accrue from day to day.

(b) If at any time during the period of this Contract of Service the payments herein agreed shall be in excess of the payments permitted to be paid by the Club to the Player in accordance with Regulations 40(b) and 43 of The Football League the payments to the player shall be the amount the Club is entitled to pay in accordance with such regulations and this Contract of Service shall be read and construed, as if it were varied accordingly.

(c) The Player agrees not without the written permission of the Club to give any interviews to nor write for newspapers or publications nor take part in television or radio and that he will submit articles etc. for the approval before any publication of the same

14. Basic Wages.

£	80	per week from 12.7.76	to 30.6.78
£		per week from	to
£		per week from	to
£		per week from	to
£		per week from	to
£		per week from	to
£		per week from	to
£		per week from	to
£		per week from	to

15. Other financial provisions:—
(Fill in as required).

The player will receive an extra £40 per week when e[?] in the First team.

Standard Club bonuses.

teams should prevent a goal at all costs with wingers like myself spending more time tracking back than pushing forward. "Safety first. Get back behind the ball," that was Bill's view. I think Bill wanted Jimmy at City to add a bit of experience. He knew what kind of player Jimmy was and the job he could do. I thought Jimmy was a hardworking versatility player. He wasn't the flair type of player we had gotten used to at City but he was reliable. You knew if he got the ball he could give it to someone and we'd build from that.

'I struggle to remember the specifics of the start of that season but I know that Tony Book wanted experience in the side for the UEFA Cup and bringing Jimmy Conway in and Brian Kidd did that to some extent. If you look at Brian Kidd's footballing career then he certainly had European experience. I wanted to start that season and I wanted to play my part. I felt I'd made a lot of progress the previous season but when the season opened I was on the left wing in the reserves at home to Wolves while the first team drew 2-2 at Leicester with Dennis Tueart on the left – his preferred side – and Jimmy Conway on the right where I'd been for most of the 1975-76 season.'

City staff member at the time Roger Reade remembers how difficult it was for young players to get into the first team at this time: 'The game was so physical that back then an eighteen or even nineteen year old couldn't come in and expect to play every game, especially not a player like Peter Barnes. It was too demanding. You'd be kicked uphill and down dale by the opponents. I think they got it

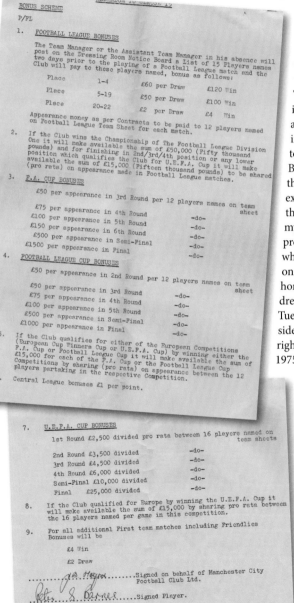

right with Peter overall. The odd game in 74-75, then the run in 75-76, and then the protection after Wembley and at the start of the 1976-77 season too.'

Peter was missing from the squad for the opening game of the 1976-77 season, a 2-2 draw at Leicester 2-2, and was an unused substitute when the Blues defeated Aston Villa 2-0, with goals from Dennis Tueart and Dave Watson, at Maine Road. Three days after that victory though Peter's chance came when he started: 'I didn't get my first team start until the third game of the season when I played on the right wing. Brian Kidd was missing from the team with damage to his knee, so Conway moved to eight and my first chance of the season came at home to Stoke on 28 August. That ended goalless and I missed the next game away at Arsenal but was back in for Bristol City on 11 September. It was an important week as we were also playing our first UEFA Cup leg against Juventus on the Wednesday night.

'Against Bristol City we opened brightly with a couple of chances early on – I remember heading narrowly wide after Tueart had sent the ball in. They'd been going well and had shocked a few. They were unbeaten in their opening four games; were in second place on goal difference. This was the first season of goal difference in the League and that meant Aston Villa were top. Prior to 1976-77 the position of teams on the same points was decided on goal average. All of this in their first season after promotion too. We ended up winning 2-1.'

Dennis Tueart had scored first in the 25th minute as he: 'swayed out to the right before suddenly cutting in and artfully lobbing the ball over Cashley. Straight from the kick off Barnes, on the other wing, intercepted a Bristol pass and beat Sweeney and Merrick before hitting a low, left-footed shot in off the post.' [4]

Peter remembers the goal as one of the best he scored: 'It was never televised but I remember it vividly because I beat three players. We'd just scored and then it was the restart. We were attacking the North Stand end of Maine Road and I remember they kicked off and I raced in to pick the ball up. I got the ball, ran past a couple of players including Gerry Sweeney, who was playing right back against me. I smacked the ball in from outside the box into the far corner netting. I know it was two goals in a minute for us but it was still an important goal because Bristol City were equal to us for most of that game.'

FIRST DIVISION

MATCH MAG

v West Ham UNITED
SATURDAY
OCTOBER 2nd 1976
K.O. 3.00 pm

PRICE 15pence

The cover of City's programme for the visit of West Ham in October 1976 shows Peter in action v Bristol City three weeks earlier.

Reports talk positively of Bristol City's contribution to the game with journalist Alan Dunn commenting: 'In the end a corrosive minute's football from Manchester marked the difference, but for the other 89 the two pounded grittily at each other and Bristol impressed everyone with their honest endeavours.' [5] Bristol scored their consolation goal in the 85th minute. For Peter his performance against Bristol was enough to ensure he retained his place for the Juventus UEFA Cup first leg four days later.

City were to compete in the UEFA Cup for the first time since 1972-73 and there were high hopes that they could enjoy a decent run in the competition, despite being drawn against Juventus. The Italian side had won the Italian league twice in the early 1970s and was developing a good reputation for the quality of its football via men like forward Roberto Bettega. Inevitably, it was viewed as a major confrontation with significant interest from the wider football world. Both the Italian manager, Enzo Bearzot, and the England boss, Don Revie, were watching from the Main Stand.

Experienced European campaigner Brian Kidd gave City the lead in the 43rd minute, but it was a painful night for Peter: 'I received an ankle injury from Claudio Gentile. Well, the newspaper and club told everyone it was an ankle injury but it was more than that really. That would've been bad enough but he'd stood on my foot as well. I tried to carry on but it was so bad I was hobbling about the place. I still suffer with my big toe now – thirty four years later! I can hardly bend it and I have to be careful with my shoes. I remember playing the full first half and was really in my stride. It was a tough physical game but I was enjoying it. Gentile was staring at me throughout the game. His eyes were

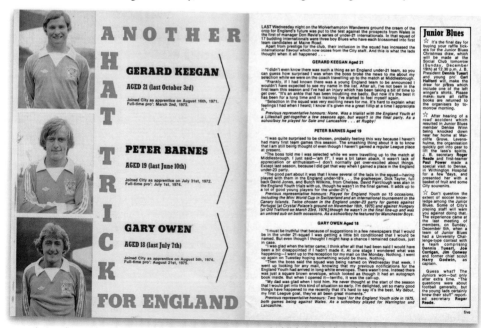

The Manchester City v Coventry programme (December 18, 1976) highlighting City's England U21s.

following everything I did, glaring at me. He elbowed me a few times and kept pulling my shirt. How could somebody called Gentile play like that? He was as hard as nails. When I was taking a corner, he came over and stood there, so I couldn't take the corner. He was everywhere I went.

'Gentile was constantly biting at me and at one point we got a corner and Dennis Tueart was taking it. As Dennis took it, Gentile came down heavy with his studs on my foot. The studs went through the leather and I remember seeing blood coming through my boot. I could hardly feel my foot I tried to carry on, but he was still tapping away at my feet and I had to go off. It seemed like Gentile would kick his own grandmother if she had the ball! I was worried when City next played them in 2010 in case he was still marking me! All night I was looking over my shoulder, checking he wasn't there!'

Peter was substituted eleven minutes into the second half, but he had performed well during his time on the pitch despite the intensity of the physical challenge he faced: 'I felt I was doing well and then the next day there were some great newspaper reports. Denis Law had been at the game too and a friend of his, the agent Gigi Peronace was with him, as was the Italian manager Enzo Bearzot. From that I was told that Juventus wanted to sign me. Dad told me that he'd been chatting with Denis and Gigi and that Gigi had talked with Giovanni Trapattoni, the Juventus manager, about me. There was a lot of talk about it but I was too young and didn't want to go to Italy at that time.'

Despite early nerves, the Blues had been on top and seemed capable of scoring more than the one goal, but Peter's substitution limited their opportunities according to journalist Patrick Barclay: 'City remained on top throughout the second half but their attack became more and more blunt, with

English centres causing Morini and Scirea a few problems. The unorthodox touches of Barnes, withdrawn in the 56th minute after a bad tackle by the ironically-names Gentile were missed; his replacement, Power, ran hard but was unable to beat defenders in the same way.' [6]

City manager Tony Book had made it clear that he had hoped for a two goal lead, but he remained optimistic with a one goal lead after the first leg: 'I am extremely confident. I do not promise victory in the second leg. Nor do I foresee defeat. The vital thing is going to be the first goal scored - the team that gets it could easily carry off the title.'

During the 1990s Dennis Tueart explained that he felt City's failure was simply as a result of European inexperience: Against Juventus we didn't do too badly in the first game, but we only got the one goal. I think that was because we were a little inexperienced compared to the likes of Liverpool. They had a European head on. They knew how to play in Europe. We didn't. We still went out with all the flair and the creative things that we had in the English League. We just didn't have the ability to play European style at that time. We weren't ready.

'We'd only just come together within 18 months and then we were in Europe. Probably from Tony Book's view as well, he was a little inexperienced as far as Europe was concerned. There wasn't any major change in tactics. We only got the one goal lead which Juventus were happy with. It would have been nice to have been drawn away first - see what we could do there - and then bring them back here. The goal was just before half-time, which is a great time to score, but we couldn't break them down in the second half. They just got behind the ball.'

Gary Owen was not selected against

Juventus, but at this period in his career he enjoyed facing physical opponents and would have loved to support Peter in his batter with Gentile: 'I always liked the confrontation. I was always protective and never liked seeing anyone get bullied. I wanted to help if I saw anyone being picked on and so on the pitch I was always keen to fight battles for the team. Peter would get kicked and I'd go for the aggressor. I was brought up that way. If someone attacked a teammate I'd make it my business to get things sorted. It was always in me to stand my corner. Many, many times when Peter was whacked by somebody I took it as a personal insult and I would seek retribution. I quite liked doing it too. I'd be chased for seasons by opponents who I'd confronted at some point – and usually it had nothing to do with me directly but I'd made it my business. That was part of my job at City. I'd like to say that whenever I got sent off it was unjust or a case of mistaken identity but I was sent off six times – that's a lot of mistaken identities! I was never the perpetrator I was always retaliating or seeking vengeance for a team mate who had been attacked in some way. I think Peter just thought it was my nature and part and parcel of the game.'

Football was more physical and while Peter often talks of the pressure put on him earlier in his career by coach Dave Ewing, Gary Owen remembers that City's physio Freddie Griffiths was keen to physically challenge younger players: 'I remember a confrontation between me and Freddie when he was bullying me. He'd say he was making me physically tougher but I didn't see it like that. We were doing exercises in the gym under the Main Stand at Maine Road. I was only small and slim then and Freddie would be physically tough on me and Peter and the other younger players. He was trying to push us in some way but I

wasn't having it. If you prod the wrong tiger you get mauled and Freddie prodded me just that little bit too much. Freddie would do stuff like kick you in the stomach when you were doing abdominals – when you were really struggling any way. Peter and the others didn't like it of course but felt they had to accept it. This day he did it to me and just me. I remember chatting with my dad when I got home – remember my dad's an ex-rugby player as well – and I told him what had happened. He asked "Did he kick anybody else?" I told him no and my dad said "Right, this is what you do. You say to him before you start the abdominals tomorrow: Please don't kick me. I'm asking you politely, please don't kick me." I listened and dad said: "If he kicks you, you get up and you hit him as hard as you can and you make sure he goes down because he'll always remember it." A week goes by and then I'm in the gym again. I remember it vividly. The first team players were doing stuff and we're all around the gym. I said to Freddie: "Please don't kick me" just as my dad had suggested. Freddie shouts out to the others: "Oh, the superstar here's saying don't kick me. Oh, right, well you'll have to see what happens won't you?" The other players are all laughing as you'd expect, so I turned to him: "I have told you. I have asked politely." He went: "Oh, he's told me! Very good! I've been told!" I started to do the work and he then stamped on my stomach. Harder than last time. Then he turned away – that was a mistake. I got up and I went sideways at him. He went flying over the dumbbells and everything. I just walked straight out in my full kit and got in my car.

'I got home. Dad asked if I'd had a speedy exit and so I told him what had happened: "Were you polite and ask him not to kick you?" I said that I had and explained it all. Dad was pleased because

Gary Owen

me. We were locked in there. There used to be a thing for an ultrasound machine. It was the only thing in there I could grab. It was quite chunky and I got hold of it. It was in my hand ready. He went "woah, woah, stop. You don't need that. I've come to apologise. I shouldn't have done that yesterday." I kept hold of the ultrasound thinking that he was trying to fool me, but he wasn't, so it was all sorted. My dad did go to see him and said to Freddie: "He did ask you politely not to kick him and you ignored that." You don't mind being told what you've done wrong but someone doing what Freddie did was not acceptable to me.'

The foot injury caused by Gentile affected Peter for a couple of weeks, causing him to miss the second leg of the UEFA Cup tie – which ended in a 2-0 defeat in Turin – and games with Sunderland and Manchester United. In the Sunderland game Jimmy Conway suffered a shoulder injury, which meant that once Peter was fit he went straight back into the team for a home game with West Ham on October 2. City won 4-2: 'I hit the woodwork a couple of times. Dennis Tueart scored a couple and Asa Hartford scored as well, but the goal of the game was from my mate Gary Owen. It was his first League game of the season and he scored on the stroke of half time. He was about thirty yards out, turned and chipped the ball over Mervyn Day in the West Ham goal! A great goal.'

Gary Owen had made his debut the previous season but this was his first League goal: 'Peter played his part in helping me score my first goal that day. Barnsey took the ball down the wing that day and knocked it back to someone who then passed it to me and I took it to the left… hit it… a nine iron over the 'keeper Mervyn Day. He desperately tried to get back and he ended up in the back of the net. I remember at half time going up the tunnel and Joe

I'd made a polite request and Freddie had completely ignored that, so his actions were not fair. It wasn't long before Tony Book phoned my dad and said "There's been an incident here." My dad said "Oh, there's been an incident all right! Nobody but nobody kicks my boy especially someone who is supposed to be on his own team. My son has been taught to fight his own corner if bullied and that's exactly what he did. Gary's seventeen and about nine stone six and Freddie Griffiths is an ex rugby player. If he wants to fight a man then I'll come and see him." Can you imagine how it was when I went to the gym next?

'I walked in and the lads were shouting stuff like "Here comes Rocky." They were all laughing and that. I needed to have strappings done and I hated having that. Freddie had to do them and I went in to the physio's room. He closed the door behind

Corrigan slapping me across the back of my head as hard as he could. He said jokingly "you'd never do that in a match would you?" because in training I always tried to chip him!'

The win placed City second on goal difference to Manchester United and the Blues would top the table briefly three days later after a 2-2 draw at Everton. Unfortunately, Peter had to miss this game due to problems with his foot. The injuries he had sustained against Juventus had been aggravated in the West Ham match. Peter: 'Once you were out of the team you'd wait for your chance. You'd do all you could to get fit and the physios would work on you but once you were fit and ready it was a waiting game. You'd be in the reserves working hard to prove you were ready again, or you'd get the call and be on the bench. Even then you weren't guaranteed any time on the pitch. Tony Book still felt substitutes were there for injuries or more of a desperate change to swing a game. Substitutes were rarely tactical then for City, so getting on the bench was no guarantee.'

Throughout the 42 game 1976-77 League campaign Book only brought a substitute on in 14 games, predominantly for injuries to players: 'Understandably he wanted a consistent team and if we were winning he was not going to change it. That was the philosophy back then. It didn't really matter whether you were a better player or not. You had to wait for your chance. The team was going really well that season, challenging for the title and my foot injury meant my chance didn't really come for several months. I was on the bench for a few games, including a crucial one against league leaders Liverpool at the end of December. We were winning after Joe Royle put us ahead but then with only a minute or so remaining Dave Watson was clearing danger by heading the ball backwards

to Joe Corrigan. Unfortunately, Joe was further forward than Dave realised and the ball sailed into the net. I sat on the bench watching. It was unbelievable and seemed so cruel. Dave was a brilliant defender and that was so unusual.'

Staff member and fan Roger Reade believed this was to have an impact for the rest of the season: 'It gave Liverpool the edge. When that own goal went in you could feel the whole of the ground deflate. It was the difference. Psychologically, if we'd have won that there would have been a difference going forward for both teams. Like when City beat Liverpool in 2018-19 those crucial games affect both the winners and losers for weeks, maybe months.'

Peter came on as substitute in the next League game, a 5-0 victory over Leicester which saw Brian Kidd score four and Mike Doyle the other. Gary Owen remembers Peter's performance that day: 'We beat Leicester 5-0. Barnsey came on as substitute but was provider for most of the goals – Brian Kidd scored four. For me it was great to have him, or Dennis Tueart on the wing. Preferably both. Tueart was substituted that day for Peter, so we didn't have both on at the same time unfortunately.

'Tueart wanted it to his feet but Peter would be happy with it at his feet or slipped inside. He didn't care because if it was slipped inside his pace would take him past the full back. He was a great crosser of the ball. He didn't just cross it like some do in the modern game, he would pick out the specific player and know exactly where they wanted the ball. Today you see people get in to areas and they just knock it but there's nobody there. With Peter he would look and then pick someone out. He knew where that ball was going and who specifically it was going to. It's no good getting there and hoping.

'Peter also had great pace and was

a wonderful dribbler of the ball. For a midfield player like me and because of the relationship we had together as professionals but also our personal relationship Peter was perfect.'

For City fan Steve Heald the game was a defining moment in his love of the Blues: 'Earlier that season my dad wanted to test the water to see how interested I would be, so I started off going to reserve games. I can't recall much of these, except for asking the usual daft questions and Peter Barnes scoring a memorable goal on a rare 2nd team sojourn. "He'll play for England one day that lad" my dad surmised. When just a year later he did I thought my dad was a footballing sage. By January 1977 my dad decided I was ready for the first team, and we embarked upon a routine that didn't alter greatly for 16 years. My first League game was the 5-0 against Leicester. I can still reel off the twelve playing for City that day. We sat in the North Stand. I recall

the expanse of heads stretching up and down the stand in front of me and behind me. And the noise, nothing I'd ever heard before. I found it so very exciting and according to my dad made a fair bit of my own, yet I don't recall this. I was hooked, and looked forward to my visits to Maine Road every fortnight.'

Despite Peter's performance against Leicester he remained on the fringes, making the occasional appearance on the substitute's bench: 'I was on the bench a few times but it wasn't until March when I came on at Old Trafford in the derby that I got the chance to keep my place.'

Peter's arrival in the Manchester derby came in the 59th minute, by which time the Blues were surprisingly losing 3-0. It had been a strange game with gusts of wind blowing the ball off course a few times and City's defence having perhaps their worst performance of the season as journalist Peter Corrigan explained: 'City are capable,

Glyn Pardoe's testimonial in March 1977. Glyn's grandson Tommy Doyle appeared for City's first team in 2020. Players are: Tommy Booth, Tony Henry, Kenny Clements, Paul Power, Peter, Gary Owen and Dave Bennett.

of course, of recovering the ground they lost in this game but their defence, which was good enough to carry them through 17 undefeated games recently, fell rather easily to United… It was hardly the scoreline one would have anticipated… City, apart from one aggressively determined run by Kidd which took him 50 yards, found the middle part of the game a time of great difficulty, which was perhaps reflected in Doyle's hacking battle of Jimmy Greenhoff, which earned him a yellow card, and a number of other signs that composure was not theirs. United took full advantage.' [7] According to Corrigan's report City seemed a more potent force once Peter had replaced Paul

Power and the Blues did manage to attack more fluidly. Royle scored a consolation goal but Book was far from happy. He was trying to maintain a title challenge and was disappointed with the performance: 'We have too many individuals out of form at the moment. It is not good enough for the championship.' [8] Looking forward to the next game, four days later against Sunderland, he added: 'We will pull out of this bad spell on Wednesday night, I promise you that.'

Losing the Derby 3-1 meant City were third, three points behind leaders Liverpool, but the Blues did have a game in hand and the two sides were yet to meet at Anfield.

Ipswich were second, a point ahead of City. United, after the derby win, were also in with a shout of the title. They were fourth, seven points behind Liverpool but with two games in hand over the Merseyside team.

The game in hand over Liverpool was won 1-0 with City defeating Sunderland via a controversial penalty scored by Dennis Tueart and given for a foul on Gary Owen. Peter: 'I started against Sunderland and it was a tough game. They were near the foot of the table but they'd had a good run and had moved off the bottom. We weren't really in our stride, but the penalty came just before half time. I know Sunderland complained about it, saying that Gary wasn't fouled, but whatever they felt we got that penalty and Dennis put it away. That gave us confidence and we went in with a bit more belief than we'd had a few minutes earlier. When the second half started I couldn't wait. The confidence was there.'

Journalist Patrick Barclay recognised this change in his match report: 'They demonstrated their full power and skill in a 10 minute spell immediately after the interval when Barnes at last managed to drift clear of Docherty on the left and send over a steady stream of the kind of centres to which Sunderland always look vulnerable.' [9]

City's title challenge remained in a difficult period despite the Sunderland victory. It was clear that the team was not functioning as well as Book hoped and at West Ham the Blues suffered a 1-0 defeat. Julie Welch reported on the latest setback: 'Fancied for the League title by a fair number of self-respecting football buffs, Manchester City had timed it badly to hit basement form. Severely rattled at Old Trafford last week, they laid into struggling West Ham yesterday with all the zing of stale biscuits, went under early on to a vintage bit of Bryan Robson, and

from then failed miserably to get a grip on a match which could have been theirs for the taking.' [10] She added: 'West Ham would surely be the first to admit that luck came their way by the slab. Their opponents hit posts, tripped up and trundled into each other; indeed, on one occasion City had three fine shots at goal blocked successively by their own players. Day, too, picked the right afternoon to be at his zippiest, and his marvellous twisting save from a Barnes volley was surpassed only by Corrigan putting paid to Bond's penalty shot.'

'That was a really unlucky game for us,' remembers Peter. 'Everything we did seem to back fire and Mervyn Day in nets was at his best that day. We should definitely have won but it was one of those that just went away from us.'

Ten days later a goalless game at Queen's Park Rangers was viewed positively by Book and seen as a step forward, although newspapers were not so positive. Norman Fox in *The Times* was surprised at City's satisfaction with a point, believing the club needed two points to sustain the title challenge. [11] He did praise Peter a couple of times in his match report of the game and felt he deserved greater support: 'Poor Barnes found himself working without support, or, apparently, the interest of midfield players who refused to explore beyond the half way line.'

The negativity towards City's approach at QPR was significant from the media but the truth of it was that Book had calculated what his team needed to do to win the title and, with crucial games against championship hopefuls Liverpool and Ipswich coming, he felt avoiding defeat at Rangers was more important than taking a gamble and pushing forwards. The point earned meant that City were in third place, three points behind leaders Ipswich, managed by Bobby Robson, and second placed Liverpool but, crucially, Book's Blues had a game in hand over both clubs and had to play them both. The City boss felt his side could win the title by gaining 19 points from the remaining eleven games.

In his programme notes for the Ipswich game Book praised Peter: 'I compliment Peter Barnes on his return. He's come through the teething problems that afflict the young learning their profession. He has taken his opportunity well since his recall and I have been very pleased with him. He knows that he has to buckle down to the job to maintain his first team status, and that's what he has been doing.' [13] Peter feels that Book sought to protect his young players: 'It had been a whirlwind year or so for me. I became a regular; scored in the League Cup final and was PFA Young Player… My family kept me grounded but the media focus had been high. We've seen this with so many young players over the years. There's a clamour for them to play every week and you get calls from the media asking you for a few words or to do some promotional work. We all want a piece of the new star and it would be easy for anyone in that position to believe the hype and to seek the limelight. Fortunately, I was shy and not really one to look for the attention and my parents kept my feet on the ground, but it is hard when you're thrust into that spotlight.

'Tony Book was keen to keep me grounded. He didn't want me to get carried away and he knew that other clubs, like Juventus, were starting to show interest. When I was out of the team it was frustrating but once I'd got back in there was no way I wanted to lose that place and, fortunately, I did enough and received enough praise to ensure I stayed in the team, but one slip up and I'd be out. That's what we all felt then.'

Injuries to Mike Doyle and Dennis Tueart put pressure on Book's team selection plans for the Ipswich game. He was forced to play Gary Owen, who was suffering with acute tonsillitis on the left wing, where Tueart would have played, with Peter on the right. Ged Keegan returned to the team for only his second League appearance of the season. It was not a great match but it was an important victory for City, who won 2-1 thanks to an opener from Kidd and the winner from Watson as the game neared its end. Granada TV's Gerald Sinstadt reported on the winner for *The Times*: 'City won 2-1, thanks to a fine goal from Watson four minutes from the end. Barnes, whose pace was one of the afternoon's brighter features, swung a corner wide and deep from the left. Watson came off a five yard run to score with a header that had more force and accuracy than much of the shooting. The goal was Watson's 50th in the league, and, in his own estimation, the best. After the match, Ipswich's manager, Mr Bobby Robson, praised the header.' Sinstadt highlighted efforts by Tommy Booth and by Peter which he felt could have settled the game earlier but, in the end, the victory was all that mattered. At one point when the match was particularly stale, Gary Owen was substituted for Tony Henry which brought significant criticism – and booing – the manager's way. At the time fans had no knowledge of Owen's battle against tonsillitis and the condition was to cause him to miss the following two League games.

Dave Watson described his goal in 2003: 'My best memory has to be the goal I scored against Ipswich in April 1977. It was such an important goal and so many fans over the years have discussed it with me. City and Ipswich were second and third in the League, and were both putting considerable pressure on Liverpool. We couldn't afford to lose, and Peter Barnes sent a great ball in. I met it about eight feet in the air and headed it in from about twelve yards out. Mick Mills said that I'd rose up and headed it in before he'd even had chance to move. It gave me a lot of satisfaction and, of course, we won the match 2-1.' [14] After the 2-1 victory, Ipswich manager Bobby Robson told Tony Book: 'If we don't win it, I hope you do.'

The Ipswich win was followed by another by the same score at home to Leeds on Good Friday. Again it was not a vintage performance but the Blues did enough to strengthen their title challenge as Derek Wallis explained: 'Manchester City clawed their way to within one point of First Division leaders Ipswich and Liverpool with two goals from Brian Kidd.' [15] City had gone a goal behind when Joe Jordan headed the opener in the 17th minute, but Brian Kidd, who had been criticised earlier in the season on Match of the Day by Jimmy Hill, proved to be one of the Blues' most reliable performers during this period of the season: 'Kidd equalised in the 38th minute after Joe Royle's pass bounced off Trevor Cherry. And he flicked in the winner after Paul Madeley headed out Peter Barnes's corner in the 64th minute.'

'This was an important win for our belief,' says Peter. 'We'd overcome the title favourites for much of the season Ipswich. Then Leeds, who were always a tough team to face back then. This meant we were a point behind Liverpool on equal games and about to play them the next day at Anfield. That was a big ask but Brian Kidd was having a great spell and I was feeling confident. I was always keen to play at Liverpool and I saw this as one of those title-deciding games. If we could win then with eight games left the title could be ours.'

Liverpool were still in the European Cup and FA Cup and they possessed great belief that they could win a remarkable treble. Ipswich were still in pole position, so the game would be some way off deciding the title but if City could get the victory then Book's side would certainly be in with a chance. Peter: 'I couldn't wait but when the team was announced I was on the bench. Gary Owen was out of course, but the team seemed more defensive than it needed to be.'

Dennis Tueart was missing as well as Owen with Ged Keegan, playing his third League game of the season, and Paul Power, who had missed the previous five, replacing Peter and Tueart. The reason Tony Book gave for dropping Peter to the bench was: 'He needs a bit of a rest and I think Paul Power's non-stop running ability could be a crucial factor today.' [16] Peter: 'Obviously, I wouldn't have

Blues Barnestormer!

Welcome back to first team action for Peter Barnes, who came on as sub in the 56th minute of the visit to Manchester United on March 5th. He impressed—and has retained his wing role since that recall.

KO Kidd

A typical power-blast by striker Brian Kidd, the type of finishing that brought him a hatful of goals only a couple of months ago. And he's deadly keen to get back in the scoring routine as this flair for finishing indicates.

Peter retained his place in the starting eleven until the meeting with Liverpool on April 9, 1977.

wanted a rest. I was desperate to play at Liverpool. I think Tony went a bit negative that day. I know there were a couple of injuries and we'd played the day before but if you think about the team it was more of a negative one. We went there to stifle Liverpool and it was a mistake. Obviously, if it had worked then that'd be fine but we had the quality in attack and we went there for a draw.'

The tactic seemed to work for much of the game but ultimately Liverpool broke the deadlock with a goal from Kevin Keegan which goalkeeper Corrigan got a hand to and almost palmed out. Despite being a goal down City continued to play negatively as they tried to match the approach many in Manchester felt Liverpool had become masters at. Injuries to Mike Doyle and Joe Royle hampered City's options and, as the game wore on Book made the decision to replace Royle with Peter. Peter soon played his part in helping the Blues equalise in the 79th minute, according to Norman Fox's report: 'City managed to get several players into the penalty area when Barnes centred low. Kidd prodded the ball across the line and for a moment the Kop was quiet.' [17] Peter: 'I used to hate coming on as substitute when we were losing. It's hard doing that. You want to go for it and you might offer something new of course but, quite often, the pattern has been set. Especially, if you've gone there to contain the opposition. I did contribute at Anfield but I never felt it was my sort of game and soon after the goal we were on the back foot again.'

Unfortunately, Liverpool managed to regain the lead within a minute and the game ended with a Merseyside win. *The Times* explained: 'Manchester City lost 2-1 after being unable to alter their tactics which were geared to a containment game... They then probably lost their

chance of the championship in one minute out of a nine months season... There were black moments when it seemed that the whole City side had abandoned any thoughts of counter-attack.' [18]

The Liverpool defeat left City third, three points behind Ipswich and Liverpool, but with a game in hand over Ipswich. The win would have placed City second but, crucially, would have meant the season was entirely within their control. Now the advantage lay with Liverpool who also had a game in hand over Ipswich. Peter: 'I know we weren't performing particularly well in the previous games but we had managed to get two wins and a draw. I suppose as this was Easter and we had three games over four days Tony had to be careful with his selections but, thinking back to that time, we were going for the title. If we'd gone to Anfield and attacked we may have come away with at least a point. The worst that could happen was that we'd lose – which we did anyway. We had players who could be physical and our defence was strong anyway, so we should have gone at them, knowing our defence would've withstood anything else. I love Tony and he was a great manager but that day I think our tactics let us down.

'Looking back I'd have loved to have started against Liverpool on either wing – I didn't mind attacking Phil Neal or any of their defenders then. I know he was a footballing full back but I never saw him a threat to my type of football. I loved a challenge and I'd have loved to play in that game. Looking back that game at Anfield was the difference. It was a bit like that game in 2012 when Alex Ferguson brought Manchester United to City and played for a draw but ended up getting beat by that wonderful header from Vincent Kompany. I always think, if you're going for the title then go for it. There's no point holding

A classic City-Liverpool game. This one is a 3-1 Maine Road victory over Liverpool, October 1977, which saw Peter leave Joey Jones tackling fresh air.

back if you've got flair players. It would be different if your entire style game after game was a defensive, negative one, but when you're renowned as a flair team – which we were in 1977 – then let the opposition worry. Maybe that's why I'm not a manager but, as an attacking-minded player, I always want to put the others under pressure.

'Liverpool were a hardworking team and had talented players. The Kop always added something at Anfield of course but on our day we could beat anybody. You only have to look at our European games against Milan in 1978 and Juventus in 76. We had a great balance in our team and we played with width. I've always believed that great teams play with width and I'm sure the likes of Asa Hartford and Gary Owen loved getting the ball out to me or Dennis Tueart out on the wings. I'm so passionate about playing with width – Mahrez, Sterling

and the others add so much to modern City while you only have to look at the struggles United have had in recent years when they've tried to play without having width. It's really important to me. When we played at home we could use width well. Maine Road was a great pitch because of its size. It was so wide and I loved it.'

Despite the defeat at Anfield, City still stood a chance and the following three games ended in victories (Middlesbrough 1-0, WBA 2-0 & Birmingham City 2-1), lifting City to second place on goal difference to Liverpool. The possibility of winning the title was back and all it needed now was for Bob Paisley's side to slip up and the advantage would swing to City. Liverpool had a game in hand over City, due to their ongoing commitments in Europe. Peter: 'Back then the pressure of playing in Europe would often affect a club's league form, especially as the First Division tended to have at least six teams who seemed genuinely capable of winning the League too. Every game in the League was a challenge – no matter who you were – and I know we felt we could still win the League, but then came our biggest slip up... Derby County! It was a terrible pitch at the Baseball Ground.'

City lost 4-0 at Derby which manager Book found particularly hard to take: 'It was a day when everything went wrong. The sand-pit of a pitch played its part in disturbing our rhythm, though I don't want that reason to justify our sub-standard performance since it was the same for both teams. Simply, we didn't put our game together and I felt that overall we had our worst 90 minutes of the season with composure finally cracking and players reacting badly to the frustrations. Brian Kidd fell for the three-card trick when he permitted himself to be provoked into being sent off shortly after receiving a booking from the referee.' [19]

The Derby defeat meant City were now two points behind leaders Liverpool, who still had their game in hand, and the Merseyside club also had a better goal difference with only four games left for the Blues to play. The title race was not over but catching Liverpool seemed unlikely. Then, on May 4, City drew 1-1 at fifth placed Aston Villa. Tueart had scored a header in the 53rd minute to put Book's side in front but 'Villa equalised out of the blue when full back Robson let fly with a speculative 25 yard drive that Corrigan seemed to touch on to the crossbar, and from there into the path of Brian Little', according to journalist Bob Harris. [20] The advantage was well and truly with Liverpool now who only needed four points, possibly three due to their superior goal difference. After the match Tony Book told the press he still felt City

had a chance of lifting the Championship trophy: 'I won't concede it until it's mathematically certain.' [21]

With three games left to play Peter felt the League could still be won: 'The situation was somewhat different to the era of City's dominance under Pep Guardiola. Back in the late seventies title winners didn't expect to win every game. In 1976 Liverpool had drawn fourteen and lost five and still won the League. The year before that champions Derby had lost ten and drawn eleven. So with four games to go Liverpool had lost seven and drawn eight – that was better form overall than the previous seasons and it gave us hope. We'd only lost seven and had drawn thirteen so, looking at past titles, it was still possible. We had to make sure we didn't drop any other points but with three games left there was still hope for us. We didn't give in and our next game was at home to Spurs.'

The Tottenham game became one remembered by fans of Manchester City for decades due to the excellent performance of Peter and because of City's destruction of the London club, managed by Keith Burkinshaw. The game began with the Blues more cautious than had been promised against a team that needed a win to stand a chance of First Division survival. In fact Spurs seemed more co-ordinated than City, who were still missing Mike Doyle through injury, during the opening minutes. Nevertheless, the opening goal came after 19 minutes: 'when centre-half Tommy Booth headed in a corner from Peter Barnes. Earlier, Pat Jennings had kept his side in the game, spreading himself to keep out a shot from Barnes with his knees.' [22] Booth was deputising in defence for Doyle and, as always, proved to be a truly dependable member of the team. Another excellent defensive performance came from Dave Watson who 'showed the eyes and disposition of a hawk as he swooped on the danger areas, obliterating them.' [23] City had other chances in the first half with Spurs' 'keeper Pat Jennings: 'a mite lucky – he stumbled into the path of Barnes's point-blank shot rather than deliberately saving it.'

In the second half Peter played his part in helping to blast Spurs away: 'So total was the change after the interval. Barnes began to bedazzle Naylor, Tueart was more involved in the action and the whole side seemed to shift forward some 20 yards or more. The effect on Spurs was like that of a hurricane on a straw hut. They were flattened and they might easily have conceded almost as many goals again.'

According to journalist Leslie Duxbury: 'It was Barnes who began the second-half romp, winning the ball from Naylor in the air and floating it into Tueart's stride on the right, for the winger to shoot fiercely past Jennings.' Peter received a great deal of praise for his performance in this game: 'Barnes upstaged everyone again with the goal of the game. He went past one defender, confronted Jennings, moved coolly wide and aimed an impudent chip into the empty net as Osgood strained desperately to protect it.'

Asa Hartford scored City's third with a brilliantly angled volley in the 60th minute, six minutes after Peter's goal. In the 85th minute Brian Kidd netted the fifth when he tucked Dennis Tueart's pass into the corner and Spurs were well and truly beaten. There was praise for every member of the City team but Tom German, writing in The Times, was particularly impressed with: 'Watson, immaculate in the air in Manchester's back four, Hartford's shrewd use of the ball in the central areas and the articulate skills of Barnes were elements of City's game which Spurs found difficulty in coping with. Like Tottenham and Hoddle, Manchester have young talent of high promise in Barnes and Owen, both skilful in the use of the ball. Barnes has added resolution and durability to his sleight of foot. He seems less diverted now by a stern challenge and, on Saturday, had a contribution to three of his side's goals. The third he scored himself with marvellous calm and control. Taking Owen's pass up the middle, he flicked it away from the Tottenham challenge, dummied to shoot so convincingly that Jennings committed himself and then chipped the ball over the prostrate goalkeeper with impish craftsmanship.' [24]

The five goals were perceived as relegating Tottenham, although mathematically that was not quite true, but they also reduced the goal difference advantage Liverpool had to only five goals. The Blues' overall performance was still some way off perfection according to some journalists however: They never played much above half pace simply because they did not need to do more than go through the motions.' [25] While the suggestion that this was an easy game was unfair – Tottenham had demonstrated their determination during the first half and faded once City overwhelmed them – it did cause fans to wonder what might have been had the Blues been so rampant at Derby, but more specifically, in their game at Anfield. Had City attacked Liverpool at will, as they had demonstrated they were able to do at various points, would Liverpool's negative approach have been swept aside like Spurs, Leicester and others had been? Peter: 'Looking back it adds to the frustration of that Liverpool game a little. We were going for the title and this game demonstrated what we were capable of.'

After Tottenham City took the lead at home to Everton through Brian Kidd but a rare mistake by Gary Owen led to the away team equalising. It also led to Joe Corrigan racing out of his goal to tell Owen exactly where he should have put the ball. The game ended 1-1 on the same night Liverpool played out a goalless game at Coventry. The Blues still could mathematically win the title but it would be tough. Peter: 'Had we beaten Everton then who knows? But Liverpool had two games left to play and a superior goal difference. We only had one match away at Coventry left and were two points behind.'

The final City game of the season ended 1-0 with Jimmy Conway scoring his first City goal, but Liverpool played out another goalless draw at home to struggling West Ham to see them over the line. As with so many Liverpool games their negative, defensive approach had seen them through according to journalist David Lacey: 'Liverpool retained the league championship on Saturday as a matter of routine, their goal-less draw with West Ham being so devoid of passion that even Anfield's rejoicing was somewhat mechanical. Neither side was prepared to risk the loss of one point in prolonged pursuit of two and so much of the game was confined to tedious sparring in midfield.' [26]

The Liverpool manager Bob Paisley admitted afterwards: 'We've played some good games and the moderate ones can be excused. The League has been foremost in the players' minds because until today there was always the thought that they might end up with nothing at all.' This season there had been a great deal of talk on the philosophy of English football with a technical research project performed on behalf of FIFA. It concluded that English football was 'a struggle for dominance in midfield with plenty of power tackling to win possession of the ball. It is as if the players were contained in an envelope which moves up and down the field. Always six or more defenders set themselves between the ball and goal when the other team is in possession.' [27] David Lacey, in his criticism of the negative approach taken, commented: 'The biggest disappointment has been the failure of those clubs with progressive ideas to achieve the results which might have persuaded others to become more adventurous in their thinking.' It is a view Peter shares: 'My whole approach was to attack. I saw that as my job and when City – and to be fair United – played with attack minded wingers we seemed to do well. When we won the League Cup reports often talked of the excitement of our game. They wanted others to play like us and we pushed forward with Dennis down one wing and me down the other. Don't get me wrong, we had decent defenders and they got us out of some sticky situations – sometimes caused by us pushing forward too much I guess. But, game after game, when we attacked we tended to come out of it well.

'Liverpool lost their last game of the season, which was after our season had ended anyway. That meant we missed the title by a point. So close! I know some would say, "yes, but if they'd won their last game then it'd have been three points." That's true, but had we got a draw at Easter or even won there, things would have ended differently and I'm sure we'd have won the League.

'If we'd have won the title in 76-77 then the changes that took place eighteen or so months later, with Malcolm Allison coming back, wouldn't have happened. The directors would have been happy with the way things were going and, after winning the League, who knows what the club could have achieved. We would not have made wholesale changes in 1979 because winning the title would have put us in a much better place. Instead of that it all imploded within two years. I'm sure there was bad luck in

Peter in action at Maine Road during 1976–77.

there and, of course, it's impossible to know what might have been, but I genuinely feel that a more positive approach against Liverpool at Easter would have swung the momentum our way and we'd have done it. I love Tony Book to bits and I don't think I'm in any position to criticise because I've never managed a leading top flight team, but looking back it does feel as if we were just a little too cautious at Anfield. We were Manchester City Football Club – the flair team – and we should have made Liverpool change their approach when they faced us. We had wingers who could attack and score goals; a creative midfield; brilliant forwards; and a great, solid back four in front of one of the greatest goalkeepers in an era of brilliant goalkeepers.

'I think we should have won the title that year. The two games against Liverpool were crucial and that home game, at the end of December, we should have won. We battered them. A brilliant City performance but we were so unlucky with their goal.'

Dave Watson took responsibility: 'We missed the title by a point to Liverpool. I scored an own goal against Liverpool that season and that point would have won us the championship. I feel responsible. Most defenders take responsibility whereas forwards don't need to. They miss chances, but our mistakes are noticed. I played as a forward and so I know how the mentality works. Forwards and defenders are different breeds, and that made me appreciate what it takes to be good in both roles.' [28]

Nine year old Ian Brightwell, who would play in the same City team as Peter a decade later, was a frequent visitor to City at this time: 'It was the team I supported and I used to go down to Maine Road. Colin Bell was nearing the end of his career when I went but there were people like Asa Hartford, Peter Barnes and Gary Owen. City were still a major side at that time. I

remember the year we missed out on the title by a point to Liverpool - we should have done it. Tony Book was manager and the players were a different class. It was great to watch and little did I realise that one day Book would coach me and I'd play alongside Barnes.'

Joe Royle was a member of the side during 1976-77: 'We went on to run Liverpool for the title. We came close – only one point in it – but that was a great side. At that time I think we all felt that City would go on and find great success because everything seemed perfect. Players like Peter Barnes, Gary Owen and Kenny Clements were coming through, so you had a nice blend of young local boys and more experienced talent.'

As both Royle and Brightwell commented this was a great City team, playing in a highly competitive era with several teams capable of winning the League or finding success in Europe. Sadly, in the years that have followed this era of Manchester City's history has tended to be overlooked in favour of the successes that preceded it or by the romance of the resurrection of a failed giant in 1999. It is a point that Gary Owen feels strongly about: 'I think one of the issues with City's history is that the mid to late 1970s isn't particularly recorded or promoted by either the club or football in general. Apart from the 1976 final people seem to be unaware of us coming close to winning the League in 1977 – not bettered until the last few years; of us being a top three supported club for most of this time; of us being an attacking glamour club throughout this period; of us challenging in Europe and having some great victories… There is more coverage of

City's struggles in the late 1990s than there is of this entertaining, challenging top flight period. Everyone talks about how low we got and not how high we were. It rankles! I often get asked about this period. Fans want to talk about it but football seems to have forgotten it and they seem to prefer the story of City were a failing club. Failing? Not while Dave Watson, Joe Corrigan, Joe Royle, Brian Kidd, me and Peter were there. We were challengers. That squad was packed with quality and we were the only team who really came close to Liverpool. We were a great club that became badly managed and then failed, not a failing club that got lucky. It is as though it never existed.'

[1] 'So tired City slip to defeat', unknown newspaper, June 1976. Cutting held in Peter Barnes' collection.
[2] Undated *Manchester Evening News* cutting, believed to be August 10, 1976.
[3] *Manchester City v Aston Villa match programme*, August 25, 1976, 4.
[4] 'Bristol destroyed in one minute', *Guardian*, September 13, 1976, 16.
[5] *Manchester City v Aston Villa match programme*, August 25, 1976, 4.
[6] 'Man City 1, Juventus 0', *Guardian*, September 16, 1976, 20.
[7] 'Passive resisters', *Observer*, March 6, 1977, 20.
[8] 'Based on sound planks', *Guardian*, March 7, 1977, 16.
[9] 'City do not impress', *Guardian*, March 10, 1977, 26.
[10] 'Ham-handed', *Observer*, March 13, 1977, 24.
[11] 'City happy despite the wastage', *The Times*, March 23, 1977, 10.
[12] *Manchester City v Ipswich Town match programme*, April 2, 1977, 3.
[13] 'Watson's best too good for Ipswich', *The Times*, April 4, 1977, 8.
[14] Dave Watson, interviewed by Gary James, 2005.
[15] 'Cool Kidd hots up title race at the double', *Daily Mirror*, April 9, 1977, 35.
[16] 'Tueart ruled out – Barnes is axed', *Manchester Evening News*, April 9, 1977.
[17] 'Paisley takes the cautious line', *The Times*, April 11, 1977, 9.
[18] Ibid.
[19] 'Tony Book Review', *Manchester City Match Programme v Tottenham Hotspur*, May 7, 1977, 2.
[20] 'Villa Park battle', *Aberdeen Press and Journal*, May 5, 1977, 24.
[21] 'Book: I won't concede title', *Daily Mirror*, May 5, 1977, 32.
[22] 'Manchester C v Tottenham H', *Coventry Evening Telegraph*, May 7, 1977, 46.
[23] 'City blast the men of straw', *Observer*, May 8, 1977, 22.
[24] 'Hoddle a lone spark as Spurs flames die', *The Times*, May 9, 1977, 6.
[25] 'Prolonging agony', *Guardian*, May 9, 1977, 20.
[26] 'Liverpool's machine clanks on', *Guardian*, May 16, 1977, 16.
[27] Project referred to and quoted from in an article on the defensive, negative style of Liverpool's title success: 'Worthy champions but few tactical advances', *Guardian*, May 16, 1977, 16.
[28] Dave Watson interviewed by Gary James, December 2009.

Peter Barnes
with Debbie
Darbyshire.
Many images
from Debbie's
collection
appear in this
biography.

Chapter Eight

A FAN FAVOURITE

> **Undeniably, the brilliant Peter Barnes was City's architect of their most crushing League win in years. Here was a potentially world class player superbly living up to that reputation with a breathtaking display of wing power that was a throwback to the days of Finney and Matthews. So potent and powerful was Barnes that he reduced his marker Graham Wilkins to such a level that the Chelsea full back was forced to resort to a string of foul tackles in his crude attempt to stop the City flyer. 'Devastating City, but...'**

Manchester Evening News, November 28, 1977

Life at Manchester City was good for Peter and by the summer of 1977 his status nationally was such that media articles would focus on his significance both to the Blues and to English football. There was much praise for his positive, attacking style of football and, off the pitch, he was proving to be a popular figure, especially with younger fans. He was perceived as a local lad with immense talent. Newspaper articles talked of him in glowing terms while fans wanted to know about his every move with several young supporters appearing wherever Peter appeared. This included supporter Debbie Darbyshire who, a decade later, would be one of the women who played in the inaugural Manchester City Ladies game at Boundary Park: 'We all loved Peter. There was a group of us who would try to get his autograph or have our photo taken with him. We always looked out for him. He was one of us. Just a normal young lad who loved City.'

On the pitch Peter enjoyed attacking and embarrassing defenders with his skill. He loved the challenge and was an expressive player but off the pitch he remained a shy, introverted person: 'I always appreciated the interest from the fans and I'd get involved in various fan related activities but I felt the acclaim was a bit too much – I was only a kid playing football. I didn't see myself as a star. Whenever people waited for me to sign autographs and things I didn't want to let them down. They paid their money to watch me do something I loved and I always felt they deserved more.'

Club employee at the time, Roger Reade, remembers the attention Peter received and the support he gave to fan related initiatives: 'After the PFA award and Wembley in 1976 the interest in Peter increased significantly. There were more people waiting for him outside the ground and I think Peter somehow managed to keep all of that within his stride. He just dealt with it. I remember the magazine Look-In doing a big feature on the Junior Blues and so we wanted to get a player involved and Peter volunteered. I can't remember if it was one day when him and Gary Owen came into the office or what, but I do remember him saying he would like to do it to help us.

'The Junior Blues was seen as the way forward in football's fight against hooliganism and Peter was happy to promote it. He didn't have to. It wasn't in his contract – that sort of thing came much, much later. It was just something he thought would help. Entirely his choice. I remember Peter being at the Junior Blues rallies at the Free Trade Hall and at Belle Vue. I remember at the second one both Peter and Gary Owen were there and were asked questions because they were two of the young players. They were both Junior Blues as well, so I think one of the questions was about being a member and playing for City. I know Peter was asked if he had volunteered to join the Junior Blues or was

he strong-armed into it and he said "no, no, not at all. I wanted to see what was going on and to understand what it was all about." That was great for us, because comments like that would help others decide to join. I never, ever had any problems with getting Peter involved. He was fantastic and it was great to work alongside him and Gary Owen and some of the others.

'There was a great camaraderie between players and staff back then. All players, staff and directors when they were around, could go to the Social Club and have lunch together. We used to sit on tables in the main room at the Social Club and were mixed in. I remember eating a fantastic steak sat with Peter and Gary [Owen]. That was how it was.'

'We used to go to Cellar Vie II on Charlotte Street in the city centre. It was a popular place for City players and staff back then. Peter would never walk in and think "everyone's looking at me." He'd just duck his head and go to the bar or find a place to sit – that was Peter as a person. Much more reserved than other players. Naturally humble. Some players would like the attention but Peter wasn't like that.'

Gary Owen remembers that both him and Peter were willing volunteers for anything Roger and other staff wanted them to help with: 'We'd get involved in activities like the Junior Blues because we wanted to. Peter and I hung around together often. We were different personalities on the pitch. We had some fun along the way. I remember once we were down in London for a game with Arsenal and we were staying at this hotel about to have an evening meal. For me and Peter it was still a fairly new experience being in a fairly posh hotel. Dennis Tueart ordered his meal and ordered some wine to go with it and then it was Peter's turn. Peter said to the waiter "can I have this minute steak, but could I have it a bit bigger

Peter's mum receives a birthday gift for him from a fan.

please?" Everyone laughed. Another time Peter was having a soup and he's scraping and scraping the bowl. I said "Peter, that's the pattern on the bowl!" He thought it was a leaf.'

Roger Reade: 'Peter was unassuming off the pitch. He didn't boast about his achievements at all. He was grounded even though he was a hugely talented player. Peter was most at home when he was in a team that was challenging for success.

That's when he would be flying too. His flamboyance, his extravagance, his 'jink' as I would call it – where he would drop the shoulder and send the full back the wrong way and he'd leave him on his backside – that was all natural for Peter. I think if a player has that it sets them above other players. He didn't score many goals but he did create an awful lot. I don't know if some fans felt that his lack of goals was an issue but to me his contribution wasn't about scoring goals himself. An attacking winger will always get some criticism if they're not scoring goals. He scored that great goal in the League Cup final and he contributed a lot in Europe during a period that was actually a great one for City. We may not have won that many trophies but we were always challenging.'

During the 1977-78 season City had opened its doors to the BBC for a groundbreaking fly-on-the-wall series of features for the magazine show Nationwide. Similar in approach to the One Show, Nationwide would cover some light-hearted content alongside investigative journalism with a variety of topics covered. During the season a series of features were filmed examining a leading professional football club from a variety of angles. Roger Reade: 'I was interviewed for one episode of the series. They were given the freedom of Maine Road. They filmed the laundry ladies and the social club… lots of areas really to get a full view of the club. It was part of Peter Swales and Tony Book's plan to widen the support.'

Initiatives like the Nationwide series increased interest in the club and also ensured the profile of players like Peter increased. He explains: 'Cameras appeared at the training ground and at various places within the club. We soon got used to it. Nowadays there are things like Tunnel Cam where players are followed the moment they leave the pitch, but in 1977 the idea of having cameras following you was completely new. If I'm honest I wanted to avoid their gaze but for City it was great exposure.'

City narrowly missed out on the League title in 1977 and there were high hopes the 1977-78 season would see the Nationwide coverage capture the Blues taking the title for the first time since 1968. To strengthen the team Tony Book brought in England star Mike Channon for £300,000, making him Book's most expensive signing. It also meant that, with a few positional changes across the team, Peter would start the League campaign on the bench. This infuriated many City fans, including G Hay of Chorley, who wrote to the Manchester Evening News Pink to complain: 'Peter Barnes is the most exciting City forward reared through the Juniors since David Wagstaffe. When finally reinstated to the team at the end of last season his breathtaking runs and dribbles and varied crosses provided both goals and goal chances for his team mates. His corner kicking was so accurate that players like Watson were able to make their sorties upfield pay with goals – a rarity at corners for City.

'Who can forget his amazing goal when he sold the astute Jennings a "dummy"? How then can Tony Book leave him out of the side or pay £300,000 for his replacement Which he has if Channon was not bought to replace Royle?' [1]

The comment about Channon is significant as the belief had been that the England international had been brought in as Joe Royle's possible replacement, which City had strongly denied, leading to the suggestion that he was Peter's replacement, especially as Peter was dropped to the bench where he was to remain without coming on for the opening three games – a draw and two victories. He did come on in the tenth minute of the League Cup tie at Chesterfield for Dennis Tueart who was struggling with a hamstring injury. Peter's first start came at home to Norwich on September 3 1977. The Blues won that game 4-0 and headed the table. The day had seen Mike Channon score his first – and second - goal for the club. The following week Channon scored again as City defeated Manchester United 3-1 with Brian Kidd scoring twice.

The Blues were in outstanding form but then faced Widzew Lodz in the UEFA Cup at Maine Road. It was a frustrating night despite goals from Peter – a great volley in the tenth minute – and Channon. City had taken a two goal lead and seemed totally in control but then it all changed. The still injured Dennis Tueart was watching from the stands: "We were 2-0 up with ten minutes to go and then Boniek scored from a penalty and a free kick. At 2-0 with ten or fifteen minutes to go we were cruising... justifiably 2-0 up. Then the free kick. He scored direct from it and then got a penalty when one of their guys dived. Suddenly it's 2-2."

Polish international Boniek's goals changed everything. A fan from the North Stand ran on the pitch and attacked the Widzew scorer and the game also saw the sending off of Willie Donachie in injury time. UEFA fined City £400. After the game the City players were quoted extensively in the club's match programme and in other sources. Most focused on the disappointment of the final ten minutes and were critical of both the referee and the Polish goals although Peter tried to focus on the positives. He was delighted that he'd scored his first European goal: 'I always enjoy scoring, but it is a special thrill to get a goal in European competition.

'We should have taken things a bit easier when we were leading 2-0. But we began to rush in an effort to obtain a bigger lead and we made some unforgiveable mistakes.'

In the aftermath of the game a nineteen year old supporter – whose name and address details appeared in the match programme - was found guilty of using threatening, abusive and insulting behaviour, and was fined £100. The club named and shamed him and also banned him from Maine Road, but City were also instructed to erect fencing behind both goals (fencing already existed in front of the Kippax terracing). Initially, the club in consultation with the police and local authority erected the fencing for only high profile fixtures, but as time went by the fences became a permanent barrier between the players and the fans. Peter: 'I hated the fences but this was a national thing. The

Peter (hidden by the grounded defender) scoring against Widzew Lodz in the UEFA Cup.

same night as our Widzew game when a fan ran on United fans caused trouble at St Etienne. That led to punishments for United but the general mood was that English fans were causing trouble. United had fences first – they'd got them in 1974 after the pitch invasions against City - and then gradually all clubs had to have them. It was awful to see the fans packed behind them. As has been shown in recent years, you can segregate and police fans without huge fences but back then there seemed to be this rush to fence people in instead of looking at sensible alternatives. The fences started to come down again after the Hillsborough disaster in 1989 as I neared the end of my football career.'

City chairman Peter Swales told the media that he believed fans wanted the fences erecting in the aftermath of the Widzew game: 'I feel sure the supporters of Manchester City would rather see these barriers round the pitch than have constant invasions and possible trouble with the European authorities.' [2]

The return leg against Widzew was miserable for the Blues. Peter: 'We stayed at a hotel. It was supposed to be the best in town but it felt as if the war was still on. We used to go for a walk from the hotel and we'd see people queuing up for bread on the pavement – a bit like when we had the shortages when Coronavirus first started to affect us in Britain [in March 2020] except this was every day and this was normal.

The queue would be fifty yards long. The shops were empty. The game itself was going okay and then Joe Royle got a chance. Somehow he fell over the ball. It was a trip and when he crash landed there was a big cloud of dust from this awful pitch. One of the players joked that it was like seeing a rhinoceros falling down in a safari. There was this big cloud of dust. It was a sitter and you could feel the blame heading his way. The press were muttering about it after the game but some of the officials seemed to feel the same way.'

The game ended goalless with Widzew going through on the away goals rule and Peter's view that Royle was to get the blame proved true. Years later Joe Royle felt he had been made the scapegoat: 'This is one European game that I was probably never forgiven for. I wasn't even due to be playing in the game, although I was in the squad, because Mike Channon had signed. The day before the game Channon pulled out with an hamstring, and I was told I was playing. So I was going to be thrown into it really. I wasn't due to be anywhere near ready.

'In the game I chased the ball down, challenged the goalkeeper, and the ball dropped. Whilst I was waiting for it to drop and then take it into the empty net, I lost it. I should have volleyed it first time. I was always blamed for that. It was City's way. The fact that we'd lost a 2-0 lead at home was the real reason we went out, but I know

Peter Barnes is suffering because of the constant clamour for new faces and instant success—Channon

TOO MUCH TOO SOON

PETER BARNES isn't the first football prodigy to discover that he can't exist on talent alone in the ruthless jungle of the First Division.

Defenders are reminding him that they aren't impressed by England caps or by rave Press notices. Bluntly, last season's electrifying winger, the pro's Young Player of the Year, is struggling. A classic case, say his critics, of too much too soon.

Questions are being about his ability

Criticism of Peter in October 1977.

what they used to say. The players used to joke about it. It was immaterial really. I knew I was on my way out of the club anyway. I knew that when Mike Channon was signed. I was probably the first of that great side to go.'

Joe Royle was to be transferred to Bristol City on November 15, seven weeks after the UEFA Cup second leg, confirming to those who had initially suspected Channon was Royle's replacement that they had been right all along.

Despite going out at such an early stage the UEFA Cup cost City in the League. The Blues' momentum was disrupted and in the games that had followed each leg they had drawn 1-1 at Queens Park Rangers and Everton respectively although there had been a 2-0 win over Bristol City in between

which had seen Peter score a classic goal: 'It's nice when people remind you of games. People often come up to me and talk about this one against Bristol City at Maine Road. It was never televised so it's great when people remember it. I ran from the half way line, beat three players, before I hit it on the left and it sailed into the far corner. I loved that goal and think it was one of the best I'd scored because I'd ran all that way, beat a few players and then smacked it in the corner. When fans bring that one up I know they were there because it just doesn't appear on film anywhere. That means more. I don't think I scored that many goals overall, not like someone like Dennis Tueart, so it's always great to be reminded of those special goals like this one. The goals against Tottenham at home in May 1977 and at White Hart Lane in February 1979 get shown a lot and were great goals, but I think this one was better.'

These results in late September and early October kept the Blues top of the table, but three days after the Everton game they lost 4-2 at Coventry, causing them to drop to second. Once they lost their dominance in the League the chance of winning the title was lost, although they did keep pace to some extent and there were some satisfying victories along the way. These included a 2-1 win at Maine Road on October 8 against Arsenal. Peter: 'I loved this because I scored one of the goals with a chip over Pat Jennings. The year before I'd chipped him – more or less

Peter collects the ball under pressure from Arsenal's Pat Rice, October 1977.

an identical goal – when he was playing for Tottenham. They were relegated and he moved to Arsenal and I did the same again! In some ways it was a better goal. I was coming in from the Kippax towards the Platt Lane. I beat Pat Rice, with Arsenal's offside trap, and I ran from the half way line but there was nobody with me. There was no one in the box who I could square it to and it was a tight angle. I thought "there's nothing on here" but I knew there was only Pat Jennings to beat, so I came in and I just dinked it. The ball went over his head and into the far corner. People often remember the Spurs goal from the year before because there's film of it but this was, to me, a much more technical goal because of the angle. I had the whole Spurs goal to go at the previous season, but here it was such a tight angle that the odds were not great. Anyway, I scored and we won the game. I don't think Pat Jennings was a fan of mine after those two games, but the goal gave me a lot of pleasure.'

Mike Channon had missed the Arsenal game but returned for Wolves on October 22. Roger Reade had viewed Channon's arrival extremely positively at first: 'When we signed Mick Channon I thought "that's it. That's the missing piece. With Peter down the wing, crossing the ball in we're going to score loads of goals and have a fantastic season." But it just didn't quite click for us for some reason. I remember BBC Nationwide were covering the Wolves game. We'd had a fairly good start and were being put across as one of the favourites to win the League but the Wolves game was one of those where the ball just wouldn't go in. We did everything right, except score. It ended in a 2-0 win for Wolves and that was the game that was featured on Nationwide. Just our luck!'

Things improved the week after when City faced reigning champions Liverpool

at Maine Road. Mansfield-based City fan Andy Wragg felt this game was a magical moment in his early support of the Blues: 'I was 16 years old at the time and my friend and I had only been given permission to go to matches alone. It's was an 110 mile return journey from Mansfield by bus, so this journey in to the relatively unknown added to the excitement of the day. Our expectations of the great mid-70s City side were high. We adored watching Dennis Tueart burn down the left wing, and Peter Barnes doing likewise on the right. From low down on the Kippax steps you got a real appreciation of their skill and you could feel the anticipation and excitement of the tens of thousands of City voices behind you whenever these winged wizards came in possession… The noise was deafening - it was the Kippax at its very best. Trailing at half-time to a David Fairclough goal, the Blues came out for the second half and stormed it. Thrilling strikes from Kiddo, Channon and Joe Royle sealed it. Barnes ran Alan Hansen in to the ground and big Dave Watson was commanding at the back.

'Anything seemed possible after that game… Years later my mind always drifts back to that day in 1977. I remember the day; I remember Gerald Sinstadt's commentary the following Sunday afternoon: "It's Barnes storming down the middle, Hansen is all over the place and now brings him down, but the ball runs kindly for Royle - bang - its 3-1".' [3]

Liverpool had only lost one of their opening 12 games when they came to Maine Road for that game. It was a great victory but, although it wasn't known at the time, it was also the final City League match for Joe Royle.

Peter, together with his mate Gary Owen, were hugely popular with City supporters as demonstrated near the season's end when City faced Derby County

Peter after scoring the first goal v Arsenal with Brian Kidd, October 1977.

at Maine Road on December 3. A dull, insipid game had come to life briefly in the 24th and 25th minutes when, first, Mike Channon scored for City then Gerry Daly equalised for Derby within a minute of the restart. Peter was on the substitute's bench and was brought on in the 63rd minute. Fans were delighted when they saw him warming up and preparing to take to the field but then their cheering turned angry as they saw that Gary Owen was to be taken off. Journalist Don Evans explained: 'The scoreline stood at one apiece when the incident occurred, a frustrated crowd, angered by the boredom that had gone before and the inability of City to take both points were delighted when Peter Barnes came on. But the delight turned sharply to disgust when it was seen that it was young Owen's number that had gone up from the dug-out.

'Cat-calls, jeers, and whistles cascaded down from the terraces who had been calling for Barnes from as early as the 20th minute. Owen came off looking upset, even angry, but Book rode the storm.' [4]

151

Ken and Peter Barnes pictured in November 1977 (above) and Peter with Tom Finney the following month (below).

Book explained his decision: 'It's my job to make changes as I feel necessary. I don't know whether the crowd understands, I don't necessarily expect them to. But there is certainly no way I would be influenced by the fans. If I had then Peter Barnes would have been on after only 20 minutes.' Many fans felt the game would've trod a different path had Peter been playing earlier, especially as once he was on City appeared more potent. After the game an unnamed City player reflected on the frustratingly negativity of the game and then said to Don Evans: 'I'm surprised you're here, and not watching the snooker', while Peter was asked about the crowd calling for him for much of the game before he came on: 'I believe they like to be entertained, and that's what I try to do.'

Unfortunately, a stomach bug prevented Peter from appearing in the following two League games but he did appear in the starting line-up for the Boxing Day meeting with Newcastle United at Maine Road. It's a game that has entered Manchester folklore as one of those games you just

had to experience to fully appreciate. All of those present that night from players, to fans, club officials to newspaper reporters, talk of this night as one of football's most emotional nights. This includes Peter: 'It was an incredible night. Not for the quality of football but for the return of Colin Bell and the ovation he received.'

The story of Colin Bell and his injury had become one of football's most discussed topics with the teatime BBC television news show Nationwide profiling Colin's story and fight to regain fitness. Viewers were touched by Colin's long, hard training schedules; his lonely runs through the streets of Moss Side and Rusholme; and by his absolute determination to return to full fitness. To them Colin's story was incredible, to City and England supporters it was a deeply disappointing and tragic story. Peter: 'I was injured for a while – Ray Ranson had tackled me from behind in training and my knee went. They kept taking me to Withington Hospital and the pain was horrendous. My knee used to blow up and they'd stick needles into the top of

Well done, Peter! Manchester City's Peter Barnes is named the North-West Sportsman of the Year by the Variety Club of Great Britain (Manchester Committee). Pictured (left to right) with him are City manager Tony Book, chief coach Bill Taylor, chairman Peter Swales and team-mate Gary Owen. Picture: IAN CURRIE.

Barnes magic takes award

By DAVID MEEK

PETER BARNES, the player with a touch of magic, is the new North West Sportsman of the Year.

The Manchester City winger weaved another spell over the annual awards to leave more experienced sportsmen standing.

The 20-year-old Barnes who has already jinked his way into the England team this season pipped former world speedway champion Peter Collins for the Variety Club of Great Britain trophy.

Manchester United's Steve Coppell, who also won his first senior international cap with Barnes against Italy, finished third.

The other nominations for the award were Red Rum trainer Ginger McCain, Liverpool captain Emlyn Hughes, Rugby Union international Tony Neary, Bolton manager Ian Greaves and Rugby League star Steve Nash.

Said Barnes today: "I was surprised to get the award.

A signed photo of Peter blasting City's opener past Alex Stepney. United 2 City 2, March 15, 1978

my knee to drain the fluid off. They had to hold me down the pain was excruciating and I hated needles too! They put me in a cast at night time. I'm sure now they'd have better treatment. Forty years on I have issues with my knee that I don't have in the other one and I think some of it was caused by the club wanting to get me back on the pitch quickly.

'We didn't have big squads then, so every player was needed out on the pitch or available for selection all the time. Anyone injured was of little value. While I was receiving treatment I could see what was happening with Colin Bell and the fight he had to get back. I'd be lying on one treatment table while he was on another being worked on by Freddie Griffiths and Roy Bailey. The noises, creaks, cracks and other sounds made me feel ill. You could hear the bones and the gristle. When you're injured and trying to fight your way back it

can be a lonely time. You'd see the fit players go out for training, practice games and the like but you'd be in the treatment room or the gym working, often on your own, with only your mind and your thoughts to accompany you. You can start to doubt yourself or doubt whether you'd ever regain your place. It's bad enough for a few weeks but Colin Bell had this for months and months. It was relentless. I don't know how he kept going. When he came back into contention we were all delighted for him and we hoped it would all work out. That game against Newcastle was a landmark moment for everyone connected with the club.'

On Boxing Day 1977 Colin Bell was named as substitute for the visit of Newcastle. Tony Book had planned to bring him on as substitute for the final twenty minutes, but an injury to Paul Power meant the manager had to take decisive action.

Peter in a race for the ball with Wolves defender Geoff Palmer, March 1978.

Peter: 'Tony told Colin he was coming on at half time in the dressing room and we all wished him well and hoped it all went well for him. As we came out for the second half fans spotted Colin in the line-up and Maine Road erupted. The Kippax began to sing his name and the whole atmosphere lifted significantly.'

The substitution totally transformed the atmosphere and the result. The game had been goalless, but the Blues tore into Newcastle as if they were playing in the most important game of all time. Dennis Tueart played superbly and scored a hat-trick, with Brian Kidd also scoring, to make it a convincing 4-0 win for the Blues. Peter: 'I remember Colin had a header which went over the bar… It would have been nice for him to score but his return was the most important aspect of that day.'

A modest Bell feels he did not contribute a great deal: 'I don't think I touched the ball. It was ten men versus eleven, but the atmosphere got to our team and we ran away with it.' [5] Bell was to start the following twelve League games, all of which Peter started too: 'I had a decent run then and I felt I was contributing

Disillusioned Barnes waits for England

DISILLUSIONED star Peter Barnes must rely on a call from England to rescue him from a frustrating period of unemployment with Manchester City.

That became clear yesterday when City manager Tony Book not only left Barnes out of today's team to meet Derby, but hinted that he

BY PETER JOHNSON

Barnes that his duty was to serve his club first and then devote any remaining energy to his country.

But the change in City's tactics in the last week has

played the previous night,' said Book. 'If he plays on Tuesday he will obviously come back into the reckoning for our final game at Chelsea on Friday.'

As expected Barnes will sit on the substitutes' bench this afternoon watching an unchanged City team trying to dismiss the last faint mathematical doubts about their right to be in Europe next season.

doubts that the youngster's future lies at Maine Road.

'We have changed our tactics in the last two games,' he said. 'But it is always players, not tactics, that count in the end.

'I have no doubt that when Peter comes back he will be just as devastating, perhaps even a more complete player, whatever the system.'

Wanted Barnes worth £750,000 —Book

By JOHN BEAN

MANCHESTER City boss Tony Book last night valued his brilliant young winger Peter Barnes at a staggering £750,000 but ...

BARNES ROCKER

City star left out again

PETER BARNES is left out of the Manchester City team again today, a victim of the squad system that led to Dennis Tueart leaving the club.

After being named as substitute for the second successive match the young England left Maine Road tight-lipped and confused.

By Bill Elliott

"I don't really want to say anything at the moment. Let's just wait and see what happens," was the talented star's only comment.

Forty-eight hours earlier, Barnes requested a talk with manager Tony Book after losing his place for the home game against Coventry.

It gave Barnes the chance to vent his feelings, but it has not got him back in the team hoping to beat Derby today and so make certain of a UEFA Cup place.

Now Barnes knows that his next game at Maine Road ...

21 team against Yugoslavia in the semi-final of the European Championship next Tuesday.

And the irony of being first choice for his country at senior and junior levels while being passed over for his own club side is not lost on him.

And all that adds up to a searching test of Peter's character as well as the extent of the commitment to the only club he has known.

Whether he decides to adopt the same position as Tueart remains to be seen.

But Book began the delicate manoeuvring to placate his player ...

BARNES PLAYS IT BY THE BOOK

WHILE Manchester City fans and the English football public at large fussed and fretted over Peter Barnes' parachute drop from the Brazil match to the subs' bench, Tony Book was lifting the boy.

In the quiet of his Maine Road office, Book reassured his prodigy by saying; "If you don't develop into a world-class player there must be something wrong. You're 20 years of age and you've achieved fantastic things already."

By John Roberts

Barnes sought an audience of his manager the morning after watching City defeat Coventry City 3—1 without him a week after his encouraging performance in England's 1—1 draw with Brazil at Wembley.

Brazilian brutality had cost ...

about the current situation.

"But certainly I am in a position to see how things go for a while yet."

Book said he could not understand what the fuss was about. "Peter didn't get picked ... ing in an

disturbed by the player's lack of tactical maturity.

"The game has nothing to do with systems. It's only to do with players," he said.

"When you have the ball you play with it and when you haven't you get behind the

Peter Barnes

☐ Barnes and City teammate Joe Corrigan are the two full caps in the England squad for Tuesday's European Under-21 game against Yugoslavia at Maine Road—although City play at ... 24 hrs earlier.

CITY 'NO' TO BARNES MOVE BY EINDHOVEN

PSV Eindhoven, crack Dutch club and UEFA Cup finalists, want Manchester City's brilliant England winger Peter Barnes.

But Maine Road chairman Peter Swales stressed today; "Barnes is not for sale at any price."

Barnes has recently discussed his future with Blues' boss Tony Book following his failure to imme-

by Peter Gardner

Peter gets a shot in v West Bromwich Albion, April 1978.

well. We won seven consecutive League games, lifting us to second place behind Nottingham Forest. Brian Clough's team were incredible that season but we felt we could catch them but we suffered a few draws in March and lost touch. We ended up finishing fourth and Forest were champions. They thoroughly deserved it but we were disappointed that we'd dropped away. At least we'd qualified for the UEFA Cup though.'

Chairman Peter Swales held the belief that this season had been another progressive one in his quest to see City dominate. He was proud of the fact that support was increasing and the Blues were the third best supported club in the League and he did all he could to help increase support further. Swales would open up

supporters' branches wherever he could: 'We opened places in Norway, and I thought if United are in Norway then we'll go to Norway. We went to the United obsessed Malta and tried there. We went to Jersey and opened one there. Went to Ireland and Scotland... Anywhere we could. It was buzzing, it was vibrant, and we brought the Junior Blues in - we were the first with a junior club and everybody used to come and see how it operated. It's been a tremendous success.' [6]

The whole trajectory of the club seemed to be upwards and Peter was perceived as being an essential part of the progression. Like City, Peter's career was developing well. In November 1977 he had made his full England debut in a World Cup qualifier and in April he had impressed with a brilliant performance against Brazil at Wembley, which led to the New Statesman commenting: 'Barnes must take a lot of credit for inspiring the new confidence. His peculiar hurtling style, like supercharged skipping, conceals an art surprisingly similar to Stanley Matthews's: he runs, that is, in more or less straight lines with little distracting thrills on them. Barnes doesn't waste time sending a defender one way and swerving the other. After his minimal feint, he simply carries on running through the place where the defender has just moved from. That is why so many of his runs make him look like a man squeezing down a human corridor. The margins are very small… He sends a full-back of the denser species both ways at once, which leaves the fellow either sitting or standing on the spot perplexedly scratching his head, adjusting his chewing gum etc.' [7]

Peter had appeared in 33 (plus one as substitute) League games and had scored eight goals. It was perceived as a great season for him personally and both the fans and the media often focused positively on his performance in games, especially a 3-1 win over Liverpool in October; a 6-2 victory over Chelsea in November; a 2-0 win over Aston Villa on New Year's Eve and a 3-2 defeat of West Ham in January. UEFA Cup winners PSV Eindhoven were impressed with Peter's performances during the 1977-78 season and made a bid for him shortly before their UEFA Cup final appearance. City valued Peter at £750,000 - £250,000 more than the British transfer record which had seen Kevin Keegan leave Liverpool for Hamburg the previous June – but this valuation did not reflect the salary he was on which, according to sources at the time was considerably lower than the majority of his teammates at Maine Road and a quarter of what he could earn in the Netherlands. [8] City had a reputation for paying homegrown players considerably less than players, such as Mike Channon, brought into the club regardless of how those players performed; their contribution to the development of the club; or even the entertainment the fans gained from the players. Peter, loved by the majority of City's match-going crowd, remained loyal to the club he loved but, ending the season on the substitutes bench despite being perceived positively by leading football figures at home and abroad at a national level, did play on his mind.

[1] 'Prize Postbag', *Manchester Evening News Pink*, undated but believed to be August 27, 1977.
[2] 'Manchester City to fence them in', *Aberdeen Press and Journal*, September 22, 1977, 26.
[3] Letter from Andy Wragg to the author during research for *Farewell To Maine Road*, posted in 2002.
[4] 'Jeers for Book', *News of the World*, April 30, 1978.
[5] Colin Bell interviewed by Gary James, February 2005.
[6] Peter Swales interviewed by Gary James, December 1995.
[7] *New Statesman*, May 5, 1978, 617.
[8] 'Barnes in "Pay me what I'm worth" shock', *News of the World*, May 14, 1978, 19.

Dad Ken took up Crown Green Bowls after his football career finished and became a member of Lloyds Hotel Bowling Club, one of south Manchester's most succesful clubs.

Chapter Nine

ENGLAND
EXPECTS

❝

'Please don't expect too much of me,' says the 20-year-old Manchester City winger, hailed as the new saviour of English football.

'Barnes asks fans: Treat me gently', *Daily Mirror*, November 16, 1977, 32.

❞

It was the 1977-78 season when Peter first played for the England senior squad after appearing for his country in various age related games, including the under 21s. He made his England under 21 debut as substitute in a goalless game with Wales in December 1976, replacing Liverpool's David Fairclough in the 70th minute. This was the first England international at that level since a restructure of football's age related international competitions, previously there had been an under 23 team. Peter was to start the following seven under 21 internationals, scoring his first goal against Norway in Bergen on June 1, 1977 and receiving significant praise in the process: 'Peter Barnes brought a smile to the battered face of English international football here in Bergen last night.' [1] The *Daily Mirror* report went on: 'Barnes, the quick and highly skilful winger from Manchester City, was very much the star turn on an evening when England gave us so much to admire.' Peter set up the

first England goal when he 'jinked past two defenders and crossed the ball for Deehan to hammer it in. Nottingham Forest goalkeeper John Middleton had to make a dazzling save from Norwegian skipper Rune Ottesen before Barnes sent England further ahead after an hour. Full back Peter Daniel pumped forward a free kick and Barnes cut in from the right to score with a thundering left foot shot.

'The exciting Barnes had another block-busting drive turned over the bar before Norway pulled a goal back.'

After Norway Peter played in a 8-1 humiliation of Finland and then was selected to face Italy in March 1978. Italian teams were beginning to play a key role in the development of Peter's career. He'd faced Juventus in September 1976 for Manchester City and had made his England Senior debut against Italy in November 1977. Played in front of a crowd of 22,241 – the largest for the U21s at the time – the U21 international v Italy at Maine Road was a tough international for Peter who said at the time: 'It was the worst experience I've ever had.' [2] He went on: 'The Italians are always like that. It was no different in the World Cup match at Wembley.' The game had been a physical one and led to City manager Tony Book, who was watching from the Main Stand, commenting: 'It was a triumph for English discipline. Some of the England skill was brilliant but the way they kept their heads was even better. I know Peter Barnes was knocked about a bit, but that was because they recognise him as a really good player.'

Gary Owen, who played alongside Peter in this U21 international, remembers the physicality of the game: 'One of their players tried to take Peter out in the first five minutes, so that was it I had a go at one of theirs a minute or two later. The ball was nowhere near us – and neither was the referee – so I went "smash" and that told him! You try to take out one of ours and I'll try and take out one of yours. That seemed fair. That's how it was in those days. We had players – both at City and with the international teams – that could do that. Peter wasn't one of those type of players. He needed to be protected, whereas I liked that confrontational aspect. I was brought up to stand my corner and that helped Peter and I worked well together.'

Roger Reade remembers: 'I was working at Maine Road the day after the Under 21 game and a photographer and reporter came down to take photos of Peter because he was black and blue after the physical battle the night before. Back then the newspaper photos were black and white. What they realised when they got down to see Peter was that the bruising didn't have enough contrast to stand out in a newspaper photo. So Roy Bailey, a renowned and respected physio at City for many, many years, got some iodine I think

Peter Barnes, Manchester City's England winger, today counted the cost of the mauling he received in last night's Under-21 match at Maine Road. And there to show him the extent of the damage was Scotland World Cup star Willie Donachie with a mirror through which Barnes can see his blackened right eye. Picture: Ian Currie. "Italian kids kick like their dads"—Page 19.

it was. It was something he had which was used to colour in Peter's bruises. He painted around his eye to ensure he had a visible black eye and the press got their photo.'

Peter played in two further U21 internationals, both draws – the return with Italy and against Yugoslavia in the second leg of the semi-final of the UEFA U21 tournament. By that time Peter had also appeared in three senior internationals with his debut coming against Italy in 1977.

City team mate Gary Owen was pleased when Peter was selected: 'I was delighted. He was my pal and it was an achievement we all shared in and loved. I was playing England youth or 21s at that point so I felt I was just a step or so behind him. I remember his senior debut and it was a really good performance. It was great to see

England Under 21 Appearances

Date	Opposition	Venue	Score	England Goalscorers	Comments
15/12/76	Wales	Molineux	D 0-0		Came on as substitute for David Fairclough
27/4/76	Scotland	Bramall Lane	W 1-0	Cunningham	
26/5/76	Finland	Helsinki	W 1-0	Peach	
1/6/77	Norway	Bergen	W 2-1	Deehan, Barnes	
6/9/77	Norway	Goldstone Ground	W 6-0	Ward (2), Deehan (2), Barnes	
12/10/77	Finland	Boothferry Park	W 8-1	Woodcock (3), Deehan (2), Simms, Daniel (pen), Cunningham	
8/3/78	Italy	Maine Road	W 2-1	Woodcock (2)	Attendance of 22,241 was the highest the U21s had played in front of up to that point. 1st leg of UEFA U21 quarter-final
5/4/78	Italy	Rome	D 0-0		2nd leg of UEFA U21 quarter-final
2/5/78	Yugoslavia	Maine Road	D 1-1	Sims	Peter's last U21 international. Attendance of 24,423 was the largest home crowd for England U21s until November 1994. UEFA U21 semi-final 2nd leg (1st leg ended in a 2-1 defeat).

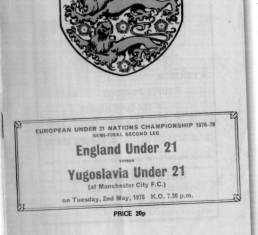

EUROPEAN UNDER 21 NATIONS CHAMPIONSHIP 1976-78
SEMI-FINAL SECOND LEG

England Under 21
versus
Yugoslavia Under 21
(at Manchester City F.C.)

on Tuesday, 2nd May, 1978 K.O. 7.30 p.m.

PRICE 20p

and, I have to stress this, he never lost his humility. He never came back from England or anywhere else and thought he was better than what he was or better than us. He kept his feet on the ground and stayed the same Peter. Maybe because of his dad's influence or his brothers he just stayed level headed.

'There were also a lot of seasoned internationals at City then. People like Dave Watson, Dennis Tueart, Willie Donachie, Asa Hartford, Mike Doyle, Joe Royle… He also had people like Ray Wilkins who he'd played at every level… but it's important to know that Peter got his chance because he was a phenomenal player at this time. He was unplayable. It's difficult finding a player today who compares. From

Gary Owen and Peter wearing their England U21 blazers.

a City perspective I suppose you'd say Leroy Sane but he's more of a Weeble – you don't know where he's going at times and his concentration lets him down but he is only a young player too. Because he's a wide player and left footed you'd say Sane compares to some extent. He can take people on, he can cross it, he's plenty of energy but only on his best days would he compare.

'Barnesy was a heals on the touchline wide player – that was him. He never wanted to be in the middle or at the back he was out and out edge of the pitch on the wing. There was no point trying to get him to go back and defend because we had plenty of people who could do that back then. Once City's defence got the ball then they could also deliver. No fullback Peter faced was ever particularly keen to play against him. Whatever they did Peter

would have an answer – if they pushed forward they knew that if they lost the ball he'd be on them and win the ball. They'd be frightened. Defenders would never want to be rushing back thirty yards with Barnes going at them. It worked great. If Peter was in a one on one with half the pitch to go at nobody would beat him. He was always going to get past that defender.'

England manager Ron Greenwood loved this aspect of Peter's play: '[Barnes] was a natural – Pacey, tremendous at going past defenders, a potential match-winner.' [3] Thinking about the Italy game, Greenwood later commented: 'I picked Steve Coppell and Peter Barnes as our wingers and Bob Latchford as the centre-striker – a first cap for each of them. Their inexperience did not worry me because I thought they had the right qualities and character for the job.' [4]

When Peter was selected for England

there was a lot of talk about wingers in the media with Greenwood being praised for selecting Peter and Steve Coppell and reintroducing attack-minded wingers in the national team. Alf Ramsey had abandoned orthodox wing play in the 1960s and his success in the 1966 World Cup then led to teams across England playing with less attack-power down the wings. According to David Lacey in the *Guardian*: 'Since then the system aped and stereotyped throughout the Football League, has tended to hold back the development of the national game.' [5]

Peter's father Ken was not a fan of negative play. In 2004 he felt that success under Ramsey had limited thinking: 'I think Peter was very unlucky. His style of football was out of fashion nationally when he hit his peak. England had won the World Cup in '66 with Ramsey's "wingless wonders" and, although that was a tremendous achievement, it meant that almost every side believed that wingers were no longer needed in the game. Managers started to follow Ramsey's approach and players like Peter had less chance as a result. Just because Ramsey had been successful it didn't mean everyone else would be. In fact it's a bit like the deep-lying centre forward tactics we used at City in the fifties - the Revie Plan. We were successful because we made it work, but if every side had adopted the Plan we'd have all cancelled each other out.' [6]

Journalist Jack Steggles asked Peter about the upcoming game and Peter was as modest as ever, telling him: 'Please don't

Ken and Peter celebrate Peter's England call up, November 1977. Photographed in the Maine Road kitchen.

expect too much or me. A lot of nice things have been written and said about me. I've had so much good publicity that people may be expecting me to beat the Italians on my own. That's a big burden and I beg the fans to give me a chance. But I'm not afraid of making my debut in such an important match.' [7] Despite these requests, some in the media were already suggesting Peter could be the 'saviour' of English football.

The Saviour? Peter: 'I came in when England needed to beat Italy 6-0. Ron Greenwood had come in as manager after Don Revie had gone off to Dubai to manage the United Arab Emirates. Ron wanted attacking football and me, Bob Latchford and Steve Coppell were all brought in. We were never going to beat Italy 6-0 but we managed a 2-0 win and it was a good game. Using words like "saviour" to describe a footballer is way over the top and puts pressure on young players. I was always pleased when other young players came in with me. Players like Ray Wilkins, Steve Coppell and so on. It made it easier and as Ron was a new manager too it made it

better for all of us. I don't think anyone expected us to beat Italy – certainly not 6-0 – so getting a 2-0 win and doing okay was fine. I think there had been so much depressing news around the England set up following Don's departure that it actually made life easier for us, but having young players I'd played with in England under 21s or at youth made it better. I was always a shy player, but having these familiar faces around me helped a lot. I had been Ray Wilkins' roommate so that helped as well once we were both in the senior England team. The manager Ron Greenwood was a real gentleman.

The Guardian's Paul Fitzpatrick took the opportunity of Peter being selected by Ron Greenwood for the Italian game to explain to readers why he believed the City man was such a good player, while also expressing some concern on the way Peter was being managed at Maine Road: 'The establishment of Peter Barnes on Manchester City's left wing has been one of Maine Road's happier stories this season. There have been times when one could not help but feel that Tony Book, City's Manager, had a distrust almost of the talents of Barnes and that other gifted youngster, Gary Owen. It was almost as if Book, who did not enter professional soccer until an advanced age, could not convince himself of the value of youth.

'Barnes, to the frequent dismay and frustration of City followers, was repeatedly left out of the side last season, and one was left to wonder whether Barnes would ever fulfil his potential sitting on the substitute's bench or playing in the Central League side. But even Book now has no doubts. So convinced is he of Barnes's

THE EMPIRE STADIUM, WEMBLEY
Association Football
INTERNATIONAL
MATCH
(World Cup Qualifying)
No ticket genuine unless it carries a Lion's Head watermark below

ENGLAND
VERSUS
ITALY
WED. NOV. 16, 1977
KICK-OFF 7.45 p.m.
YOU ARE ADVISED TO TAKE UP
YOUR POSITION BY 7.15 p.m.

TURNSTILES
E
ENTRANCE
1
ROW
31
SEAT
196

CHAIRMAN
WEMBLEY STADIUM LTD

NORTH TERRACE SEAT
£8.00
TO BE RETAINED   SEE PLAN AND CONDITIONS ON BACK

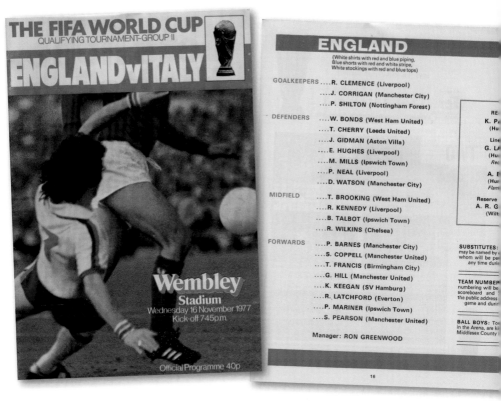

ability and his maturity that he lost little time in accepting Dennis Tueart's transfer request last week. That would have been an unthinkable situation last season.' [8]

Fitzpatrick continued: 'Barnes is physically stronger now than he has ever been. His ability, which he possesses in enviable quantity, has never seriously been questioned since he made his debut as a frail 17-year-old. But there have been doubts about his ability to survive the buffetings of the harshly competitive First division where seasoned defenders take unkindly to having the ball pushed through their legs by an impudent young upstart. Happily Barnes has proved beyond all reasonable doubt this season that he not only has the ability but the character to survive at the highest level.'

'The Italians knew all about me because of the UEFA Cup tie against Juventus and so they knew what I was capable of and they knew what to watch for but I didn't really think much about that. I was just delighted to have been picked and to be appearing in front of 92,000 at Wembley. I loved the feeling of being on that coach, heading towards the twin towers. I was so proud. My dad came to watch with Tony Book and a few others from City.'

The staff at City were proud of Peter's contribution in this game. Roger Reade: 'Every time a City player played for England – whatever the level – we loved it. The Italian team had a nucleus of players from Juventus – who we'd played a year earlier - who were physically intimidating. Peter played in that game as if he had no fear

167

whatsoever despite the kicking he received. He made it look like he'd been playing international football for years in that game.'

The Italian game ended in a 2-0 England victory with goals from Kevin Keegan and Trevor Brooking and in the press later that week respected footballing figures Tom Finney, Joe Mercer, Jimmy Greaves and Bob Wilson were asked for their views. [9] They all praised Ron Greenwood for including young players like Steve Coppell and, of course, Peter, leading to Mercer specifically commenting on those two wingers: 'They will be great players if we persist with them. What we must not do is start making wholesale changes.' Finney was also supportive: 'Greenwood must strive for a settled side. That means giving the same players an extended run. As a winger and long-time advocate of using the flanks, it was heartening to see Steve Coppell and Peter Barnes do so well.'

A few years later Ron Greenwood remembered: 'The victory was a wonderful shot in the arm for us and I could see promise in the method we had used. I felt if we could keep it going it would mature into something really good. Variations and subtleties would come with time. Coppell and Barnes were essential to the pattern and I believed they were part of England's long-term future. They gave us width and flair, they were the edge to our blade, and I would have kept them in the team as long as I was in charge.' [10] Unfortunately injury cut short Coppell's career while Peter's move away from Maine Road in 1979 would limit his opportunities.

Peter's second international was a 2-1 defeat by West Germany in Munich. Peter: 'I remember Berti Vogts was up

LÄNDERSPIEL

Preis 1,–DM

PROGRAMM

22. Febr. 1978
Olympia-
Stadion
München
20.15 Uhr

Deutscher
Fußball-Bund

DEUTSCHLAND – ENGLAND

Titelfoto: Tor durch Karl-Heinz Rummenigge (FC Bayern München) beim 2:1 gegen Italien am 8. Oktober 1977 in Berlin. Torwart Dino Zoff greift ins Leere. Links Giacinto Facchetti.

against me in Munich but he couldn't do anything right that night and I went past him time after time. I was always taught to run with the ball with my head up. To look around and not put my head down.' Peter's memory is correct as newspapers highlighted his contribution time and time again with journalist Bob Harris writing: '[Barnes] gave the experienced Berti Vogts a harrowing time, and twice raced past him and almost put England into the lead with a fierce shout that skimmed across the face of Zepp (sic) Maier's goal.' [11] Germany had a brilliant chance to score via Rummenigge but: 'England were still matching them skill for skill and Pearson came equally as close when Barnes again turned Vogts on a sixpence and crossed to the far post for Pearson to head in to the side netting. The patient build-up of Ron Greenwood's relaxed side eventually paid dividends when Pearson headed them into the lead four minutes before the interval with a move that began with goalkeeper Ray Clemence.'

Germany equalised and then, after Kevin Keegan had gone off injured, Bonhof scored a dramatic late winner for the home team. Peter: 'We were disappointed with that after all the effort we'd put in. It was a free kick and there was an argument with the ref about the distance the wall had to be. We were pushed back further than we thought we should. Bonhof was excellent at curving balls around walls and he took the kick while the argument was still going on. The ball curved into the top corner, past Clemence, and that was that. It made the complaints increase of course and I think a draw would've been a fair result.'

There had been snow on the ground which angered Ron Greenwood: 'We played well on a pitch that hadn't been properly cleared, Peter Barnes gave that gutsy and knowing little full-back, Berti Vogts, a

real running, and a Stuart Pearson header gave us the lead.' [12]

After West Germany came a 1-1 draw with Brazil which started a run of fourteen unbeaten games for England. After the Brazil game Peter was described as: 'England's international discovery of the season who scared the pants off Brazil, Italy and West Germany.' [13]

Peter: 'I had a good game against Brazil. We lost but it was personally a good game for me. Their team was packed full of successful world stars.

'I loved playing for England at this time and I am

THE FOOTBALL ASSOCIATION
LIMITED
Patron: HER MAJESTY THE QUEEN
President: H.R.H. THE DUKE OF KENT
Chairman: SIR HAROLD THOMPSON, C.B.E., F.R.S.

Secretary:
E. A. CROKER

Telegraphic Address:
FOOTBALL ASSOCIATION, LONDON, W2 3LW
Phone: 01-262 4542
Telex: 261110

16 LANCASTER GATE, LONDON, W2 3LW

Our Ref: JJB/TJ/   *Your Ref:*   7.8.78.

Dear *Pete*,

I have much pleasure in forwarding to you by Registered Parcel
Post *ONE* International Cap(s) awarded to you for ....
.................................*England v. Hungary*...

Will you please complete the enclosed acknowledgement slip and
return it to me immediately you receive the Cap(s).

Yours sincerely,

Jim Burie

for Secretary

*All the best at Derby.
Hope to see you next month.
J.*

Encs.

Registered Office: 16 Lancaster Gate, London W2 3LW
Incorporated in London: Registration Number 77797

so pleased that Ron Greenwood believed in me. He loved playing with wingers and encouraged me. Ron Greenwood was dignified... knowledgeable... a true football man.' Ron was also a big fan of Peter's and he was impressed with his performances throughout his first couple of years with England. In February 1979 he commented:

'Peter Barnes has only missed one game for England since I took over and I don't think that he has ever let us down. Perhaps the advent of Laurie Cunningham has geed him up a bit.' [14] Cunningham was proving to be an exceptional talent on the wing for West Bromwich Albion and this clearly placed pressure on Peter: 'Laurie had

England Senior Appearances

Date	Opposition	Venue	Score	England Goalscorers	Comments
16/11/77	**Italy**	Wembley	W 2-0	Keegan, Brooking	World Cup Qualifier
22/2/78	**W Germany**	Munich	L 1-2	Pearson	
19/4/78	**Brazil**	Wembley	D 1-1	Keegan	
13/5/78	**Wales**	Ninian Park	W 3-1	Latchford, Currie, Barnes	Home International Tournament
20/5/78	**Scotland**	Hampden Park	W 1-0	Coppell	Home International Tournament
24/5/78	**Hungary**	Wembley	W 4-1	Barnes, Neal (pen), T Francis, Currie	
20/9/78	**Denmark**	Copenhagen	W 4-3	Keegan (2), Neal, Latchford	European Championship Qualifier
25/10/78	**Rep of Ireland**	Lansdowne Rd, Dublin	D 1-1	Latchford	European Championship Qualifier
29/11/78	**Czechoslovakia**	Wembley	W 1-0	Coppell	
7/2/79	**N Ireland**	Wembley	W 4-0	Latchford (2), Keegan, Watson	European Championship Qualifier
19/5/79	**N Ireland**	Windsor Park, Belfast	W 2-0	Watson, Coppell	Home International Tournament
26/5/79	**Scotland**	Wembley	W 3-1	Barnes, Coppell, Keegan	Home International Tournament
6/6/79	**Bulgaria**	Sofia	W 3-0	Keegan, Watson, Barnes	European Championship Qualifier
13/6/79	**Austria**	Vienna	L 3-4	Keegan, Coppell, Wilkins	
12/9/79	**Denmark**	Wembley	W 1-0	Keegan	European Championship Qualifier
17/5/80	**Wales**	Racecourse Ground, Wrexham	L 1-4	Mariner	Home International Tournament
25/3/81	**Spain**	Wembley	L 1-2	Hoddle	Peter came on as sub for Trevor Francis
12/5/81	**Brazil**	Wembley	L 0-1		
20/5/81	**Wales**	Wembley	D 0-0		Home International Tournament
30/5/81	**Switzerland**	Basle	L 1-2	McDermott	World Cup Qualifier. Came on as sub for Dave Watson
9/9/81	**Norway**	Oslo	L 1-2	Robson	World Cup Qualifier. Came on as sub for Glenn Hoddle
25/5/82	**Holland**	Wembley	W 2-0	Mariner, Woodcock	Came on as sub for Paul Mariner

immense talent and I loved the challenge that presented. As time moved on the newspapers would often highlight the two of us, plus Steve Coppell of course, as examples of the great future English football should have. Things didn't work out how any of us would have liked with England in the end, but for a while there was a real buzz about England's possibilities.'

Peter managed fourteen England internationals while with Manchester City, increasing to 22 in the years that followed. This meant that at the time he made his 14th international appearance he had made more England appearances than any other homegrown City player. In fact Scotland's Willie Donachie was the only homegrown City international player to have made more appearances for his country than Peter while at Maine Road. In addition, Peter had helped England win two British Home International Tournaments – perceived as a major competition for almost a century between England, Scotland, Wales and Northern Ireland (playing as Ireland for most of the competition's existence).

[1] 'Peter puts England on glory road', *Daily Mirror*, June 2, 1977, 32.
[2] 'Barnes blast for Italians', *Daily Mirror*, March 9, 1978, back page.
[3] Ron Greenwood, *Yours Sincerely* (London: Willow Books, 1984), 38.
[4] Ibid., 37.
[5] 'Greenwood's revivalist meeting?', *Guardian*, November 16, 1977, 24.
[6] Ken Barnes, interviewed by Gary James in April 2004.
[7] 'Barnes asks fans: Treat me gently', *Daily Mirror*, November 16, 1977, 32.
[8] 'Coppell rewarded', *Guardian*, November 8, 1977, 20.
[9] 'Now bring in the kids', *Sun*, November 18, 1977, 32.
[10] Ron Greenwood, *Yours Sincerely* (London: Willow Books, 1984), 39.
[11] 'Battling England go down fighting', Newcastle Journal, February 23, 1978, 14.
[12] Ron Greenwood, *Yours Sincerely* (London: Willow Books, 1984), 42.
[13] 'Barnes in "Pay me what I'm worth" shock', *News of the World*, May 14, 1978, 19.
[14] 'England stay put', *Guardian*, February 6, 1979, 24.

Chapter Ten

BARNES' STANDARD

> £1.5 million Barnes Offer Denied: A report that
> the Italian champions, Juventus, are ready to offer
> £1.5 million for Peter Barnes was angrily denied yesterday
> by the Manchester City chairman, Peter Swales... Whether
> Barnes is one who would be tempted to move is another
> matter. He said last night that he was settled at City and
> did not want to play for anyone else.

'£1.5 million Barnes Offer Denied', *Guardian*, December 8, 1978, 20.

With his appearances for England and his contribution to Manchester City, 21 year old Peter was perceived as an established first team player by the start of the 1978-79 season. PSV Eindhoven, Juventus and other clubs were interested in signing him but this was bringing him a recognition that his earnings at City were somewhat less than some of the players who had been brought in, such as Mike Channon. While Peter had no issue with Channon or any other arrival, he did find players at England would discuss their earnings and club contracts and differences between players of similar ages and playing for comparable clubs became obvious. Journalists, looking for a story, would ask Peter about his earnings and the player would be open and honest.

In the days before media training for players, footballers would often chat to journalists without considering how their comments may appear in print. This would occasionally cause issues between a player and his club, while some journalists would seek to create a series of articles out of a player's comments with one featuring a player expressing discontent over his earnings, followed by a comment from the club's manager on another day and then another by the player. These articles would create a situation where fans would think a player is about to walk out on a club or has a serious disagreement with the direction of the team. At Manchester City the mid 1970s had seen articles on several star players appear dissatisfied with their place at the club, including Rodney Marsh, Dennis

Tueart and Mike Doyle. Whether these articles properly represented discussions within the club are not clear but neither Tueart nor Doyle left when those stories first emerged, while Marsh was dropped from the team and then transferred as a result of issues in the dressing room, not stories in the media. Inevitably, as Peter's status nationally increased so did the volume of articles on him, leading to frequent comments about his earnings and, at times, lack of opportunities. [1]

Talking to individual reporters was something that happened as part of every day life with journalists often popping in to Maine Road. Chairman Peter Swales encouraged promotion of the club and saw the value in close relationships with the media but, of course, this openness meant that fairly minor disagreements between the players and the manager or elsewhere within the club could blow up into national, headline grabbing stories. As Peter was perceived as a major asset, wanted by many clubs and was already being asked about his salary and aspirations on a regular basis it would be inevitable that when things started to go wrong at the club his name would appear as someone who was likely to leave. As the 1978-79 season progressed the club would enter a difficult period, leading to player dissatisfaction and widespread media coverage. In October, for example, Tony Book expressed his anger at media reports which were suggesting Peter was about to leave: 'A lot of fuss was made last week about my second half substitution of Peter Barnes. It's the age-old press gimmick of stirring up the waters, creating the drama when things aren't going quite so

Members of the City squad, including Peter, welcome Paul Futcher to Maine Road.

smoothly for the subjects of their attention. The Headlines were harsh and without foundation when they said that Peter was on the point of a transfer show-down.

'Their imaginations may be fertile when they write such news, but if you look at how many times their speculative stories have ended up barren you'd realise that there's not much to admire in that kind of reporting.'[2]

Journalists in 1978, as with those in the 2020s, had to find content and any minor disagreement or substitution that angered a player or fans often became big news. With limited television coverage of games, those that could not attend matches gathered their football content from radio commentaries and newspaper reports, which shaped minds. Manchester City's match day programme, particularly the manager's comments pages, often contained material commenting on issues that by 2020 were no longer covered in official material. Match programmes were, of course, promotional publications produced by the clubs but, in Manchester City's case, the 1978-79 match programme editor was never afraid to publish material attacking the media or indeed criticising a player. That whole approach changed significantly as television coverage of games increased and clubs considered how their brand could be impacted. City was a club that always welcomed the media in the 1970s but it did so to broaden the club's supporter base, using action on the pitch to promote a positive, dynamic looking club. Any negativity within the media about team selections, player disagreements and the like would be challenged within the club's own publication, knowing they were talking directly to match going fans and media.

Peter remembers 1978-79 as a season that started with lots of rumours: 'It was a tough season and we seemed to be in the papers often. In fact, despite the speculation about Eindhoven, Juventus, Manchester United and others wanting me, I looked forward to City developing further. I thought we stood a real chance of winning a trophy. Colin Viljoen, Paul Futcher, and then his brother Ron, joined us and I thought we were progressing. The club were trying to sign the great Polish World Cup star Kaziu Deyna too. I was disappointed that Dennis Tueart and Joe Royle had both left the previous season, but it felt like Tony Book had plans to strengthen the team further and we had no reason to be concerned about that – maybe our own place in the team but a challenge was always healthy.'

Some of Peter's concerns about his own place at the club were satisfied in June, around the time of his 21st birthday, when the club offered him a new contract. That removed some of the worries that had plagued him at times: 'It meant I knew I had a future at City – or at least that's what I thought and that's what I was told. I didn't want to leave, despite the media suggestions that I wanted out. That was all paper talk and any comments I made towards the end of 1977-78 were really a frustration about being dropped after playing so well for England. Plus the difference those of us who had come through the ranks were treated contract wise to new arrivals.'

Peter, wearing the number 11 shirt, was on the wing for the opening of the 1978-79 season, with Mike Channon on the opposite wing. There had been an injury scare for Peter: 'I had knee ligament issues which kept me out of the pre-season but was fit enough to play in the 1-1 draw at Derby in the first League game.'

The opening weeks of the season were not great with City earning three points from their opening four fixtures, but a 3-0 win at home to Leeds on September 9

Peter in action at Twente Enschede.

seemed to be the start of a decent spell and was followed by a 1-1 draw at Twente Enschede in the UEFA Cup. Peter: 'The UEFA Cup became the most likely trophy for us to win that season and we won the second leg 3-2 at Maine Road with Brian Kidd and Colin Bell being our stars. Joe Corrigan had been great over the two games too and that European experience that those three possessed was vital. Asa Hartford was playing – he'd played in the World Cup in Argentina that summer and was another with a strong understanding of the game outside Britain. But it's worth remembering that our team for this UEFA tie had included me – just 21, Gary Owen, Roger Palmer and Paul Power. All locally produced kids.

'After Twente came Standard Liege. The first game was something special. I loved

those European nights at Maine Road. Maine Road was special for European nights. They were always different from the norm and I loved them. You took it all in as you got to the game. You'd see the mounted policemen outside the ground, the lines of buses dropping fans off, the smell of tobacco around the ground… The greatest experience of course was coming down the tunnel and charging towards the Kippax. The noise would hit you and, no matter how many were in the ground, it felt like a cauldron for those European nights. I couldn't wait to get out on to the pitch. These were special nights.'

Against Liege Scotland star Asa Hartford scored in the 13th minute but, despite several attempts that was all that separated the clubs up to the 85th minute. City surged forward, keen to increase

The golden goal that started the rush . . . Brian Kidd slots Manchester City's second against Standard Liege from the penalty spot.

A late, great show by City

Daily Mail, Thursday, October 19, 1978

Reaction following the 4-0 home win over Standard Liege.

ORTSMAIL EUROPEAN SOCCER SPECIAL

Magic spell

By RONALD CROWTHER

Manchester City 4
Standard Liege 0

FIVE minutes of magic last night left the way wide open into round three of the UEFA Cup for amazing Manchester City.

In those dramatic dying moments of a first leg game in which they appeared to have lost their way against Belgium rivals Standard Liege, Brian Kidd hit two goals and Roger Palmer helped himself to a third to give them what must surely be an impregnable lead for the second leg on November 1.

Superb

Most of the magic in this striking transformation came from England winger Peter Barnes, who suddenly took the game that had appeared to be fading from City's grasp by the scruff of the neck.

First he forced a corner and when he floated over the kick it led to a penalty award for City as Belgian centre-half Poel handled the ball to prevent Dave Watson from striking with a header.

From the spot Kidd tapped

...bly to head his second goal and City's third at Maine Road.

their lead and that late rally saw three goals in four minutes to create a decisive and emphatic victory. The transformation was heralded as a high point in Peter's developing career and he demonstrated his skills superbly as he made Liege suffer with attack after attack. Peter Gardner writing in the *Manchester Evening News* commented: 'Twisting, turning, tormenting and teasing the harassed Belgians, Barnes paved the way for that final three-goal fling with Kidd grabbing two and Palmer the last. It was Barnes at his brilliant best although Hartford and Watson were also heroes on a night when City proved that patience always pays.'[3]

Peter in action against Standard Liege at Maine Road.

The *Mirror's* Derek Wallis reported: 'England winger Peter Barnes inspired a fantastic late change. First Dave Watson rose to head a Barnes cross which Theo Poel fisted away and Brian Kidd hammered in the penalty. Barnes set up Kidd for a header and then created the opening for Roger Palmer to clip No.4. Not surprisingly Barnes… also made City's first, which came from an Asa Hartford header on twelve minutes.' [4]

After the game Liege's manager Robert Waseige commented: 'Barnes is a world class player who can do enough to win any match on his own.' [5] Others were glowing in their praise too including the *Guardian's* Michael Carey who described the player's role in the final two goals: 'Barnes made his way wonderfully past three defenders, like someone weaving through a minefield, before providing a cross which Kidd headed home and two minutes after that Barnes produced something similar, only this time down the right, to enable Palmer to seal his own fine performance with a goal.' [6]

In the weeks that followed Peter talked of his performance in that game: 'That was probably my best display of the season. I can feel the pressure around me. Everyone expects miracles from me every Saturday

Peter during the 2-2 draw at Bolton, October 21, 1978.

but I'm afraid in this standard of football it's just not possible.' [7]

Looking back in 2020 Peter remembers: 'There was a lot of expectation around me. If I had a quiet game that was a story. If I had a great game that was too. I couldn't hide from the media attention. In that first leg against Liege I enjoyed the final flourish. Everything just clicked. We suddenly were able to attack and nothing seemed to get in our way. If there was one disappointment for me it would be that the game finished when it did. I'd have liked another five minutes or so to see what score we could've achieved that night. I got a lot of praise after

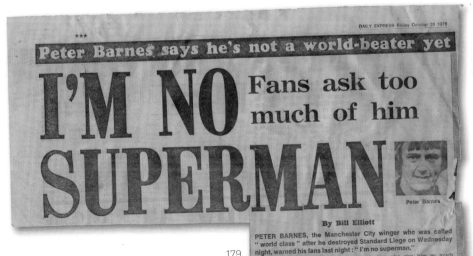

that match but Roger Palmer had a great game. I was pleased he scored the fourth.

'After such a convincing win we didn't foresee any problems in the return leg but we lost 2-0 and one of their goals came from a penalty when Asa Hartford was supposed to have handled a clearance. Then Gary Owen was sent off – he wasn't too happy with the tackles that were coming at us.'

Gary Owen: 'Asa Hartford was about to be deliberately trod on and I could see this. Asa was "fouled" and so I chased after the player and ended up reacting. I've never intentionally gone in over the top or anything like that. I have at times gone to punch someone – and caught them – but that's always been retaliation for something that's happened to me or a team mate. Against Liege Asa Hartford was about to be deliberately trod on and I could see this. Asa was 'fouled' and so I chased after the player and ended up reacting. I got sent off. I'd had a few bookings in the League and they took it all into consideration and it looked like I was a nasty piece of work.' [8]

Owen's dismissal came in the 86th minute, resulting in a five match European ban and led to journalist Peter Gardner commenting: 'Manchester City were poised to graduate with European honours… until Gary Owen failed the test of temperament. His sending off in Belgium was the one souring note of a magnificent Blues performance.' He explained: '[Owen] chased fully fifteen yards to aim a flying kick at Phillipe Garot, the Belgian international defender who had fouled Hartford. Gary should have known better. He had missed the first leg because of a one match suspension... and the authorities rightly took this into account when reaching the decision of a stiff five match ban.' [9]

After Standard Liege came AC Milan with the first leg staged at the San Siro stadium. The game should have been played on Wednesday November 22, but the conditions were poor with thick, swirling fog forcing the referee to postpone the game until lunchtime the following day. Not everyone was happy with the delay but the game simply could not be played as planned. The fans that had travelled from Manchester had to hastily rearrange their plans with some on a City Supporters' Club charter having to leave the replayed game at half time to make sure they made their flight. For Peter the delay brought some hope that he could play: 'I had a muscle strain and was out of the match but then the fog caused the delay and City hoped I could make it, but it was an impossibility really. Had I been anywhere near fit enough I'd

Barnes is £1½m Italian target

A PETER GARDNER EXCLUSIVE

PETER BARNES, Manchester City's brilliant England forward, could feature in a sensational £1½m transfer to Italy.

I understand reigning champions Juventus are poised to move for the 21-year-old wonder winger once the Italian FA ban on the import of foreign players is lifted.

Juventus have had Barnes watched at regular intervals this season, and plan a

have played because I was desperate to appear at the San Siro.'

The prospect of Peter appearing was covered in a variety of newspapers with the *Reading Evening Post* claiming that: 'Manchester City were today making a desperate bid to include England winger Peter Barnes in their side.' [10]

Peter missed a classic City away game which saw the Blues race to a 2-0 lead thanks to goals from Brian Kidd and Paul Power, who was playing his first game since injury in the League Cup at the start of October. Milan did fight back and the game ended 2-2 but it was perceived as a great European night for City. Years later Kenny Clements remembered: 'We had the audacity to go two goals up at the San Siro thanks to Kidd and Power. It was a tough ground to play at. Fireworks going off and an intimidating atmosphere. No one ever beat them at home, but we were. They came back at us and it ended 2-2.' [11]

The Maine Road return came on December 6 and Peter was fully fit and ready for this game: 'Getting the away goals meant we had the advantage but playing a team like Milan was always going to be tough. We knew we had to score. There was no point trying to hold out and hope the advantage remained.'

In the days leading up to the second leg transfer speculation suggested Juventus were about to launch a £1.5m bid for Peter. This was an astounding amount at the time and led City chairman Peter Swales to suggest the story had been whipped up by the Italian media to try and unsettle City prior to the match. He commented: 'If this is the result of a plot to upset our players, it will not work, but I'll tell you what – it has damn well upset me.' [12] When asked about it at the time Peter commented: 'This business will certainly not affect my performance tomorrow night.' Looking back Peter believes the timing was aimed at unsettling

Peter, with Kenny Clements in the distance and United's Martin Buchan close by, at Old Trafford, September 1978.

City: 'There was a ban on foreign players in the Italian league at the time. That was to be lifted the next summer, so the transfer gossip was all far too early. I know Juventus were definitely interested but breaking that story so close to our second leg with Milan was only ever someone's idea to unsettle us. It was great to be connected with continental clubs like this – and it happened frequently around then – but the timing was all wrong.'

Despite the transfer rumour, the return leg saw City demolish the Italians 3-0 with goals from Tommy Booth (14th minute header), Asa Hartford (a wonderful 20 yard effort that dipped past Milan's keeper in the 31st minute), and Brian Kidd (42nd minute). According to journalist Peter Gardner: '[Milan] were dead and buried by half time in a third round tie that became so one-sided it was embarrassing.'[13] Peter: 'It was a great night although I was kicked quite a bit! Collovati and Maldera were both tapping away at me. I'd played against Collovati earlier in the year in an England

U21 game and I told Ronald Crowther from the *Daily Mail* that he "was all elbows in that game, and my face looked as if I had been in a boxing ring." Then in this game with Milan he hacked me down early on. Maldera was the one who fouled me to give us a free kick which led to the opening goal. That set the tone – Milan kicking at us and us kicking at goal. It was funny though because I'd done a piece with the *Sunday Mirror* a few days earlier saying how Milan were a clean side and wouldn't resort to kicking!'[14]

In that article Peter commented: 'I rate them as the cleanest Italian side I've seen. They concentrate more on football than fighting. And that's a formula that's bound to help my game – I can't wait to play them.'[15] Journalist Peter Gardner was critical of Milan in his report: '[Milan] resorted to old habits with cynical fouls aimed mainly at Peter Barnes... And for Barnes there was satisfaction of another personal drubbing of Italians against whom he appears to thrive on tormenting. No wonder Juventus want to buy him… and of this display they'd pay £2m, never mind the reported £1.5m. His world class touches were a pleasure to watch.'[16]

The result put City through to the quarter finals of a European trophy for the first time since 1971 and chairman Peter Swales was delighted. In October 1995 he explained: 'These were great times for City, playing the best in Europe and winning. I think the supporters had more fun then than they're having now. We were intent on getting bigger crowds then and overtaking United. We made some mistakes, but that period was exciting.'[17]

These exciting times saw City paired with top German side Borussia Monchengladbach in the UEFA Cup. Peter: 'They were a top side but after beating Twente, Liege and Milan we feared no one. Every team we played that year in the UEFA Cup had been viewed as a tough opponent and, apart from perhaps Twente, all the other teams had been expected to beat us over two legs. Despite the quality in our side we hadn't really received the positive coverage others had but the two games against Milan had changed that. Now we were ready to face any team. We really didn't care. Tony Book had learned as a manager what it takes to challenge in Europe and we had a great mix of European experience and youth. I couldn't see anything going wrong.'

[1] Throughout 1977-78 Peter was often quoted in the media in articles that talked about his position at City; his wages and potential moves. These included 'Disillusioned Barnes waits for England', *unknown newspaper*, April 29, 1978; 'City "No" to Barnes move by Eindhoven', *Manchester Evening News*, May 8, 1978; 'Problems all the way now for Peter Barnes', *Weekly News*, April 1, 1978, 28; 'Barnes rocker', *Daily Express*, April 25, 1978; 'Barnes in "Pay me what I'm worth" shock', *News of the World*, May 14, 1978, 19.

[2] 'Tony Book talking', *Manchester City v Blackpool match programme*, October 10, 1978, 5.

[3] *Manchester Evening News*, October 19, 1978.

[4] 'Barnes has a stormer', *Daily Mirror*, October 19, 1978.

[5] 'Regis double sparks Albion', *Coventry Evening Telegraph*, October 19, 1978.

[6] 'Barnes Storming', *Guardian*, October 19, 1978, 26.

[7] 'Just the job for Barnes', *Sunday Mirror*, December 3, 1978, 45.

[8] Interview with Gary Owen by Gary James in February 2020.

[9] Peter Gardner, *The Manchester City Football Book 1979* (London: Stanley Paul, 1979), 48-9.

[10] 'New chance for Barnes as City and Milan try again', *Reading Evening Post*, November 23, 1978, 28.

[11] Interview with Kenny Clements by Gary James in November 2003.

[12] '£1.5 million Barnes Offer Denied', *Guardian*, December 8, 1978, 20.

[13] Peter Gardner, *The Manchester City Football Book 1979* (London: Stanley Paul, 1979), 50.

[14] The article Peter referred to was: 'Marked man… But Barnes is not scared', *Daily Mail*, November 22, 1978, 47.

[15] 'Just the job for Barnes', *Sunday Mirror*, December 3, 1978, 45.

[16] 'Asa – Euro ace!', *Manchester Evening News*, December 7, 1978.

[17] Peter Swales interviewed by Gary James in October 1995.

Chapter Eleven

ALLISON RETURNS TO WONDERLAND

"
To get rid of our two most valuable assets in one
fell swoop as Manchester City have done must raise
questions we upset fans want answering. I object to
Tony Book and the board getting rid of our brightest ever
home-grown product so recklessly. Surely an effort could
and should have been made to settle things, especially
as Barnes wishes to stay. Fans miss out every time.
We are only moneybags and likes and dislikes are
ignored. We expected great attacking things from
Malcolm Allison when he returned. So far the only good
he's done is to get things right for Mike Channon and
sign Barry Silkman.
"

Supporter **JOAN MARSLAND** writing to the Pink Postbag,
Manchester Evening News, May 5, 1979, 7.

With victory over Milan in the UEFA Cup and life at Maine Road seemingly settled, everything appeared positive at City for Peter by Christmas 1978. Results in the League had become worrying with five consecutive defeats causing the club to slip down the table – at the end of October the Blues were fifth but had dropped to fourteenth by Christmas Day – but Peter felt there was enough quality in the team to change City's form. Peter: 'Our League form was worrying in November

and December 1978, there's no doubt about that. But we were convinced we could change things around. We were doing well in the UEFA Cup and we'd got through to the League Cup quarter-final but lost 2-1 at Southampton – I came on as sub for Kazzy Deyna who had signed earlier in the season. He was trying to adjust to the English game and I think it was tough for him. A lot was expected of him and the Southampton tie was only his second game.

'The way we had played in Europe

and earlier in the season, showed what we were capable of and I didn't really have any doubts. Others may have done but I don't think me or any of the other players felt too much was wrong. We were the same people. We hadn't suddenly turned into a bad team. Look who was in there – Joe Corrigan, Dave Watson, Willie Donachie, Asa Hartford, Brian Kidd, Mick Channon… all internationals. Channon wasn't having the best of times at City as far as the fans were concerned but we knew what he could do. As far as I was concerned at Christmas 1978 we were in a bit of a false position in the League. A few decent results and we'd move up the table – plus we were in the quarter finals of the UEFA Cup. That was definitely within our grasp. Sadly, the directors of the club felt differently.'

In the match programme for the visit of reigning League champions Nottingham Forest, who ended the League in second place, on December 23 Tony Book wrote of his disappointment of how the season was progressing. He concluded: 'If a manager has the confidence and the ability to put things right, he will survive all the crises that the game has to offer. This is the worst one I have suffered. Yet it is far from a calamity. I'm sure that in future years there will be grim spells when I search every decision to see whether I would do it differently. Up and downs, brickbats and bouquets have been going as long as League football itself. I have no intention of losing my nerve. Or my belief that it can quickly be put right and City can go into 1979 with reputation restored and produce the brand of soccer that our fans have always been proud of.' [1]

A 1-1 draw at Bristol City on December 30 brought to an end 1978 for the Blues and

on New Year's Day journalist Peter Gardner wrote his verdict on the state of City: 'There is not much currently wrong with the club that a string of thumping good results will not put right.' [2] He commented on the team's disappointing League form during November and December before focusing on Europe: 'The UEFA Cup mission has been one of outstanding successes so far with three seeded and powerful teams eliminated on the way to the last eight of a competition that was once a graveyard for City hopes.'

Behind the scenes the feeling within the boardroom was that Gardner's view that a string of good results would change everything was not correct and that a significant change was needed within the team's management structure. There was no suggestion that Tony Book would lose his position, but there was a view that coaching had to improve. On City's board of directors at that time were several Malcolm Allison fans, not least Ian Niven, a publican who had been part of a takeover launched in November 1970. That takeover had led to Niven becoming a director and part of the board that relieved Joe Mercer of the manager's position at Maine Road in preference to his number two Malcolm Allison. Hindsight shows that this was a mistake for the club.

In 2003 Ken Barnes explained: 'Ian Niven was always a Malcolm Allison fan, as were one or two of the others. He has a pub in Marple and in it he has a bar named after Allison. He wanted him to come back to City [in 1978-79] but Tony Book had done a wonderful job over the years. So what if we were going through a bad month or so? That happens to the best of teams and he'd have got it right. Chelsea and Birmingham were struggling and looked doomed and there were other teams below us that had less about them, so it was unlikely we'd have

got relegated. Plus Tony had that UEFA Cup quarter-final to come… win that and all would be forgotten.' [3]

Sadly, City's board did not give Tony Book the chance to see how the European tie would play out and as January started Ian Niven and other directors began to suggest to chairman Peter Swales that it was time to act. Back in 1995 Peter Swales explained: 'That's when I made my biggest mistake - well I think it was my biggest mistake - Malcolm Allison. Definitely! I got talked into that! Instead of sticking with Tony Book who, when you think of it, gave us second place which today would make him a king, wouldn't it? One or two on the Board started to say "well, if we could just get Malcolm we could do the final push." Final bloody push all right!

'Tony Book wasn't the best manager we've ever had at City but Tony was the right man who loved the club. Total dedication. He should never have been moved out of the job and moved to number two. That was a mistake because Tony could have taken us through the early eighties. He had tremendous respect from the staff and fans. He's always retained his dignity. He would probably have done a lot better as a manager if I'd allowed him to. That was a mistake. It was a mistake giving Malcolm the job and it was a mistake taking Tony out of the job. Definitely.

'Malcolm was probably the best thing to ever happen to Manchester City - him and Joe Mercer as a team. I think Joe was probably a bigger influence than a lot of people think he was, but they were a great team. It doesn't mean though that ten years later you can pick that lad out of the crowd, and bring him back, and expect him to be the manager of the whole set up. I think Malcolm was a terrific motivator and a terrific coach, but he needed Joe. I think Joe made him what he was - he didn't know

Malcolm Allison

that, and a lot of his supporters didn't. There are still a lot of them today - even directors of Manchester City. I don't know how old Malcolm is - a lot older than me - he must be 67, but they'd bring him back now! Because they are real fans you see. They can't get over what he did for them in the late 60s. You can't bring old managers back.'[4]

Director Eric Alexander, a member of the Alexander family which had been actively involved with the club since 1894 and was a former chairman at this time, did not want Allison to return: 'I wanted results to improve, of course I did, but when you've been involved with football as long as I have you have faith in the players. The team we had contained quality throughout and Tony Book was a great manager. Bill Taylor was his coach and, not only that, he

was the England coach... I know England have made mistakes over the years but Bill Taylor wasn't one of them. So, with England's coach and a trophy-winning manager who knew the club inside out why would we want a change? I liked Malcolm Allison and we trusted each other but I did not want him back. At the club's Centenary Dinner [held in 1995] I told Malcolm that if it had been down to me he wouldn't have come back. We are still friends but it was a mistake to bring him back and that's down to his fans on the board talking Swales into it.'[5]

As far as Allison was concerned Ian Niven was the man, or at least one of the men, who told Swales that he wanted the former manager back at Maine Road. The discussions between the Allison-supporting directors and Swales took place over a few days and reached the conclusion that bringing Allison back would be the right thing for City. Swales was obsessed with overtaking Manchester United and throughout his tenure to this point the gap between the two clubs had been narrowing. City had been more successful in terms of trophies than United during the 1970s and the Reds had, of course, spent time in Division Two. City's support had increased with the Blues typically the third best supported League club, averaging over 40,000 in both 1976-77 and 1977-78. 1978-79 was showing a similar pattern in a season that ended with United averaging less than 47,000, although City's average dropped a little by the time the directors were discussing Allison. Swales: 'I'm a Manchester lad - grew up in Ardwick. I understand how a supporter feels when you're losing matches. It's the hardest thing there is. I grew up being baited by Manchester United supporters and all through the Busby years. The hardest thing for me as chairman was having United rammed down my throat. I wouldn't want to say publicly that I hated them, I didn't. But they were the rivals. In 1977 we were runners up in the First Division by a point and we got to United on support. We averaged 40 odd thousand and we almost caught them, and I thought well next year we'll win the Championship and we'll do it. We didn't - we finished fourth - but I felt we were close.' [6]

The idea of bringing back Allison seemed a possible way to close the gap with United and Big Mal, as he was often referred to at this time, wanted the challenge. While many of those there at the time, including Allison and Swales, held the view that Ian Niven was the man who predominantly wanted Allison back, Niven has since claimed it was not his idea to appoint Allison as coach in January 1979: 'I

was amazed when the chairman asked him back... the next thing I remember was the chairman asking me to lunch and saying, "I am thinking of bringing Malcolm back. What do you think?".' [7]

City supporter and staff member at the time Roger Reade knew of Allison supporters within the board: 'There were a couple who loved Malcolm and idolised him to some extent. I'm not certain if the whole board wanted him back but we never heard any dissenting voices at the time. The whole board seemed to be keen. As a fan I recognised that Malcolm had achieved so much for City the first time around and there were certain aspects that we all liked about him – I loved how he'd go to Old Trafford and say there's nothing to fear here. Pep Guardiola is similar. There's nothing to fear.' [8]

Despite those positive attributes Roger did not feel that bringing back Allison at that time was right for the Blues: 'I felt we were creating a bit of a dynasty with City challenging for trophies year after year while developing young talented players like Peter Barnes and Gary Owen. We had a group of seasoned professionals that were working well overall under Tony Book. They knew the game inside out and they would have given you another couple of years at least of top four football. I'm not saying they'd have won many trophies or anything like that but we'd have been there or there abouts.'

Manager Tony Book knew little about the plan but when he heard about it he was not happy: 'It came about because two directors who were very staunch Malcolm fans went to the chairman and got it through. It was the last thing I wanted.' [19] Book explained: 'The first I heard of the plans to bring back Malcolm Allison was at a board meeting, when the chairman informed me they had already spoken to

Malcolm and said I was to go and meet him in Bristol and sort it out. I made the journey feeling sick because I knew deep down that this was the end of management at Maine Road for me.' [10]

Gary Owen remembers how he first heard the news of Allison's return: 'We came in for training and there was like an eerie feeling. Something wasn't right but you couldn't put your finger on it. Bill Taylor came in with an uncomfortable looking face. Then Tony Book came in and was followed by Malcolm Allison. All brash, like he'd never been away. He told us he was here to improve things and I looked across at Bill Taylor's face and he looked horrified and disappointed. He looked as though he hadn't been told until that morning. Disappointed isn't the right word… more like a sad realisation that this was happening, Malcolm took us out on the pitch and don't forget we were a team of established internationals at various levels all the way through. We all knew the game. Allison was speaking in "footballing terms" which some would say was ahead of his time but others would say he was out of his mind. Only those who worked with him can know for sure which one it was and in my opinion he wasn't ahead of his time! If you could see what we worked on… well, it just didn't make sense.'

The news broke on Friday January 5 with Granada Television revealing that Allison had accepted an offer to return to Maine Road from Tony Book at an afternoon meeting. The following day almost every newspaper carried the story and reasons for Allison's return with many claiming it was Book's idea to bring Allison back. This was done by the club to ensure the view remained that Book was the one making the decisions but

it was some way off the truth. Nevertheless, this was the image portrayed. [11]

Allison was delighted with the return: 'I have always had an affinity for Manchester City and I am delighted to be back. My first job will be to get the players together to talk about objectives and aims. I want to find out from them what is wrong, if anything, and how we can put it right together.' [12] When he was asked if he was happy returning to Maine Road as coach he brashly replied: 'I am not just a coach I am a scientist. My training is brilliant and, like all scientists, I can make things work.'

Peter was initially excited by the prospect of working with Allison: 'Everyone told me how great it would be. They said that he loved working with wingers and, of course, we all knew what he'd done at City previously. Everyone was positive and I couldn't wait. But then he arrived and it was all so different to what we thought it would be. He had such weird ideas and at training all you could hear was him shouting, barking instructions at us. The team had done so well in the previous couple of years

189

and I don't think there was a lot wrong with the team. We were having a bad patch in the League – but that had only been November and December really. Before that we'd only lost two of our opening thirteen League games and we'd progressed to the quarter final of the UEFA Cup and the League Cup. There wasn't too much wrong and we'd been such a wonderfully happy club, then Allison came back. I know he achieved a great deal in his first spell but let's not forget he had Joe Mercer as his manager. He was a great football man and knew the game inside out. In 1979 Allison seemed to be on a mission to self-destruct. That was my impression at the time. The saddest part is that the club began to fall apart.'

Like Peter, Roger Reade felt somewhat deflated with Allison's return: 'To be fair to the directors I could see what they were thinking by bringing Malcolm back to help Tony but it was the wrong decision because he was a different fella when he came back. There was the difference to what we were used to. With Peter Barnes for example – if I was walking up the corridor and he was walking the other way he'd stop and have a chat. He'd be interested in what was going on; how I was doing and what was happening around the club. With Malcolm he wasn't bothered. You'd see Malcolm coming your way in the corridor and he would ignore you. It was as if you weren't

Peter listening to his records in a staged photograph for Scoop magazine.

there. I took an instant dislike to him, which was annoying for a lot of us at City who had never really known him or met him before. Those that knew him from his first spell worshipped him and couldn't wait for him to come back but those of us who hadn't were so disappointed.'

Within a week of Allison's return City's popular coach Bill Taylor handed in his resignation saying that he felt unable to work under the new set up. It was disappointing news for Peter who enjoyed working with Taylor both at Maine Road and with England: 'I didn't want the change and so I didn't want Taylor to leave either. Everything was disrupted and instead of us working our way out of a difficult spell we seemed to be heading for turmoil.'

On January 13, Allison's first game as coach ended in a 1-1 draw at Leeds. The next game, his first at home, was also far from successful as the Blues played out a goalless draw with Rotherham in the FA Cup third round. The replay ended to the satisfaction of the new coach with Brian Kidd scoring twice and important goals from Gary Owen and from Peter, bringing a 4-2 victory. It was the first win in 14 games and led some to think that all was well, but it was not. Goalkeeper Joe Corrigan: 'When Malcolm came back… I was angry more than anything else. I wasn't happy with the underhand way things had been done and wasn't about to hide my feelings.' [13] Captain Dave Watson's wife Penny wrote a couple of years later: 'Right through the club the atmosphere changed to one of suspicion, and the place swiftly became miserable… I hated Malcolm Allison for what I could see he was doing to Dave [Watson] and to Manchester City.' [14] Dave Watson himself commented: 'In my opinion the club was never the same. It was the end at City for all the players who had made a name for themselves – all the internationals.' [15]

Peter agrees with Dave's view: 'You could sense it straight away. Things were different and our mood changed. The mood just wasn't right. As a younger player I didn't understand what was wanted at times. There were also some strange activities, for example, Malcolm brought in a guy called Lenny Heppell. He was a champion ballroom dancer from Newcastle. He was about nine stone and must have been in his sixties. Malcolm told us Lenny would be giving us extra training. Lenny took us all out on the pitch at Maine Road, facing the North Stand. He stood at the front and he'd get us to sprint out to the right a couple of metres then back in. He'd shout left or right depending on which way he wanted us to go and we had to rush left or right and then back. He started to tell us how to run. He had us moving around like ballerinas. One day he took Mike Channon into the gym and tried to get him and Gary Owen to walk around with books on their heads, telling them they were not straight backed enough! "Stretch your neck up!" he'd be shouting. It was like a finishing school for young ladies. Can you imagine what Mike Channon was thinking? Lenny took Willie Donachie to one side one day and gave him advice on how to turn the television over: "Don't walk over to the TV to change channels, sprint there and sprint back." We had this guy with us for a couple of months. We'd arrive at the ground and we'd see him: "Oh, it's Lenny Heppell today. He'll be getting us to curtsy now!"'

Gary Owen remembers: 'Lenny Heppell had Mike Channon and Asa Hartford in twos doing dance movements. When you walked through a door you couldn't just walk through it normally. You had to walk through sideways in a particular movement. In tactical discussions he drew so many lines on the board that it looked like the tracks at the busiest railway station gone wrong! There were lines everywhere in different colours that didn't match how any game was played. You have to have patterns of play and you have to be tactically strong – but this wasn't that. This was confusion and Malcolm was the instigator. The atmosphere was wrong right the way through the club. We all knew that this was not right. That Malcolm wasn't going to work out. Malcolm had already decided that some players were too old and couldn't take on what he wanted to put over. He wanted to change the players and in that group he obviously felt were myself and Peter. I was only about 21.'

The rumblings were to continue for some time with media speculation appearing frequently on which players would be leaving. It was a troubling time for many of the players in the squad, including Peter: 'It was such a change and I felt my days were numbered. Malcolm kept trying all these different ideas. One day he walked in: "All right lads? Today after training I've got a guy coming in. He's a professor coming to talk to you about the brain, so when you've got changed get up there as soon as you can." We all walked into the players' lounge after training with wet hair and so on. This professor was stood there in his shirt and tie ready to give us a lecture on the brain. We all wanted to go home. We'd finished training and we all had plans, as you would do back then. We sat down and waited for the professor to start, looking at our watches. The professor draws the brain on this board and starts to talk about it, using different colours to mark different parts. He starts talking about memory loss, positive thinking and so on but none of us were interested. Me, Paul Power, Kenny Clements, Gary Owen… we're the young ones and we're sat there all polite but looking at each other, knowing what we're all thinking. I started looking

around the room at the older players - Mike Channon, Brian Kidd, Dave Watson and so on… The professor keeps going and starts telling us that we're losing too many games because our brains are not positive enough and so he goes on and on. You can imagine what happens. After about twenty minutes enough is enough and Mike Channon stood up "I've never heard so much shit in all my life" and he walks out. Once he's gone the other older players start filtering out one by one: "I've got an appointment", "My wife's expecting me", "I need to take the dog to the vets".…. They'd had enough. The youngest players were the last to leave.

'There's a place for psychology and exploring ideas like this but at that time, in that environment and in the way it was all carried out, it was wrong. Maybe Malcolm was ahead of his time, but back then the way it was all explained to us was confusing. Were we supposed to follow Lenny Heppell's ideas, the professors he brought in, Malcolm or the boss Tony Book? The message wasn't clear and all those influences seemed to contradict each other anyway!'

Peter and the others were open to new training ideas and anything that would give City an advantage or improve matters but this was different. It was not simply a new coach adding well proven techniques, it seemed to be a wholesale change with everything that had helped the Blues challenge in recent seasons thrown out and disregarded, while other ideas were tried for a day or two before they were also discarded. The majority of players felt either confused, bemused or unwanted. Gary Owen decided to ask Allison what his plans were: 'I asked him if he was looking to sell us, meaning me and Peter and some of the others. I'd just signed a new six year deal and genuinely wanted to see that through at least. Malcolm told me: "Nobody's for sale but if anybody comes in with an offer

Mirror Sport

'There's no way I'm going to stop taking on defenders'

Tuesday, January 23, 1979   (No. 23,316)
Manchester (STD code 061) 832-3444

PETER BARNES

SELFISH SLUR ANGERS BARNES

By ALEC JOHNSON

PETER BARNES, Manchester City's England winger, hit back angrily yesterday at suggestions that he was "a selfish player."

Young B a r n e s was nettled at TV criticism during City's 2—3 defeat at home to Chelsea when it was put to coach Malcolm

Allison that Barnes was being greedy by hanging on to the ball too much.

Barnes told me: "I know full well that I'm not playing as well as I can do, but I resent anyone saying I'm a greedy player.

"I'm in the City team be-cause

happy with my game since the Milan match a couple of months ago. I'm determined to get it back to its previous stan-dard.

"But there's no way I'm going to stop taking on defenders.

"I think everyone in the team knows he can play better right now, but we've got to keep try-ing to play our natural

we'll put it to you." I asked if that was for me or for all of us and he said: "It includes everybody." So, straight away he had that negative vibe that he doesn't want you because he'd have said something like "oh, no. I want you to stay." Even if a manager doesn't want you, he might say that to keep you motivated but Malcolm didn't say anything like that. No comments about a future for any of us.

'I went to speak with Peter about it and told him what was said. Peter wasn't confrontational and so he wouldn't have gone in to ask him. I said to Peter that if anybody came in for any of us he was going to sell us. Slowly but surely that's what happened. Over the coming months the mood dropped significantly and the whole club seemed unsure of where it was going or what was happening. What we had was nothing like what we'd had before. It was unbelievable how Malcolm had changed it. I know those who played under Malcolm during his first time at City rightly love him for what he did back then, but I'm sure they'll agree that he wasn't the same man when he came back in 1979. Don't forget he was supposed to be the coach when he

came back but he acted like the manager. He believed he was the boss and that was how he acted.'

It is no wonder that within this environment the club struggled. Gary, Peter and the rest of the City team remained committed on the pitch but Allison's coaching and various initiatives were not delivering. City struggled in the League and were knocked out of the FA Cup by Third Division Shrewsbury Town. It was an embarrassing 2-0 defeat and led to Allison being dubbed 'the mouth' by some in the media. [16]

Peter: 'The conditions against Shrewsbury were poor and I don't think the game should have been played. The TV cameras were there so I guess that influenced the decision but there's no mistaking this was a poor day for us. I started on the left and was switched to the right wing after we'd gone a goal behind in the ninth minute. They scored their second about twelve minutes into the second half and there was no way back.

'Understandably, the mood was awful. I remember Joe Corrigan was asked by the press about the game and he said it was a disaster. Which was right as far as the players were concerned. Players do take responsibility for defeats – and that's right, they should – but that Shrewsbury game was more about the way the mood around the club had changed. There was a lot of negativity and the week before the FA Cup tie we'd been beaten by Chelsea 3-2 in the League. Highlights were shown on the telly and I was called "selfish" in an interview with Malcolm Allison – that really upset me because I was playing the way City wanted. I don't think Allison defended me enough and the tension was building. The *Daily Express* claimed City were "superstars who forgot the basics" – that may be how it appeared to the outside world but that was really brought on by the confusion at the club.' [17]

After the Shrewsbury game Peter Swales called an emergency meeting with Allison and Book to determine where the Blues were failing. Peter Swales: 'I didn't know [Malcolm] like some of the others knew him. I knew his reputation and I knew

what he could do. I knew about the late sixties and early seventies of course, but he'd had an in-and-out career in the middle seventies. It was unbelievable really though. It was untrue what happened really. He used to talk a language that was alien to me. I knew I made a mistake… A month, maybe two months in. He'd probably say that we had no money or something and he'd say it was me not him. It wasn't going to work with him and it was all wrong. It was tragic really.' [18]

By the time of the meeting, Allison had already attempted to change the playing personnel with Mike Channon transfer listed only 18 months after his £300,000 arrival. Players did not know whether they were part of City's plans or not and everyone seemed to be available if another club was interested. Confusion reigned throughout the club. BBC North-West cameras were frequent visitors to Maine Road and City's training facilities at Platt Lane and with almost every visit the local reporter would ask about the management

A 'SPOT PRIZE'!
City snatch point with a penalty OUTSIDE the area

Manchester City .... 2 Norwich City 2
MANCHESTER CITY were saved from another home defeat and Norwich deprived of their first away win of the season by a penalty that WASN'T at Maine Road last night.

It happened in the 90th minute when City winger Peter Barnes was brought down just OUTSIDE the penalty area by Richard Symonds, but referee Bert Newsome of Shropshire pointed to the spot.

By BOB RUSSELL

"SPOT PRIZE" for Manchester City as Peter Barnes is brought down just OUTSIDE the penalty area by Norwich's Richard Symonds, but referee Bert Newsome awarded a penalty and Gary Owen scored his second goal in the 2–2 draw at Maine Road   Picture: GERRY CROWTHER structure. Swales, Book and Allison would be asked at regular intervals who the manager was; what titles were being used; how the structure operated and so on. Depending on who was being interviewed the answers varied. Sometimes Allison appeared to be the one making all the decisions while Book would be described as the man in ultimate charge at other times. Officially, Book remained the manager at this point with Allison acting as chief coach, or 'coaching overlord' as the coach was often dubbed, but at various times between January and September 1979 changes would be made. [19]

Roger Reade believes the lack of clarity over roles was an issue: 'You look back and you realise that was an error from the start. I watched the BBC films at the *Boys in Blue* film show last year and Malcolm was asked a few questions about his role, more or less, "What's your role? Is Tony Book the manager or are you the manager" and he avoids answering. He ends up saying something like "I'm Malcolm Allison" and it shows there's an issue. Malcolm was in charge but Tony Book was the manager at first. When it was announced about Malcolm's return those of us working there were asking similar questions: "Well, how's it going to work?" We wanted to understand the relationship.' [20]

Peter remembers: 'There was a lot of confusion. You'd be told one thing by Tony Book and then Allison would change that. The players were rightly criticised for the Chelsea League defeat and then the Shrewsbury tie but the mood across the club was not right. Over the next few weeks it all started to fall apart with players either being told to leave or wanting to get away. It wasn't long before Brian Kidd moved on and transfer listed Mike Channon was constantly being tipped to move, though that didn't happen for a while. The team was

starting to break up and Kiddo leaving was a major loss… he wasn't the last either!'

Before Kidd left City, the Blues had their UEFA Cup quarter final with Borussia Monchengladbach to play. The first leg at Maine Road saw Allison perform one of his many shock moves when he announced that 18 year old Nicky Reid would be making his debut. It was an amazing decision and saw the youngster move virtually from the 'A' team to one of the most important club fixtures of the decade. Allison selected him to mark Allan Simonsen. City took the lead in the 25th minute when Peter sent a pass to Channon who scored with a fierce drive. Sadly, Lienan scored an equaliser for the German side in the 67th minute. Peter: 'They'd had a goal disallowed by Simonsen only two minutes earlier and we were under a lot of pressure at that point. It was quite a physical game too – Klinkhammer kept having a go at me and I ended up retaliating. As Gary Owen was suspended I had to do my own retaliation and I got booked. Klinkhammer walked away with nothing!'

The game ended 1-1 and City knew the second leg would be tough, especially with the mixed messages and lack of clarity within the club. Kaziu Deyna, the experienced Polish World Cup hero, had not played in the UEFA Cup first leg and media reports followed saying that he wanted to leave. [21]

Peter: 'There seemed to be stories of players leaving all the time and that eventually included me before the end of March. It was all a distraction. There were lots of strange stories in the press after Allison had joined us. There was one concerning a well-known hypnotist called Romark – apparently he'd put a curse on Malcolm!'

The Romark story saw the hypnotist offer to lift his Allison curse for the second leg of the UEFA Cup tie. The relationship between the City coach and Romark went back to Allison's time at Crystal Palace when the hypnotist had been asked to work with Allison's players to give them confidence and help them to victory. There was a fall-out between the club and Romark which led to the hypnotist cursing Allison and working with teams that opposed Palace to help them to win. In March 1979 Romark claimed his curse could be lifted if Allison wanted but, seemingly, the City coach refused, leading to the hypnotist criticising Allison publicly: 'Romark remarked unflatteringly that if Allison had eleven one-legged players he would play a two-legged man as substitute.' [22]

The Romark-Allison conflict lasted for some time and, in 1980, the hypnotist was credited with helping Fourth Division Halifax Town to FA Cup victory over Allison's City – at that time the most expensive team ever assembled in England. All of that was for the future but in March 1979 it added to the distractions and chaos surrounding City. Peter: 'As professionals you try to focus on your game and ignore everything else but it was all too much. I was beginning to feel unwanted, as were many of the others. I was frustrated that Brian Kidd was about to be sold and it seemed like any one of us

SHOCKS FOR BOOK

Asa, Barnes in big City showdown

By DON EVANS

DOUBLE trouble for Manchester City last night. Scottish international Asa Hartford has asked for a transfer, and a "disgusted" Peter Barnes is ready to move, if the right offer comes along.

HARTFORD . . .request

Hartford, 27, cost City £200,000 from West Brom nearly five years ago and has made more than 200 appearances, as the midfield general, for the club.

I understand that Hartford is bitterly disillusioned with the tactics at Maine Road that include the playing of two "new boys" instead of experienced stars for the vital UEFA Cup clash against Borussia.

American soccer giants New York Cosmos and Washington Diplomats are reported ready to double that fee to around £400,000 for the Scot. Though several top home clubs will be alerted.

England winger Barnes, shaken to the roots by his ommission yesterday from the side that drew 1—1 at Arsenal, told me last night : "I feel insulted and disrusted. I feel at times as if I'm being treated as a child.

'RUBBISH'

"This has been going on, on and off for two years. I've never said much before, just bitten my tongue and talked about fighting back, but this time it's different.

"There's so much rubbish being talked about me. That I drop my head. Absolute nonsense. That I've lost my confidence. I have never lost confidence though you may lose it in the people you work for.

"Believe me, if the right offer comes in then I'll take it, but I never thought it would come to this."

England's top clubs will move swiftly for him. Q P R are already considering their offer, Arsenal and Leeds have long time back interest in Barnes, whilst abroad.

Yesterday Barnes played for City reserves in a home game against Nottingham Forest reserves.

But now the good news. Mike Channon, scorer of yesterday's goal for City, is ready to listen to manager Tony Book's suggestion that he comes off the list.

"I cannot join a better club. The team has been reorganised and things are looking better."

BARNES . . . ready to go.

CHANNON . . he'll stay

They say I've lost confidence. I've never lost confidence, though you may lose confidence in the people you work for

PETER BARNES

could be sacrificed. The second leg against Monchengladbach was our last chance of winning a trophy that season and we should have been going into that game with the same optimism and spirit we had for the games against Twente, Liege and Milan. Our game with Aston Villa had been postponed on the Saturday before our game in Germany, so we weren't tired or anything. We knew a 1-1 first leg had made it tough for us but with the right team selection and tactics we could do it. We had experience in our side but it didn't go the way any of us hoped. The tactics were wrong and some of our most experienced European stars were on the bench!'

Peter's views are backed up by newspaper articles pre-match which criticised Allison's selections such as John Roberts' piece in the *Guardian*: 'Malcolm Allison gambles with new men and tactics.' [23] Those gambles, according to Roberts, included the retention of Nicky Reid, who was to make his League debut eleven days after the tie, and the selection of Tony Henry: 'a 21 year old striker who has played only one League match, against Wolves last season… preferring Henry to the vastly experienced Brian Kidd.' [24] Worse, claimed the journalist, was Allison's tactical plan: 'Henry will be required to adopt the ambitious role of a deep-lying Hidegkuti (sic) or Revie in Allison's tactics for the match. Basically, City will play 4-4-2, with the midfield players Viljoen, Henry, Reid, and Hartford, taking turns in moving upfield between the flank men, Channon and Barnes.

'Allison's descriptions of the plan sounded like a distant echo of Willy Meisl's "whirl" in which players with all round ability rotated with emphatic freedom of expression.' [25]

Allison told the media he was convinced this approach would bring City a two goal victory but the *Guardian* article suggested his tactics, combined with his team selection, was somewhat naïve and ended: 'The situation would, however, seem to demand more than the potential offered by Reid and Henry – indeed it has been suggested that Gladback's (sic) markers will be keeping their eyes focused on the City's substitutes bench in case Kidd, Deyna or Bell, should make an appearance.' [26]

Leaving experienced European campaigners Kaziu Deyna, Colin Bell and Brian Kidd on the bench seemed ridiculous in the media, especially as Paul Futcher, the club's record signing from the previous summer, was also missing from the starting line-up.

Despite the media criticism of the tactics and team selection, Peter feels that City began well before a spot of bad luck changed everything: 'Our confidence was improving as the first half progressed. We were doing well and felt we could win the tie. About a minute before the break Tony Henry had a shot which looked like it was going in but somehow it deflected off the right hand post. Borussia got the ball and broke away and scored! An awful time to concede a goal and we were so unlucky. I felt so sorry for the fans who had travelled out there. We had a decent following behind the goal and I could see their reaction. It was a real blow and after that we were chasing it. Six minutes into the second half we conceded another. I looked at the bench and we had Deyna, Kidd, Bell… all experienced European players. They didn't look happy – and they were right to be unhappy.'

Reid was substituted by Deyna in the 62nd minute, but another goal was conceded nine minutes later. In the 79th minute Deyna provided a consolation goal – a spectacular volley. City were out of Europe. Peter: 'Everything we'd hoped for had gone. From challenging Liverpool for the title only a year or so earlier we were now struggling in the League and had no chance of trophy success. The club was in disarray… Let's just say that at the end of the game a few of the players didn't hold back with one shouting: "there's your tactics Mal!"'

Kenny Clements, who had appeared in the opening seven UEFA Cup games of the season before breaking his leg was now fit but, like the experienced internationals, was not selected for this tie. He remembers: 'I broke my leg a few weeks after Milan so that made life a bit difficult for me, but the big problem was the return of Malcolm Allison. I know he was a great coach first time at City, but second time he really did ruin everything. All the older players told me it'd be great having him back, and then when he was back they all admitted they were wrong. I think he'd become too hung up on new ideas that he forgot about the basics. I remember he used to give us homework. He'd tell us to go home and write "I must win" or "I will win" a thousand times, then the next day he'd ask us if we'd done it.

'I always used to say 'yeah', but some of the younger, more impressionable lads would produce their lists and some would even write out twice as many lines! He insisted we drank coffee before a game to keep us alert, and brought in lots of motivational people. It didn't motivate me I'm afraid! By the time of [Moenchengladbach] I was fit but didn't start, and then for the second leg both Brian

Kidd and I had to sit it out while Nicky Reid made his debut marking one of the greatest players of all time. When we were two goals down Kiddo threw his shirt at Allison in anger.' [27]

Brian Kidd never played for the club again and was sold to Everton before the transfer deadline later in the month. Channon was already transfer listed while Asa Hartford was also made available. Peter: 'I was dropped for the Arsenal game four days after the UEFA Cup defeat and I was added to the transfer list. I didn't want to leave but I didn't want to stay if the squad was being dismantled like this. It was a tough time. After being dropped I asked for a meeting with Tony Book to see where I stood. It all appeared in the papers – and City's match programme – as if I'd demanded a guaranteed first team place but that wasn't what I wanted to know. I wanted to know if I was part of the club's plans going forward. I wasn't daft enough to ask for a guaranteed place – no one can expect that. I was disillusioned with the way things were going and it wasn't long before Gary Owen was dropped too.'

Owen was dropped for the meeting at West Bromwich Albion on April 4 which ended in a 4-0 defeat. Journalist Patrick Barclay commented: 'Owen was ordered not to comment by the City manager, Tony Book, but it is safe to assume that he has joined the ranks of those disaffected by events… The arrival of Malcolm Allison as assistant to Book in December (sic) was seen by some as a panacea. Instead, it has proved the prelude to crises involving Mike Channon, who was transfer listed; Brian Kidd, transferred to Everton; Asa Hartford; Dave Watson who has expressed interest in going to North America; and Peter Barnes, who declared himself disillusioned after being dropped… Meanwhile, the dissatisfaction of players such as Kazimierz Deyna and Paul Futcher, passed over in favour of inexperienced youngsters, has simmered on as what seems a constantly experimental side attempts to keep one step ahead of the shadow of relegation.' [28]

With eleven games to go City were sixteenth on 28 points, seven higher than the relegation zone. It was understandable that Book and Allison would want to select players they believed would help the club earn enough points to guarantee their First Division survival but tactical changes and playing relative novices seemed crazy. Chairman Peter Swales was getting somewhat worried: '[Allison] played with a different system almost every week. He had some amazing plans. I used to wonder and I thought "the way we're going, we're going to play without a goalkeeper one week" because he'd tried everything else. I expected him to come in and say we're going with eleven outfield players. It was a definite mistake. I don't want people to think he didn't do anything for City because

MANCHESTER CITY MATCH MAGAZINE · 13

The Cheadle & Gatley Junior Blues Drum Majorettes have caused quite a stir among members of their branch this season . . . and not just the Junior Blues, either. President Asa Hartford, City director Chris Muir and winger Peter Barnes were full of praise for their super marching display at Cheadle's first local branch meeting of the season early in September. Peter (pictured with the girls on the front lawn of Cheadle Hulme High School where the meetings are held) admired their co-ordination and colour . . . the girls all wore uniforms of sky blue tops with white skirts and matching Junior Blues sashes.
With a bit of luck the members of the troupe may be making further appearances at meetings around the City. So keep your eyes peeled.

DRUMMING UP SUPPORT

Our apologies to the thousands of you who have sent in renewal subscriptions to the Club and who haven't yet received either your newsletters or your membership certificates. These will be on the way to you shortly. Secretary Jessie Ward and assistant secretary Jan Rochford, have been working overtime getting through a flood of applications. They should be all issued within the next week or so.

Junior Blues News

The winner of the "Ain't he cute?" competition in the Tottenham Hotspur match magazine was Celia Cramer, of Heald Avenue in nearby Rusholme. Celia, aged 14 correctly indentified the baby as being a younger version of City's midfield star Gary Owen.
Thanks to everybody that took part, and watch for details of another competition shortly. Incidentally Celia's prize is a Super City autographed football shortly on its way.

Birthday Greetings

Happy Birthday to all our members who have had birthdays in the past few weeks. Especially to players Ged Keegan (3rd October), Mark Leigh (4th October) and Dave Watson (both 5th October).
Willie Donachie (both 5th October).

Diary Dates

Next Sunday (October 15th): Wythenshawe Branch hold their first meeting of the new season at 10-30 a.m. at Poundswick Upper School on Simonsway in Wythenshawe. Several City personalities will again be in attendance.

199

Peter Barnes on using the sole

'It's the sort of skill you learn when you're playing 20-a-side games in the park as a kid.'

The ability to roll the ball around the foot, using the sole of the boot, has always been the trademark of the game's 'ball players'.

It makes opponents feel uneasy because the player in possession is saying, in effect: 'This ball is mine and there's no way you're going to get it.'

Peter Barnes, Manchester City's England winger, says it often. He stands on the ball momentarily near the touch-line and tempts the full-back to lunge for it. The advantage is with Peter because he has possession and can dictate the play.

'I only do it when a defender is trying to get right and pinch the ball,' says Peter. 'Then, if I get past him, he might think twice the next time and give me that vital yard or two.'

Peter is already a hardened pro but he says that it's this type of skill that's the icing

Graham Taylor : Practising with the sole of the boot is one of the best ways of getting the 'feel' of the ball. On your own you can move with the ball in a centre circle and drag it back now and again. The important thing is to maintain control, and you'll find that it's also a question of 'sorting your feet out'.

on the cake for him.

'It's the sort of thing you learn when you're playing 20-a-side in the park as a kid, and it's sad that a lot of that kind of thing is knocked out of youngsters.'

'The skill is also useful for switching the play. Anyone who finds himself in a situation where there's 'nothing on' can drag the ball back with the sole and look for other alternatives.'

A typical situation with Barnes with the ball by the line...

As the defender gets tight, Peter drags it back...

With such a skill, it's very much a question of...

... now you see it, now you don't—and I'm away Peter.

The Football Handbook asked Peter to demonstrate 'using the sole'.

he was great with City in his first spell. He was fantastic for City. But I maintain it was a mistake to have brought him back and I hold my hands up.' [29]

Despite his concerns, Swales kept faith with Allison and would strengthen his position as the year progressed. Unfortunately, it wasn't only Big Mal's tactics that confused the fans though. His transfer activity added to fan frustrations. The departure of Brian Kidd, replaced by Barry Silkman, suggested to some that there seemed to be a determined effort to reduce the club's status as one of England's elite. Roger Reade was not impressed by this move: 'With the greatest respect in the world, Silkman was not a player that

was fit to compete with players like Kidd, Channon, Hartford… He was an ordinary player – and I mean no disrespect by that but when you're comparing him to those men it has to be accepted. None of us could understand why the change was being made. Next thing we're hearing rumours that the player was going to be Malcolm's eyes in the dressing room. I don't know whether that was true or not but that was one of the rumours circulating within Maine Road and, whether it's true or not, players heard that and were bound to think it was time to move on.' [30]

By this time both Gary Owen and Peter, who had combined perfectly at various levels for City and also for the England

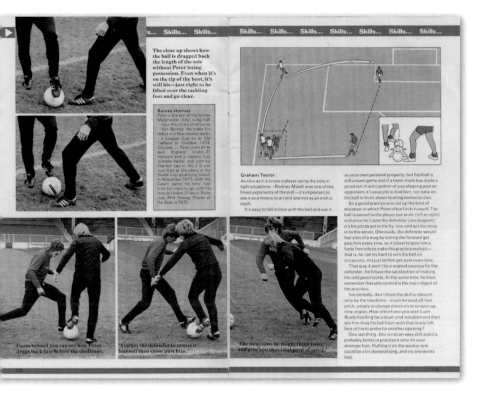

U21 side, were no longer seen as first team players and would only ever play one more game together for the Blues. That was a 3-1 victory over QPR in which Owen scored two of City's goals. It turned out to be the final game of the season for Peter.

Three days after the QPR victory the chaos at City hit the headlines again. Under the headline 'Book reads weekly riot act', the *Guardian* reported on several players who either wanted to leave or who no longer appeared wanted at City. [31] The list included Hartford, Owen, Watson and Peter but the article also talked of the dissatisfaction fans were feeling, commenting that 'supporters have been baffled by the tactical upheavals' since Allison's arrival. Peter: 'I didn't want to leave and I remember going up to Tony Book to explain that prior to a game with Middlesbrough (April 24) and I'm sure he wanted me to stay but I don't think he had the final decision.'

On April 25 the City directors met and agreed to put Peter on sale at £750,000, despite his desire to stay. Book was quoted: 'we thought it was in his interest and the interest of the club that he should be made available.' [32] The board also decided Asa Hartford could leave but insisted that there would be no change to the managerial team which surprised some in the media: '[this] means that Allison, the coach, can continue with his extensive redevelopment plan. In spite of a veritable square dance of tactical manoeuvres at Maine Road recently, Allison says he has yet to put his deeper notions into operation.' [33]

Within days of City putting a price on

Peter's head, Allison was interviewed by Patrick Barclay and gave his views on the players he found at City: 'When I arrived they were very introverted and defensive about themselves, as disappointed sides always become. After the two previous years they had believed they were going to be very successful... In fact, I think they had been on a slight decline for two years, getting into a rut with a short passing game that relied on one or two people up front to tear teams apart, but the stars were not that good.'[34]

It is fair to say Allison's views were somewhat different to the international managers, including England boss Ron Greenwood, who had picked many of the City team for key internationals and to those in charge of some of the biggest clubs of the era who expressed interest in Peter and many of the other players. His views were also at odds with fans who had enjoyed watching those players challenge for the League in the previous two seasons. As Barclay commented: 'City's supporters remain restive, concerned about the

impending loss of Barnes, Hartford, and possibly Dave Watson, and still largely as baffled by the modern style as the players have often appeared to be.'

For Peter it was clear a move had to happen and, at the start of May, eventual League champions Liverpool entered into negotiations with City's Tony Book and Peter Swales meeting Liverpool's manager Bob Paisley and chairman John Smith on May 2. The Merseyside Reds offered £650,000 – some £200,000 more than their record signing (Kenny Dalglish) - for the player but City demanded £750,000. There was a suggestion that Liverpool might offer a player exchange, such as David Fairclough, to the deal to meet the Blues' asking price. Peter: 'I didn't want to leave City – and I explained this to the papers at the time. I loved the club and had supported them since boyhood but it was obvious I wasn't wanted and had to go. The Liverpool move would've been ideal as I could have stayed living in the north west and I'd be playing for a team challenging for trophies – as City had throughout my time prior to 1979. Unfortunately, the board did not want a player exchange, insisting on the cash and Liverpool, despite their status, couldn't afford what City wanted.'

Liverpool certainly wanted to sign Peter with Bob Paisley frequently discussing the potential transfer: 'Barnes is the right age and has the sort of ability we are looking for. So we will be seeing how things develop.' According to Liverpool supporter and author Stuart Kelly, fans on the Kop did not want the Merseyside Reds to sign a player from Manchester's Blues and vented their feelings during a game. Kelly claimed: 'they started chanting, "If you hate Peter Barnes clap your hands", and the whole Kop chanted it. It was never mentioned again.' That view is somewhat different to the view from Manchester and indeed what was reported in Liverpool newspapers however, with the *Liverpool Echo* talking of transfer negotiations continuing after Anfield had staged its last League game of the season. Peter: 'They may well have chanted abuse after it had broken down but Liverpool simply did not want to pay the full asking price and City did not want a player exchange or part-exchange. From the messages I got before the transfer broke down from everyone I knew at Liverpool or who was a fan of Liverpool, then it was clear they wanted me to sign – and I'd have loved to have signed. It broke down between Liverpool and City over the transfer fee, not through my actions or those of the fans.'

'After Liverpool Dave Sexton wanted me to join United but City's valuation increased.'

By the time Manchester United tried to lure Peter to Old Trafford at the 1978-79 season's end, City's board had decided the Reds would have to pay £1m or £750,000 plus Steve Coppell. Peter: 'It was clear as the close season began that I wasn't wanted and I was unlikely to be at Maine Road for 1979-80. It was a worrying time. I couldn't understand why I wasn't wanted and you can't help but doubt yourself. I had no idea where I'd be or what would happen, but I knew that if I had to leave I wanted to stay at a challenging club within traveling distance of Manchester. I didn't want to leave the city.'

[1] *Manchester City v Nottingham Forest match programme*, December 23, 1978, 5 & 7.
[2] *Manchester City v Middlesbrough match programme* (postponed game), January 1, 1979, 10-11.
[3] Interview by Gary James with Ken Barnes at Maine Road, 2003.
[4] Interview by Gary James with Peter Swales at his home, October 1995.
[5] Interview by Gary James with Eric Alexander at Maine Road in 2003.
[6] Interview by Gary James with Peter Swales at his home, October 1995.
[7] Ian Niven quoted in David Tossell, *Big Mal* (Edinburgh: Mainstream, 2008), 268.
[8] Roger Reade interviewed by Gary James, January 2020.
[9] Tony Book quoted in David Tossell, *Big Mal* (Edinburgh: Mainstream, 2008), 268.
[10] Tony Book and David Clayton, *Maine Man: The Tony Book Story* (Edinburgh: Mainstream, 2004), 160-61.
[11] For example see 'Mal back at City!', *Daily Mirror*, January 6, 1979, 32.
[12] *Manchester Evening News*, January 6, 1979.
[13] Joe Corrigan, *Big Joe: The Joe Corrigan Story* (Ayr: Fort Publishing, 2008), 122-23.
[14] Penny Watson, *My Dear Watson* (London: Arthur Barker, 1981), 86-87.
[15] Dave Watson quoted in Penny Watson, *My Dear Watson* (London: Arthur Barker, 1981), 91.
[16] 'Mouth O-Mighty', *Coventry Evening Telegraph*, January 27, 1979, 49.
[17] The article Peter refers to is: 'Manchester City flop again: Miserable', *Daily Express*, January 22, 1979, 30.
[18] Interview by Gary James with Peter Swales at his home, October 1995.
[19] A collection of BBC films held at the North West Film Archive at Manchester Metropolitan University demonstrate the confusion. These have been shown publicly by Gary James and Will McTaggart in a series of film shows called *The Boys in Blue* held at the Cornerhouse and Dancehouse theatres in Manchester between 2011 and 2019.
[20] Roger Reade interviewed by Gary James, January 2020.
[21] 'Polish star unhappy', *Coventry Evening Telegraph*, March 13, 1979, 29.
[22] 'Hypnotist Romark', *Daily Mirror*, March 9, 1979, 31.
[23] 'Allison's tactical gamble', *Guardian*, March 20, 1979, 26.
[24] Kenny Clements interviewed by Gary James in November 2003.
[25] 'Now Owen joins the reserves' club', *Guardian*, April 5, 1979, 22.
[26] Peter Swales interviewed by Gary James, October 1995.
[27] Roger Reade interviewed by Gary James, January 2020.
[28] 'Book reads weekly riot act', *Guardian*, April 24, 1979, 24.
[29] 'Barnes on offer', *Guardian*, April 26, 1979, 22.
[30] 'City malcontents', *Guardian*, April 28, 1979, 26.
[31] 'Liverpool go for Barnes', *Guardian*, May 3, 1979, 24.
[32] 'Barnes fee delays Paisley move', *Liverpool Echo*, April 27, 1979, 36.
[33] Stephen F Kelly, *The Kop: Liverpool's twelfth man* (London: Virgin, 2008), 40.
[34] 'Soccer', *Guardian*, May 17, 1979, 20.

Chapter Twelve

LEAVING CITY

> **Barnes Can Start Packing His Bags:** Manchester
> City's proposal to transfer Peter Barnes, lately troubled
> but still the most potent force in Mancunian football since
> George Best, as a means of raising money towards the
> purchase of the comparatively prosaic Steve Daley from
> Wolverhampton Wanderers, may become reality
> within the next few days.

'Barnes can start packing his bags', *Guardian*, July 13, 1979, 24.

The 1978-79 season ended with Manchester City fifteenth in England's top flight. This was the club's worst final league placing since 1967 when, ironically, Malcolm Allison was City's chief coach. Rumours of player departures surrounded the club and for Peter this was a worrying time: 'I didn't know where I was going to be in August. By this time my life had seemed settled. My career was going well. I was playing regularly for England and felt I had a lot to give to City. The fans had supported me throughout and I loved how they had backed me all the way. I was living in the city I loved. I was in a good relationship and my family were nearby. I didn't want to leave City – and I'd told them that – and if I had to leave I didn't want to go somewhere where I had to move home. But I didn't really feel I had a say and, for a footballer or in any walk of life, uncertainty and lack

of control can affect you mentally. It was a difficult time, especially that feeling that I wasn't wanted. That hurt the most.'

Peter, clearly a sensitive young man at this point, did not talk publicly about the way his potential departure was affecting him and, if anything, the media coverage that surrounded him at this time tended to focus on a search for a new club or dissatisfaction with City's decision-makers. It did not talk about his mental wellbeing and, in general, the football industry thought of players as assets that could easily be taken from one environment and placed in another, but for the young men in these situations it was difficult. For so long Peter had been promoted as a player with a brilliant future, destined to be an England winger for many, many years and, while he remained level headed, it was difficult for him when the realisation dawned that

he was no longer wanted at the club he loved. For Peter and his friend and team-mate Gary Owen these were exceptionally difficult times.

Before the end of May Gary was on his way. [1] Peter found out it was happening when he arrived at Maine Road one morning: 'One day I walked into the main entrance at the ground and saw West Brom's manager Ron Atkinson waiting. I couldn't understand why he was there. "Surely, we're not selling a player" I thought. Then I heard Gary Owen was off to West Brom. I was shocked. Six weeks later I was on my way there as well. Regardless of how things went at West Brom, this was such a major disappointment. I couldn't work out why I wasn't wanted and why the others were transferred.' Gary Owen: 'When you're younger you don't calculate your life or your

plans in the same way. I remember thinking that if Malcolm didn't want me then I'd go. If I was older I may have acted differently but then Ron Atkinson contacted me and smooth talked me to go to West Brom.'

Along with Mike Channon, Gary Owen had been joint leading City scorer with 11 in the League in 1978-79 and, inevitably, supporters were angry when it was announced that he was to move to West Bromwich Albion for £450,000. That figure looks small in comparison with the fees that surrounded the club over the coming years but it must be stressed that this was a huge figure for a young player. In fact it was the highest fee ever received by City at that time, but fans felt that was no compensation for losing the England Under 21 team captain. Owen's departure brought much criticism but the summer saw further

ROY'S STAR TEAM...1979

Striker: PETER BARNES

This man is a match-winner! On his day he is devastating! Fast, tricky and with a thunderous
shot, the Manchester City and England star will thrill crowds anytime, anywhere!

departures including Peter's. Peter: 'You get to the point where you realise you can't stay. There'd been the interest from Liverpool and from United – I'd have been happy with either of those moves at the time but City couldn't agree the fees for whatever reason. I was disappointed, then through Gary Owen I heard that West Bromwich Albion were interested and I agreed to talk with them. My logic was that it'd be better if I chose the club rather than having it chosen for me and having Gary there helped enormously.'

The importance of going to a club where Peter was already close to someone should not be overlooked. The realisation that City no longer wanted him affected him considerably: 'I'm quite a spiritual man and I try to find ways of reassuring myself. During this time doubts appeared and I needed reassurance. Moving to West Brom seemed the way forward and with Gary there it seemed ideal – if I had to leave City! If there'd have been a way to stay I would've but it was clear that for the first time in my life I wasn't wanted.'

Gary Owen remembers: 'Ron Atkinson asked me to have a word with Barnsey because he wanted him at West Brom. Peter and I had a good relationship. I went through it with Peter, talking about the team – a real attacking team at that time. Barnsey came – Ron had smooth talked him as well. I remember before I left City Steve Daley, who is a mate of mine, called me to tell me that City were interested in signing him. He said that it'd be great playing with me and Barnsey. We talked about his fee and wages and it all seemed sensible. Anyway, by the time he'd signed his fee had rocketed and we'd all been moved out of the club. It was a shock to him because he arrived, expecting us all to still be there and we'd gone! It wasn't the team he thought he was joining. He

was a really good player but he stood no chance at City once Malcolm had done his transfer business. They sold all the assets and in any business if you sell your best assets and don't replace them then you will fail. Everybody went. It was unbelievable. Allison lasted until October 1980 before being dismissed. After that he went to Sporting Lisbon and he called me to ask if I would go to Sporting and play for him! I remember thinking what I'd thought at City – was Allison "ahead of his time" or "was it madness?" He was happy to move me on at City but then wanted me in Portugal…. It doesn't make sense.'

City chairman Peter Swales recognised this as a major turning point in the development of football in Manchester when he was interviewed in October 1995. He described how up until the return of Allison the balance of power within Manchester was swinging City's way and how the 'mistake' of bringing Allison back killed the momentum the Blues had been building. Although City remained typically the third best supported club in the League and had won more trophies than United in the Seventies, all of that stopped once Allison was allowed to rip City's team of predominantly internationals apart. Swales resignedly expressed the view in 1995 that: 'Nobody ever will catch Manchester United now. I couldn't manage it and nobody else will ever catch them up because they are going to be there for good now, never mind my day.' [2]

Club employee back in 1979 Roger Reade saw the departure of his friends as a devastating blow personally and professionally: 'Peter and Gary were the young princes who, at Maine Road, were destined to be heroes for many years, but we also had these seasoned pros who were quite humble. Brian Kidd was a lovely, lovely guy. Many of the others similar.

Malcolm shipped out so many players that it was madness. The die was cast and we could never really compete at the same level – well not until the successes following the 2008 takeover – again. The big fees Allison paid for the replacement players crippled the club. We had a too generous bank manager who always seemed keen to lend City money. By 1983 the club was in a desperate state because of the debts and problems which began when Allison returned.

'The 1978-79 season was so hard because of Malcolm's return and the repercussions of that. It led to me questioning my own future. I loved City. Absolutely always have and always will, but I was looking at the situation and thinking that Malcolm is harming my club. The club I love. When Peter and Gary went that was it. I thought "no, I can't watch him destroy the club." I knew I had to leave. I left in the summer of 1979, literally around the same time as Peter. Some of the people

who worship Allison overlook what he did second time round. They suggest it was going to happen anyway or similar but for me that second period was a disaster. The killer for me was when Peter and Gary signed for West Brom within weeks of each other and they were both literally in tears. They didn't want to go. They loved City and of course I loved them as mates. It tore the heart out of the club and City never got it back. Eventually, relegation in 1983 was as a direct result of this philosophy.'

Roger's anguish was felt by many and he remains convinced that Allison's return was to impact the club for decades: '1978-79 was an iffy season and Malcolm was making these big decisions that would have long term impacts. If Tony had been in total charge he would not have made those decisions. It fell apart so quickly. I think looking back on it now that Malcolm genuinely thought he was the best coach in the world and the only way he could prove it when he came back to City was to get a

Peter caught by Debbie Darbyshire's camera on matchday.

new dynasty of his own. In other words players that he was personally responsible for and not someone else's players. So he personally looked to change everyone that didn't fit the "made by Allison" mould. Brian Kidd, Mike Channon, Asa Hartford, Dave Watson… Don't forget that Tony Book was capable of forging his own team and moving on any that were no longer vital. When he first took over he had the task of transferring some of his old mates with players like Francis Lee and Mike Summerbee transferred out. He also wasn't afraid to discipline and sell Rodney Marsh, so it's not as if he couldn't do the job. He'd put so much effort into ensuring he had a blend of talented young players and experienced internationals and was good at doing that, but then Allison seemed to push forward with plans to lose all the experienced men.' [3]

Peter agrees: 'That period set City back for years… decades even. The directors who wanted Malcolm back caused this. Their decisions were tearing the club apart and those of us that left, like player Gary Owen and office staff member Roger Reade, were distraught. To us it was the greatest – and friendliest club!'

Fans were dismayed at the departures, while others felt City lost their entertainment

value at this time. United fan, but regular Maine Road attendee in the Seventies, Terry Christian seemed mystified: 'I stopped going to City home games not long after Allison came back. I think he got rid of players for the sake of it. I remember thinking it was weird – I'd never seen Asa Hartford have a bad game and Dave Watson? With Allison it had to be his team. It's a real shame that Peter wasn't allowed to develop at City. Why when you have two young players like Barnes and Owen do you get rid to replace them with what? Fortunes were spent by City and they ended up with a much worse team.'

Peter's transfer rumbled on for a while before reaching completion on July 17, 1979: 'I never had an agent. None of us did. We used to get help from the PFA and that was very useful but I took a friend of my dad's when I signed for West Brom because

The stars who won't shine for City again

FLASHBACK : Father and son at dad's testimonial game.

MANCHESTER CITY have rocked the world of soccer by transfer-listing their two most valuable " assets," Peter Barnes and Asa Hartford.

For Barnes, it is the beginning of the end of his days at the club he joined straight from school in 1972.

The sands of time would also appear to have run out for Hartford—the brilliant little Scottish international midfield player who joined the Blues from West Brom in August, 1974, for £250,000.

The name Barnes, of course, was famous with City fans long before young Peter appeared on the scene. His father, Ken, a stylish wing-half who captained City in the late 1950s, is perhaps best remembered as "the finest player never to win an England cap."

By PAUL HINCE

Clearly, father Ken had an enormous influence on his son's early development, and by the time Peter was 13, clubs were already queueing up to land the promising youngster. In fact, Leeds United, whose manager at theO time was Don Revie, a former team-mate of Ken Barnes at

finally overwhelmed by his fellow professionals 24 hours later when he was voted the footballers' Young Player of the Year.

Peter's nerve cracked when he

Oddly enough, while Peter has gone from strength to strength for his country, his career at club level has not run so smoothly.

He did sign a six-year

this was the first time I'd moved anywhere and dad said I'd need some support and advice. He was John Doherty, an ex-United player who was working for an insurance company in Hyde. He eventually ran the United Former Players' Association and helped a few people with their contracts and transfers over the years. John was a big friend of my dad's and dad confided in him. He told him about my proposed move and, because John was good with figures, he helped. He had a wonderful brain and helped a lot of players over the years, including organising a charity game for the families of the Munich victims in 1998. Sadly, he died of lung cancer in 2007.

'John went with me to see Ron Atkinson at the Hawthorns. We went to the boardroom – it was all dark wood panelling, beautiful – while we waited for Ron. Ron came in wearing his tracksuit. Larger than life, as you'd expect. It was the era of flash managers. He introduced himself to me and John and then said: "Peter, I believe you're quite quick over ten yards?" It was the first thing he said and I shyly reply: "Yeah, not bad. Mr. Atkinson." Quick as a flash he says: "Well, just sprint over there and pour the teas out then!" Straight away I knew I was going to like this guy. He had a great personality and he knew how to keep our feet on the ground too.

'Ron had been known as the Tank as a player at Oxford and years before he'd been in Villa's reserve team when Joe Mercer was the manager there. Years later, Joe Mercer went to Maine Road when Ron took one of his teams there and dad was talking to Joe when Ron walked in after the game. Ron walked up to say hello to them both and turned to Joe and said: "Joe, I've got a question for you. How come I never made it at Villa? How come you never gave me the chance to get in the first team?" Joe turned to him smiling and replied: "Because you

weren't good enough Ron." Dad loved that and used to tell the story often.

'Ron was great for my career and I loved playing for him. We had issues at times but he loved attacking, flair football and I enjoyed listening to him. He was a big personality, like Malcolm Allison but the difference was that Allison seemed to want me out, whereas Ron thought I had something to offer. That was why I signed for him at West Brom.'

Over the years that followed Ron and Malcolm would often be compared or asked about the other in some way. Both were perceived as big personalities, though in 1979 Allison was the one who had found success during his post playing career, while Atkinson was still searching for major trophy success. At that time Peter felt Ron was the one more likely to find glory in the years to come, while Allison felt that Peter, like the other players transferred out of Maine Road that year, had little to offer. In August Allison explained his transfer activity: 'I made all the changes in the close-season because City needed that type of restructuring. Little had been achieved for a long time with the squad that was here last season, despite reputations, and I could not see anything being achieved with it in the future. I have my beliefs and I back them.' [4] Allison obviously felt that winning a major trophy, finishing second and fourth in the League and reaching the quarter-finals of the UEFA Cup were not achievements.

As for Albion, the club had seen two of their influential players transferred with Laurie Cunningham moving to Real Madrid for £950,000 and Mancunian Len Cantello moving to Bolton for £350,000. Peter and Gary were viewed as direct replacements, though it would always be tough replacing such an iconic and heroic figure as Cunningham. Albion had finished third in 1978-79, nine points behind

Peter in the colours of West Bromwich Albion.

Ron saw what Malcolm Allison was doing at Maine Road: 'I took advantage of their clear-out. With the Cunningham finances, I took on board Peter Barnes and Gary Owen and also waiting in the wings was David Mills. He was my ultimate transfer disaster, the player who subsequently declined to such a degree I called him my albatross.'

Unlike the signing of Mills, Atkinson felt that Peter and Gary's signings proved successful for West Brom, commenting that they were: 'sound purchases, with Barnesy notching thirty goals as a winger in two seasons, and Gary playing at West Brom for seven years.' Peter's transfer cost West Brom £750,000 – an Albion record until June 1997 when the club signed Kevin Kilbane for £1.25m – eclipsing their record transfer paid by over £230,000. 'At that time I didn't care how much anybody paid because it was immaterial. I just needed to go to the right club for my mental wellbeing. I knew it was a record but it wasn't a record I wanted. Footballers never have a part to play in how much a club pays or receives. I think West Brom always claimed it as £748,000 and City as £750,000 – I don't know why. Usually it's the buying club that says the higher figure because of tax payments they've had to make. Whatever the actual amount paid, this remained an Albion record for almost twenty years. I don't think it directly added pressure on me but I think it did affect the way other players, the media and some fans felt. A bit like today when Manchester City buy a player for £50m some in the media will focus on that amount and constantly talk of it when the player isn't delivering as much as the price tag suggests they should. That then influences others and before you know it a player is being viewed differently than they had been before. The amount seemed to upset others.'

champions Liverpool but eight points ahead of fourth placed Everton. The team had led the table earlier in the season but the player departures meant that the summer of 1979 had seen manager Ron Atkinson seeking to replace two of his popular stars. In 1998 Atkinson looked back at this period: 'The odds were heavily stacked against me in the summer, seeking new energy and purpose after the title disappointment the season before. Due to contract freedom, I lost Cunningham to Spain and Len Cantello, an impressive midfield anchor, to Bolton Wanderers. Tony Brown, a finisher who lurked in the shadows and pounced with better effect than any rival of that era, had packed his bags for America. Just as bad, Regis and England fullback Derek Statham were laid up with knee injuries that ruled them out for months. In other words, half the team that put us in with big-league potential had been wiped out. I needed to put the roof back on, even if the foundations remained sound.' [5]

There is no doubt that Peter was going to be viewed by Albion players and fans differently because of the amount paid. As with the transfer activity at Maine Road, Peter would be judged by some based on what had been lost at the Hawthorns. The circumstances were different but the result was similar – both Manchester City and West Bromwich Albion had lost popular players who had delivered for their clubs. Any player coming in to either of those clubs would be watched and compared to what had been lost by both fans and players.

One of the men who seemed unhappy with Atkinson's transfers was West Brom's longstanding centre-half John Wile who later commented: 'We'd lost Len who was a grafter and Gary Owen never quite did that, He was like a dog with a bone for an hour, all over the show, but he faded late on in games. Peter Barnes was very erratic. Good players both of them, no question. But they weren't as consistent as the guys they'd replaced.' [6] Wile also had an issue with another Atkinson signing that summer, striker John Deehan. Deehan, who Atkinson claimed repaid his investment once he played as centre-back, had arrived from rivals Aston Villa with Wile expressing the view that Deehan: 'came in on a lot of money, more than the rest of us. He was twenty-two and living in a big house outside of Birmingham. People like Ally Brown, Alistair Robertson and me were ten years older, had smaller houses and were getting paid less. That upsets the dressing room. As a player, you don't mind so much if someone comes in and will give you thirty goals a season. But when they don't make a huge difference it eats away at the spirit of the team.' Peter: 'It's often frustrating when a player signs and earns more than someone who has been at the club a while. We had it at City when Mike Channon arrived but instead of moaning and whinging about it you have to focus on your own game. If you're delivering then bring it up at contract renewal or demand a show-down with the boss. If you don't get anywhere then leave. There's no point sitting there and letting it affect your career. I don't remember animosity when I arrived – in fact I remember a good welcome from Cyrille Regis, Derek Statham, Bryan Robson, Brendon Batson… Good players. Good professionals.'

Gary Owen was well aware that not all the players were positive though: 'There was a great group of players there when Peter and I signed but, inevitably, there were one or two who made it known how much they resented what the new signings were being paid. There were some strong words said and a few arguments. I remember saying "well, get off your backside and prove what you're worth but don't start moaning because I was given a better contract" to one particular longstanding player.'

The transfer to West Bromwich Albion meant that, initially, Peter and Gary were to stay in a local hotel. Gary Owen: 'We both moved in to a hotel that the club used. The Europa Lodge it was back then. We both had sponsored cars which were Fords from Gordon Ford in Stockport. One morning

we woke up at the hotel and Barnsey had gone out to his car and he came back in and told me that he'd had some wheels stolen. When I got to my car I'd had two wheels stolen. He'd had three, so between us we didn't have enough wheels to even get to training! The cars were on bricks – I'd got two wheels and he'd got one! I said to Peter "they obviously like me better than you because they've only nicked two of mine!"

'We phoned the club and someone collected us. It was a big joke of course at training and it also got into the local newspaper. The Europa Lodge is next to junction one of the M5 near the road to the ground, but the hotel is in like a bowl, so you'd come off the motorway, go round and then go round and down. When the *Express & Star* was delivered that evening it told the story of how the new signings had had their wheels pinched and then the next evening the five missing wheels came rolling down the slope back to the hotel car park. Nobody saw who sent the wheels back. All we knew was that they were rolled down the hill – like a coin, circling for a bit before going down on its side.'

Peter: 'Gary likes to laugh about the tyres and how I'd had more 'borrowed' than him.'

1 'Soccer', *Guardian*, May 17, 1979, 20.
2 Peter Swales interviewed by Gary James, October 1995.
3 Roger Reade interviewed by Gary James, January 2020.
4 *Manchester City v Crystal Palace match programme*, August 18, 1979, 6.
5 Ron Atkinson, *Big Ron: A different ball game* (London: Andre Deutsch, 1998), 87-88.
6 Paul Rees, *The three degrees: The men who changed British football forever* (London: Constable, 2014), 199.

Chapter Thirteen

ALBION

" I'll never be a robot. I've no wish to be an ordinary player. I'll know that has happened when I wake up the day after a match and I don't need a long, hot bath to bring out the bruises. I'm satisfied enough with my form since joining Albion. There hasn't been a game when only one man has marked me. "

'Barnes bears marks of his genius', *Daily Mirror*, September 7, 1979, 31.

Staying at the Europa Lodge, Peter tried to focus on life at his new club: 'I wanted to get going straight away. I felt I needed to prove that Malcolm Allison was wrong and I couldn't wait for the first game. At the start of August we played China and we won 4-0 but importantly I felt I'd had a good game.' Reports credited Peter with a good performance and he played a hand in at least one of the goals while also finding the net himself with a '30-yard swerving drive.'[1] Peter's goal came eleven minutes from time in the friendly on August 1. Ten days later Peter scored the only goal as Ajax were defeated in Albion's centenary game. This time Peter: 'scored a magnificent 8th minute goal after beating two men and sending a curling left-foot drive into the far corner.'[2]

'I know they were only friendlies but I enjoyed those first few games', says Peter. 'The goals against China and Ajax were considered impressive by journalists and

fans, so that was pleasing. Having Gary Owen there helped and we made our home at the Europa Lodge, though we'd both get back to our families as soon as we could after games. At the hotel Gary seemed to get involved with everything. If he was bored he'd go behind reception and work there for a while. He wasn't asked to or anything, he just decided to do it. There were some good people there and they made us welcome. West Brom used the hotel a lot and Mick Brown, Ron's assistant, was also staying there. I got on well with him. He was quite a traditional coach and, obviously, a figure of authority to us. So it must have been a bit of a shock to him one day when he called down to reception and Gary answered: "Europa Lodge reception. How can I help?" I think Mick wanted some room service and so Gary took his order: "So that's a chicken salad sandwich. Is there anything else to go with that? No, okay, Mr Brown we'll get that sent up." Mick interrupted: "Is that Gary Owen? What are you doing?" He couldn't believe it, but it was just what Gary did. He loved to get involved and I'm sure some people thought he was an employee.'

'We had some fun with Mick at the hotel!' Gary remembers. 'He was a traditional football man and he loved Barnsey. I was right in your face and always about – working behind reception or whatever - but Peter would never dream of doing anything like that. I was outgoing but Barnsey was reserved and I think Mick liked him more than me.'

Gary talks with affection about his time helping out at the hotel: 'I wasn't paid to do it. I just did it, but it wasn't only reception - I did everything! I had a badge made which I wore "Executive Consultant to the General Manager". I worked really hard when I was there. Peter will say that I did it for fun but there was a bit more to it. I liked the humour of doing it of course, but I'd always been interested in business and I wanted to see how it all worked. So I worked behind reception, then in the offices. I used to sit there and listen to what was going on. It was fascinating. I did an accountancy course at Walsall – it was a bit basic, more like bookkeeping, but I was keen to learn. My view was that if I ever did a business I'd know the basics and be able to ask questions of any accountant or anyone else I dealt with. I was probably a bit young to be doing it but business was getting into my head and so staying at the Europa Lodge gave me the opportunity to see what was going on. Everyone knew we were at the Europa Lodge. We'd be in the bar at night playing pool, not drinking, and fans would come in and play with us.'

Peter: 'I walked down to reception one

day looking for Gary: "Where is he?" The receptionist replied: "He's in the staff room on his break" On his break! He wasn't on the payroll but they'd started allowing for his breaks. I half-expected a fire drill to go off one day and Gary being there taking the register of staff! It was a comical time at the Europa. There was one day when Gary & I were having breakfast and Mick came down with a cut nose and blood all over his face. It looked horrific and we wondered what happened. He told us, all matter of fact: "I was shaving and I fainted." As he'd fainted he'd banged his face on the sink. We just started giggling. It seemed so funny at the time.'

The 1979-80 League season commenced with Ron Atkinson boasting that he felt that he would manage the Baggies to the League title. In an article in the Daily Mirror he went through his logic, focusing on the players he believed would make the difference. This included Gary and Peter: 'Owen was a snip. I'll stake my life on him doing a good job for us. I'm absolutely astonished City let him go. You see Barnes in action and he excites you. OK, there might be days when I'll feel like strangling him. There will be a lot more when I'll want to carry him off shoulder high. The other lads are thrilled to have Gary and Peter at the club.' [3]

Both Gary and Peter played in the opening goalless draw with Derby. Peter: 'We had a difficult start because we had lost Cyrille Regis with a cartilage problem which kept him out for the first three months or so. He was our leading target man and without him it was tough. His injury came in the China friendly and it made it difficult for the team.' Inevitably, the close season transfer dealings came under the spotlight with Regis himself critical in later years: 'Why would you let Laurie go and buy Peter Barnes? Why sell Len Cantello and get Gary Owen? It was bizarre. But it was out of our hands.' [4]

Gary Owen remembers how difficult these opening weeks were: 'It was tough for Peter at the start because they'd had Willie Johnston, who was a hero plus Laurie Cunningham – a legend at the club – and then Barnsey. I don't think Peter started as well as he would've liked, so there was pressure on him all the time. I was in midfield and had Bryan Robson alongside me, so if I was not having a particularly good game having him alongside me would help enormously and vice versa. I think I

New signings Peter Barnes and Gary Owen turn out for the WBA team at a cricket game in July 1979.

It's not all fun being a footballer! Mum makes sure that me and brother Mike always lend a hand with the washing-up!

Peter's life was regularly featured in magazines such as Scoop.

Relaxing after training or after a match is a real necessity. Music and a game of chess with Mike always help me unwind.

started off better than Barnsey did through circumstance and opportunity I guess.'

Peter: 'Obviously there was the departure of Laurie Cunningham. It's always tough when a hero and a hugely talented player leaves. From West Brom's point of view maybe the money offered for Laurie was too good to turn down. I suppose they saw it as good business but for me that wasn't an issue because they'd signed me. I felt wanted and I couldn't worry about what had happened before I arrived. I understand that fans would think about it but on the pitch I had to get on with my game. I had to focus on my career and what I could do to help West Brom be successful.'

While the departure of Cunningham has over the decades since been viewed extremely negatively, former Albion goalkeeping hero John Osborne gave a slightly different interpretation in the press in the months that followed: '[Cunningham and Cantello] decided that they no longer wanted to play at The Hawthorns and Ron Atkinson had no alternative but to let them go. Most fans I've spoken to think that the alleged £1 million Albion received from Real Madrid for Laurie was a good deal, but it will take more than that now to replace his talents.' [5] He added: 'Most people accepted that it would take the new boys, Peter Barnes and Gary Owen, a few games to settle in, but I wonder if they realise how difficult it is for the other lads in the team to adapt to the loss of the powerful precision play of Len Cantello or the silky skills of Laurie Cunningham. Without detracting from the two signings from Maine Road, who I'm certain will prove to be bargain buys before the season is through, I do not think there is a team in the country who would not have suffered from losing two players of the calibre of Cantello and Cunningham.'

Gary Owen believed that, even with the loss of Cunningham, the team he joined with Peter in 1979 was one of true quality: 'We shouldn't overlook that Ron already had a great team. Derek Statham was probably the best left back in the country. If he'd have been playing for Arsenal and Kenny Sansom for West Brom Derek would've had more caps than Kenny. He was as good as Sansom. We had Ally Robertson and John Wile who were veteran centre-backs who would kick anything if they had to. They were good defenders. We had Brendon Batson – the most underrated right back ever! He was linked with England a few times but with any other club he'd have played without a doubt.'

Peter was asked about Batson and also Cyrille Regis for a book in 2014: 'Both of them are terrific characters. Brendon was a great talker in the dressing room. He was very serious about his game when he went out on the pitch, but a joker off it. He was always taking the mickey out of people and smiling and laughing. Cyrille was more of the silent type… He was a nice guy, very charming and mild-mannered. But put him on the field and if someone upset him, he'd be like a man-mountain.' [6]

'Don't forget we had Tony 'Bomber' Brown – rightly a legend at the club for all the brilliant goals he scored,' remembers Gary. 'There was Bryan Robson and Barnsey of course… Cyrille Regis and Alistair Brown, who scored plenty of goals. Football wise you can understand why both me and Barnsey went there.'

Despite the quality of Atkinson's team, the opening weeks were tough. The fixture list had not been kind with the opening day goalless home draw to Derby, quickly followed by a 2-0 defeat at Manchester United; a 3-1 loss at Liverpool and then a home 5-1 defeat to Midlands' rivals Nottingham Forest. These were amongst the toughest fixtures to face for any club at the

David Mills and Gary Owen with Peter.

time, but for a team that had lost its regular number nine through injury and had sold a hugely popular and talented player in Cunningham, these were nightmare matches. Despite the gloom, Peter did score the club's only League goal in their opening three games – that was at Anfield - while Gary Owen netted their goal against Forest. Peter: 'The Liverpool game was poor for us and I received some criticism in the press. I did score but it was a consolation goal really, coming in the 63rd minute when we'd already let in three.'

After the match at Anfield a Liverpool fan wrote to the *Liverpool Echo* with the news that Peter's goal was the first by an Englishman at the Anfield Road end of the stadium in 31 games – not a fact that many connected with Liverpool, or West Brom for that matter, particularly cared about but at least it was a step in the right direction. [7] There was also some positive news in the League Cup with Fulham defeated 2-1 on aggregate. Peter played

in both legs, which came either side of the Forest match. After the away leg Peter was profiled in the *Daily Mirror* where he commented on the fact that in most games, including the game at Anfield, he had been marked by multiple players: 'I almost felt neglected at Craven Cottage. Fulham didn't have more than two doing the job. At the Hawthorns the previous week they had been queuing up to mark me in the first leg. Against Nottingham Forest last Saturday I was doing well, beating Viv Anderson and getting my crosses over. In the second half they had Martin O'Neill coming back to double-mark. It gets a bit depressing at times. But when I feel sorry, it's not for myself… it's for the way the game is going.' [8]

Peter often talked about his worries for the future of football. Inevitably, he tended to focus on his dissatisfaction that attacking wing-play seemed to be out of fashion at some clubs. A goalless game with Bolton followed Forest and, as with any club struggling in the League, it was relatively easy to lay the blame at the selling of players or at those who were recent arrivals. Parallels with Manchester City's plight were clear – both clubs had lost players who were idolised. John Deehan and Peter, as recent Albion arrivals and attacking players, were always likely to be criticised when the club was not scoring enough, but it wasn't the attackers who had let in eight goals in the games with Liverpool and Forest. Nevertheless, they were held accountable by some. Ironically, Albion's next League game after Bolton was against Manchester City. This was to be an important game for both Peter and Gary Owen. Peter was asked about the game by journalist Ian Willars: 'We don't feel that we have anything to prove to Manchester City or Malcolm Allison, although we obviously did not feel we had a future at City as far as Malcolm was concerned. But we have never been so happy since joining Albion and even though we have had a bad start – for a variety of reasons – we have every confidence that we will get off the mark tomorrow. And what could be better than against City.' [9]

'I remember us playing City fairly early in our time at West Brom' says Gary Owen. 'We beat them 4-0 and I scored. It was satisfying beating City after what had happened. Today people say "don't celebrate if you score against your former team" but trust me. I am loyal to whichever club I am with and will do everything I can for them. Of course City was my team and I'd want them to win unless I was playing against them. I'm professional and I'm a winner, so of course I'm going to celebrate. I think fans wouldn't want anything less. When we beat City at the Hawthorns it was an unbelievable feeling to come out on to the pitch for both me and Peter to hear the away fans singing "There's only one Gary Owen" or "One Peter Barnes". Then the West Brom fans were singing "Thank you

very much for Gary Owen" and "Thank you very much for Peter Barnes". I loved that. It was unbelievable and it meant so much.'

About a month into his time at the Hawthorns Peter was asked his thoughts on the club. He commented that they were 'a happy club. And they are an ambitious club. That suits me. It's a club where you come through the players' entrance and you almost need to walk out on the pitch to reach the changing rooms.' [10] He added: 'We started badly at Albion but we're through to the third round of the League Cup and I think we've turned the corner.' Sadly, the League Cup run ended with a 3-0 defeat to Norwich in a fourth round replay.

There was also disappointment in the UEFA Cup with Peter missing the first leg through injury: 'We played Carl Zeiss Jena in East Germany and lost 2-0. I was suffering from a hamstring injury I'd picked up in our 4-0 win over City at the Hawthorns and so missed that leg, but I did return for the leg at the Hawthorns. John Wile scored but we lost 2-1 and were out of Europe. That was deeply frustrating for us.' Peter was also finding living in a hotel difficult: 'I had three months in the Europa – Gary and I had bedrooms next to each other – but I wanted to move out. I wanted to settle but couldn't do that in the hotel. I'd broken off my relationship with my girlfriend because it was difficult with the traveling – we ended up getting back together and we got married later - but it was tough maintaining the relationship at first after the move. Whenever a game was over I'd be desperate to get back to Manchester. If we played on a Wednesday we'd have Thursday off and so I'd go home, back to my flat in Bramhall. I'd see my parents and friends. I was homesick. I moved into digs and stayed with Mr & Mrs Weaver – she was South African and he was from Birmingham. Lovely people but it was difficult for me. I'd bought a lovely flat in Bramhall, overlooking the park, and had been looking forward to settling there, but then I was transferred and ended up in digs. A complete change. It was like starting again and that was tough. I'm a massive family man and I missed that. I always wanted to get back.'

Peter had moved into his digs by the end of November but it remained an unsettled time for him. In addition to his domestic situation there were a few murmurs around the club that Peter wasn't welcome. 'Me and Gary had been at City for years and that was the only football club we knew. It takes time to settle in. As well as the football there are the domestic situations – is your family okay? Where are you going to live? It takes time but when you arrive shortly before the season starts and you're expected to deliver straight away you don't have the time. People forget that.'

There was some criticism of Peter's performances, prompting Ron Atkinson to defend him shortly before Christmas: 'This player is loaded with ability, believe me, more than I realised he had when I signed him. The supporters are now seeing glimpses of the real Peter and they'll soon grow to love him, because they like players of his class here. I am prepared to have that sort of player in my side. I made my own mind up that Peter is a matchwinner, and that's what we needed. He can drive you up the wall the very next match but I'll put up with that.

'I'm not a manager who'll just pick 11 ordinary players because then I'll just have an ordinary side. I don't want that. The fans have got to be as patient as I am.' [11]

Atkinson's faith was rewarded a few days later as Albion defeated Bristol City 3-0 with Peter netting twice and Gary Owen scoring the other. Post-match the manager commented: 'All three goals – Peter's two and the one by Gary Owen – were all marvellous. But Peter began to look sheer class. There didn't seem to be anything on for his second goal, but he just hit it, and the next thing we knew the ball was in the back of the net. He has been threatening to show top form for several games, and now I feel we are about to see the best of him. All this talk about his future has not been helping the lad, and as far as I am concerned, suggestions about his leaving is a load of rubbish.' [12]

According to the *Birmingham Post*: '[Peter's] goals yesterday gave him new heart. "It was nice to score twice in front of my own crowd and I hope it will help to put us all in good spirits for the visit of Liverpool on Saturday." The standing ovation he was given at the end of the game can have left him in no doubt that the Albion fans want him to stay at The Hawthorns.' [13]

Over the years it has been suggested that Albion supporters did not take to Peter but the evidence during 1979-80 suggests otherwise. Peter: 'I've always had a lot of time for West Brom fans. They did make me welcome and I loved their support. On days when I was feeling homesick their support cheered me up considerably.'

Gary Owen remembers how difficult it was for Peter at times during this period. 'As well as his homesickness, there were problems in the dressing room occasionally. One of the longstanding players had an issue with both me and Peter because they'd brought us in and we were on bigger money. Typically, players brought in got better contracts than those that had been there some time. It's the way it works and that's that. Whether it's right is another thing but that's how it happens. I knew this particular player had an issue but he didn't say anything to our faces and then one particular day it all came out.

Barnsey would let it all wash over him and wouldn't say anything really but I would tackle something head on. There'd be sneaky little digs at either me or Peter and Barnsey would say "ignore it. Leave it" but I couldn't. In general the mood at the Hawthorns was good but there were one or two who had an issue with me or Barnsey from before we even arrived – that's how silly it was.'

By December, criticism of Albion's form had, inevitably led to discussion about the previous summer's transfer activity with some criticising the manager for selling Cunningham and bringing in Peter. It was an easy criticism to make, especially as rumours circulated that Peter wanted to move clubs again: 'I was homesick - I won't deny that - and some stories appeared in the press suggesting that Manchester United were about to sign me.' What appears to have happened during this time, and at others when Peter is quoted criticising his manager or club, is that a journalist had asked him how he was feeling and, instead of remaining guarded and holding back, Peter would often comment on being homesick or he'd make comparisons between clubs or managers. These would then be reported in a sensationalist manner, suggesting either he wanted to leave or that a club closer to Manchester was interested. As Manchester City had only sold him that summer, the obvious club was Manchester United. The *Birmingham Daily Post* carried one such story which claimed that United 'had made a move for the £650,000 winger and been given first option by Albion if they should ever release him.' [14]

Atkinson was understandably upset by this constant speculation: 'I am becoming extremely angry about these stories. Barnes is settling down very well now and has started to show his best form. But the constant barrage of speculation connecting Barnes with Manchester United is not calculated to help him. I am fed up reading about it and denying it.'

It is clear that this type of reporting – and Peter's honesty with the press – added to the pressures on him. Those, together with the regular criticism of West Brom by some in the media, affected his play, although he would always deny that. Every time a story appeared suggesting Peter was not the right player either at Albion or any of the other clubs he played for, then it would intensify his own doubts or negative feelings. He did not often talk about this at the time, although there are some comments such as these: 'I have found it difficult to settle here, and I'll admit there were times when I went on to the field in the wrong frame of mind. There was also the worry that I might be leaving Albion. I kept picking up newspapers and reading that I could be on my way, and in the end I started to believe that I had no future here.' [15]

Gary Owen was asked to comment in the local press about Peter feeling homesick: 'I can appreciate Peter's problems in settling in because he has always been a more reserved person than me. I'm the type who goes down into the hotel bar, has a game of pool and soon makes friends whereas Peter tends to take a back seat.' [16] In 2020 Gary remembered this period: 'We were both homesick and whereas I built relationships straight away – I've still got some great friends now that I made back then – Peter didn't. He'd keep himself to himself. We were both young and all our friendships initially were in Manchester. Our lives were there and we'd both go back after games. Barnsey may not have started off as well as he'd have wanted but he did have some great games for West Brom.'

November and December were months when West Brom received a great deal of criticism, although as Christmas approached Peter's own form impressed. Against Arsenal on December 15 he was judged to be the man of the match as Albion played out a 2-2 draw. Peter was not on the scoresheet but he set up Bryan Robson for the opener and he thrilled down the wing, skipping past John Devine time after time. The Arsenal player was eventually booked for hauling down Peter at one point in the match.

By December 22 Albion were 16th out of 22 clubs in the First Division but, crucially, only three points above the relegation zone after playing 21 games. Ron Atkinson: 'We were producing some good football but nothing seemed to go right for the team… I believed firmly that if I should show the slightest concern at our predicament, the players might panic. I worked hard and long on boosting confidence at every opportunity. [Peter and Gary], who remembered bad times at Manchester City when the place became oppressive and depressing, would often sit open-mouthed in the dressing-room. The two of them just couldn't believe how light-hearted the atmosphere remained at the Hawthorns, despite our predicament.' [17]

Albion had lost seven and had not won a League match since November 10 with Peter receiving some criticism. This led to Peter having a conversation with Ron. In April 1980 he looked back on that chat: 'I asked the boss for a different role. I told him it was no good me standing out on the wing waiting for the ball. I wanted to be involved.' [18]

Some talked of Peter having more freedom in the weeks that followed which improved his play considerably, starting with the League game with Bristol City on Boxing Day. That day Peter scored two and Gary Owen one as Albion won 3-0 before 19,590 at the Hawthorns. This was described as a turning point in the season: 'Since Peter asked Atkinson in December for more freedom on the pitch, he has been a revelation.'

League defeats at home to Liverpool (2-0) and away to Ipswich (4-0), together with a FA Cup replay loss to Second Division West Ham (2-1), followed, before Albion travelled to Midlands' rivals Nottingham Forest on January 12. Forest's Viv Anderson remembers that games between the two teams were often considered significantly clashes: 'There was always a rivalry between West Brom and Forest. We always had battles with them going back throughout my time at Forest. Those games were always high profile. These were great days for Forest of course, but West Brom were seen as a major rival at the time. They had some great players like Derek Statham, Big Cyrille, Peter of course… and we had some really good games against them. They were a good footballing team too. Ron Atkinson liked to play football the right way, as did Cloughie of course. For a spectator or a neutral it was wonderful to watch and always a good

Gary Owen, Peter and 'Tucks' Trewick pose reading the WBA annual at the start of 1980.

game. Peter had a trick so you never knew which way he was going to go and so was tough to play against. He could chip you; go inside; go outside… you had to be really on your mettle when you played against him because he was a really, really good player. He wasn't the sort of player who would kick you. It was the other way round with Barnsey, we'd be trying to get one in on him first to let him know we were there. His dad brought him up to play football the right way and it's been like that wherever he's been and whoever he has played for. His aim was to entertain the crowd and that's what the game is about.

'Obviously Peter and I were mates with England but that means nothing when you're playing at a club level. I remember in that specific game in January 1980 that the ball was going behind the two of us

and I sort of pushed him away as I'm going to run for it. Somehow I poked Peter in the eye with my finger. He stopped and said "What are you doing, Viv?" because we were mates and I'm going "it was an accident Peter". He's going "I can't see, Viv. What've you done?" It was just before half time and I don't think he came out for the second! It was a complete accident but I was relieved when he was substituted because you wouldn't want him to run riot. Forty years on Peter still mentions it whenever he sees me!' [19]

Peter was substituted and Albion lost the match 3-1. 'Peter's a very shy person but he expressed himself on the football field,' Anderson remembers. 'He was completely different on the pitch than off it. In a game he'd be flamboyant; would take risks; would entertain the crowd – if he could go back and beat you for a second time he'd do that. He had no problem demonstrating his skills on the pitch. Off it he was very, very quiet. That was just his personality. He liked a laugh and a joke but he kept himself to himself. But don't let any of that detract from what a great, expressive, entertaining player he was.'

The Forest defeat brought pressure on Albion with the side dropping to 18th out of 22 teams after 24 games. Even Allison's Manchester City were above them – and they'd just lost a FA Cup tie to Fourth Division Halifax Town. A 2-2 draw at Crystal Palace followed before Albion faced Peter's old club City at Maine Road. Peter: 'Going back to City with both teams struggling was not ideal. When I walked into the ground I could feel the negative air that surrounded City at the time. A few fans said hello to me as we arrived and that was good, then during the game Cyrille Regis gave us the lead after about 30 minutes. It was a dour, tough first half, but I managed to increase our lead just after half-time. City came back at us and Stuart Lee scored, but five minutes from the end I scored our third – I dribbled around Joe Corrigan!'

Peter's sister Susan was sat in the Main Stand that day: 'It was great to see Peter back at Maine Road. When he played for City I used to go to all the home matches and sometimes I'd travel with him to the game. I couldn't get to see him at West Brom but then I was there for the game when he scored two against City. A bloke behind me shouted: "What's Barnes doing? He's never scored two goals for City ever and he comes back here and does that!" There was a lot of abuse being muttered in the background.'

The mood at Maine Road after the 3-1 Albion victory was not great, although it wasn't all Peter's fault of course. After the match City fans demonstrated with chants of 'Allison Out', 'Sack the Board' and, possibly for the first time, 'Swales Out', adding to the pressure on Malcolm Allison who, when asked if time was running out for him, responded: 'I won't feel that until the day they bury me!' [20] Peter: 'It wasn't nice to see but, as a West Brom player, I was satisfied with the win. We needed the points as much as City.'

Remi Moses, who had only made his League debut the week before was perceived as the star man, but Peter's performance in the 3-1 victory brought much positive coverage his way. This helped him personally and as the season progressed he proved his value to Albion on numerous occasions, causing Ron Atkinson to comment: 'Peter is a far better player than I thought when I bought him.' [21] Those comments came in April, shortly after eight goals in six League games. Four of those were penalties, with two coming in an entertaining 4-4 draw with Bolton.

SIMON PEPS LATICS   ENGLAND RU GLORY

Barnes nails City:
3-1 super Reds

Worst yet for Mal:
United's late blast!

PETER BARNES, the winger sold to West Brom for £600,000 in the close season, nailed crisis club Manchester City on a two-goal return to Maine Road today.

By STEVE

Peter scores for Albion at Maine Road.

Susan, Peter's older sister, knew how talented and flamboyant her brother was on the football pitch but she also knew that off the pitch he was somewhat different: 'I remember Ron chatting to dad about him. He said: "The way Peter plays you'd think he was a right cocky so-and-so off the pitch but he's such an introverted lad. He needs an arm around the shoulder." That was true. Peter liked to do the tricks and make opposition players look a bit foolish at times. He'd entertain and appear to be full of himself but he was nothing like that off the pitch.'

By the time Albion faced Arsenal at Highbury on April 26, the team had climbed to ninth in the First Division following a run of ten games without defeat. Gary Owen, who had captained the side on occasion during 1980, remembers that Ron Atkinson had encouraged and pushed them throughout that season: 'Ron was a great manager. He was a winner and wanted to win every game. Ron was good for us and knew how to get the most out of us. He even coped with a typical Barnsey moment

when we played Arsenal away. We had gone down, had our breakfast – in those days Cyrille Regis would have two rounds of toast with beans, two eggs and steak! After that we went back to our rooms, got our bags ready and then down for the team meeting at 12. We were in the team meeting and Ron was going on about the Arsenal players and what he'd want us to do. He was turning to each of us in turn telling us what he wanted from us: "Cyrille, use your power.… Barnsey when they get to you I want you to… Where's Barnsey? Gary, where's Barnsey?" I replied that when I'd left our room he was supposed to be right behind me. Ron used a few expletives and then said "well, anyway, the less he knows what we're doing the more chance we've got!" Later I see Peter and he says "what time's the team meeting? Are we having one today?" Ron didn't even tell him off afterwards. He just rolled his eyes. That was typical Barnsey. As a roommate Peter was so laid back. He thought I was often "busy" because I was always up doing something, ready to go. He'd be saying "Do you want

ALBION 3, CRYSTAL PALACE 0
TUESDAY, 1st APRIL, 1980
This game produced three fine goals; one from
John Trewick and two from Peter Barnes (shown here).

9

a cup of tea" and he'd be taking his time doing that while I'd be getting up, having my shower, getting dressed. He'd still be stirring the tea, taking his time while I'm making phone calls, popping in everybody else's room…. I'm always buzzing about, seeing what's going on but Peter's approach was different. Life happened to him whereas I was always looking to find it.

'I've always liked Barnsey and he's always been in my life somewhere. I remember going on a holiday with his family to the Isle of Man when we were youngsters at City.'

Despite Peter's laid back approach and missing the team meeting that day he put in a superb performance at Highbury. The game ended in a 1-1 draw on April 26 with Peter netting Albion's goal in the 19th minute. His performance was described as 'simply exhilarating' with journalist Harry Miller claiming Peter was 'better than Laurie Cunningham and essential to Ron Greenwood's European Championship plans.' [22] Peter: 'I enjoyed that game and I do remember being surprised pre-match

that we weren't having a team talk! I think Ron said something like "perhaps you should miss all my team talks in future if you play like that afterwards." There was quite a lot of humour flying around that day and I was on the receiving end of some good natured banter.'

The goal at Highbury was Peter's fifteenth in the League that season – his best return for either City or Albion – after 37 (plus 1 as substitute) taking his goalscoring ratio to 0.395 goals per game. That season centre-forward Cyrille Regis only managed to appear in 26 League games, scoring eight (ratio of 0.308 goals per game), due to injury which meant that Peter was the club's highest scorer.

Albion finished the season tenth on 41 points. It was a disappointment after the previous campaign had seen them finish third, but missing Regis for the opening four months had limited the club's opportunities. 1980-81 was anticipated to be a better year for the club and for Peter: 'I was feeling more settled and was happy with the way 1980 had progressed so far.'

1   'China losers so friendly', *Coventry Evening Telegraph*, August 2, 1979, 19.
2   'Flyaway Ivan still in dark about a move', *Birmingham Daily Post*, August 13, 1979, 11.
3   'The big sting', *Daily Mirror*, August 18, 1979, 16-17.
4   Paul Rees, *The three degrees: The men who changed British football forever* (London: Constable, 2014), 199-200.
5   'Let's see that smile', *Sports Argus*, October 6, 1979, 16.
6   Paul Rees, *The three degrees: The men who changed British football forever* (London: Constable, 2014), 199-201.
7   Letter from W Youds published in 'Sports platform', *Football Echo*, September 8, 1979, 8.
8   'Barnes bears marks of his genius', *Daily Mirror*, September 7, 1979, 31.
9   'Out: Mills bombshell', *Birmingham Daily Post*, September 15, 1979, 14.
10 'Barnes bears marks of his genius', *Daily Mirror*, September 7, 1979, 31.
11 'Albion on the rocks?', *Sports Argus*, December 22, 1979, 16.
12 'Revival is in the air – Atkinson', *Sports Argus*, December 29, 1979, 13.
13 'More freedom deal for Barnes is a winner', *Birmingham Post*, December 27, 1979, 10.
14 'Barnes stays here say Albion', *Birmingham Post*, December 24, 1979, 14.
15 'Peter looking the part', *Sports Argus Centre Spot*, December 15, 1979, 5.
16 'We'll soon start to climb – Gary', *Sports Argus Centre Spot*, December 15, 1979, 5.
17 Ron Atkinson with Joe Melling, *United to Win* (London: Sidgwick & Jackson, 1984), 57.
18 'Barnes joining the Brady bunch', *Sun*, April 5, 1980, 31.
19 Viv Anderson interviewed by Gary James, January 2020.
20 'Moses leads Albion on', *Daily Mirror*, February 4, 1980, 31.
21 'Barnes joining the Brady bunch', *Sun*, April 5, 1980, 31.
22 'Peter finds his old magic', *Daily Mirror*, April 28, 1980, 30.

Chapter Fourteen

THE END OF ALBION

❝
Albion winger, Peter Barnes, has his sights set
on Spain – not for a holiday but for the World Cup Finals
in two years' time. Barnes is one of an Albion contingent
who are part of England's plans at the moment, at all levels,
and he makes no secret of the fact that the position he
wants is at senior level. There was no doubt that his call up
for the 'B' internationals this season, against America and
Australia, prove he still figures in Ron Greenwood's plans,
even though his games at senior level have been restricted.
He firmly believes that wingers have a vital part to play
in England's bid for World Cup glory, and at the moment
his biggest rival would appear to be former Albion ace,
Laurie Cunningham.
❞

'Peter Barnes', West Bromwich Albion v Grimsby Town match programme,
January 3, 1981, 12-13.

For 23 year old Peter 1980-81 was hoped to be the season when he strengthened his claim for a place in Ron Greenwood's England squad for the 1982 World Cup; became settled at the Hawthorns; and married his girlfriend Alison Garrathy. Peter had met Alison while he was playing for Manchester City. The introduction had come from his City and Albion teammate Gary Owen: 'Alison used to live at the back of where I lived. I introduced the two of them… I don't think he's ever forgiven me for that! No, I'm joking. I didn't really know her, other than she lived at the back of our house, but I did introduce them. They seemed to hit it off and then they started going out together.'

Peter remembers: 'We met at a nightclub in the basement of a hotel which was then called the Valley Lodge, near Manchester airport. A few of the City players used to go there. One night

September 10 1980. Peter: 'I'm not certain why we picked the date we did but at the time it seemed to make sense. It was a Wednesday. As a footballer it was always important to check if there were any games planned and Albion had nothing scheduled and we weren't aware of any other clashes. Other players did get married in the football season, so it didn't feel like it was an issue to us. I asked Gary Owen to be my best man and we made our plans.'

Peter was keen to get married and find a permanent home in the Midlands. He wanted to settle at Albion and felt that, despite a few issues at times during the 1979-80 season, he had started to adjust to life at the club: 'West Brom was a wonderful club. Training was good. We played attacking football with Regis and Brown. A good, good side. Ron was excellent. I could see a bright future.'

I was there with Gary Owen who knew Alison's friend from his home town. We got chatting and I asked: "are you coming here next week?" She said she was and so the following week we went there and I expected to see her but she wasn't there. I had a bit of a go at Gary saying: "Your friend's friend never turned up!" A few days later he bumped into his friend and told her that Alison didn't turn up: "You need to tell her that Peter's been in the first team three or four times!" Gary was showing off for me, along the lines of "Doesn't she know who he is? He's a first team player!" It makes me laugh now.

'We met up the following week I think and that was that then. We started going out.'

The relationship developed but Peter's move to Albion affected plans and Peter and Alison stopped seeing each other for a period. They soon rekindled the relationship though once they were back together and they made plans to marry on

Despite Peter's hope of settling down, two days before the 1980-81 League season opened it was reported that Manchester United manager Dave Sexton was about to bid for him. Journalist Bob Russell claimed: 'United's interest, which goes back beyond Barnes's move to the Midlands 13 months ago, intensified when they lost the battle with Juventus for Liam Brady. Old Trafford boss Dave Sexton was also promised first refusal last December when the news started spreading that Barnes was having trouble settling at West Brom. Barnes's form problem appeared to resolve itself when he switched to a deeper, freer left-sided game which brought him both a rush of goals and an England recall. But the hankering for a return to the Manchester scene remains.' [1]

Sadly, every time a story like that appeared some Albion fans assumed Peter was angling for a move and this affected their view of him: 'Obviously, I was still missing Manchester but as the new season started I wanted to plan for a future at

West Brom. Newspaper stories of United's interest were unsettling.'

The opportunity to join United was mentioned often during the new season and hampered Peter's progress at times. The opening month was a little frustrating on the pitch too, as Albion lost their opening game and drew their next two, with the first victory coming at Brighton in the fourth game. Before the following fixture, the news broke that Peter had been selected to play for England against Norway in a World Cup qualifying match after missing out earlier in the year in the European Championships. Neither he nor Laurie Cunningham had been named in the 22 man Euro squad

with Greenwood selecting 24 year old Tony Woodcock instead for the national team. Peter's selection for the World Cup qualifier was something of a surprise, especially as the date of the game was the same day Peter was due to marry Alison! According to the *Daily Mirror*, Ken, Peter's father, felt the choice was a simple one and that his son should play for England. [2]

'Dad would have put the international first', believes Peter's eldest sister Susan. 'When my parents married dad was a City player. They were married at the Manchester registry office in the morning and then dad played a game in the afternoon. I think it was for the Reserves.'

Although some of the specifics are sketchy for Peter, it does appear that as he wasn't selected for the England squad that was to play in the 1980 Euros, the prospect of then being selected for a World Cup qualifying match seemed unlikely. At the time the wedding was arranged Peter couldn't possibly have known that Ron Greenwood would change things around for an early season important international. Peter: 'I don't remember why we planned to get married in the football season. I do know that was seen as a blank day at the time, but then I was selected for the England game. We did discuss cancelling it, but we knew we couldn't. The arrangements had been made and we felt it had to go ahead. I telephoned Ron Greenwood to explain. It was a difficult call to make but Ron was really nice about it. He seemed to understand and he said it wouldn't be a problem, so that was a relief.'

Peter Barnes and his fiancee, Alison Garrathy.

Star switches his match of the day

By Peter Gardner

SOCCER STAR Peter Barnes has put possible World Cup glory with England before his marriage to Warrington model Alison Garrathy.

Barnes, West Bromwich Albion and former Manchester City winger — recalled by England boss Ron Greenwood for the qualifying match against Norway at Wembley a week

tomorrow — had considered withdrawing from the squad because his wedding was on the same day.

But after talking with his father, Ken, chief scout at Maine Road and himself a one-time City player, Peter is now planning a postponement so he can link up with England.

Peter said today: "I thought that as I didn't go to Italy for the European Championship finals, my England chance had gone.

"That's why we went ahead with wedding arrangements for September 10, not realising that was the date of the World Cup match

The newly weds, Peter and Alison, with best man Paul Futcher.

Laurie Cunningham was drafted into the squad at the last moment, though it was 22 year old Graham Rix who actually played in Peter's position, making his first England appearance. Rix retained his place for the next international, again a World Cup qualifier, against Romania on October 15. Peter wouldn't get his chance again until the following March when he came on as substitute in a friendly with Spain.

Further issues followed for Peter when West Brom arranged to play a friendly in Naples on his wedding day. Peter was given approval to stay behind but there was a question mark over whether Gary Owen had to travel: 'I said to Ron that I was Peter's best man and asked if I could stay behind. Ron said "No, you're not missing this trip" and he took me off to Italy.'

A little over 24 hours before he was due to marry Alison at Penketh, Warrington, Peter heard the news that he needed a new best man. He asked former Manchester City midfielder Paul Futcher, then with Oldham, if he would step in: 'Paul became my best man when Gary had to go off with West

233

Brom – he scored a goal in the friendly at Napoli! Maybe in hindsight I should've cancelled the wedding, but can you imagine the problems that would've caused for the families?'

After their wedding Peter hoped he and Alison would settle: 'We rented a detached house in Stourbridge. A lovely part of the world. I still owned the flat in Bramhall and we were happy renting our new home. We were settling in to married life and things were going well for West Brom too – After losing to Arsenal on the opening day we only lost to Liverpool in our next ten League games. I'd scored the only goal in a win over Coventry on October 8th and things seemed good.'

After defeating managerless Manchester City – Malcolm Allison and Tony Book had been sacked with their club in the relegation zone – on October 11, Albion were fifth, two points behind leaders Ipswich. Then

came a 2-1 defeat at Nottingham Forest during which Peter suffered a hamstring injury which kept him out of the following three games. Due to five draws in eight games Albion lost pace a little, although they were not beaten again in the League until December. Peter had returned to League action at home to Villa (0-0) on November 8 before scoring in a 2-2 draw at Arsenal. Gary Owen scored the other goal from a penalty. Gary also netted a penalty in the next League match – a 3-1 win over Leicester. Peter: 'We felt that was an important win. We went sixth. Five points behind leaders Villa but we had a game in hand. The First Division was exceptionally tough back then and any one of about eight clubs could win it. Liverpool were always strong and Nottingham Forest were at their height, but then there was Bobby Robson's Ipswich – an incredible team at the time. Villa were doing well and teams like Arsenal

Liverpool v Albion, 13 September 1980 – Avi Cohen chases Peter.

and Everton were in with a chance. United, of course, were desperate to win the title and their fans were getting somewhat frustrated, but that meant you'd often be up against it.

'Despite the strength of all the other teams we felt, under Ron that we could do it. I was feeling really positive about life at the Hawthorns. We'd been married two months and everything seemed to be going well. After the home win over Leicester we left Stourbridge because it was my sister-in-law's 21st birthday. We went to Warrington. We came back late on the Sunday night and as we pulled up you could see something was wrong. The curtains had been drawn and I knew we'd left them open. We opened the door and the house had been ransacked. Everything was turned upside down. It was a horrible feeling. We'd been burgled.'

According to newspaper reports over £6,000 of personal items had been stolen but, more significantly, the burglary was to have an effect on both Peter and Alison's wellbeing: 'All the feelings we'd had about being settled had gone. Understandably, Alison was then nervous about being at the house alone while I was at games. My mother-in-law bought us a dog – a Doberman – and that helped but we knew we had to move. You feel unsettled knowing someone has been through your things and been all over your house. Brian Hassall, who acted as an agent to some extent and had helped me with things like boot contracts, lived at Upper Longdon, Cannock Chase, so we moved there because it meant we knew someone nearby.'

A week after the burglary Peter netted

Peter Barnes

Albion winger, Peter Barnes, has his sights set on Spain — not for a holiday but for the World Cup Finals in two years time.

Barnes is one of an Albion contingent who are part of England's plans at the moment, at all three levels, and he makes no secret of the fact that the position he wants is at senior level.

There was no doubt that his call up for the 'B' internationals this season, against America and Australia, prove he still figures in Ron Greenwood's plans, even though his games at senior level have been restricted.

He firmly believes that wingers have a vital part to play in England's bid for World Cup glory, and at the moment his biggest rival would appear to be former Albion ace, Laurie Cunningham.

It is fair to suggest that Albion fans have not yet seen the best of Barnes, but it is obvious that the potential is there for him to be one of the finest exponents of wing play in the country.

Barnes shot to prominence at Maine Road, with Manchester City, and he was voted the best young player by the Professional Footballers Association a couple of years ago.

Before today's match with Everton, the winger had scored five goals for Albion and each one had a touch of class about them.

Barnes is determined to reclaim his England spot and he knows that this can only be achieved by showing the England manager, at club level, that he is on top of his form.

BOB DOWNING—*Sandwell Evening Mail*

the third in a 3-2 victory at Spurs, who had been unbeaten at home. West Brom had been leading 3-0 before a fightback from Tottenham which journalists suggested made Ron Atkinson angry but the manager completely dismissed that view when he answered a critic: 'Disappointed? How the hell could anyone be disappointed after the way we played? The only reason we conceded goals was that we were chasing more of our own.' [3]

That win put Albion fourth, three points behind leaders Villa, but defeats to Leeds (2-1) and at Coventry (3-0) and a goalless draw at Sunderland quelled some of the talk of an Albion title success.

Peter was the star man when West Brom picked up their next points with a 3-1 victory over Manchester United on December 27. According to *The People* newspaper: 'England winger Peter Barnes pulled out some surprises from his bag of tricks to send Manchester United into the New Year with a hangover. Barnes' wizardry was the decisive factor as these giants wrestled with each other. He scored one and set up another for smash-and-grab Albion.' [4]

Atkinson's assistant Mick Brown was full of praise after the match: 'He is what the game is all about. He is an entertainer. The crowds go away either loving or hating him, but they all talk about him during the week.' [5]

Despite the positivity on the pitch, the unsettled feelings following the burglary continued to affect Peter: 'I think, even after moving to Upper Longdon, we had the view that we'd be moving back to the Manchester area. When something like that happens it affects you more than perhaps you realise at the time. I worried about Alison whenever I travelled away and if we both left the house there was the worry that someone would break in. It had nothing

BARNES STAR IN A CLASSIC

By CHRIS MOORE: West Brom 3, Man Utd 1

NIKKI JOVANOVIC
—Consolation goal

RED TROUBLE from an old Blue ... Albion's Peter Barnes beats Manchester United's Gary Bailey and Jimmy Nicholl ... it's number two in the net.

to do with West Brom, but it affected our thinking at a time when I had wanted to settle and felt comfortable with the way things were going at the club.'

While Peter gave his all for Albion, the unsettled feelings just wouldn't go away. These were not helped of course with the realisation that England boss Greenwood was not picking him for competitive internationals. According to Ron Atkinson: 'I still believe that, in his day, Barnes could have made a major contribution at international level if the players around him had been carefully selected. His idiosyncrasies, no matter how irritating, could have been tolerated as long as there were enough ball-winners, runners and engine-room players willing to earn the right for him to play and produce the skills. We had such men at West Brom in Bryan Robson, Gary Owen, and later Remi Moses, and Barnes' scoring record with us was excellent. While at the Hawthorns he had a better record for hitting the back of the net than many of the leading strikers in the country.'[6]

If only Greenwood had possessed the same level of determination as Atkinson had for a style of football that brought out the best in Peter. Fortunately, things began to improve for Peter internationally when Greenwood brought him on as substitute in a friendly over Spain on March 25. He was in action for only seven minutes, but it was a step in the right direction. Fans of both West Brom and Manchester City wanted to see him regain his international place, while neutrals genuinely seemed excited whenever he played. This led to numerous articles and discussions on his abilities and on the value of attacking wingers in the media. Peter's place in the England set up seemed to prompt debate on the value of traditional styles of play and, inevitably, he was often asked for his views. Shortly after his appearance against Spain he was quoted: 'Wingers have got to come back. They can excite the crowd as well as produce the goals and Spain showed on Wednesday just what damage a wide player with speed can do.'[7]

Peter's frustration was clear to see in the article: 'I have always been a winger, but sometimes I feel like a dinosaur. There aren't many what I call true wingers around, and I blame the coaches. They keep telling the youngsters to pass the ball instead of letting them develop any natural ability to take people on and run past them. That's what frightens defenders and what players are encouraged to do in South America and on the Continent. If a player is blessed with the talent to run quickly and take the ball past defenders he should be allowed to use it.'

Greenwood's selection of Rix, rather than Laurie Cunningham, to play when Peter was getting married suggests that Peter's views on the type of player the England boss wanted to wear the number eleven shirt were valid. Cunningham was recognised, like Peter, as a great attacking force and for neutrals who wanted to see thrilling, attack-minded wing-play it was clear that either Peter or Cunningham was the man England should choose.

Back at the Hawthorns, Albion still stood a slim chance of title success, although Villa looked to have the title in the bag. A 2-0 win over Everton at the end of March was followed by a brilliant 3-1 victory over treble-chasing Ipswich Town. As reporter John Dee explained: 'There was not the semblance of fluke about it. Albion won simply because they were the superior side.'[8] West Brom, unbeaten at home since December 6, took the lead in the ninth minute when Ally Brown netted. Sadly, Ipswich equalised through Alan Brazil moments later, but the game swung back in Albion's favour shortly before half time when Peter picked up a rebound off the legs of Ipswich defender Kevin Steggles:

Peter returns to Maine Road as a West Bromwich Albion player.

BARNES STORMER

Peter Barnes (West Bromwich Albion) v Tottenham, Football League Division One at the Hawthorns, May 2, 1981.

WITH a shuffle of the feet and a shake of the shoulders, Peter Barnes wriggled through the Tottenham defence to score the kind of goal they'll be talking about in the West Midlands for years.

Spurs might have had one eye on the twin towers of Wembley beckoning them to the Cup Final a week later but that shouldn't detract from this brilliant solo effort which left Ricky Villa, Mark Hazard and Don McAllister sprawling in the winger's wake.

Ally Brown had put Albion ahead in the eighth minute before Barnes stormed through ten minutes from the interval.

From a throw in, he took the return from Batson and set off on a mazy dribble like a serpent through sand, finally shaking off Hazard's tackle and wrong-footing McAllister before blasting a left foot shot into the roof of the net.

It was a goal which not only made the fans snatch their breath and inspired Albion to a 4-2 victory, but which also caught the eye of England manager Ron Greenwood, who immediately re-called Peter to his squad against Brazil.

Golden Goal

NEXT WEEK:
● The goal that clinched glory for Liverpool

MATCH WEEKLY

Peter's brilliant solo goal against Tottenham turned out to be his last for Albion.

'Barnes scampered to the near post where, incredibly, full-back Batson spectacularly headed his first League goal in 115 appearances.' [9]

Brendan Batson played a crucial part in this match, being heralded as the star man, and he prevented John Wark from scoring an equaliser shortly after the break. The *Sunday Mirror* reported that soon after Peter ensured a home win: 'Barnes provided the killer touch for Albion's 13th home win of the season after 56 minutes. He popped up on the right wing, cut across two defenders and unleashed a shot that deflected off Terry Butcher to leave Cooper helpless.'

Off the pitch there were reports that Peter put in a transfer request, which it was claimed was turned down by Atkinson. Newspapers also claimed that Peter's form appeared to suffer in the games that followed - a 2-1 defeat at Manchester United and in a 2-1 home win over Sunderland – and as a result it was suggested by journalist Denis Sunley that Peter was to be dropped for a crucial League game with Leeds at Elland Road on April 25. Ron Atkinson was quoted by Sunley: 'After putting in a written transfer request a couple of weeks ago, he has not looked as though he is in the right frame of mind to play for Albion. And, with us entering such an important time in our bid for Europe, I cannot afford to play anyone who is not in the right frame of mind.' [10]

At the time Albion lay third, five points behind second placed Ipswich with leaders Aston Villa nine points clear of Atkinson's team. Leeds were tenth on 41 points, eight points behind Albion. With only two games to play, West Brom knew they couldn't catch either of the teams above them in these days of two points for a win, but any of the four clubs below them could still leapfrog Albion. It was a tense time

and Ron had to ensure his strongest team played, but this seemingly left Peter in the cold. Fortunately for the player the Leeds game was postponed due to poor weather and was rescheduled to take place on May 6, four days after the campaign had been due to end. There's no doubt Peter would have missed the game had it been played as planned but the postponement gave him hope.

Ultimately, Peter played the final two games of the season, even scoring against Spurs on May 2. This became Peter's last competitive goal for Albion as Tottenham were defeated 4-2. Four days later Peter played in a goalless draw at Elland Road. The point was enough to ensure Peter's team finished fourth – Arsenal had leapfrogged them – and qualify for the UEFA Cup, one point ahead of Liverpool. West Brom had also reached the quarter-final of the League Cup where Manchester City defeated them 3-1 in December.

In between the postponed Leeds game and Albion's meeting with Spurs on May 2, came England's fourth World Cup qualifier. This was against Romania at Wembley and Peter had been named in the squad. Peter's older sister Susan was rightly proud of her brother's international recognition: 'We were all so proud. Sadly, Dad was never selected for England, though many people said he should've played, but whenever Peter was picked it meant so much to us all. It was a major honour, not something to take lightly. When he was first picked for England I remember mum putting a giant English flag up in the living room. She was so proud and we watched that game together. We talked about how he was so dedicated. He never went out anywhere and would go to bed at 9 O'clock… doing everything he could to help his career develop.'

While it has often been forgotten in

the years that have followed, in April 1981 Peter's selection for the squad brought much positive coverage his way. The *Daily Mirror*, for example, reported on the hope that Peter would appear and even quoted Manager Greenwood in a manner that suggested the England boss wanted to play in a positive manner: 'The pattern we played when Italy were beaten 2-0 three years ago, with Barnes and Coppell playing wide, was ideal. If we had qualified for Argentina, taken that system there, and it had gone right, others might have copied us... I would love it if we could go back and play it like that again. But Peter got transferred and it affected him. He should have been going forward and getting better.' [11]

Unfortunately, Peter never made it off the bench and England played out a dour goalless draw. This was seen by the British media as an extremely negative performance with some calling for Ron Greenwood to be sacked. Journalist Bob Harris felt Peter would have made a difference, especially as the only player who appeared to make any headway in attack was fellow winger Steve Coppell:

'[Coppell's] efforts on the flank made me wonder just what Peter Barnes might have achieved had he, instead of Terry McDermott, replaced Brooking in the second-half.' [12]

After the international Bob Harris asked Peter for his views and he admitted: 'I had the impression at half-time that I was to go on for the last half-hour and I was desperate to get the chance because I really fancied my chances.'

Over the following month Peter started an international friendly over Brazil which ended in a 1-0 defeat at Wembley and a Home International game with Wales that ended goalless. John Bond, the Manchester City manager, enjoyed Peter's performance against Brazil: 'I thought Barnes had a marvellous match. He was magic.' [13]

Peter also came on as substitute during a 2-1 defeat in a World Cup qualifier against Switzerland, but he was never given much opportunity. This seemed surprising to many fans and the media at the time and added to criticism of Greenwood who, it was felt, was still playing too negatively. After the Switzerland defeat the *Liverpool*

By HARRY MILLER

ENGLAND are ready to wing their way to the World Cup finals. That was the broad hint from manager Ron Greenwood yesterday.

He may announce today that Rumania will be attacked on a wide front, with Steve Coppell and Peter Barnes playing as genuine wingers.

Barnes, brought back for seven minutes against Spain last month and dropped by West Brom last Saturday, is set for a full recall at Wembley tomorrow.

He insists he is in the mood and Greenwood pushed aside mounting injury problems to remind us: "The pattern was played when Italy were beaten 2–0 three years ago, with Barnes and Coppell playing wide. It was ideal.

"If we had qualified for Argentina, taken that system there, and it had gone right, others might have copied us. It is a pattern that is easy for the players to understand. But you can't keep picking people if they are not playing well."

Affected

"At the time we had Kevin Keegan coming back from Germany like a Messiah and setting everyone alight. I would love it if we could go back and play it like that again. But Peter was transferred, and it affected him."

That Wembley win over Italy saw Barnes win the first of his 17 caps with a stunning performance. Shortly afterwards Barnes and Coppell played wide, with Trevor Francis in the middle, as Hungary were beaten 4—1.

It is tempting for Greenwood to try the formation again as England go looking for vital World Cup points.

Barnes, who recently asked West Brom for a transfer, insists: "I'm in the right frame of mind and I feel I'm ready to return.

"If I get the chance to prove myself I've got to take it. I know I've got the ability. I'm 23 now and I know I'm at the crossroads."

Skipper Kevin Keegan

Echo blamed Greenwood and suggested he needed to think about giving Peter more starts, especially in the crucial Hungary game coming on June 6, but the England boss told the media prior to a Home International meeting with Scotland on May 23 that the players had told him: 'that if we were going to keep near the pattern we had decided upon then one of the wingers had to go. I was happy to do that as it is easier to play that way, to compromise and do what everyone else in world football is doing. This is a pattern that suits them.' [14] This seemed ludicrous to some as the manager was, in effect,

saying that some of the players were picking the team, even though results had been poor with England only winning two of the nine games played, with five defeats, between September 1980 and the end of May 1981.

Peter was the winger who was dropped (Steve Coppell retained his place) for the 1-0 defeat to Scotland at Wembley. At the time Peter told the *Daily Mirror*: 'If one winger had to go it was bound to be me, because Steve works harder at the defensive side than I do. I thought I'd played well against Brazil and Wales.' He added: 'I know only one way to play. That is taking on people, getting to the line, and putting the ball over. I still say the game is about skill.' [15] In that article journalist Harry Miller spoke for many fans when he commented: '[Peter] remains adamant at a time when work-rate rather than skill, and resource rather than the way the game is played, have become depressing fashionable again.'

It is worth highlighting that Peter's predecessor at West Brom, Laurie Cunningham, was in a similar position as far as England was concerned. Cunningham had moved to Real Madrid partly because the 1982 World Cup would be played there and he felt the experience would add to his attempts at securing an England place but, with wingers of Peter's and Cunningham's style seemingly out of fashion, the former Albion player had barely been given an opportunity. For some fans Greenwood's left wing should either

Brazil's manager Tele Santana said: "We liked several English players — principally Barnes. He is a player with plenty of ability and vision.

"I saw the last two England matches against Rumania and Spain and I thought England played better against us."

Acclaim

But as the final whistle sounded, the Wembley crowd fed on dismal failure in recent matches, stood to acclaim this England performance.

They were delighted to see an England team they could at last identify with. One with two wingers and an old fashioned centre forward.

One of those wingers, Peter Barnes, was a constant probing menace to the Brazilian defence. He was prompted from midfield by a marvellously inventive Graham Rix.

The attack was constantly supported from the back by an outstanding Bryan Robson and a bold-running Kenny Sansom.

Proud to be English

I FELT proud to be British after the game against Brazil at Wembley.

It was one of the best games I've seen and was full of attacking football. Brazil were back to their best and it was a joy to see our national team playing two wingers, Steve Coppell and Peter Barnes.

Most of all, the fans at Wembley were terrific. The way they applauded and cheered their team on was in great contrast to the last two performances there.

Lee Boyall, Kettering, Northants.

Left: West Brom winger Peter Barnes — thrilled the England fans against Brazil.

MATCH WEEKLY

have seen Peter play or Cunningham. If Peter couldn't play then Cunningham ought to be in and vice versa.

Greenwood's decision not to use two wingers added to the unsettled feeling Peter had in May 1981. He felt he had a lot to offer but football at the highest level seemed to be moving away from the notion of using flair players, wide on the wing. Peter: 'The burglary had unsettled me, and a move seemed the only option. Before the second season at West Brom came to an end John Bond wanted to sign me. A return to Manchester City then would've been perfect. Dad was still working at Maine Road of course and he told me that Bondy was interested. It was a bit embarrassing that messages were coming to me through Dad.

'I received a call from Bond where he introduced himself and said that he had told my dad he wanted to sign me. He talked about what he wanted to do and asked me to be patient, but I was still a bit bitter about City selling me in the first place. I didn't know what to make of it but a move back to Manchester would've been good for me and my wife. The problem was that City had let me down and I wanted it all sorting out quickly. I didn't want to wait and I didn't want promises to be broken.

'Unfortunately, West Brom wanted cash rather than player exchanges or anything like that. They'd paid a lot of money for me and, with transfer fees still at high levels compared to only a couple of years earlier, they needed the right money to do their own squad changes. Bondy kept offering different players in part-exchange but they didn't want that. Under Bond City were playing attacking football and I wanted that, but the deal wasn't going anywhere. Manchester United were also interested at that time. I'm not quite certain why that didn't progress, but I think it was a similar situation with player exchanges and so on. I know some of the newspapers tried to pass it all off as a battle between City and United for me but, as the player involved, it was deeply unsettling. It's a game to some in the media but for those whose futures were at stake it was serious.'

According to journalist Peter Gardner West Brom wanted £1m for Peter: 'John Bond has run into a £1m stumbling block in his bid to sign a first recruit in his Manchester City staff strengthening… "If that's the case, I think he's priced the player right out of the market." Said Bond as the Blues returned to Manchester today following last night's FA Cup Final replay defeat at Wembley. "I don't think any club in the country would be prepared to pay that much for him, and in that event, Peter Barnes could well have to stay with Albion for the rest of his career," added Bond.' [16]

Peter: 'Once that deal fell through I was happy to stay at Albion. Ron Atkinson was a great manager to play for and things were going well on the pitch, but then Ron started talking to United about being Dave Sexton's replacement.'

In 1984 Atkinson admitted that the first contact he had about the Manchester United manager's job came in May 1981, and that by the time of the European Cup final on May 27 he had formally applied for the role. [17] He also claimed he'd been approached by Manchester City the previous October about joining the Blues. Peter: 'Ron left West Brom at the start of June. He took Mick Brown with him and then you start hearing rumours of who is coming in as manager, but also which players were leaving. Bryan Robson was supposedly going, and I started hoping that Ron might take me. Ronnie Allen, a former West Brom player, came in as manager – he was a complete contrast to Ron. Ron was flamboyant, loved having a laugh and a joke

I should've done the same. It's easy to say that now but I do wonder what would've happened if I'd stayed.'

While Gary Owen had a good career at Albion and enjoyed his time there, he does feel that Ron's departure changed life significantly for the club: 'Where it all went wrong was when the manager left. Mick Brown, Ron's assistant went, as did other backroom staff. Robson and Moses followed and suddenly it's not a team that's building with the aim of winning something. I remember Ron saying if he could transport the entire West Brom team to Old Trafford he would've done. He knew what he had.'

For Peter the summer of 1981 eventually saw him move north but, instead of joining one of the Manchester clubs, he moved to Yorkshire: 'Out of the blue Leeds United showed interest. I got a call from Allan Clarke, the Leeds manager. He told me that West Brom had given him permission to speak with me. He knew that I was unsettled and, because of all the talk about signing for United or City, he decided to act. Leeds was my second club – going right back to boyhood and the trials there – and it would mean returning north. Eddie Gray, one of my heroes, was still playing at Elland Road.

'It seemed perfect.'

with you and was a great guy to be around, while Ronnie was the opposite. Quite serious and dour. An old school manager. I just couldn't hit it off with him. I knew he'd had a good management career at Bilbao and in Portugal, Greece and Saudi Arabia, but it was difficult for me. The arrival of any new manager, no matter who it is, can be unsettling and so Ron's departure meant it was time to leave.

'In hindsight, perhaps I should have stayed longer at the Hawthorns. Gary Owen stayed about five years and, maybe,

1 'Back for Barnes', *Daily Mirror*, August 14, 1980, 28.
2 'Love wins the day for Barnes', *Daily Mirror*, September 3, 1980, 28.
3 'Hell raisers', *Daily Mirror*, December 1, 1980, 30.
4 'Barnes nip', *The People*, December 28, 1980, 47.
5 'Peter has a Barnes stormer', *Sunday Mirror*, December 28, 1980, 46.
6 Ron Atkinson with Joe Melling, *United to Win* (London: Sidgwick & Jackson, 1984), 56.
7 'Peter Barnes makes a plea for wingers', *Aberdeen Press and Journal*, March 28, 1981, 20.
8 'Batson star in great win', *Express & Star*, April 6, 1981.
9 'Ron: "Bet on Villa"', *Sunday Mirror*, April 5, 1981, 47.
10 'Albion drop winger Barnes', *Express & Star*, April 24, 1981.
11 'Ron's wide boys', *Daily Mirror*, April 28, 1981, 28.
12 'Knives are out, but Greenwood stays on', *Newcastle Evening Chronicle*, April 30, 1981, 28.
13 'Bond bids to land Barnes', *Manchester Evening News*, May 13, 1981.
14 'England desperate for victory over Scotland', *Aberdeen Press and Journal*, May 23, 1981, 18.
15 'Peter will keep his old style', *Daily Mirror*, May 29, 1981, 32.
16 'Barnes "priced out of market"', *Manchester Evening News*, May 15, 1981.
17 Ron Atkinson with Joe Melling, *United to Win* (London: Sidgwick & Jackson, 1984), 66-69.

244

Chapter Fifteen
LEEDS, LEEDS, LEEDS

> The Leeds United manager, Allan Clarke, has made a £750,000 offer for West Bromwich's England winger, Peter Barnes. Albion have accepted the bid, but Barnes appears to be set on rejoining Manchester City. He said yesterday 'Out of courtesy, I'll speak to Leeds, but the only reason I want to leave Albion is to go back to City.'

Leeds United, managed by Allan Clarke since September 1980, had drifted somewhat since the departure of Jimmy Armfield in 1978. Armfield had taken the club to the 1975 European Cup final, but many analysing Leeds suggested the club had never quite been the same since Don Revie left to become England manager in 1974. Whatever the truth, the appointment of Clarke had been viewed by many as a return to the days of Revie, though respected journalist Frank Taylor felt differently: '[Clarke] faces an uphill fight. These are desperate days for the Elland Road club.' [1]

Clarke himself had told the media that he would win a major honour within three years. Something journalist Tony Hardisty found hard to accept. Writing a year after Clarke's appointment he commented about the trophy claim: 'Confidence or lunacy? There were many who shook their heads and suggested that the 34-year-old might

well have bitten off more than he could possibly chew. "If he's as good as he talks he will do a good job – but I doubt it. The chances are that he's nothing more than a smart mouth. Time will tell." One wise old manager told me.' [2]

By the 1981 close season Clarke seemed ready and able to bring in several new players to shape the team the way he wanted. One of the players he wanted was Peter: 'Allan Clarke met me in the Manchester Post House at Northenden, along with a guy called Martin Wilkinson. Wilkinson had never played professional football but he had been Clarke's assistant at Barnsley. I had a lot of respect for Clarke as a player with Leeds and England, and he told me that he was planning to create another Revie-like era for Leeds. He told me Joe Jordan was coming back.'

Jordan was at Manchester United and Leeds did make attempts to sign him but he eventually moved on to Milan that summer.

Peter was also told that Tony Woodcock was going to join from Cologne and others, including Frank Gray, would be purchased. Peter: 'It all sounded positive and he told me that Leeds had money to spend and would be bringing in several key players.

'He talked about the men on the board and the money they had and that they were prepared to spend. I was thinking that this was great. Leeds made their offer and I joined the club. Frank Gray signed as well and Kenny Burns arrived, so he'd bought two defenders and me. The names mentioned to improve his midfield and

attack did not arrive and that was it. We needed a striker more than anything else. There was talk of Andy Gray signing – if that had happened then we'd have done well and I think I'd have played well with him, but it didn't. We did have Derek Parlane and he was a good, Scottish striker but he was having a few injury problems when the 1981-82 season started which added to the issues in attack.

Demonstrating the growth in transfer fees during this period, Leeds paid £930,000 (including tax and levies) for Peter. This was more than double Leeds' previous highest transfer fee paid – that was £400,000 for Alan Curtis in May 1979. Peter remained Leeds' record buy for almost nine years with the £1m transfer of John Lukic in May 1990 overtaking Peter's fee.

Peter: 'We didn't get much advice at the time and I think my heart ruled my head. I wanted to move back north and I saw the club as the Leeds of old where one of my heroes

Leeds nip in for Barnes!

LEEDS UNITED have lifted £750,0000 England winger Peter Barnes from under the noses of his hard-up hesitating former club Manchester City.

The deal I can reveal will go through this morning with the highly gifted 23-year-old ex-City idol beco record signin

What was to be purely call by Barne turned into a coup for you boss Allan Cla the West Bron covered a set-u ing with the salary which y premier club w ing.

The Main e minded Barnes, stand, only dec give Leeds the o out of deference determined Clark

"The only re want to leave Wes is because I want back to Manchest

By BOB RUSSELL

insisted at the weekend. But with City unable to up their bid beyond £650,000 and Leeds agreeing terms with Albion's new boss Ron Allen events suddenly took

PETER BARNES

gress and I'm confident of having Frank in my team for Saturday's friendly against Bohemi r i e n d l y   a g a i n s t Bohemians in Dublin," said Atkinson

SHOWDOWN

By PETER COOPER

A FINANCIAL showdown — even a power struggle—was last night's new backdrop to the race for Peter Barnes.

Manager Allan Clarke withdrew from Leeds United's pre-season tournament trip to Spain, to win 48 hours' grace, barely one jump ahead of the England winger's former club Manchester City.

Leeds claim they have Barnes on ice. West Brom, who now accept they will not get £750,000 cash, are said to be willing to help Leeds.

Clarke in fight to sign Barnes

He said: " I think Peter will sign for them to-morrow, though I am keeping John Bond in the picture following City's earlier interest."

club with average gates of only 21,000 should realistically be seeking three players for that much money.

Clarke looks certain to bump heads with chairman Manny Cussins.

● New manager Emlyn Hughes makes his debut w i t h Rotherham United's Third Division champions at Burton Albion tonight.

● Stoke City midfielder

September 5 1981 – Leeds v Wolves: Peter takes on Geoff Palmer with Ken Hibbitt looking on.

Eddie Gray played, overlooking any doubts, issues or potential flaws. The connection of those early years of my footballing life was what I considered, not the reality of the present day.'

'I remember Barnsey going to Leeds,' says Gary Owen. 'It was for a record amount but I remember thinking that it was the wrong move. He told me he was off to Elland Road and he asked me if I fancied going there because they'd asked him about me, like Ron Atkinson had asked me to put in a good word with Peter in 1979. I thought about it. City were interested too, but I stayed at the Hawthorns.'

As Gary suggested, this was not the transfer that a traditional attack-minded winger, who felt he could still have a role to play in England's World Cup ambitions, should have made. Peter: 'I remember thinking "why had he bought me?" because he had Carl Harris, the outside right for Wales, and Arthur Graham, Scottish international winger who could play left or right. It didn't make sense. Why buy another winger? I was the Leeds United record signing but he didn't need me. I was so desperate to move north that I didn't think logically and everything he had told me about the plans he had, the players he was bringing in and so on, seemed perfect, but it wasn't. It never happened.'

Despite his misgivings Peter looked forward, determined to settle at Elland Road: 'My debut was at Swansea, who had just been promoted under John Toshack. There was a lot of interest in how 'little' Swansea would fare against 'mighty' Leeds and about six thousand Leeds fans travelled down for it. Before kick-off I walked down the tunnel in my suit just to get a feel for the ground and the day. All I could see were Leeds fans all in place, making noise. It was about 1.30pm and the rest of the ground was mostly empty but the away sections were packed. The noise was unbelievable and I felt fantastic. What a club to join – that's what I felt at that moment. At full time I felt something completely different! It turned out to be a bad day and we lost 5-1 with Bob Latchford scoring a hat trick for Swansea. They topped the table that night and the story of that day was all over the press.'

After the Swansea defeat Clarke had dropped his new signing Frank Gray with reports saying that Gray had been told that he'd have to fight for his place. [3] The suggestion being that the Leeds manager held him responsible for the 5-1 defeat.

Peter retained his place and against Everton at Elland Road he produced the cross that led to Arthur Graham scoring a 37th minute goal for the club. Sadly, the game ended 1-1. A 3-0 home win over Wolves followed, again with Graham scoring all Leeds' goals. Clarke was full of praise for Graham at this time: '[he] is marvellously quick and skilful. Jock Stein must be kicking himself for leaving him out of the Scotland squad after what he saw against Everton. Arthur was head and shoulders the best player on the field.' [4]

Clarke also had some positive words about Peter: 'Barnes is one of the game's most exciting talents. To see him cross the ball perfectly when he's going at speed is something special.' [5]

Sadly, the second away game of the season saw Coventry City trounce Clarke's side 4-0. Leeds were already in the relegation zone and were clearly lacking

Peter, with a little twist, sends Coventry's Danny Thomas spiralling, September 1981.

something. Assistant manager Martin Wilkinson went public and claimed that Peter was mainly to blame, lambasting the player to journalists. [6]

It was totally unprofessional for Wilkinson to do this and, understandably, Peter spoke with a journalist at the West Midlands' based *Express & Star* who allowed him to get his side of the story across. The newspaper reported: 'Things have not gone well since my move to Yorkshire. It appears the manager is putting all the blame on me for our 4-0 defeat at Coventry on Saturday. I am being played out of position at the moment – they want me to play deep in midfield. That is not my game. I need to be out on the wing – that is where I can do most damage. But despite these problems, I am staggered to find out that Clarke wants to let me go. He knew when he bought me what sort of player I am. He knows my strengths and weaknesses, and I would have thought he would have played me to my strengths. I want this whole thing sorted out before we go any further. I hope this whole thing is not going to turn sour on me – otherwise I would never have moved from Albion.' [7]

The truth was that Leeds were missing an out-and-out striker. Andy Gray had been expected to sign, according to Peter, but Leeds wouldn't meet their asking price. Peter could be blamed as much as Wilkinson or Clarke wanted but until they could sign a true centre-forward then the side was bound to suffer in attack. It was a point journalist Tony Hardisty recognised and commented on after the Coventry defeat: 'A target man in the mould of Peter Withe or David Cross is the critical piece of the jigsaw Clarke needs so desperately to make use of the Barnes-Graham service.' [8]

The Monday following the embarrassing Coventry defeat, there were clear the air talks at Leeds according to the *Express &*

Star: 'Clarke and Wilkinson spoke to all the players after Saturday's setback. "I'm sorry Peter got the brunt of it after the match. But he must take his share along with the others and we must take ours – we are all in this together."' Wilkinson was the man quoted in the article and he added: 'It would be suicide to buy a player and then try to make him do things he can't. There is no way we want to make Peter Barnes a defensive player. We want him to make more positive runs into the box – but he feels he is lacking in a bit of confidence at the moment.' Peter disputed that he was lacking confidence: 'Since I came to Leeds I have played four games and in two of them I have played well. So many managers and coaches talk about work rate – but that's what is killing the game.'

Peter was already rueing his move from Albion and ended his interview thinking about the team he had left behind: 'Just pass on my best wishes to all the Albion lads. My thoughts will be with them.' This led to Peter being fined £750 for making disparaging remarks about the club.

According to the *Guardian* in 2009, Wilkinson publicly criticised Peter at other times that season. Wilkinson is alleged to have said: 'We are not asking Peter to run his blood to water, but we do want to see him get a bit of a sweat occasionally.' [9]

In 2021 Peter's view of this time is that Wilkinson was not supportive of his style of play at all and that the assistant manager's own background and lack of professional football experience was an issue: 'He didn't know how to handle professional players and we had doubts over his knowledge and experience. In my career I worked with many coaches and, even if I didn't like what they were doing, such as Malcolm Allison, I couldn't argue that they didn't have any coaching experience at the highest level. With Wilkinson it was different.

'When you're an attacking winger and in a team that's losing games the pressure on you increases,' says Peter. 'We're constantly trying to get the ball and then if we did and it was fired across to me the expectation would increase. Every mistake gets noticed and you're the one who has failed. When it was one on one that was fine – I was happy with that. I had confidence that I could win in any duel like that but when you're losing the opposition would tighten up and so you'd suddenly find there'd be two players

on you. Sometimes three. This added pressure brought more frustration and if the ball was taken from me then it'd be "oh, he's lost it!" When that happens when you're in a struggling team it's so much worse than in an attack-minded, challenging team because you knew that you'd be under pressure for some time. The mentality of a struggling team is so different from a team that's used to winning. At Leeds that season we were not very good at keeping the ball and so we were in a downward spiral rather than an upward one.

'Sometimes I wouldn't get a touch of the ball for twenty minutes because the opposition would have all the play. I know some will say that I'd cost all that money and so on, but it wasn't just about me. The mood was wrong and the team suffered. I really felt for the fans. I'd wanted to play for Leeds for so long. I admired the club in lots of ways and wanted things to work perfectly for the fans.

'We used to have a meeting every Monday in the boardroom at Elland Road with Allan Clarke. We'd discuss the previous game. Clarke would have a board up and would be going through everything that had gone wrong. It felt like a grilling every week to us players.

'We'd end training each day with a five-a-side. Clarke would play and he'd also bring out this yellow jersey. The idea was whoever had had a bad game would wear the yellow jersey. Clarke would insist: "you had a crap game, so you're in the yellow!" Then as we played the five-a-side he'd be calling for the ball all the time. He wouldn't leave the training ground until he'd scored a goal and then celebrate! It was like that teacher played by Brian Glover in Kes and he'd run down the touchline celebrating "Clarkie's done it again. Never leaves you!" Then it would be game over and back in the changing rooms.'

'I desperately wanted my Leeds move to work out. From a young age Leeds was a team that meant a great deal to me. I idolised their players and, after Manchester City, I saw them as my team. I wanted to join them as a boy and I'd always been impressed with the club. Their fanbase was impressive – always passionate, always significant – and at the time I joined them they were truly a giant of the game. It felt like the sort of club where fans would love my normal style of attacking play – and I think they would – but from the start it was clear that I was not going to get the freedom I needed. It was so different to my thoughts before joining them. I felt sorry for the fans. They deserved more than they got from the Leeds I joined in 1981. This was a major club that needed success. I know people often look back on the Leeds team of the late Sixties and early Seventies and talk of a negative approach but it wasn't like that. They had some hard players, but with people like Eddie Gray they had a great attacking nature too. How I wish I'd been able to play in a Leeds team like that. That's what the fans deserved but instead they had a frustratingly negative, defensive Leeds in 1981. That was a major shame and something I felt awful about. Football is all about the fans and their enjoyment – we didn't give them any enjoyment and I desperately wanted it to be different.

'When I joined Leeds they were still loyal to Don Revie. His influence was still there. I don't remember them singing his favourite "Bye, Bye Blackbird" but we did play carpet bowls in the long lounge at Elland Road. That was Don. He did it with England too – throw the jack, then the bowl…. All quite serious too. Then there was Bingo. We were all sat there with our cards: "is it a line or a full house we call House for?" All traditional northern entertainment I guess, but that's what we

did. We were mostly working class lads who would've been away with our parents playing games like this, so it was all part of our culture. It did take your mind off the football and it did help build a spirit between us I guess – unless you were the one who never got a full house! Though it does seem so strange now.'

Many of the protocols and procedures in place at Leeds during Peter's playing days had been developed or passed down from Don Revie's hugely successful period there but as time passed by many of these activities faded. Maybe it was when Leeds lost the direct connection with Don and his former players that caused the club's decline. Peter: 'Leeds should have won more trophies – even under Don – than they actually did. They were so unlucky. There was that European Cup final against Bayern Munich at Paris. Bayern were reigning European champions and won 2-0 but that Leeds team was incredible. We should never forget that Leeds were only the second English team, after Manchester United, to reach the final of the European Cup. People think Europe's all about United and Liverpool but Leeds were there before Liverpool. They were just unfortunate to come up against Bayern. Lorimer had a goal disallowed that shouldn't have been. The referee had awarded the goal and then Franz Beckenbaeur argued and the ref disallowed it! Bremner had almost scored before that. We also shouldn't forget that both Leeds and Manchester City had both won major European trophies before Liverpool – that's often overlooked when people suggest Liverpool had a European history but City and Leeds don't!'

During the opening months of 1981-82 further struggles occurred, including a 4-0 defeat at Manchester City on September 23. Peter: 'It would be wrong to say I didn't leave Maine Road that night wondering "what if?" about John Bond's interest in me only a few months earlier.'

As the season progressed Leeds' attacking problems were clear and Peter was moved further forward: 'I was a winger, not a main striker. Every team needs a good striker and we had no one fit who could do it consistently. When Clarke told me he was playing me there I couldn't believe it. He tried me as an inside left and kept putting me in different positions. I was an outside left – I could play as an outside right but I was no good with my back to the goal. My skills were elsewhere and I completely lost my confidence. I was Leeds' most expensive signing and so much was expected of me, but I was out of position, we were losing and my confidence just went. It drained away. Our season went from bad to worse and I couldn't do anything to change it.'

By the time Leeds faced Bobby Robson's impressive Ipswich team in the League Cup on October 7, stories emerged that Clarke was preparing to sell Arthur Graham to bring in Andy Gray from Wolves. Leeds clearly needed a target man but selling Graham, a hero to many fans, was not going to be taken well. Inevitably, the Leeds fans made their feelings known during the Ipswich game. The match ended in a 1-0 defeat but, as far as fans were concerned, the result was more of a side show for the main event which was to let Clarke know the strength of their feeling. Journalist Mike Green described the scenes: 'Leeds United supporters let manager Allan Clarke know in no uncertain terms last night that they don't want Andy Gray at the club if it means Arthur Graham leaving. Clarke has offered Graham in part exchange for the £1,000,000 striker, but "we'd rather keep Arthur Graham" was the chant of the fans throughout the League Cup-tie with Ipswich. The former Aberdeen winger was cheered every time he touched the ball while Gray's name was the target for ridicule. Not surprisingly, Graham responded to all this hero worship

January 1982 and Peter plays for Leeds Reserves against Derby County in front of 150 fans at Elland Road.

by turning in a fine display. With England winger Peter Barnes also in impish form and veteran Eddie Gray a commanding figure in midfield, Leeds did not look like a side destined to have a hard time this winter. Certainly, it was hard to believe that 20 clubs separate Ipswich at the top of the First Division from Leeds at the bottom.' [10]

As Peter tried to settle into life at Elland Road he continued to think about his international career and was hopeful of having a place in Ron Greenwood's World Cup 1982 squad. In November England were due to play Hungary in their qualification group and as part of the build up to that the *Daily Star* compiled a World Cup Dossier of players they believed should be in contention. Inevitably Peter was analysed, with ratings given for Skill, Effectiveness and Competitiveness. Overall, Peter scored 25, which was higher than most other players including, for example, Bryan Robson, Steve Coppell, Mick Mills, Russell Osman, Kenny Sansom and Dave Watson. Peter had been assessed by the newspaper during his Leeds 1-0 home win over Notts County on November 7. Comments from the newspaper's assessor included: 'Barnes's close control was superb and his crosses into the box were generally accurate and well timed… Ran defender Tristan Benjamin dizzy and was involved in the build-up that led to the only goal of the game… Can rarely have shown more appetite for the ball, although he did quieten down in the last 15 minutes.' [11]

Despite the positive coverage Peter was not selected for the England-Hungary squad with Aston Villa's Tony Morley taking his place. Peter knew that Morley had enjoyed a good season so far and recognised that, no matter what efforts he made, it was difficult to shine in a struggling Leeds side. He publicly wished Morley well and the Villa man made his international debut,

coming on as substitute: 'England qualified for the Spain World Cup and, after that night, I felt it was going to be me or Tony in contention,' remembers Peter. 'It was like when we all thought it was me or Laurie Cunningham for the Euro squad in 1980. In the end neither of us went and… I think you can guess what happened in 1982. I felt sorry for Morley. He'd had a good season with Villa and, as a pro, I wanted him to do well. Obviously, I wanted to be in the squad and to play but I wanted the best for every England player.

'When I played for England there were no cliques in the dressing room, not like at Leeds where certain players stayed together in the dressing room. Players like Kevin Keegan treated us all the same. He was a great role model and helped some of us younger players, but he also helped the older guys too. Even when he was European Footballer of the Year there was no cockiness about him and that's what I liked about him. I loved being around players like that with England.'

It looked as if Peter's chance of making the World Cup squad had gone for good: 'As the season progressed my mood worsened.

Seemingly I'd dropped out of the England squad and I'd signed for a man who had been a great player but was not the best manager, if I'm honest. Allan Clarke tried – I know he did – but I'd come from West Brom, who'd had Ron Atkinson, and City with Tony Book. It just wasn't right and I kept thinking back to those players who were supposed to sign but they never came.'

In November the victory over Notts County lifted Leeds to 16th and in January a 2-0 win over Swansea gave the club their highest position of the season – 14th, but the struggles were never far away. Peter: 'We were heading for relegation but it was tight with three clubs – us, West Brom and Stoke - able to still go down on the day we played our last game. Of all the places to go

it was the Hawthorns against West Brom on a Tuesday night. If Leeds won then we'd be safe and West Brom would be more or less down, though they had another game against Stoke to play. So it was all a bit messy.

'I was unhappy at Leeds because I had been played out of position, dropped from the team and the arrivals Clarke had promised never materialised. We'd taken Frank Worthington on loan for a few months and he'd scored a few goals which had helped lift us – there was a 4-1 win at Villa and a 3-3 draw at home to Birmingham and Frank had scored a couple in each of those games. We were eighteenth after winning 2-1 at home to Brighton on the Saturday, then it was West Brom on the Tuesday. I thought that with Frank in the team we'd do enough to survive, but the day before the game there was a League disciplinary meeting and Frank got a one game ban for reaching twenty disciplinary points. It was poor luck.'

PETER
BARNES
Leeds Utd.

What made the ban worse as far as Leeds were concerned was the fact that several players who had reached the twenty disciplinary points mark at other clubs escaped with warnings, including Terry Fenwick at QPR who would've missed the FA Cup final had he been banned as Worthington had. Leeds' assistant manager Martin Wilkinson commented: 'The decision seems a bit harsh because Worthington hasn't got a bad disciplinary record over the years. He did not make a personal appearance but sent a letter asking for

Peter races past Sammy Lee as Leeds take on Liverpool in February 1982.

leniency and pointing out that he had taken a whole season to reach 29 points with us and Birmingham.' [12]

'Playing West Brom added to the feelings I had,' remembers Peter. 'I know they were struggling too but being there for our last game made me think about everything that had happened since I'd left the Hawthorns. We knew we had to win but we were losing 2-0 – Cyrille Regis and the former City player Steve Mackenzie scored. There were only a few minutes to go when things turned nasty.'

Five minutes before the end of the match Leeds fans managed to pull down an 8ft iron fence as they tried to force their way on to the pitch. They were frustrated with the way the season had gone and, according to newspapers of the period, they sought to invade the pitch: 'Hundreds of youths pelted police with missiles. Officers responded with baton charging – pouring over the flattened fence and forcing back the fans.' [13] Superintendent John Mellor, who was in charge of match day policing, claimed every member of his 100 strong force had been injured by fans, mostly by objects thrown at the police from the terraces. In total 46 arrests were made. [14]

Peter hated the way this day developed: 'We could see what was happening with the fans. Mounted police were there and it was all turning sour. My move to Leeds had been the worst move I could've made and the scenes unfolding really affected me. I understood and could feel the frustration of the fans but to see this conflict going on really upset me. I knew the fans were frustrated and I knew they wouldn't do anything silly to us the players, but their actions typified the mood around the club at the time. It felt like we'd all lost

Frank Gray watches with interest as Peter Barnes features in the action against Stoke City in the home game at Elland Road.

something. My world caved in that day. Being at the Hawthorns added to it. I'd gone back to where I'd had two good years – I only left because we'd had the break-in then Ron had moved on. My England career seemed to be stuttering – this was a World Cup year too! My team was about to be relegated and I was unhappy with the way things were turning out. I had no idea what to do. I felt angry at the promises that hadn't been fulfilled and I felt absolutely sick. It was as if I'd been shot. It just hit me! It was heartbreaking.

'The mood in the dressing room was flat. I was stunned. I'd never, ever thought that any side I'd played for would get relegated, but it was happening. All our heads were down. Someone brought a pot of tea in and said "Come on lads, get a cup of tea inside you." We had a lovely trainer

called Barry Murphy who had come from Barnsley with Clarke and Wilkinson. He tried to get us all going again. He was a proper, track-suited trainer and he kept trying but it was too late. We could hear the fans outside. We didn't know what was going on but you could hear the noise and a few sirens. It was awful.

'I felt hard done to. I know I was the big signing that season but I felt that Allan Clarke had let us all down. All the players. The mood was not good. It was Trevor Cherry's testimonial year and Trevor was a lovely fella. We all liked Trevor and I got on well with him. He'd been Leeds' captain for a few years and was well respected within the dressing room but Clarke took the captaincy off him and gave it to Kenny Burns within a month of Burns signing from Nottingham Forest. Regardless of whether Burns was a good captain or not, a move like that can upset the dressing room. Trevor Cherry was a legend at Leeds by this time – and deservedly so – so you don't go taking the captaincy off someone like that who lived and breathed the club, knowing everything about it. Not for a new signing. Decisions like that have a big impact and I don't think it's any coincidence that we struggled that season.'

Burns had been made captain by Clarke almost immediately on his arrival. [15] Decisions like that affected Peter: 'I think all players like to trust their manager. If he appears to treat everyone with respect and fairly then you are happier. If you're happy then it improves the whole team and morale is good. Seeing how that captaincy was changed had an impact on me. It may have affected others either consciously or sub consciously too. You can't help thinking "well, if he's done that to him, what will he do to me? I've not been here as long; I'm not a Leeds legend. Will I be cast aside?" It was tough. If you like the manager and he's fair with the squad then you'll give him an extra twenty percent. I loved playing for Big Ron at West Brom because he was positive and understood what each player gave. A manager has to know his players. I didn't think we had that at Leeds in 1981-82.

'My confidence drained away off the pitch and then of course on the pitch we were losing games, so that caused more confidence to drain away. Then I was played out of position at times, so the drain on my confidence continues. It goes on and on – that's when a good manager acts. That's when a good manager takes you to one side and gives you a pep talk. A bad manager takes a different approach and stories can get in the papers too.'

A week after the season had ended in relegation for Leeds, Peter suddenly felt he had an opportunity to show what he was really capable of when Ron Greenwood included him in a provisional forty man squad for the World Cup. This would be whittled down through a series of four games over a two week period, starting with a friendly against Holland at Wembley on May 25. A Home International against Scotland at Hampden Park and further friendlies with Iceland at Reykjavik and Finland in Helsinki would follow: 'I knew my form wasn't great. It was a struggle at relegated Leeds but I was included in the provisional squad and joined the rest of the players at training. Ron told me that I'd be playing in the game with Holland and I knew this was my big chance. I couldn't wait.

'In the lead up to the match we were training at London Colney and the squad was split into two teams for a game. I put everything into it. I knew what I needed to do and at one point I had the ball. I dodged four tackles and then I dummied another player. I hit the ball from about 25 yards out and it flew past Peter Shilton into the top corner. I was really pleased with that but as I moved I realised I'd pulled my left calf. It was agony and I had to hobble off. We were playing the next day and I had to say to Ron Greenwood that I couldn't start.'

Journalist Bob Harris had seen the incident and described the scene in a newspaper article exactly as Peter remembers it. Harris added: 'It was ironical that [Peter] should suffer just at the moment he was poised to return to the international scene against Holland at Wembley tonight.' [16]

The injury meant Peter was dropped to the bench, although even that seemed to be an unwise decision by the manager, and he came on as substitute, as had Graham Rix. England won 2-0 with goals from Mariner and Woodcock. Peter was still struggling with his leg and was unable to achieve much in the game. Bob Harris reported: 'Barnes had a token seven minute spell in place of Mariner. It was hardly enough time to make him a serious challenger for Spain.'[17] Peter ended up being sent home to receive treatment after the game and missed the match with Scotland the following Saturday. As so many international games were scheduled for May and early June, Peter had little opportunity to regain full fitness and show what he was truly capable of again.

Despite being in Greenwood's squad for the friendlies with Iceland and Finland, Peter never played another minute of international football for Greenwood, missing out when the manager announced his World Cup squad at the end of that week. 'Ron was going to phone me and, although I was hopeful, I knew what was coming,' says Peter. 'I remember the call: "Peter, it's Ron Greenwood here." We exchanged pleasantries and then he said:

"Peter, you were really unlucky pulling your calf and missing out on starting the Holland game. The way Leeds have struggled this year has caused you to lose confidence and I know Allan Clarke has had you playing outside of your natural position. He's probably not the right man to be playing for." He told me he wasn't taking me and then added: "I've got some advice for you – Get yourself away from Leeds as soon as possible! The move hasn't done you any good." He was a nice man and it felt good to know he was offering this advice, though I was upset that I wasn't going to Spain.'

Journalists were surprised with some of Greenwood's final selections, with Bob Harris writing: 'England manager Ron Greenwood is going to Spain without a left winger. Naming his final squad of 22 for Spain, he decided to do without both Leeds' Peter Barnes and Tony Morley of Aston Villa.'[18] Ron Greenwood told the media

BARNES WAITS IN THE WINGS!

RON WILL WAIT FOR INJURED BARNES

By HARRY MILLER

RON GREENWOOD has delayed naming his England team to give Peter Barnes a chance to claim a place in Spain.

All the signs pointed that way after the Leeds winger suffered a slight hamstring in training.

He spent the afternoon having treatment and Greenwood waits until this morning to announce the side to play Holland

By FRANK CLOUGH

PETER BARNES is ready to crash the pain barrier tonight in a bid for a World Cup spot.

England's forgotten man showed flashes of his most dynamic form yesterday during the final training session for the Wembley clash against Holland. But then he pulled up with a thigh injury.

Even though Ron Greenwood had 25 players in his squad, he immediately decided against naming his line-up until later today – a fair clue that Barnes is in the forefront of his selection thinking.

Cold

"I'll name the side in the morning," he said. "Peter's injury doesn't look too bad and Graham Rix has also come into consideration after training this morning."

Barnes has been out in the cold for 12 months

since his transfer from West Brom to Leeds. But he shrugged off the heavy strapping on his thigh as "precautionary" and said: "I don't think it's too serious, but I'll have to wait and see if there's any overnight reaction."

Forgotten man on World Cup drive

BARNES ... hoping

And the 24-year-old added: "I'm running out of time and I would desperately like the chance to show I can still do it.

"If Barnes can get through a fitness test this morning, I'm sure he will play.

Type

The Dutch, beaten finalists in the last two World Cups, should provide interesting opposition, even though they failed to qualify

258

WONDER WINGER!

PETER BARNES

Captured in superb action, Peter is one of the country's finest touchline raiders. With wingplay a fast disappearing part of our game, it is a tremendous sight to see Peter in full flight ... weaving his way past defenders, with incredible close control. He's certainly a big favourite with ROY OF THE ROVERS readers and that's why he's featured in Roy's Quiz ... inside!

that he had selected Graham Rix for the left wing but most journalists pointed out that the truth was that England were not going to play with wide men and that the style of play was more like Alf Ramsey's 'wingless wonders'.

In 1984 Ron Greenwood explained that he had changed England's tactics when he selected Rix during the 1981-82 season: 'Rix told me he didn't like playing wide and forward on the left, so he was accommodated in an orthodox role in midfield on that side.' [19] That ultimately was

the reason why neither Morley nor Peter were to go to Spain. Greenwood, of course, gave a different view as to why he didn't pick Peter for the World Cup: 'Barnes, sadly, did not keep going. Poor Peter seemed to get knocked sideways when he left Manchester City. He was a Manchester lad, through and through, and had he stayed in his home town I think he would have got better and better. He needed people to believe in him. His ability was given its point by confidence, and when he lost his conviction he was not the same player. It

Super Focus

PETER BARNES
Leeds United

FULL NAME: Peter Simon Barnes
BIRTHPLACE: Manchester
BIRTHDATE: June 10, 1957
HEIGHT: 5ft 10ins
WEIGHT: 11st 7lbs
MARRIED: Yes, to Alison
CHILDREN: No, but I have a beautiful Doberman Pincher, Heidi
CAR: Datsun
PREVIOUS CLUBS: Manchester City, WBA
JOB OR TRADE BEFORE TURNING PRO: None
NICKNAME: Barnsey
FAVOURITE NEWSPAPER: Daily Mail
FAVOURITE PLAYER: George Best
A PLAYER FOR THE FUTURE: Terry Connor (Leeds)
FAVOURITE OTHER TEAM: Barcelona
FOOTBALL HERO OF CHILDHOOD: George Best, Denis Law, Colin Bell, Mike Summerbee, Francis Lee.

Peter Barnes' England debut against Italy at Wembley four years ago.

Harvey Smith

Terry Connor (Leeds)

FAVOURITE OTHER SPORT: Golf, tennis, riding
OTHER SPORTS PERSON YOU MOST ADMIRE: Harvey Smith — good character
YOUR BEST EVER ALL-TIME XI: Banks, Wilson, Beckenbauer, J. Charlton, Cooper, di Stefano, Hartford, Kempes, Law, B. Charlton, Best.
MOST MEMORABLE MATCH: My England debut v Italy, November 1977
BIGGEST DISAPPOINTMENT: None to date
FRIENDLIEST AWAY FANS: Manchester City
BEST STADIUM PLAYED IN: Olympic Stadium, Munich

FAVOURITE FOOD AND DRINK: Salads, steak, fish. Orange juice, milk
MISCELLANEOUS LIKES . . . DISLIKES: Winning, taking Heidi for walks . . . Smoking, washing-up
FAVOURITE SINGERS: Christopher Cross, Frank Sinatra, Fleetwood Mac, Beatles
FAVOURITE ACTOR/ACTRESS: Paul Newman, Sophia Loren
FAVOURITE HOLIDAY RESORT: Jamaica
FAVOURITE TV SHOW: Coronation Street
BEST FILM SEEN RECENTLY: Tribute (Jack Lemmon)
FAVOURITE ACTIVITY ON DAY OFF: Shopping, resting, seeing friends
BIGGEST INFLUENCE ON CAREER: Mum and dad for their support and help in early years
SUPERSTITIONS: None
PRE-MATCH MEAL: Chicken
INTERNATIONAL HONOURS: 20 full England caps
PERSONAL AMBITION: To be remembered in football
IF NOT A PLAYER, WHAT JOB WOULD YOU DO? Go into selling cars with my father-in-law
CAREER AFTER PLAYING: Don't know yet
WHICH PERSON IN THE WORLD WOULD YOU MOST LIKE TO MEET? Pele

SHOOT!

was not the sort of problem the England manager could do anything about.'

Gary Owen, who had captained the England under 21s, felt that players from certain clubs stood little chance of breaking into the England first team. It's a view that has been expressed by many players over the years with Gary commenting: 'At that time I think the England manager picked players from teams that were doing well. If you played for Arsenal or Liverpool you'd be in, whereas if you were at West Brom or Leeds you wouldn't make it. I remember Ron Greenwood picking six of the Liverpool team early on in his reign and I think that was a sign. In those days it was all about whether the club was doing well. Look at Cyrille Regis – how did he not get more England caps? He got five, but he was at West Brom. Barnsey was the same. At Leeds he was never going to develop his England career.'

Back in June 1982 Peter was quoted in the papers saying that, because of the injury and lack of opportunity, he had expected Greenwood not to select him but, rather than focus on his own feelings, Peter took time to express sympathy for Morley missing out. It demonstrated the compassion and caring nature that the winger regularly displayed for his fellow professionals. 'It's awful missing out on a World Cup opportunity,' says Peter. 'I thought my world had fallen in. The summer of 1982 was miserable. Ron Greenwood was a gent, as always, and I know that there are plenty of players who haven't had the chance to play for their country, but that didn't take away the pain I felt. Playing for your country in a World Cup would've been a tremendous pinnacle of my career. But it wasn't to be. Twenty-two caps for England at that time was hard to achieve but I still felt I could add something for England. I was deeply hurt.

'During the summer of 1982 I did a lot of thinking. I watched the World Cup wishing I was there.'

1   'Frank Taylor at large', *Daily Mirror*, September 15, 1980, 30.
2   'A 5-1 thrashing but Leeds boss still feels he is on a winner', *Sunday Express*, September 6, 1981.
3   'Champions crash again', *Belfast Daily Telegraph*, September 3, 1981, 25.
4   'A 5-1 thrashing but Leeds boss still feels he is on a winner', *Sunday Express*, September 6, 1981.
5   'Barnes takes five minutes to "clear the air" at Leeds', *Express & Star*, September 15, 1981, 26.
6   'The joy of six', *Guardian*, June 12, 2009.
7   'Angry Barnes has problems at Elland Road', *Express & Star*, September 14, 28.
8   'Barnes takes five minutes to "clear the air" at Leeds', *Express & Star*, September 15, 1981, 26.
9   'The joy of six', *Guardian*, June 12, 2009.
10 'Leeds fans want Graham to stay', *Aberdeen Press and Journal*, October 8, 1981, 24.
11 'Mac's hit-and-run job', *Daily Star*, November 9, 1981, 25-26.
12 'Ban hits Leeds', *Newcastle Journal*, May 18, 1982, 12.
13 'Police baton charge as fans invade pitch', *Aberdeen Press and Journal*, May 19, 1982, 1.
14 'Fans in court after English football riot', *Aberdeen Evening Express*, May 19, 1982, 3.
15 'Operation for Burns', *Aberdeen Evening Express*, November 7, 1981, 10.
16 'Barnes adds to England worries', *Aberdeen Press and Journal*, May 25, 1982, 24.
17 'Dutch treat – now Spain beckons', *Newcastle Journal*, May 26, 1982, 28.
18 'Greenwood's squad has Ramsay look', *Aberdeen Press and Journal*, June 5, 1982, 20.
19 Ron Greenwood, *Yours Sincerely* (London: Willow Books, 1984), 39.

Chapter Sixteen
EL RUBIO

"
Leeds and England winger Peter Barnes will join Spanish club Real Betis – provided Leeds' terms are met by the Spaniards. Barnes, who spent two days this week looking around the Spanish set-up, said last night: "I shall fly out to sign on Sunday, provided both sides are fully satisfied." Leeds are believed to be insisting on a down payment of £115,000, with a further £235,000 at the end of 12 months. If the Spaniards don't come up with the second payment, Barnes would be free to return to Leeds.
"

'Barnes: I'll go', *Daily Mirror*, August 6, 1982, 27.

With Leeds' relegation in 1982, Peter was expected to move on. It seemed inevitable that he would join a First Division club but Leeds' financial situation was an issue. The transfer market had collapsed to some extent with only one player, Adrian Heath (£700,000, Stoke to Everton in January 1982), costing more than £500,000 since October 1981. The main reason for the collapse was that there had been significant debate about curbing the spending of clubs after a number of well publicised £1m+ moves with fees paid in instalments. This led to the Football League changing their rules at their AGM on June 11, 1982 to insist that 50% of any transfer had to be paid immediately with the balance being paid within a year.

The idea was that the change would control future spending but it also meant that clubs which had spent huge sums in the previous year or so were unlikely to recoup

OLE! BARNES

most expensive purchase by an English club. The transfer fee rule change may have protected the game from wild inflation at the time, but it did nothing to help those clubs that had bought at the height of the market.

Leeds knew that they needed to make changes following relegation and Peter was, in effect, their greatest saleable asset but they were never likely to recoup their investment. Peter: 'Allan Clarke was sacked at Leeds and Eddie Gray came in – my idol. A wonderful man. He called me in and explained that attendances would be dropping; income would reduce and that he had to sell players. He explained that either I'd need to take a pay cut or I'd have to leave. Obviously, I had my mortgage to pay and had other commitments, so a pay cut was going to be an issue. I told him that I understood his situation and that I knew it wasn't his fault. I said that I'd need to move on. I still believed I could play at a higher standard than the Second Division and I also still felt I could play for England but I knew that wouldn't happen at Leeds – Ron Greenwood had told me that – and it certainly wouldn't happen if I was in the Second Division. I know that's not how it should be – talented players should be able to play for England regardless of the club they're at or the division they're in – but that's how it was.'

Gray, an admirer of Peter's style of play, had been keen to keep him but he knew that if a decent offer came in, the club would need to accept to ease their

their investment if either the player or the club felt the player should move elsewhere. This meant that any potential move by Peter could see Leeds make an enormous loss, as clubs were unlikely to pay 50% of the fee Leeds had paid West Bromwich Albion up front. Club finances were stretched across the board and would remain so for some time.

The impact of the high transfers of the late seventies and early eighties was felt by many clubs for years with some, most notably Leeds, Manchester City and Wolves, suffering for a decade or two, maybe longer. Perfectly demonstrating the effect the change had on transfers is Peter's own transfer to Leeds. The 1981 total transfer cost of £930,000 was the 11th highest fee paid by an English club at the time and, by the end of May 1988 this was still the 15th

A REAL HIT

financial worries. There was also the issue of reducing the wage bill. Loan spells could help ease the burden to some extent.

'Out of the blue I received a call from someone working for Ambrose Mendy, the agent to Nigel Benn, the boxer' remembers Peter. 'He said to me that Real Betis was interested and I remember discussing it with my wife. We both thought that it would be a good opportunity. This team seemed to want me and that had to be better than staying at Leeds. For me it was always quite simple – if a team wanted me then I'd talk. I just wanted to play football at the highest level possible all the time, so this was an opportunity to do that.

'I went out to Seville to talk to Real Betis. It's a beautiful city but it was so hot on the day I went over. It was something like 40 degrees and they put me in a wonderful hotel called the Alfonso XIII. It was a gorgeous hotel and both me and my wife loved the place. It felt like I had to take whatever they offered simply for the chance to play in Spain and in this great city. At that time the Spanish league had some of the greatest players in the world including Maradona, who joined Barcelona that summer. I also thought that it would suit my style of play too.

'They found me a bungalow with a swimming pool to rent in a town called Dos Hermanas, which means "two sisters", which was only about fifteen minutes from the ground. I signed a three year contract but there was a get-out clause after a year which meant I could go back to Leeds if I couldn't settle. It was more like a loan deal for a year then it'd be permanent. Leeds made about £300,000 from the deal and, more importantly, they got me off their wage bill.'

The transfer was recorded as 23 million pesetas with a further 48 million due to Leeds if Peter stayed more than a season,

estimated by the British press as a total of approximately £300,000. It was classed as a prominent transfer in Spain at the time because it was still relatively unusual for an English player to join a Spanish club. An interview with Peter appeared in the sports newspaper *AS*, eleven days before he made his debut in the semi-final of the Carranza trophy against Real Madrid. All seemed positive but then a few worrying comments began to concern him. At training he was told to play as a centre-forward. He discussed his move with friendly British journalists and was later quoted in the *Daily Mirror*: 'I reckon the club bought me without ever watching me because when I got here, they said they wanted me to play centre forward. I've heard of being versatile… but that's ridiculous!

264

El Rubio takes his place on the back row of the Real Betis squad photo.

'The problem is I think Betis bought me on the basis of watching a couple of video films of me playing for England. They didn't realise I was a left winger – they couldn't have done because they've already got two left-sided players. Gordillo, the Spanish international, plays left back and likes to get forward down the wing. The captain also likes the left side, and so I was put in at centre forward in practice.' [1]

Real Betis struggled in its opening games of 1982-83, adding to Peter's frustrations: 'They're near the bottom of the table, lost their first two games and I haven't yet made a full League appearance. When I played in practice matches at centre forward, I didn't know what to do… The truth is the club didn't do their homework on me. If they'd done so they would have known they needed a central striker. We've only got three forwards in the whole club, including me. It's a bit of a farce and it may have been a political move to buy me.'

The frustrations felt at the time of the transfer have eased somewhat over the decades that have followed and Peter looks back fondly on his time in Spain: 'Seville has a great football history and rivalry with two clubs – Betis and Sevilla. Andalusian people are so warm and welcoming. It's a great place to live but Betis were never going to win the league. Top ten would be the aim, maybe a UEFA Cup place or a good cup run, but that was it really. We had some great players – Gordillo, the left back, went to Madrid a year or so later for a million, which was still a lot of money for a left back then. He made 75 international appearances for Spain. Julio Cardenosa was an inside left, who played in the 1978 World

Cup. Sadly, he missed an open goal against Brazil which led to Spain's elimination and never played again for his country as a result, but he was a wonderful player. Esnaola was a brilliant goalkeeper. There were four or five really great pros with international experience.'

On 24 September 1982 the sports newspaper *AS* asked Betis' manager Antal Dunai, a former Hungarian international, about Peter's arrival and form (translated to English): 'I had never seen him play. But a player who has been international in a country with a very tough league, where it is played hard, it is logical that I considered him important and that I expected him to be a reinforcement, which I am still waiting for. However, you have to take into account many circumstances, many changes in your life: new club, different game, different climate, another language, and also a month-long delay in preparation for joining later... I am convinced that he

is a good boy.' When questioned further Dunai claimed that language issues were the reasons he had not played Peter as often as the fans and the media had wanted, before adding: 'He started strong, training hard. Proof that he was not injured, but then he has not overcome the mentioned circumstances. The problem now for this man is that he has to respond, and he does not have time to overcome the inconveniences.'

Regardless of what Dunai thought of Peter's opening weeks, the player did last longer at Betis than the manager: 'The language was an issue but I worked hard on that. Dunai had gone half way through the season and was replaced by French goalkeeper Marcel Domingo. He had a great name as a coach. An experienced man who spoke Spanish and French, but he'd gone at the end of the season as well. I know there had been managerial changes during my time at City, West Brom and Leeds but

this felt different. This felt part of the culture of the game in Spain whereas, at that time, English clubs tended to stick with managers a little longer – usually, anyway!'

The same day as Dunai's *AS* article was published, Peter appeared in the *Daily Mirror* denying that he was about to return to England. He did admit that new Leeds manager Eddie Gray had called him to say that he could come back whenever he wanted, but Peter was far from impressed with some of the rumours he had heard doing the rounds: 'I was angry when I heard someone had suggested I'd be home soon because it was a shambles. People must think I'm a right fool coming all this way and then heading straight home again. Well, they can forget it. I hope to sort it out and stay.' [2]

Peter's move to Spain seemed sensible for Leeds at the time but the club still owed West Bromwich Albion £160,000 from his initial transfer to Elland Road. This caused the Football League to ban Leeds from any other transfers until that outstanding balance was paid. They eventually paid £140,000 in January with the rest promised in March, ensuring the ban was lifted, but the club's financial issues were concerning and likely to influence any future discussion about Peter's value to the club. Already, the media coverage of his opening months in Spain suggested the initial deal for a year at Betis would not be extended into a permanent move.

Life in Spain was enjoyable but the overall experience of playing football there was somewhat different to what Peter had

Peter in action as Betis defeat Osasuna 4–2 in April 1983.

experienced at Leeds: 'You never seemed to get a day off. It was play a game on Sunday... in for a massage Monday... every day there was something... "Concentration Friday". It was too much at that time. Things have changed since then in England but our culture back then was much more laid back. Particularly on a match day when you'd be chatting with fans or signing autographs on the forecourt before getting into the ground about two hours before kick-off. In Spain we'd arrive on a Friday; leave our cars at the ground; get on a coach for a trip into the mountains to somewhere like Cordoba where we'd stay in a parador – an old castle converted into a luxury hotel. We'd be there from Friday until the game at 4pm on Sunday. I remember thinking "my wife's in the house. She can't speak Spanish. She's got no one to talk to." I couldn't speak Spanish. We didn't have an interpreter and I couldn't talk with anyone so I'd pick up the hotel phone and call my wife. There were no mobiles and I'd be in the lobby calling from the public phone, asking how she was. Just hearing another English voice gave me a boost. It was hard doing these weekends away for home games – you expect travel for away matches but back then in England we never stayed away for a couple of days for a home match. After games the Spanish players wanted to get off home because they'd been away from their families like I had. In England, we'd go for a post-match drink and that would help new players settle, but in Spain then that didn't happen. There was no players' lounge at Betis and so there was no opportunity to socialise for us or our families.'

Domestically other changes were on the cards which concerned Peter: 'We were expecting our first baby and I used to worry about Alison being on her own. I went to see the club secretary Pedro and I said to him in broken Spanish: "My wife…mi mujer is in the casa… house on her own. She's pregnant… con una bebe. In England we report to the ground two hours before kick off… dos horas ante partido… you'll get more out of me by leaving me with my pregnant esposa and letting me come dos horas ante partido. The response was always "No" and it would be explained that I was part of the team and that this was the normal way to prepare for the game. I couldn't do anything but accept it.'

It was difficult for Peter to settle in this situation: 'I met a ship builder who was English and we used to go to his house, but as a couple we were both lonely. There weren't many English in Seville back then. I used to speak basic Spanish and that took me about five months to learn. I wasn't fluent but I could get by. If someone went into a deep conversation they'd lose me but I could get by. For the first few months the team talks went straight over my head. I didn't have a clue what they were saying to me. There were a lot of gestures and that's how I got to understand what was needed. There was one bloke who spoke English really well – he'd been learning it – but no one else did. It was always Spanish – as it should be in Spain – and it took me some time.'

Despite those issues Peter did enjoy being out on the pitch: 'I loved playing in Spain but after about five months we knew we'd come back to England. My daughter, Eloise, was born while we were there. She

was born March 29, 1983. My wife was from Warrington and my daughter was born at the Mill Road Maternity Hospital at Everton, Liverpool. We knew we wanted to have the baby in England and so my wife went home to her family, to have the baby there. Because of the football season I had to stay out in Seville of course. That was difficult for us both. When my daughter was born I was in England though because they'd let me fly home for a week. I stayed at my in-laws and it was magical when our daughter, Eloise, was born. A wonderful time, but footballers couldn't take much time off and I had to get back for a game. There weren't direct flights then, so you'd go to Madrid and then on to Seville. It was hard leaving Alison and Eloise but I had no choice. I ended up alone in Spain while my wife and daughter were back in England. I wanted to be with them.'

As suggested, Peter always wanted to put his family's happiness first which, according to an interview in *Shoot* shortly after Eloise's birth, was part of his decision process in leaving Spain in the first place: 'My wife Alison has just had our first baby. And she's not entirely happy about settling in Seville for any length of time. It's something we've got to talk over, but the odds are on us being back in England next season, because the happiness of my family is very important to me.' [3]

In terms of the football, Peter has a few strong memories of the 1982-83 season: 'I remember two games in particular. We drew at home 1-1 with Real Madrid in March and I scored the opener in the 66th minute. To score in a league game against Real Madrid meant a lot to me. I also scored another but it was disallowed. It was a perfect goal but for some reason it was disallowed and we were not happy about that. There was nothing wrong with that at all. I knew I'd beaten Madrid's offside trap

Peter and Alison with Baby Eloise, April 1983.

and I smacked it past the 'keeper but no… they claimed it was offside.

'The following week we played Barcelona at the Nou Camp. It was a magnificent experience. 90,000 people. Maradona was playing. He'd been out for a while with hepatitis. For us this was a major game – it'd be like Southampton playing at Old Trafford when United were winning everything. It was a David and Goliath type of game. No one expected us to do anything. We had a good history, excellent coaches and some success over the years but Real Betis were not perceived as a giant of the Spanish game, not like the Madrid clubs or Barcelona.'

Playing league football at the Nou Camp was exhilarating: 'It was such a wonderful experience to get changed, go down that tunnel, down the stairs – there was a cage so that you didn't come into contact with their team. You go up to the pitch and then you see the magnificent stadium. Incredible place and, at the time, much bigger and better than anything in England. I couldn't wait to get on the pitch.

'We conceded a goal early on – it was about the third minute – but I was getting plenty of the ball and was enjoying it. We equalised after 24 minutes and things seemed to be getting better for us. We put three defenders on Maradona – two behind and one in front of him – and that was working. He wasn't getting much of the ball but he was such a genius when he did. At one point I managed to nutmeg him. He came to tackle me and I stuck it through his legs. I was in a daze: "I've nutmegged Maradona… I've nutmegged Maradona." It was the closest I'd ever got to him in my career and was the pinnacle for me. I was stood there in a daze and then the ball was taken off me! I'm still dazed thinking "I've nutmegged Maradona" while everyone's shouting "Pedro, trabajo!" at me and play

is going on! Never mind the rest of the game… I've nutmegged Maradona!

'We ended up drawing the game 1-1 at the Nou Camp and the directors came in afterwards. They took out envelopes, threw them down on to the table and they were full of cash. It was divvied out between us. That never happened at Maine Road or the Hawthorns! To draw at Barcelona was like winning the FA Cup. It was a major achievement. It was unheard of. I think I was still in a daze… I've nutmegged Maradona!'

Peter's comments are typical of his nature. Rather than talk triumphantly of facing Maradona he has played down the moment over the years that have followed and turned it in to a humorous memory. This shows his humility. While others would have boasted, Peter creates a more down to earth version of the truth. This happens often throughout Peter's footballing life.

As the Maradona incident perhaps shows, this season was really one of two halves for Peter. Under Dunai he hardly had an opportunity to do anything, but once Domingo took over things had changed. In April 1983 Peter explained: 'I'd expected the first four or five months to be difficult – I think they are for any player who goes abroad – but I was unlucky that Betis had a poor start to the League, and this put pressure on [Dunai].

'Results were more important than entertaining the fans, and I had trouble getting a place in a defensive line-up. When I got back after Christmas, Dunai had been sacked and the new boss, Marcel Domingo, took us out to dinner, had a heart-to-heart chat, and since then I've been in the team. Maybe it's just coincidence, but we've shot up the table!' [4]

By the time of that comment, Peter had scored against the League leaders and eventual champions Bilbao – a 65th minute goal in a game Betis won in spectacular style 5-1 in March. This was typical of the entire season for Betis: 'We finished 11th out of 18 clubs and our striker Poli Rincon was the league's top scorer. Who knows how the season would've gone had Domingo been the manager at the start. Mind you, he may not have signed me!'

Although Peter had not played too many games for Betis, he has been remembered by some fans. Features appear on his career on fan websites and, in 2020, his eldest sister Susan remembered: 'My son lived in Spain for eight years and a few of the old men that he got to know knew who Peter was from his time at Real Betis. They talked about him and called him El Rubio which means the blond one. We were surprised that he was still remembered there.'

The season ended with El Rubio knowing he would return to England: 'I still had a house near Wetherby in Yorkshire. It was all locked up and at the end of the season I said to my wife that we should go back. We hadn't settled as well as we'd hoped, despite loving the area, and then there were the managerial changes. I'd already seen two managers dismissed during that season and didn't know what to expect going forward. Now there was my daughter to think about too and I wanted stability in my life. As the Leeds-Betis agreement allowed me to return after one season it seemed sensible to leave Spain.

'After having Eloise, my wife returned to Spain on my birthday, June 10th. By that time everyone at Betis knew I was going back to Leeds, so they all said goodbye to me. We packed up the house. Sold the car – a Renault 5 – and planned for the return to Leeds. The three of us travelled back to Manchester together. It was sad leaving Spain.

'I think if it was today I would've stayed and appreciated Spanish football more. The world seems a smaller place now. Technology would've kept us in contact with family and friends back home. Football clubs spend time on player welfare now – that was unknown then. I was getting used to the language and was getting used to things. I'd started to meet more people but I was settling more than my wife because she'd been back in England for a few months after my daughter had been born. It was a difficult time for her, being pregnant and then a young mum without family or friends around. Overall though it was a great experience. I got on well with the team and I think they knew that it was difficult due to the language problems and so on.'

When Peter returned to England there were several issues with bureaucracy which meant he missed some of Leeds' preseason games in the build-up to the 1983-84 season. He also needed the assistance of the PFA to ensure he received wages owed to him by Real Betis. According to reports PFA secretary Gordon Taylor acted on Peter's behalf and in July 1983 it was reported that Taylor: 'negotiated the £25,000 owed to [Peter]'. [5]

At Leeds Peter was keen to make things work. He idolised Eddie Gray as a player and wanted to do a decent job for him and the Leeds fans: 'When I returned Eddie Gray was still the manager, so that was good. Because I'd earned a decent wage in Spain I was happy with a lower offer at Leeds. The club was still in the Second Division and were having financial issues, so I understood that. Money was not an issue to me and I was happy to see how things would work at Elland Road this time. The fans had remained loyal and, as someone who had always considered Leeds to be my second club as a boy, I was keen to play my part. I still wanted to play at a higher level, of course, and there were no secrets between me and Eddie Gray – he knew that if a top flight team came in that Leeds would listen and that I would possibly want to go. He also said to me "Peter, you're going to struggle here to get the ball. We've got some kids in the team learning their trade and it'll be difficult for us to challenge for promotion. We'll be under pressure most games and we won't get the distribution you need."

'I appreciated the honesty. It was a tough time for Leeds and the Second Division was more about defence for us, not flair. Other clubs did show interest –

Graham Taylor tried to persuade me to go to Watford but the need to be in the north was great at this time for me and my family, so I turned him down. He had a great team at that time and it would've been good to experience that but it just wasn't the right time.'

Watford had been prepared to pay £200,000 to sign Peter: 'Watford boss Graham Taylor has already put the money down. But Barnes, just back from a bitter spell in Spain with Real Betis, is reluctant to move his family yet again. Taylor, an open admirer of wingers, is not worried by Barnes' reputation. Barnes has all the skill but has yet to use it consistently through a season.' [6]

According to reports at the time Manchester City, Sunderland, West Ham and Aberdeen were interested during the 1983-84 season. Peter did not move to any of the interested clubs and remained at Leeds United throughout 1983-84, although he was desperate to join a top flight club where he hoped he would have the chance to resurrect his England career. Leeds, still struggling in Division Two, was not the best club to be at to fulfil those ambitions especially as he found it difficult getting into the team at first due to a groin injury. Then things began to change and Peter was given a chance. He began to shine. According to the *Liverpool Echo*, when he returned to the first team Leeds enjoyed: 'eight League matches without defeat, after an opening spell without Barnes that had seen the team desperately near the relegation zone.' [7]

The report went on: 'In a game devoid of talented players capable of being match-winners, and in an era when the once common phrase "wizard of dribble" had become defunct, even the thought of a return to vintage form

Peter fends off Newcastle's John Anderson on 27 August 1983.

by Barnes sets the taste buds watering…
After nearly three years of disappointment
at Leeds and Seville one sense that his
confidence needs resurrecting. And Yet
the fact remains that England have never
replaced him.'

The article waxed lyrical about Peter's
strengths and included comments from
his former West Bromwich Albion boss:
'There is no doubt that Barnes can still do
the business and last week his old boss Ron

Atkinson came back from watching Oxford
v Leeds and told me: "Barnes got over four
absolutely world-class centres but there was
nobody to put the ball in the net for Leeds."
In top class football critics also tend to
overlook Barnes' goals, and in his last two
seasons with West Brom he scored 30 goals
when he had good players around.'

After the footballing frustrations of
the previous couple of years Peter was
feeling optimistic about the future by this

time and he told the *Echo*: 'My object now is to get back into the swing of regular League football. Leeds are not too far off the promotion zone and it would give me enormous pleasure to be involved in helping them back into the First Division. I think we are capable of doing it this season.'

Looking back over his career since he left Albion he added: 'Perhaps to some extent I was a victim of the period when the game drifted into ultra-defensive tactics. But I feel it is all changing now for the good. The game seems to be crying out for ball players and wingers again, after a period where there have been too many run-of-the-mill players, and as a result there is more entertainment. I was puzzled and frustrated by what happened to my career, but I have never doubted my ability, and I know that when given the service I can still turn it on. I still have time to hit the heights again, but I prefer not to build up too many hopes.'

Despite his hopes, Leeds finished tenth in the Second Division that season with Peter scoring four goals in 25 (plus 2 as substitute) appearances. In May Ron Atkinson took him on loan to play in an end of season tour with Manchester United, but the move was never likely to become a permanent one. The following October he joined First Division Coventry City with a transfer fee reported as £65,000. 'Coventry City came knocking with Bobby Gould as manager,' says Peter. 'It seemed like a good opportunity – a First Division club. Lovely training ground – probably the most futuristic training ground in English football at the time. There were some really good players already there too. I knew Dave Bennett from our time at Manchester City and Cyrille Regis was about to sign from West Brom, so that all helped make my mind up. For me, I always wanted to sign for a team where I knew some of the

Pater celebrates scoring Leeds second goal v Barnsley, 23 October 1983.

274

players. It helped me settle and Coventry seemed right because of that.

'We bought a house at Kenilworth, ten minutes from the ground. It's a beautiful part of the country and everything seemed positive. I was settling in well.'

When Peter, Alison and young daughter Eloise moved into their new home they needed some work doing to the house. As with anyone moving to a new area Peter decided to ask his new team mates if they could recommend any tradesmen: 'I thought we'd get someone reliable to do some electrical work for us. We needed some lights fitting and so I went into training one day and said "Lads, anyone know a good electrician? We need some lights fitting?" Up pipes one of the younger players, Stuart Pearce. He says: "I'll do it, Peter. I'm a sparky."

'I couldn't believe it but I thought I'd give him a go. He came round. Did an excellent job and when I came to pay him I asked, "how much?" He refused payment but I gave him about ten quid. He did quite a few jobs for players and it was great to see his enthusiasm.'

Pearce, of course, went on to be a committed England international and manager of Manchester City. He did several electrical jobs for players during the early years of his career.

While Peter was pleased with Pearce's work, the winger was also content with the public utterances being made by manager Gould. Gould was delighted to have Peter at Highfield Road and told journalists at the time: 'I have been after Peter since I arrived here. I contacted him when he returned from Spain, but nothing came of it. He should have gone with England to the 1982 World Cup finals and he would have come back as a world-class player. You don't lose his kind of ability in three years.' [8]

Peter made his Coventry debut in a

1-0 victory at Watford on October 6, 1984. Journalist Neville Foulger described Peter's debut as 'a triumphant return to Division 1 football' and talked positively of his skills: 'which are going to excite and delight City's fans and torment opposition defences in the months ahead. Not since Tommy Hutchison have the Sky Blues had such a richly gifted player. Even after three years in the wilderness, Barnes remains a soccer artist capable of bringing people to the edge of their seats the moment the ball arrives at his feet... there was enough in his performance at Vicarage Road on Saturday to suggest that City have landed an absolute bargain.' [9]

After the victory, Foulger asked Peter for his views on the game and the new Coventry winger was full of positivity for his new club: 'We have the nucleus of a very good team here and I was very impressed. I really enjoyed the game... With a bit of luck we could have had two or three goals and if some of the younger players start to have a bit more belief in themselves we can go places. There are no great sides around in the First Division any more. Watford have

proved that. They only arrived in Division 1 a couple of years ago and in that time have finished runners-up and reached the FA Cup final at Wembley. That just shows what can be done.'

Three days after the League win at Watford Peter made his home debut in a League Cup defeat to Walsall. The next day Cyrille Regis signed and both men played in a 1-1 home draw with Newcastle the following Saturday. Jim Brown, the chair of Coventry City Former Players' Association, believes that both Peter and Regis were great players: 'It was clear that both Peter and Cyrille were class players but Bobby Gould's tactics didn't really suit either player.' [10]

A little over a month after arriving both Peter and Regis scored against their old club West Bromwich Albion. Sadly, the game ended in a 5-2 defeat. 'These remained tough times for Coventry' says Peter. 'We were in the relegation zone and didn't seem able to put together enough wins or draws to lift us out of it permanently. Bobby Gould, the manager, was a deep thinker and used to get the Subbuteo pitch out every Monday morning. He was desperate to work out what was going wrong and who was to blame. We'd all be in his office or the players' lounge, stood around this board. He'd be reliving the game step by step. He'd also put videos on of the game and pause it, rewind it and go through it in detail.

'We were struggling. Gould had already brought in Don Mackay as assistant. He was a former goalkeeper from Scotland and later went on to manage Blackburn for a few years but in 1984 he arrived at Coventry, supposedly to help us strengthen defensively. I didn't really like Don's approach at this time. We went to Luton at Christmas and lost 2-0 and Bobby Gould was sacked and Mackay takes over. There was a 2-1 defeat to West Ham and then

Mackay puts me in the reserves saying "You have that much talent, you shouldn't be here. We can't afford to play you because we need scrappers and we can't get the ball to you" – It was an odd thing to say and I thought "here we go again." Wingers would be sacrificed for defensive play. I get it. I understand why, but when you're an attacking winger it's tough. For Coventry then it was defend at all costs. Don't concede a goal. It was too negative and I think there was a general fear in football at that time.

'My dad came down with Tony Book, who was back at Maine Road of course, to watch a Coventry reserve game. I was playing and had a good game. There were a few scouts there watching and I felt confident that I'd done enough in the game to either get my place back in the Coventry team or to attract another club. Tony and dad were in the directors' box and Don Mackay was there. Don had no idea who my dad was, but he recognised Tony. He went over to them and started chatting. Dad stayed silent, listening as Tony and Don chatted. Tony asked, "How's Peter Barnes doing?" Don replied: "It's frustrating. We need results and I can't afford to play Peter in the first team. He's a bit of a luxury." That's how the game was for many clubs then. It annoyed Dad. He felt the problem wasn't that I was a luxury or too good a player for that team. Instead Dad thought that it was the managers and coaches who weren't being brave enough.'

According to Jim Brown: 'When Mackay took over the style of play didn't change and Peter was dropped after Mackay's first game in charge. He was replaced by Mickey Adams. Peter and Mackay had a "clear the air" meeting in early March with Peter unhappy to be playing in the reserves. But there was no recall until April when City were in desperate straits. He scored a volleyed goal in his penultimate game v West Brom, but was subbed at Tottenham in the next game. He took no part in Coventry's amazing escape when needing three wins to stay up they stunned the bookies, fans and Norwich – who were relegated – by beating Stoke, Luton and champions Everton. I suspect Mackay preferred Adams to Peter for the relegation scraps required – and believe me they were scraps!'

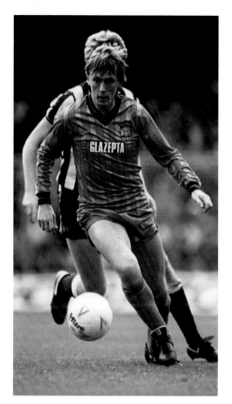

In total Peter made 19 first team appearances, scoring twice, for Coventry that season. He would have liked to have stayed at the club but it was clear Mackay saw no place for him. According to Brown: 'Sadly, we only saw glimpses of Peter's talent at Coventry. English football was pretty agricultural in those days. Regis almost moved that summer as well.'

As for Peter the end of the 1984-85 season caused him to worry: 'With a young family I wanted stability but it wasn't happening. I wondered where I'd end up next. I needed rescuing and, fortunately, Big Ron came and saved me.'

[1] 'Comic capers', *Daily Mirror*, September 24, 1982, 26-27.
[2] Ibid.
[3] 'Wing wizards set to return', *Shoot*, April 30, 1983, 2-3.
[4] Ibid.
[5] 'The Godfather', *Sunday Mirror*, July 17, 1983, 33.
[6] 'Barnes on hook', *Daily Mirror*, July 5, 1983, 28.
[7] 'Wizard of dribble casts a new spell', *Football Echo*, December 3, 1983, 3.
[8] 'Bob gets his man', *Daily Mirror*, October 4, 1984, 30.
[9] 'We can go places', *Coventry Evening Telegraph*, October 8, 1984.
[10] Correspondence between the author and Jim Brown, November 2020.

Chapter Seventeen

BIG RON'S UNITED

Peter Barnes kept faith even in the days of his deepest despair. When it all went wrong at Leeds... When it was so hot in Seville... When coach Frank Upton, at Coventry, went on and on about aggression, he never stopped believing. Believing the ability that once made him an England star, and one of the most exciting players in Europe, was still there. That one day, someone, somewhere, would recognise he wasn't yesterday's man.

'Keeping faith with yesterday's man', *Daily Mirror*, October 11, 1985, 30.

The end of the 1984-85 season left Peter pondering the future: 'I felt stuck in the reserves at Coventry and couldn't see that changing. Then, out of the blue, Ron Atkinson wanted to talk. I was 28 that close season and felt I still had something to offer if I could get to the right club. I'd had enough of being in struggling teams at Leeds and Coventry and wanted another chance in an attack-minded team. Big Ron saved the day and I was on my way to Manchester United. A move to Manchester was ideal and I knew what a great, inspiring manager Ron had been at West Brom, so it seemed perfect. The big negative of course was going to be the reaction of Manchester City fans. I knew they wouldn't like it but I

had to think of my career and I don't think many begrudged me the opportunity. I hadn't wanted to leave City in 1979 – in fact I had wanted to stay in that first team for a decade or so. I'd wanted a testimonial for long service because it was my club, but in 1985 City were not calling for me. United were and they were managed by someone I knew and enjoyed playing for. It was a no brainer.

'It boosted my confidence knowing that United wanted me. They were honest with me from the start, because I wanted to know would I be a regular or not. I went to Ron's house in Bamford, Rochdale on a Sunday morning. He sat there in his flip-flops, watching the football. He was

Peter reunited with Ron Atkinson.

a different Ron Atkinson from his time at West Brom. He was definitely Big Ron now with all the swagger that suggested.

'We discussed my career after Albion and talked about England and all of that. It was a case of us both trying to understand how I'd ended up in the reserves at Coventry. Ron told me he could offer me a two year contract but that I wouldn't be guaranteed a first team place. They already had Jesper Olsen, a Danish international, and on the right wing Gordon Strachan, so I knew it would be tough. I wanted the challenge. I felt that challenging other, quality international wingers would bring out the best in me. We talked salary and I'd get a company car for my wife to drive.

'Even though I've been a Blue all my life I was always a George Best fan and so to get the opportunity to wear his shirt meant a great deal to me. Number 11 – Best's United shirt! A footballer I'd aspired to be like all my life. I couldn't wait to sign and I knew players like Arthur Albiston and Bryan Robson. Lads I'd played with or against for years. It was a good side with talented players and others coming through.'

Peter's elder sister Susan was delighted that he was moving back to the Manchester area: 'It was great to have him back locally but, importantly, he was going to play for Ron Atkinson. Peter often needed an arm around the shoulder as a player and I think Ron recognised that back then. After leaving West Brom, the teams Peter was at seemed to be more intent on not losing than trying to win. Attacking wingers were often cast aside with managers looking for more defensive rather than expressive players.

'Because of the way Atkinson wanted his football to be played then it was perfect for Peter. Peter had impressed Ron on the pre-season tour he did in Australia with United and so it was inevitable Peter would join him if he was asked.

'Peter's a bit of an homebird and coming back to Manchester and being around us would help him. Of course, Peter wasn't the first of the family to be at United. Keith had been there as an apprentice at the same time as Sammy McIlroy. They're both about the same age. Keith was a good player but it just didn't work out professionally.'

United had won the FA Cup in 1983 and 1985 with Atkinson but the club was desperate to win the League. United fan Pete Boyle remembers the expectation that was developing at Old Trafford: 'Atkinson wasn't the first choice but he did well for United. The problem was that the expectancy was increasing year on year

that we were going to win the League. Winning the FA Cup was great but it wasn't the League. Make no mistake about it we needed to win the League and 1985-86 was the year.'

'There were some good sides around, like Everton, and Ron had done well,' remembers Peter Barnes. 'He was getting closer to winning the title which was of course the number one priority for United then. They hadn't won it since 1967 – the year before City – and had seen Liverpool suddenly become the dominant force. Ron was getting close and there was a definite feeling United would win the title sooner or later under him. I felt it. It seemed to be in touching distance.'

Peter quickly found life more positive. Back in Manchester suited him and his family: 'We lived in what had been Arnold Muhren's club house in Wilmslow at first. We knew we were going to find our own house, so we lived with unpacked boxes everywhere for about a month or so. We later bought a house in Altrincham. Once I signed I was convinced I would get into the team. At Coventry it felt as if I stood

Barnes turns back clock

PETER BARNES rolled the years back with a dazzling second half debut as Manchester United flexed their pre-season muscles with a 3-2 win at Cambridge United last night.

The enigmatic winger wore the red of United, but turned on as true blue style that was the hallmark of his great days with Manchester City.

Barnes, a £50,000 capture from Coventry, came on as substitute for Jesper Olsen for the whole of the second half after the scores had been level — in a hard fought first half.

But this was the signal for United to cut loose with a display of flowing, attacking football that

Peter Barnes

280

hardly any chance and even if I did play I was playing a negative game, but here at United it suddenly felt that I would have the opportunity. It just felt right. I was doing well in the reserves and was waiting for the opportunity. Brian Whitehouse was the trainer who had been with my dad at Wrexham, so he knew all about me. We were trained hard. I was getting fit – not just match fit but United fit. Fit enough for a team challenging for the title.'

As Atkinson had suggested, Peter's opportunities would be limited and the player began his United career in the reserves. In his first Central League game on August 24 Peter performed well and was praised in the *Manchester Evening News* report: 'Peter Barnes outshone everyone in Manchester United's Central League game against Aston Villa, but it was not enough to clinch victory at Old Trafford today. Right from the outset Barnes caused havoc in the Villa defence every time he came into possession.' [1]

While playing in United's reserves

seemed a more positive experience than being in Coventry's, Peter ached for a first team opportunity: 'United had started well – 4-0 against Villa; 1-0 at Ipswich; 2-1 at Arsenal; 4-0 over West Ham – they were like a train. Going really well, and then I got the call that Jesper Olsen had injured his ligaments and would be out. Ron told me I was playing and the elation I felt that day is indescribable. It felt like my career was now at the point it should have been at. All those years earlier with City and West Brom I felt like I was moving forward in teams that could win major trophies. I'd lost that when I moved to Leeds – the biggest mistake of my career.'

It was at Nottingham Forest that Peter made his debut. It was a memorable 3-1 victory which United defender Mick Duxbury saw as a classic: 'For a second, I lost myself, and felt like a supporter in the stand, marvelling at what I'd seen my colleagues do. Peter scored his first goal, a debut goal in a 3-1 win… It was unbelievable. The confidence was really

Peter joins FA Cup holders United in 1985.

beginning to rub off on us all and we were all raising our own games as a consequence.' [2]

Dedicated United supporter Pete Boyle was keen to welcome Peter as a United player: 'I was a football obsessive at a young age. My dad took me to United when I was four and I remember Peter Barnes as a really good player with City. Back then you couldn't call a derby game in advance. Sometimes it'd be City, sometimes United. When he joined United he was still an attractive player. I'm sure some fans didn't want him at first because of the rivalry but he did well when he got in to the team. There was the Forest away game, which was his debut. Forest was a bit of a bogey team for us and so when he scored and we won that match 3-1 you felt it was going to be a good season.

'Peter's best years had already been I guess, but he did well enough for us before his injury to deserve his chance. I'll always see him as a City great but I did see him more favourably than say City fans saw Sammy McIlroy. They saw him as a Red through and through but I didn't feel like that with Peter. I thought he gave everything for us and I liked Peter. I loved Big Ron's team.'

Peter: 'Scoring on my debut meant a lot obviously. It helped me settle and may have won over a few fans who doubted my commitment to United. It was a wonderful feeling to play with Mark Hughes, Alan Brazil, Frank Stapleton… Strachan, Whiteside, Robson, Moses… the team was packed with stars. This was like going back to the team I was in at City in 1975. Men who were great players, capable of success. Hughes, Robson, Whiteside, Strachan… eleven star men – not me as the expensive new signing. The pressure was different – we were all under pressure at United of course, but the manager wasn't looking at me as the expensive signing. I felt there was a freedom because when you are surrounded with great players you can thrive. It was exciting. I remember Mike Summerbee coming a few times to Old Trafford to watch us and I'd get a message off him "Go on Peter, show them what you can do".'

United went ten consecutive games without dropping a point. 'We were obviously top but the nine point lead we had established was a sign of how well we'd done,' remembered Mick Duxbury in 2015.

For chairman Martin Edwards this season felt so positive and, although the

Barnes dream debut

PETER BARNES made it a dream debut with a goal in a sizzling Manchester United victory at Nottingham Forest today.

The ex-England and Manchester City winger scored the second goal in the fourth minute, as the rampant Reds — maintaining their 100 per cent record — streaked into a 3-0 interval lead.

The others came from Mark Hughes and Frank Stapleton, with Barnes generally in scintillating form, before Peter Davenport (46 minutes) pulled one back for Forest.

DEBUT GOAL for Peter Barnes as he slots in a rebound after five minutes.

club were being cautious and not talking about the title, it seemed the championship was on its way to Old Trafford. Edwards felt the football played was breathtaking: 'It was just so exciting. We had Gordon Strachan and Peter Barnes on the wing; everything seemed to be going for us. We were playing so well and taking teams apart.' [3]

Sadly, injury at West Bromwich Albion on September 21 caused Strachan to miss most of the following two months. During his absence a 1-1 draw at Luton on October 5 brought the end of the winning run. Six days later the *Daily Mirror* named Peter as their player of the month saying that: 'The month that followed [Peter's debut] was stunning for United, sensational for born-again Barnes as the Old Trafford machine left the rest of the First Division trailing in their slipstream.' [4] The newspaper described him as 'England class' based on those performances and asked him what his favourite moment had been during the month. The response surprised journalist Harry Harris. It was in the Screen Sport Super Cup game to Everton: 'I got to the by-line and pinged over a lovely cross for Frank Stapleton to score with a header.'

The Screen Sport Super Cup was a competition established in 1985 by the clubs who would normally have qualified for European football but would not be able to compete because of the ban which had followed the deaths and crowd violence at Liverpool's European Cup final appearance at Heysel, Belgium. The competition

GOAL ACE — United winger Peter Barnes (right) raises his hands to the crowd to salute his goal

MY WAY — Barnes (below) shows just how he did it as Oxford defenders look on.

was criticised by many but an Old Trafford crowd of 33,859 (higher than United's home League game with Sheffield Wednesday the following April) watched Everton win the game 4-2 and led to the *Liverpool Echo* suggesting the competition should become a permanent fixture.

The day after the *Mirror* article, Jesper Olsen returned to United's first team but, instead of Peter being dropped, Atkinson decided to play them both. 'Even when he was fit I managed to keep Olsen out of the team,' says Peter. 'Then Ron put the two of us – me as outside left and Olsen inside forward – in the same team. We beat QPR 2-0 but it felt like we'd really hammered them. He kept it like that for about six games with Strachan usually on the right wing as well. It was great to be in that attack minded team.

Peter was enjoying his life and football. Everything seemed to be going well and the move to United was an extremely positive one. His judgement on moving to the Reds was spot on and, while the most obsessed

supporter of United – or City for that matter – may have felt it strange seeing Peter in a red shirt rather than a blue one, no one could dispute the boost the move had to his career. Finally, after the difficulties and frustrations he had experienced after joining Leeds, he was playing and delivering at the level he deserved.

'There was talk of me getting back in to the England squad,' remembers Peter. 'Everything was going well and I was loving it. Absolutely loving that time at United.' The comment about England is true with Bobby Robson going to United's game at Luton on October 5, specifically to watch the winger. [5]

In November the England manager came close to picking Peter for a critical World Cup qualifier with Northern Ireland but instead selected Chris Waddle who had appeared low on confidence. It seemed a strange decision to some with Robson himself admitting that Peter was on form whereas Waddle was not: 'I plan to speak to Chris before the game to boost up his confidence. Sometimes a pat on the back can work better than threats and that is one of the reasons why I did not call up Peter Barnes so that Chris can go out there and not have to look over his shoulder all the time.' [6] Robson added that Peter was: 'the next choice winger. But I didn't want to put Chris in a flap. That wouldn't be right for the boy in this case.' [7]

As early as September 22, articles had appeared suggesting Peter should be given his England chance again. At that time Robson was asked if Peter could return to the England fold and he said that he already had John Barnes and Chris Waddle but he would be open to another winger convincing him he could do a job for the national side. Atkinson responded by saying: '[Peter's] recent performances haven't surprised me one bit. Peter for

England? Anything is possible. There isn't a winger in the country playing better than him.' [8] Atkinson added: 'There's more to come. I know the lad's capabilities. He's only touched the tip of the iceberg.' In the same piece praise came from an unlikely source. Peter's former Leeds' manager Allan Clarke: 'He's better than Waddle and John Barnes. He crosses the ball better than both. He's not a tackler or grafter but top class players around him will make him flourish. They'll find the benefit of his unusual skills.'

Everything was positive and then came a game on November 16, 1985 that was to affect Peter's United career: 'We played Tottenham at Old Trafford. I suffered a calf injury during the game but I was awarded the man of the match award. I'd had

MILK CUP SPECIAL

Barnes on target to wreck Coppell dream

COPPELL: "Typical Barnes"

SORRY PAL

By HARRY HARRIS: C. Palace 0, Man. Utd 1

PETER BARNES last night scored a brilliant goal to wreck the Milk Cup hopes of his former England team-mate—Palace boss Steve Coppell.

Barnes has been transformed from a £1 million flop into the steal of the season by United manager Ron Atkinson, and is now in contention for a World Cup place.

And Coppell, who made his England debut in the same World Cup match

as Barnes in 1978, believes the winger can challenge Tottenham's Chris Waddle and John Barnes of Watford for a place on England's wing.

Former Manchester United winger Coppell said: "That was typical of Peter Barnes Magnificent touches And he'll always score goals even when you think he's having a quiet time.

"He's always likely to produce one or two blinding games but he's got to prove he's consistent over 10 or 15 games if he wants to get back in the England team."

Barnes and Coppell figured in former England boss Ron Greenwood's two-winger formation, and it is only a matter of time before Bobby Robson is watching the trickery of Barnes.

Atkinson caused a major stir when he paid £50,000 to Coventry for Barnes when sceptics felt that it was money down the drain.

But Barnes collected his third United goal in six games with such panache that even Danish star Jesper Olsen can't complain if he is left out of the team again when United continue their relentless march on the League championship at home to Southampton on Saturday.

Punch

A highly entertaining Cup-tie was settled by Barnes' 59th minute goal which Coppell described as "a sucker punch."

After a delightful thirded move Barnes deceived goalkeeper George Wood into thinking he was about to cross the ball and he scored at the near post.

Coppell, one of the youngest managers in the League, can be proud of the way Palace performed against his former club.

Goalkeeper Gary Bailey made four outstanding saves, breaking the

BARNES STORMER: Goalscorer Barnes is congratulated by Norman Whiteside (left) and Arthur Albiston.   Picture: MONTE FRESCO

It's England class Barnes

By David Meek

PETER BARNES, the wandering star who lost his way, is back in the big-time.

Last night's Milk Cup winner for Manchester United at Crystal Palace has set the seal on a frustrated footballer's rehabilitation.

Barnes has now proved his ability to compete at the highest level again, after six games in which he has scored three times and produced moments of

REDS' PICTURE PARADE — p 38

probably the bargain buy

a great first half, putting crosses in, beating the full back, creating opportunities for Frank Stapleton.'

The Spurs game was regarded as one of Peter's best for United and, symbolically, it placed him on the same pitch as one of his rivals for the England squad, Chris Waddle. According to the *Sunday Mirror* the Spurs man was given a masterclass of what wing play should be at a leading football club: 'Waddle can't have left Old Trafford happy. He was obliged to stand back and watch a superb performance from his United rival Peter Barnes.

'Even Waddle would agree that the forgotten man of football has become a real threat to his England place. Barnes turned Gary Stevens inside out. It wasn't his fault that little was made from the string of crosses he dropped invitingly into the goalmouth. He was unlucky, too, when another fine run ended with a shot into the side netting.' [9] The newspaper made Peter the man of the match but the injury brought to an end what had been a brilliant sequence of games for Peter.

'When he got in to United's team, Peter hugged that left wing.' Remembers broadcaster and United fan Terry Christian. 'He was really good in that great run United had but then he got injured. Players used to just kick him back then. I remember him playing against City at Maine Road and we won 3-0 in September. Albiston, Duxbury and Robson scored. Peter playing for United at Maine Road against City seemed so odd at the time though.

'I was at university in Derby at the time, so I didn't get to many of Peter's games at United but my mates back home used to talk of him hugging that touchline, making the runs and creating space for Robson, Mark Hughes or whoever to run through. But there were so many injuries for United that season that we just fell away.'

As Terry says, over the weeks that followed Peter's own injury others to dog United's challenge included Arthur Albiston, Gary Bailey, Mick Duxbury, John Gidman, Graeme Hogg, Kevin Moran, Remi Moses, Jesper Olsen, Bryan Robson, Gordon Strachan and Frank Stapleton. These were all missing for significant spells that affected United's ability to challenge throughout that season. There is no doubt this damaged United's title aspirations and, for Peter, his own injury limited his chance of returning to the England squad.

'England manager Bobby Robson had been developing his squad and wouldn't have thought about me at all because of what had happened at Leeds and Coventry, but then suddenly my form was good,' considers Peter. 'I was in a winning team and the media talk was really positive. Bobby had Chris Waddle and John Barnes as options and they were really good players, so there seemed to be no chance of me breaking back into that team before I played for United. Then it all changed. Everything was going well for me and then the calf injury came and that was it. No chance of playing for England then and my chances for United disappeared too. I was out for about five or six weeks and then ended up in the Reserves, managed by Brian Whitehouse, waiting for my chance to return.'

Peter's niggling injury kept him out of action for months: 'On the day of my injury when we played Spurs in November it seemed likely the title was coming to Old Trafford. The injuries changed everything but back in November I was convinced the title was coming. I know people will always think about me as a City man and, obviously, I've been a City fan all my life, but I desperately wanted to help United win the title that season.'

When Peter made a return to the

reserves in January he was still considered as a contender for a possible dramatic return to the England team, as well as United's first team of course. The *Irish Independent* still believed he was 'a Mexico outsider after a superb start to the season.' [10] That was more hopeful than possible at this stage because of the injury but it still demonstrates what an impact Peter had made in those opening months at United.

Looking at this period, even the most critical football commentator would view Peter as extremely unlucky. Without the calf injury he probably would have returned to the England squad, potentially as back up for John Barnes or Chris Waddle. Looking back on this time Ron Atkinson told writer Wayne Barton that he felt Peter deserved an England call-up: '[Peter] only cost us £30,000 and if he hadn't been so stupid he would have got back in the England team. I always thought it was worth sometimes taking a little punt on somebody giving them a little chance to see what they could do.' [11]

The stupidity Ron refers to is unclear. Maybe he was thinking about Peter's time at Leeds, Coventry or in Spain or maybe he felt the calf injury could have been avoided. Whatever Ron's view, it must be hard for Peter to come to terms with how the 1985-86 petered out: 'I was personally unlucky, but I think we all were that year. The momentum we had in the early months of the season was lost through injuries and then reverting to a more defensive formation. I was desperate to get back into the team but it wasn't to be. You learn to live with these things as time goes by and I try to keep positive, but it can be difficult when it's happening.'

'Ron began to play more defensive after my injury and Colin Gibson, who was a left back or defensive midfielder, played on

United ace in 'derby' blow

BARNES BLOW

But injured United star insists: I've proved the doubters wrong

KEVIN FRANCIS reporting

FLYING winger Peter Barnes last night came out fighting after being grounded by the latest blow to his jinxed career.

Barnes' stunning run in Manchester United's table-topping team comes to an end at Leicester today where a hamstring injury has ruled him out.

But Barnes told me: "Although I'm disappointed at missing out I'm delighted with the way this season has gone for me. I've the wing a few times. Dad, who was never afraid to speak his mind, told Ron later that season that he'd gone too negative. He told him he should have gone back to the formation that he'd had at the start of the season that had put him well clear at the top. As much as I loved Ron as a manager and enjoyed playing in his teams, I was disappointed that he didn't go back to his 4-4-2 attacking beliefs. It was that swagger the team had for those opening three months that had made us championship favourites by some way. We'd hammer teams. These were not defensive games with the occasional goal. Dad was right. Ron should have continued as he started that season.'

Ken Barnes was not the only person to question Atkinson's tactics that season. Whether it was the injuries or the fear of losing out on the title but the United manager appeared to make a series of hasty purchases that season. Maybe it was an attempt to bolster both morale and the diminishing title challenge, but the second half of the season had seen new arrivals Colin Gibson from Aston Villa, striker Terry Gibson from Coventry City, and defender John

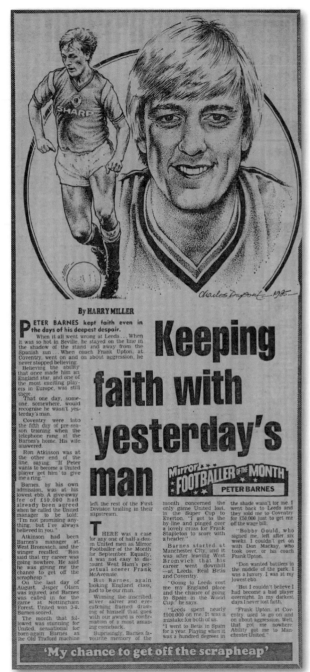

By HARRY MILLER

Keeping faith with yesterday's man

PETER BARNES kept faith even in the days of his deepest despair.

When it all went wrong at Leeds... When it was so hot in Seville he stayed on the line in the shadow of the stand and away from the Spanish sun... When coach Frank Upton, at Coventry, went on and on about aggression, he never stopped believing.

Believing the ability that once made him an England star, and one of the most exciting players in Europe, was still there.

'That one day, some-one, somewhere, would recognise he wasn't yesterday's man.

Coventry were into the fifth day of pre-season training when the telephone rang at the Barnes's home. His wife answered.

Ron Atkinson was at the other end of the line, saying: "If Peter wants to become a United player get him to give me a ring."

Barnes, by his own admission, was at his lowest ebb. A give-away fee of £50,000 had already been agreed when he called the United manager to be told: 'I'm not promising anything, but I've always believed in you.'

Atkinson had been Barnes's manager at West Bromwich, and the winger recalled: 'Ron said that my career was going nowhere. He said he was giving me the chance to get off the scrapheap.'

On the last day of August, Jesper Olsen was injured, and Barnes was called in for the game at Nottingham Forest. United won 3-0. Barnes scored.

The month that followed was stunning for United, and for a born-again Barnes as the Old Trafford machine

left the rest of the First Division trailing in their slipstream.

THERE was a case for any one of half-a-dozen United men as Mirror Footballer of the Month for September. Equally, it was not easy to discount West Ham's perpetual scorer Frank McAvennie.

But Barnes, again looking England class, had to be our man.

Winning the inscribed silver salver and eye-catching framed drawing of himself that goes with our award is confirmation of a most amazing comeback.

Suprisingly, Barnes favourite memory of the

month concerned the only game United lost, in the Super Cup to Everton. "I got to the by-line and pinged over a lovely cross for Frank Stapleton to score with a header."

Barnes started at Manchester City, and it was after leaving West Bromwich that his career went downhill —at Leeds, Real Betis and Coventry.

'Going to Leeds cost me my England place and the chance of going to Spain in the World Cup,' he says.

'Leeds spent nearly £900,000 on me. It was a mistake for both of us.

"I went to Betis in Spain for a year. Playing when it was a hundred degrees in

the shade wasn't for me. I went back to Leeds and they sold me to Coventry for £50,000 just to get me off the wage bill.

"Bobby Gould, who signed me, left after six weeks. I couldn't get on with Don Mackay, who took over, or his coach Frank Upton.

"Don wanted battlers in the middle of the park. I was a luxury. I was at my lowest ebb.

'But I couldn't believe I had become a bad player overnight. In my darkest days I never lost faith.

'Frank Upton, at Coventry, used to go on and on about aggression. Well, that got me nowhere. Ability got me to Manchester United!'

Mirror FOOTBALLER OF THE MONTH
PETER BARNES

'My chance to get off the scrapheap'

Charles Dupont 1985

Sivebaek. Then, on March 12, Peter Davenport, Hughes' intended successor, had arrived from Nottingham Forest for a fee of £750,000.

As well as the injuries and the tactical changes there was something else that affected the club that season. It gained quite a bit of coverage at the time but over the years since then people have tended to forget what a negative impact it had on performances and that was the Old Trafford pitch. Peter has no doubt whatsoever that the pitch limited United's progress: 'United should have won the League and I put it down to that pitch. The undersoil heating didn't work and we had a really poor pitch. It was blamed on the high roof and few gaps for the wind to blow in, but it wasn't just that. There was an undersoil system with wires all over the pitch which seemed to be uncovered at times. The centre of the pitch was muddy and the wings were rock hard in the winter. It was a really poor surface and, as you can see today with the pitches at the Etihad and Old Trafford, great players need good surfaces. If the pitch is poor then it can hamper the team's style and opportunities.

'United fans often talk to me about the QPR game at Old Trafford when I had a great chance to score. I picked the ball up in my own half. I jinked past three or four players and I hit this ball and it's going towards the corner of the goal. Perfectly placed to the side of the 'keeper, but then I see it hit something sticking out of the ground. It diverts the ball and it goes slightly wide of the post! The crowd went mad. They all knew it was the pitch!'

Peter's attempt against QPR was described by journalist Peter Ball as a 'run of which even Best would have been proud.' [12] In that report Ball waxed lyrical about United's unbeaten run of twelve games, adding: 'On the wing Barnes revived memories of more classical days.' Writing for the *Guardian*, Patrick Barclay was even more impressed, commenting that 'Barnes played delightfully' while detailing his impressive attempt: 'There was so much to savour on Saturday, perhaps above all a run of 60 yards by the revitalised Barnes, who left several Rangers trailing, drew the goalkeeper, and rolled a shot inches wide as 40,000 people tried to blow it home.' [13]

The Old Trafford undersoil heating system was commented on several times during the season, particularly during the early months of 1986. In March Peter Ball discussed the advantage the Merseyside clubs had over their main rivals because of the quality of their surfaces and, in particular, their undersoil systems: 'While Manchester United's and Arsenal's systems have broken down, or failed to be switched on early enough in one case, Everton and Liverpool have been playing on perfect pitches. "They do things right at this club," said Peter Reid, and it is an unarguable opinion.' [14]

Whether the rest of football believed the Merseyside clubs did things right or not is open for debate but it was a fact that United's undersoil heating system had struggled throughout the winter months. By February it was only heating part of the pitch, causing United to spend £12,000 on covers to protect the rest of the pitch.

At the start of 1986 United secretary Les Olive answered questions from journalists about the worrying nature of the Old Trafford surface, causing him to comment: 'We have exposed some of the connections under one part of the pitch and they are corroded and burned out. We have our own electricians working on the job.' [15]

The pitch issues and the injuries meant that United's chance of title success faded. Peter: 'We'd lost that momentum that had pushed us forward at the start of the season.

Suddenly, the pressure on Ron is mounting and both Everton and Liverpool were motoring. Liverpool were way off the pace but they'd been grinding out results and suddenly we'd gone from title-certainties to fourth placed and Liverpool, of all teams, had taken the League. We were so unlucky that season. If we'd have kept fit and that pitch had held up then that title would have been ours. There was one other thing that went wrong that season though. Mark Hughes, who was our number nine and absolutely vital, had signed to join Barcelona in the summer. I fully understand the ambition and the desire… I had no issue with that, but it was rumoured in January and became public when our season still had a couple of months left to play.'

Mark Hughes' transfer was agreed in January and was common knowledge some time before it was formally announced on March 21, 1986. [16] A few days later journalist Stephen Bierley was highly critical of the situation at Old Trafford: 'Whatever the rights and wrongs of [Hughes'] transfer to Barcelona, one point is certain. United's reputation, jaded anyway in recent years, has slipped another notch. Hughes will become a rich man: others connected with Old Trafford will bolster their bank balances; the fans have been taken for mugs. Atkinson and his chairman, Martin Edwards, may well have balanced the books but where is the championship winning team?' [17] Bierley added: 'Hughes, if he had to go, should have been sold in the close season. Instead the news leaked out in January and predictably his form has suffered. No player, with a million pounds at stake, is going to take unnecessary risks.'

After the news of his transfer broke Hughes scored four goals in ten games but, crucially, only three of those final games end in victory (prior to Christmas he had scored 12 goals in 21 League games). United

were third by this point, six points behind leaders Everton, but only four behind Liverpool who had played two games more. There had been other rumours of major changes in the national media, including a potential move for Ron Atkinson himself. Reporter Ken Lawrence claimed Real Madrid had approached Ron in February and that they had intensified their efforts in March. [18] Lawrence added that another Spanish club was interested: 'Atkinson has also been linked with the Barcelona job which will be vacated by Venables on June 30.'

Peter had been missing from the United League team since mid-November following his hamstring injury, but took part in a friendly in Israel in early March. This was seen as a sign the player was about to be selected for the first time and, indeed, he was due to start the Manchester derby on March 22, 1986. Unfortunately, in training he broke a bone in his hand and became an injury doubt once more. Ron Atkinson: 'Peter was very much in my plans because Olsen has been a little out of touch.' [19] Peter remained hopeful of starting the game and commented at the time: 'While there is a broken bone in my right hand, the doctors have already told me I could play. There is no great pain and I would have to have my hand tightly strapped. Obviously, I'm desperate for another chance.'

Peter did start the game and it opened in dramatic style with City conceding a careless free kick some 25 yards out after only 90 seconds. New boy Colin Gibson sent a swerving shot around the wall and beyond City's Eric Nixon into the net. Later Strachan scored a penalty to make it 2-0 but, despite that lead, it was not a great day for the Reds as they lost their lead. The match ended in a 2-2 draw, although Peter had been substituted by that time. He had set United up with a few

Manchester United's team of internationals.

chances, but his role in the game brought conflicting reports from journalists with Derek Hodgson expressing positive views, such as: 'Barnes, who had been floating teasing crosses into a stiff breeze, soon saw he had no one to aim at, for Hughes and Davenport were auditioning for the same role. By half time, all the singing was coming from the visiting end.' [20] In a piece that seemed determined to criticise United throughout, Stephen Bierley felt somewhat differently: 'The former City and England winger had voluminous bandages around his right hand; they might just as well have been around his eyes. He wandered blindly around in search of the ball, allowing Reid

complete freedom to attack down the right.' [21]

Peter remembers: 'It was my first League game since mid-November, so I had been desperate to play. It wasn't a great game for us in the end because we let a two goal lead go. United were 2-0 up – Colin Gibson and Gordon Strachan scored. Strachan's was a penalty. Arthur Albiston went to clear and he skewered the ball and it went in – own goal. He's my pal Arthur and we played each other at every level.'

It says much about the state of Manchester football at the time that this 2-2 draw was celebrated extensively by City. Much of the praise went to City manager

Billy McNeill who enjoyed telling the media that he had picked what he described as a Mancunian team against Atkinson's multi-million pound United. Much was made of the fact that the City side that day had cost £287,000 whereas United's was in excess of £3 million. McNeill reminded the media that City paraded eight Mancunians, while Peter was described as the only United player from Manchester. The discussion of expenditure added to the pressure on Atkinson but there was still hope the season would end in League glory. United were now third, three points behind Everton after 33 games with Liverpool second. League success still seemed possible.

Sadly, Peter's substitute appearance in the derby was the last time he appeared on the pitch in the League that season. Results deteriorated for the Reds with 14 points dropped in the nine games that followed, leaving Atkinson's side fourth, 12 points

behind champions Liverpool. It was a frustrating finish for United and for Peter: 'When I played against City I wasn't really back to full fitness and I didn't even get back on to the subs bench. It was frustrating not to be directly involved in those games and it was disappointing to see us lose the title like that. I hoped the 1986-87 season would see me return to first team action and I hoped to play a part in another title challenge. I'd enjoyed the season until my injury and wanted more. It's fair to say that Ron resurrected my career at United. If Old Trafford had possessed a good pitch – or even a half decent one – and some of the injuries not happened then United would have won the title for the first time in 19 years. Ron would have been given an extended contract and the momentum may have led to other major successes.'

Terry Christian believes the injury problems United had faced that season had been insurmountable. He felt that the Reds had coped better than some of their title rivals would have done: 'If Liverpool had suffered the injuries we had then they'd have finished fifth. Atkinson was really unlucky. There was a lot of bad luck that season. The balance just wasn't there all season but we were still in with a shout of winning the League up until about March, but Robson's injury and the rest. These weren't the days of squads either, so you tended to play your eleven plus a sub of course.

'United were good to watch and Big Ron was such a good manager. People forget that he finished top four every season with United.'

When considering resources, support, quality of team and so on, Ron should have won the League with United but fate seemed to play its part each time. Pete Boyle: 'Maybe Ron didn't quite have enough to win the League but these were exciting times. We'd get close and then fall away a bit. When the 1985-86 season fell away I started to think we were never going to win the League. If Ron had signed Peter a couple of years earlier, say in 1983, then I think he'd have flourished for United. He'd have been part of the team that won the FA Cup twice and who knows how things might have gone in the League too?'

1   'Slack Reds pay price', *Manchester Evening News Pink*, August 24, 1985.
2   Mick Duxbury with Wayne Barton, *It's Mick, Not Mike* (Durrington: Pitch Publishing, 2015), 158.
3   Wayne Barton, *Que Sera Sera* (Durrington: Pitch Publishing, 2019), 293.
4   'Keeping faith with yesterday's man', *Daily Mirror*, October 11, 1985, 30.
5   'Just another game says Atkinson', *Aberdeen Press and Journal*, October 3, 1985, 20.
6   'Carry on Chris', *Newcastle Journal*, November 12, 1985, 14.
7   'Waddle: I'll fight back', *Daily Mirror*, November 12, 1985, 30.
8   'Barnes dance', *Sunday Mirror*, September 22, 1985, 42-43.
9   'Quality Street', *Sunday Mirror*, November 17, 1985, 47.
10 'Bailey is back for Atkinson's sentimental return', *Irish independent*, January 11, 1986, 15.
11 Wayne Barton, *Que Sera Sera* (Durrington: Pitch Publishing, 2019), 310.
12 'A red shirt catches fire', *Observer*, October 12, 1985, 48.
13 'new masters of the screen', *Guardian*, October 14, 1985, 26.
14 'Everton turn on the heat', *Sunday Tribune*, March 9, 1986, 12.
15 'Rovers look no match for smart Luton', *Reading Evening Post*, January 7, 1986, 11.
16 'Hughes joins Spanish giants', *Aberdeen Evening Express*, March 21, 1986, 20; 'Spain drain', Star, March 22, 1986, 32.
17 'Dog's life for Ron', *Guardian*, March 24, 1986, 28.
18 'Madrid in new moves', *Star*, March 22, 1986, 32.
19 'Barnes' sad break', *Star*, March 22, 1986, 31.
20 'City express', *Observer*, March 23, 1986, 50.
21 'Dog's life for Ron', *Guardian*, March 24, 1986, 28.

Chapter Eighteen
THE HAIRDRYER

❝

United, their wings literally clipped with two
nasty tackles on first Barnes, then Olsen by a bludgeon
called Hodges, did create two chances from those flanks,
both of which Stapleton wasted... United's most threatening
aggressive move was the switch from a grandstand seat
to a touchline bench by manager Alex Ferguson to start
the second half.'

❞

'Vince makes mince of United', *Observer*, November 30, 1986, 49

The close season of 1986 brought a few inquests on what had occurred during the previous season, however for Peter there remained optimism. 1985-86 may not have ended with trophy success but it did see him earn rave reviews and play his part in a phenomenal run at the start of the season. Injury limited his chance of building on this as the season progressed of course, however the chance to contribute to United's next title push encouraged him.

'I was determined to play my part at Old Trafford,' remembers Peter. 'I felt that under Ron we still had a chance to win the League in 1986-87 but because we'd missed out on the title the pressure was on. It had been so long since United had won the League title that it ate away at some. There was also the added pressure from Merseyside - not only were Liverpool finding success but Everton were too. That made it even more unbearable I guess.

'I always felt that chairman Martin Edwards had a lot of time for Ron and supported him but others thought he was quite flash and were probably thinking that he'd had enough time. He'd been there for a few years and the title was still going to Merseyside and not to Old Trafford. Ron was larger than life - that was great when trophies were being won but when they weren't I think some resented that. When the 1986-87 season started I think his critics were waiting. There seemed to be a pressure that I hadn't noticed the previous year. It felt as though the season had to start as well as 1985-86 did to give Ron a chance. Any slip-up would give those who wanted a change the ammunition they needed, but we'd lost Mark Hughes to Barcelona. That was a big loss!'

Supporter Pete Boyle was aware of the general mood around the club: 'After missing out on the title it seemed like Ron was on his last legs. There was just a feeling that we wouldn't win the League.'

Both Pete's and Peter's views seem accurate and when the opening three games ended in defeat the pressure increased. In fact only one victory (5-1 v Southampton) and one draw (1-1 at Leicester) came in the opening eight League games. Peter had not played in any of these fixtures, but he did return for the second leg of the second round League Cup tie at Port Vale on October 7. He put in a good performance, scoring a goal as the Reds won 5-2 (7-2 on aggregate). He kept his place for the following League game, which ended in a 3-1 victory over Sheffield Wednesday, and for the 1-0 win over Luton and a 1-1 draw at Manchester City. He also played in a goalless League Cup third round tie at home to Southampton on October 29. Seven days later Ron Atkinson was dismissed. 'We could see how things

---

Cyril Chapman
P Vale 2, Man U 5
(agg : 2-7)

Storming Barnes sinks Vale

For an hour Port Vale faced up honourably to a daunting task last night, but then their defence went to pieces. United scored three goals in six minutes and gladdened the heart of manager Ron Atkinson by taking the tie 7-2 on aggregate.

Port Vale's chief tormentor was Peter Barnes, playing only

A Red revolution from little boy Blue !

PETER BARNES — whose brilliant wing displays won the approval of Old Trafford fans after his arrival at the start of last season.

By PAUL HINCE

EVEN friends of Ron Atkinson thought the Manchester United manager had finally flipped when he dipped into the club's coffers to bring Peter Barnes from Coventry to Old Trafford.

"He's paid good cash for a has-been" was the common cry. "Barnes is a luxury we cannot afford."

And those critics had a point. For a career which began brilliantly at Manchester City where Barnes earned the first of his 22 England caps before

had any faith in the ability of this old fashioned winger to mesmerise defenders with one swivel of the hips.

One was Barnes himself. And happily for Barnes in particular and soccer in general, the other was Ron Atkinson.

Inside story on the troubles at Old Trafford

MANCHESTER UNITED CRISIS
WHY RON MUST GO

SOCCER SPECIAL

BEST'S BLAST
By JACK STEGGLES

Golden glow is fading so fast
By BOB RUSSELL
who has reported United for 15 years

CELT MIS
From ALEX CAMER...

Game's giants are in a mess

CLIFF IN THE DOCK

could go because the mood had changed,' remembers Peter. 'The pressure had been on and the atmosphere had turned sour and low. Ron came and said goodbye to us all. He was disappointed and I think most of us were. Then we heard that Alex Ferguson was coming in. The only person who seemed to know anything about him was Gordon Strachan, because he'd been at Aberdeen with him. He warned us all that Alex was a different type to Ron. Whereas Ron would have a laugh and a joke with you, Alex was a serious man. He told us that things would change. When Alex arrived you could see how he was going to be. The culture would change, no question.'

Ferguson accepted the United offer and became the club's new manager within 12 hours of Atkinson's dismissal. At the time the new boss told the media: 'Money did not enter into it. It is just that Manchester United were the only club in the world capable of drawing me from Aberdeen.' [1]

For Peter the change brought mixed feelings, though he was keen to see his career develop under the former Aberdeen boss: 'Although I was sad to see Ron go I did think that Alex would at least give me a chance. I knew he'd played with width at Aberdeen and that he seemed to like wingers. I was quite positive about his arrival. We had a meeting downstairs at

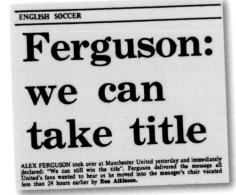

the Cliff. It was a big room and we were all there – first team, reserves, apprentices and Alex stood there. He said about coming down from Aberdeen and made comments like: "I expect you to wear that badge with pride. This is a wonderful club with a great history… Sir Matt Busby, the Busby Babes, Munich… you have to want to play for that shirt. Anybody steps out of line, you have to deal with me!" That's how it was run.

'When Ron got sacked the culture was bound to be questioned. Football was changing and the idea that players could go out drinking was beginning to stop. The press were beginning to notice and articles would appear and, of course, a new manager likes to instil his own discipline and ways. The change in the dressing room was enormous.

'Under Ron there was a lot of laughter and banter in the dressing room. A positive atmosphere with Ron very much a part of all of that too. Then under Alex it changed completely. Everything was serious. You could tell from the moment he arrived at the Cliff. Then when Archie Knox joined us a couple of weeks later as his assistant he was a tough task master too. He was like a sergeant-major. He didn't say much but he didn't need to. We knew just by a look.'

As Peter suggested there was a cultural change beginning at United following Alex Ferguson's appointment. Under Ron – as at many clubs – players had been able to enjoy a few drinks and, so long as they performed on match day and did nothing illegal, no one particularly cared. By the time of Ferguson's arrival though some were suggesting that there was a drinking culture that was affecting performances at United. 'Most footballers liked a drink back then and you'd go into the players' lounge after the match,' says Peter. 'Compared to the rest of the team at United me and Arthur Albiston were not

Alex Ferguson

great social animals. All the players would go out, of course, back then. You'd have a few beers and then go home. Because a few of us lived out Altrincham way we'd go for a few drinks after a game together and, after a couple, me and Arthur would be trying to sneak off home to our families. I was never going to be the last man out or still be there at the end of the night. I wasn't a late stay-out.

'Me and Arthur would plan to go home but the last dropping off spot was Paddy Crerand's pub, The Park, in Altrincham. There'd usually be a band in playing Irish music. By the time I made it home I'd had four or five pints and then, after that, me and my wife Alison would be off out for our own night out.

'Some of the players would carry on of course but me and Arthur Albiston were lightweight. I have to say that most of the players who did stay out and drink handled it well in terms of not letting it affect their match performance. If they delivered on match day no one would query what happened after the game. As long as players were performing that was it.'

Initially Peter seemed to benefit from the arrival of Ferguson: 'I was back in the team and had played three of the previous four League games, then Alex Ferguson arrived. He actually came to our house in Altrincham one night shortly after arriving. Gordon Strachan, Bryan Robson, Arthur Albiston and others came to a house party we'd organised and I'd also invited the new boss of course. He came with his wife, which was great for us.

'I played the first four League games of Alex's management at United. We played Oxford away and I was number eleven. We lost 2-0. Then there was a goalless game at Norwich and we beat QPR 1-0.'

That QPR victory was Ferguson's first League game at Old Trafford. The *Liverpool Echo* reported that Ferguson: 'was given a terrific reception when he was introduced to the fans before kick off.' [2] United's goal came in the 32nd minute when: '[Sivebaek] scored direct from a 20 yard free kick, awarded for a foul by Terry Fenwick on Peter Barnes, which earned the Rangers player a booking.'

Perhaps demonstrating the pressure that any United team was under at this time, the victory did prompt talk of United mounting a serious challenge for the League despite being seventeenth after sixteen games. United fan Pete Boyle was hopeful that a League challenge would occur under Ferguson but he was not convinced that the managerial change would alter the general direction for some time: 'I was not convinced. In fact right up to 1989-90 and that 5-1 defeat to City I felt we were as inconsistent as we'd been under Big Ron. I felt at times we were papering over the cracks. Back then all I wanted as a fan was for someone to bring us one League title… of course we all know what's happened since but for some time even that one League title looked unachievable.'

Back in 1986 those fans and media who thought League success was possible were brought down to earth somewhat on November 29 in a tricky away game at Wimbledon. 'It was the first time United had ever played them in the League and we lost 1-0 at Plough Lane,' remembers Peter painfully. 'This stands out vividly in my memory. We got off the coach at Plough Lane and walked into the dressing room and Wimbledon had put water all over the dressing room floor. We were treading water. All the time the Wimbledon players had their ghetto blaster on at maximum volume – you could feel it in our dressing room.

'It was a small dressing room with wooden pegs and a treatment table in the middle of the room. The tea urn comes in and Alex pours himself a cup of tea while we're all getting ready. He takes a mouthful and spits it out across the floor: "The dirty f***ing b*stards!" They'd put salt in it! Welcome to Wimbledon! Alex was fuming.

'When it came to the team talk he said things like "this team don't deserve to be on the same park as you!" I was starting. Bryan Robson was back for his first game after injury but he was on the bench. I'm outside left, doing okay but it wasn't a good game for us. It was a bit of an ordeal. More like a cup game against a Fourth Division side. A real battle.'

According to the *Dublin Evening Herald*, United's only opportunity of note in the first half came from Peter: 'Peter Barnes curled a dangerous cross to the far post, where Frank Stapleton at full stretch, shot into the side netting.' [3]

Three minutes before the break Wimbledon took the lead through a goal on his home debut for Vinnie Jones, then known as Vince in the media, a bargain purchase from non-league Wealdstone. Peter: 'The mood wasn't great at half time, but we went out for the second half convinced we could get something out of the match. Nothing really changed though. I was being kicked quite a bit – we all were - and after about sixty minutes I saw the number 11 go up. I didn't really mind because Bryan Robson, the captain, was coming on after his injury… and I'd been kicked enough! Nowadays I joke that when I saw the number 11 go up I shouted across to the bench "do you mean me or all the team?" It was that kind of game!

'Robson went on and I went down the tunnel, thinking that I'd get in the bath and get ready. I thought it would help. I get in the bath and sit there washing. After a while I could hear the studs coming up the tunnel and I knew we'd lost 1-0 because there hadn't been any cheering. You'd hear them in the dressing room if there had. You could hear the other United players coming into the dressing room. It was all subdued. I thought I'd best get out. I wrapped myself in a towel and went towards the door, but it was already hanging off its hinges – it was an appalling changing room. Then, before I had chance to prise the door open, I heard Alex start talking. My peg with my clothes on was in the far corner, so I'd have to walk directly in front of him to get to it.

'I start to make my way around but he's angry and he's talking loudly at us about the game. As I move he kicks the door and it almost comes off. I can feel him staring at me but I'm passing him and everybody else with my towel around me, "excuse me, pardon me." Who knows what he thought at that moment, but I soon found out! This was the real hairdryer treatment. He'd only been there a few weeks but he went around the room telling us each what he thought. He laid into almost everyone – Bryan Robson was saved from any criticism because he'd only come on as sub and was coming back from injury.'

The dressing room rollicking went on for a full thirty minutes according to the *Guardian's* Martin Thorpe in his report the following Monday. Ferguson, who had watched the first half from the directors box but moved to the dugout for the second period, could not have been in the best of moods that day because he had flown in from Glasgow that morning as his mum had died the previous night. [4] Nevertheless, the hairdryer treatment was something that many players would come to experience over the years. Despite respecting Ferguson and recognising his talents as a manager it was not an approach Peter was likely to enjoy. Peter's youngest daughter Jessica believes her father benefitted from a different approach: 'I think there should always be room for compassion and support for players. There are different approaches taken by managers and I think dad preferred those who took time to consider a player's wellbeing. Some players seem to respond to being shouted at but dad worked better when someone listened to him and tried to be more the "arm around the shoulder" type.'

'I always got on with managers who built your confidence,' says Peter. 'I struggled if managers came in and shouted, that wouldn't work with me at all. I needed an arm around the shoulder approach. I enjoyed managers with humour. Ron Atkinson used to hear laughter in the dressing room and he'd come in: "What's going on lads; What's the joke?" and

he'd join in. Mick Brown, Ron's assistant, would often be getting in on the act too. I remember John Gidman seeing Mick on his way to the dressing room and John laughed: "Watch out lads, ET is coming", because Mick had a squashed nose and lived-in face. Mick and Ron would be a part of the humour, but it was clear Alex was different. Managers don't need to be popular and, all these years on, we can see what Alex brought United... what he achieved. He took them to the League title, which was absolutely vital, and so much glory, so his approach worked for the club and for many players.

'I respected Alex and he gave me those four games in the first team after he arrived. So I was hopeful that I'd play a part going forward. I felt I was still fit but I started to see that he would be bringing in his own players – which is totally understandable – and so a move seemed likely.

'I only had a few months left on my contract and Alex called me to his office for a meeting. He was polite, respectable and dignified. He said to me: "Peter, I respect you as a pro but I have to tell you that you are not in my long term plans. Jimmy Frizzell, from across the road [City], is interested and they're going to come in with a cash offer. Would you be happy to speak with Jimmy?" Would I be happy? Of course. This was City and if I wasn't going to be part of Alex's plans at Old Trafford then it was an obvious move for me. My family was settled and I wouldn't have to move. It was perfect. I shook hands with Alex and that was that. I could see entirely where he was coming from and it was obvious, just from my brief spell under him, that he was going to make big changes in the way things were done there.'

Peter returned to Manchester City on January 13, 1987 but it was not the end of meetings between the United boss and members of the Barnes family: 'In the nineties, long after I'd left United, my dad used to pop in and see Alex. Obviously, dad and Denis Law had been close since 1960 when Denis joined City. Dad was captain back then, and over the years he was often allowed to pop in at the Cliff or Old Trafford.

'Alex would sometimes get the players to sign balls or shirts for dad to take to his soccer school in Malaysia. There was one day Alex was with dad when the United players were all getting their food in the canteen… Roy Keane, Beckham and so on. Alex shouted across to the lads: "Hey, you lads! You don't know this man do you? Well, this is Ken Barnes, chief scout at City. Now he was a player! He knew how to pass the ball. If you have the dedication this man had then you may, just may, get somewhere in the game. You wouldn't have got a game in his day." Dad loved it. I think Alex knew how to make him feel good and I respect him for that.'

Due to a close relationship with Denis Law, Ken Barnes was comfortable and

COMEBACK PETER

ANOTHER GREAT EXCLUSIVE

By BOB RUSSELL

UNHAPPY Peter Barnes is heading back to his first love, Manchester City.

The Manchester United winger is angry after his shock axing against Coventry on Saturday.

Barnes has kept a discreet silence over the way he has been repeatedly discarded between

Barnes could lift the Blues

By PETER GARDNER

PETER BARNES is the man to rekindle Manchester City's flickering fortunes.

He is also one of the few players who could attract back many of the missing Maine Road drifters.

Hints of a Manchester United clear-out following manager Ron Atkinson's massive recent spending spree include a possible departure for the one-time Blues golden boy.

In that event manager Billy McNeill could be first in the queue for a

player his club unloaded for £600,000 at the height of the Malcolm Allison upheavals seven years ago.

Barnes featured brightly under Atkinson at West Brom then lost his way in spells with Leeds United, Seville and Coventry before United threw him a career lifeline.

Peter the great accepted it with both hands and was, many close to

Old Trafford firmly believe, instrumental in their early season successes.

And it has to be asked whether it was more than coincidence United's star waned when Barnes was injured last autumn.

Atkinson paid Coventry a mere £35,000 to bring him back north during the close season . . . a fee even hard-up City could have well afforded but refused the gamble.

Now even a £50,000 Maine Road outlay for Barnes would be realistic for a player who would welcome a return to the club that gave him his first big chance.

I understand that Barnes, now 28, was unhappy at being left out of the United side last welcome at both the Cliff and Old Trafford over the years. Peter's elder sister Susan remembers that Denis had been a frequent visitor to the Barnes' household during his earliest days in Manchester: 'Due to our dad, famous footballers used to pop in when we were kids. When Denis Law signed for City in 1960 he was always at our house. Until about ten years ago I was still calling him Uncle Denis!

'Peter's too young to remember Denis at City, but when Denis joined United Dad took Keith and Peter to see him at his house. Keith was a United fan and idolised Denis and wanted to hear him talk about the great United games. Diane Law made some cheese sandwiches – Keith hated cheese but because he was at Denis's house he ate them all! Peter mustn't have been that bothered about Denis's United stories though because when they turned to Peter he was fast asleep in an armchair!

'Keith once took Peter on to the Stretford End to watch a United-Liverpool game. In the middle of the Stretford End Keith started pointing at Peter singing a song about him being a City fan. Peter was so embarrassed and tried to hide but that was the difference between Peter and Keith.'

[1] Ian Morrison and Alan Shury, *Manchester United The Complete Record 1878-1990* (Derby: Breedon Books, 1990), 44.
[2] 'Title pretenders maintain challenge', *Liverpool Echo*, November 22, 1986, 30.
[3] 'Wimbledon v Manchester Utd', *Dublin Evening Herald*, November 29, 1986, 39.
[4] Ibid.

Chapter Nineteen

WE NEVER WIN AT HOME

❝ Peter Barnes steps back into the Manchester City spotlight at Maine Road after an eight year absence. The 29-year-old former England winger – signed from Manchester United on Wednesday – is pushed straight into the team to face Liverpool for the most testing debut in his six club career. Barnes made his first professional debut for City as a 17-year-old 12 years ago. **❞**

'Post Sport', *Reading Evening Post*, January 17, 1987, 32..

On January 13, 1987 Peter officially re-signed for City from United. The move was heralded in the media as the return of a prodigal son and City fans were delighted. There were almost eight years between Peter's last appearance in 1979 and his return in 1987 and those seasons had seen the status of the club fall somewhat. In 1979 the Blues were perceived as a major club, able to challenge for the game's top honours but in 1987 they were struggling in the top flight and heavily in debt. In between there had been the 1981 FA Cup final appearance but a shock relegation in 1983 encapsulated the general feeling and mood of the place.

Support had remained high with the Blues being the fourth best supported team in the entire League in 1985-86, as they had been in 1978-79. City's attendances, like support across all of football, had dropped from 36,203 to 24,229 but only United, Liverpool and Everton, all of whom were winning trophies, had better figures than City. Despite this strength of support the damage caused by Malcolm Allison's doomed rebuilding plans of 1979 were evident across the club. 'When I look back I realise that the contrast between the City I'd left in 1979 to the one I'd joined in 1987 was great,' remembers Peter. 'It was sad to see how the club had declined. I left a rich, successful club and returned to one that had lost its way with no money. There were buckets to catch rainwater in the corridor at the Platt Lane training complex! I love City and it was hard to see how things had changed.'

By the time of Peter's arrival the City manager was Jimmy Frizzell, who had been Billy McNeill's assistant, moving into the new role when McNeill left for Aston Villa in September 1986. Peter: 'Jimmy was a lovely man but they hardly had any money and he had to buy cheaply. He couldn't build a team, plus they were relying on the young kids far too much. With Tony Book and Glyn Pardoe, Dad had helped develop the players who won the FA Youth Cup in 1986 by beating United in the final. It was a great achievement but that success seemed to go to the directors' heads and they thought these lads could be thrown into the team and play game after game. I used to think back to my early career and, although I was impatient at the time, Tony Book had given me and the other young lads a few games, then rested us. He protected us I guess, but in 1987 City couldn't do that.'

The way Tony Book had managed the early careers of Peter and others in the mid-1970s had been perfect and similar to the way Pep Guardiola managed the development of Phil Foden during 2019 to 2021. Book had wanted to get the most out of those players by protecting their long term development. Sadly, in 1987 Manchester City's talented youngsters had to be thrown in and deliver immediately. They had won the FA Youth Cup in 1986, under the direction of Tony Book and Glyn Pardoe, but pressure from the top meant that manager Jimmy Frizzell had little choice but to play many of these talented youngsters. Five of the eleven who started the Youth Cup final first leg appeared in the League during 1986-87 with Steve Redmond making 30 League appearances, David White 24, Paul Moulden 20, Ian Brightwell 16 and Paul Lake 3. Many of these were making a significant number of reserve and youth appearances as well. No matter how impressive these players were – and they were - the pressure on them to deliver in what was a season of struggle was immense.

'There were some good, seasoned pros there too,' stresses Peter. 'Men like

STICK WITH SOCCER'S TOP TEAM

GREAT TO BE HOME

MAINE MAN . . .
Barnes signs as boss Jimmy Frizzell looks on.

I'm staying this time—Barnes

PETER BARNES went home to Maine Road yesterday. And after completing a £30,000 move, he admitted: "There have been plenty of times in the last few years I wished I had never left."

Now Barnes, 29, is ready to finish his career with Manchester City, convinced the short trip from Old Trafford can be the last move for the winger who has never quite lived up to his vast potential.

Barnes stormed into the headlines over 12 years ago as a 17-year-old wonder boy, but in 1979 was sold to West Brom for £650,000—the first leg or a

John Gidman and Kenny Clements. Jimmy brought John in to help the young lads in October. I tipped my dad off that he was going on the transfer list when we were both at United. I got on really well with him and he was a good footballer. He wore his heart on his sleeve but fell out with Ron Atkinson though and was put on the transfer list. I said to him that I could have a word with City and see if they'd be interested and so I rang my Dad. Dad was the City Chief Scout at this time and he had a word with Jimmy Frizzell and he signed. That was that. John was good in the dressing room. He had a good way with him and made the young lads more relaxed. He cracked a few jokes.

'The quality of signings being made in general by City was not a patch on the team we had in 1979, before Allison broke it up. I suppose, if I'm being brutal, it was a mixture of talented youngsters breaking through, experienced players who were past their best and journeymen footballers. Jimmy Frizzell was unlucky - the club had no money but he was expected to work miracles. Jimmy didn't have a strong football management personality but he knew his stuff. Dad loved him and Jimmy had a great sense of humour. A really nice man but perhaps not strong enough for top flight football. He talked to the players as

a pal and needed someone alongside him who was tough with the players. A sergeant-major like Ian Macfarlane or Archie Knox, Jimmy didn't have that.'

For Peter the move was on paper a good one, although it did bring a realisation that one of his dreams was now over: 'As great as it felt to return to City I realised that my ambition to play for England again was over. I'd come so close at United, but the calf injury ended the opportunity. I was still hopeful of course but the 1986 World Cup happened without me and, after that, the chance had gone. Moving to Maine Road though allowed me to live in the same house and keep my family settled. My eldest was four and so moving to City meant we could think about schools and so on.'

Peter and Alison were also expecting their second child at the time and the following May Jessica was born at Wythenshawe Hospital. Being able to spend time in Manchester with his wider family was great for Peter. His elder sister Susan knew how much it meant for Peter to be settled in the area at this time: 'Peter likes to be close to the family and Manchester. He had always been a City fan and it meant so much for him to play for the club but, as football had been significant to our family all our lives, I don't think it ever changed Peter. He was grounded because our family life had just been normal.'

Four days after signing Peter made his second City debut against Liverpool at Maine Road. Frizzell had picked an adventurous attacking formation against reigning champions Liverpool. Sadly, there was no happy return as Ian Rush netted in the 72nd minute. As for Peter's performance

CITY'S WING AND A PRAYER

BARNES... fall guy

PETER BARNES wings his way back into top flight action today — and that could be good news for Jimmy Frizzell and Manchester City.

By KEVIN FRANCIS and MATT D'ARCY

Frizzell explained: "Peter has said he could have saved Ron Atkinson his job at United if he had been in the team regularly . . . I just hope he can save Jimmy Frizzell's job at City.

"Peter is a player of tremendous experience and ability, a crowd pleaser who people will come to watch. He was a

"People like Peter have become the fall guys of football."

Ken Barnes, City's chief scout, said: "For years now, wingers have been made the scapegoats when things have gone wrong.

"I'm not saying that just because my son is a winger . . . heaven knows, I've given him more rollickings than anyone.

the *Sunday Independent* reported that he, like City, had been mostly subdued in what was a tough match but 'Barnes made one thrilling 60-yard run to set up Imre Varadi, but the City striker wasted a clear opening.' [1]

Playing on the opposite wing for City against Liverpool was 19 year old David White who was delighted that Peter was back at Maine Road. Years later he commented that he was 'thrilled to discover that Peter Barnes had re-joined the club. [Peter] would be competing for my position, of course, but as far as I was concerned it was a pleasure and a privilege to rub shoulders with one of my childhood heroes. "Watch and learn," advised Dad. "You won't find a better professional than Barnsey".' [2]

The following Tuesday, January 20th, Peter made his second appearance for City when Frizzell decided to include him, Kenny Clements, Mark Seagraves and Trevor Morley alongside predominantly their talented young stars, such as Ian Brightwell and Paul Moulden, in a Central League game against Liverpool. This time the Blues defeated the Reds 5-0 with Peter netting the fifth ten minutes from time.

Peter's third game in a week came for the first team away at Wimbledon on January 24. It was a dour goalless draw and was City's twentieth consecutive away League game without a win. That run would eventually stretch to 34 games, ending at Bradford on October 21, 1987, during which the chant 'We never win at home and we never win away; We lost last week and we lost today; We don't give a F*** because we're all P****d up; MCFC OK!' grew in popularity. It became a rallying call to some extent during those fruitless, dismal away trips and would frequently be aired, especially after the Blues had gone a goal behind or during the final five minutes or

Peter and Ian Rush, during Peter's second debut for City.

so of an away game. For fans it was a way to demonstrate their loyalty and the longer the run of away games continued without a win the larger City's away following became. Fans just had to be there when the win eventually occurred.

'The fans were brilliant throughout my time at City but especially during this time,' says Peter. 'The mood had certainly changed around the place in between my two spells at City but I think what kept the club going was the loyalty and humour of the fans. I know there were demonstrations against the board – and that was grim to see but understandable – but as players we got a lot of support. Nothing had changed there. The fans knew the players were trying their best and there was a mutual respect. The problems at City were not the fault of the fans and, as a player, I truly felt for them. They'd been badly let down – not just in 1987 but ever since Malcolm returned in 1979.'

Peter played in eight first team games and thirteen Central League games, scoring eight, that season. The reserve team finished fourth but the first team struggles led to relegation. Peter: 'You should never go back. I love City. Always have. It was great playing for Jimmy Frizzell, but it hurt that we were losing more games than we were winning. Within a few months of arriving in 1987 we were relegated and millions of pounds in debt.

'That season it was difficult at times because some of us were heading towards the end of our careers and the young lads were at the start of theirs. We would try and help the lads but sometimes you were struggling yourself and had to focus on getting your game right. You need a good blend in a team but that was difficult to maintain at City due to the club's financial situation.'

Relegation brought a change to the management structure with the Norwich coach Mel Machin brought in and given the title Team Manager while Jimmy Frizzell was appointed General Manager. It seemed a strange set up to fans but also to members of the playing staff, especially when the two men seemed to take it in turns to face the press. Even City's match programme alternated the manager's column - one game Frizzell gave his views, the next Machin. It was odd as the they had never previously worked together, but the City board decided that was the way it was to be.

'When City were relegated they should've brought a strong coach in alongside Jimmy – or even replaced Jimmy with a new management set-up, but the club was skint,' suggests Peter. 'Instead they kept Jimmy in the role and brought in

Mel Machin. Machin was supposed to be coming in as Jimmy's number two but Mel wanted to be the manager and wouldn't come if he was the coach. Instead of moving on and looking elsewhere they appointed Mel as manager but kept Jimmy as well. There was confusion – it was a bit like when Allison returned and no one quite new who the boss was. Jimmy became a sort of number two to Mel and that was wrong!'

Peter enjoyed playing for Frizzell but Machin's coaching did not impress him: 'Mel had these stupid passwords for play. It drove me mental! Sid, Fred and Jack! He'd get us to the University Grounds and would go through his plans. Sid was when you let it flow through your legs; Fred was a flick… It was ridiculous. You'd be training and then he'd shout "Fred" and you had to do whatever that was, or your partner in the session would be behind you shouting Sid so that you'd let it through your legs.

'He told us he wanted these passwords to be used out on the pitch in competitive matches. The older players are looking at each other thinking "what is all of

this nonsense?" I'd been there with Malcolm Allison's strange coaching ideas a decade earlier, I didn't need it again. To be frank Machin was no Allison either. Understandably, the younger players did what Machin demanded – well, they had to. They were young and wanted to be picked. Totally understandable, but those of us who had been around a bit couldn't believe it.'

Even the younger players were dissatisfied with Sid, Jack and Fred. David White later wrote: 'I despised it, particularly when we played Norwich City, Mel's former club. Their players would be well versed in the gaffer's daft drill, of course, and would yell "Sid", "Jack" or "Fred" to befuddle us and wrest possession while the crowd wondered what the hell was going on. It was progressive coaching gone mad.' [3]

The 1987-88 season opened with Peter scoring twice as City Reserves beat Aston Villa 3-2 in the Central League but no opportunity came to appear in a first team League game. In fact the first chance of any first team action came in the first leg of the second round League Cup tie at home to Wolves. That night Peter came on as substitute for Paul Simpson in the 73rd minute of the 2-1 defeat but that was his final first team appearance for the Blues. Peter: 'I enjoyed seeing Paul Simpson's career develop. Years before we were both in the same City squad I popped in to Maine Road to see my dad, who was Chief Scout at the time. I knocked on the door and dad introduced me to the lad who was sat there. It was Paul and he was about to sign for the club. Dad talked about him being a winger and I had a few words with him, wishing him well. In fact I gave him a pair of boots. It seemed the right thing to do and I always wanted Paul to get opportunities. When we were both playing for Mel Machin I was dissatisfied with the friendlies and then the start of the 1987-88 season because Mel

didn't seem to give either of us a chance. Paul was still a kid so wouldn't be in a position to challenge the boss, but I did. I went to see Mel and said that if I wasn't to be given a chance then Paul should be but the manager didn't seem to appreciate our type of wing play then.'

Paul Simpson's first start of 1987-88 came in the sixth League game but even then he wore the number 5 shirt and was not on the wing in the 11 shirt. It should be noted though that Mel was picking attack-minded David White on the opposite wing from the start of that season.

Peter's sister Susan felt that manager Machin had written off Peter as soon as he arrived: 'It was disappointing when Peter was back at City because I don't think Mel Machin particularly liked him. He didn't give him the chances that he needed. With Dad being at City at the time it was difficult. Dad was always keen to ensure his boys stood on their own two feet and he would hate people thinking that they were given chances because of him. He was the opposite really. He wanted them to prove themselves as individuals.

'Dad never went overboard and would often play things down. Even when he was Chief Scout he used to remind players, not just Peter, that things could go wrong at any point. He tried to keep everyone's feet on the ground. During Peter's spell at West Brom Bill Shankly, the former Liverpool manager, was talking to Dad about Peter and said: "Oh, Ken, You've got a good'un there!" Dad told him that Peter had a chance but played it down completely.' According to Ken in later discussions, Shankly went on to say 'Don't let the coaches get hold of him, Ken!' To which Ken replied: 'Don't Liverpool have coaches then Bill?' 'The only coaches we have at Anfield are the ones with wheels that take us to away games!'

Peter's best game following his return to City was a 1-1 draw with Spurs in April, 1987. Here Gary Stevens brings down Peter, leading to a penalty which Neil McNab netted.

Both Ken and Shankly believed talent should be encouraged and worried that some managers were trying to coach players into becoming robots. They wanted players to use their natural abilities and flair.

In 1987's Manchester the development of young players was a primary concern as City needed their youngsters to shine. 'Mel wanted the kids in without thinking about guidance, experience, support,' remembers Peter. 'Some of the experienced players felt that he couldn't handle them. You can imagine what John Gidman thought. There was a pre-season game and John was on the coach playing cards with some of the younger lads. Now, John was a good pro who had been successful with Villa, Everton and United. He knew football but Mel didn't like him playing cards for money with the younger players. It wasn't much money and it was just to pass the time, but Mel marched down the coach: "John, you can't be taking money off these players." John turned and said: "You must be joking! If they don't want to play they won't play will they? They've got their own minds!" Mel shot back up to the front of the coach and ended up getting a couple of bottles of champagne. He gave them to John and apologised for shouting at him. For me the whole situation was wrong. First, he shouldn't have had a go at John, but secondly once he had decided to do that he had to follow through. He was the manager. I can't imagine Alex Ferguson backing down like that. The authority's gone straight away.'

Peter had a choice to stay in the reserves or to move on again: 'For a while I ended up captain of the reserves with Tony Book as the manager. I was only thirty but Mel had put me in the reserves where I was doing well. I decided I had to get away. I didn't want my career to end like that. Mel had most of the 1986 FA Youth Cup winning

team in the team and I could see what he was doing – if they succeeded it was a masterstroke; if they failed then it's only to be expected because they're kids.

'For me it was wrong. Those players were exceptional talents and they should have been protected and introduced for a few games then rested. Like Tony Book had done with me at the start of my career; like Ferguson did with Beckham and Co. later; like Pep's done with Foden... Young players are eager and keen to play but the Second Division was not an easy place for them to develop their careers. Not every week, which is what it became for some of them. The youth players became the first team and while quite a few of them did exceptionally well – Paul Simpson, Paul Moulden, Steve Redmond, David White, Ian Brightwell, Paul Lake, Andy Hinchcliffe for example – I can't help thinking that every one of them was impacted by Mel's rush to play them game after game in a tough league at a time when they needed nurturing and protecting for the future.

'Those young players got both Mel and City out of jail in 1989 when the club was promoted. I would've loved to have played with them more in 1987-88. I wanted to help nurture them through – that's how I saw my role developing, but I wasn't allowed that opportunity. There was real talent at the club amongst the youngsters. I could see that and, like all City fans, I was thrilled that they got their chances but they needed nurturing. Sadly, the City of the late 1980s was struggling financially and they were not given the time and support they needed.'

Peter went on loan to Fourth Division Bolton Wanderers on October 8, 1987 who were managed by Phil Neal. Neal told the media of his plans for Peter: 'He will play eight games for us in his loan period, and if he performs as I know he can, I will do everything to keep him.' [4] Sadly, things did

Peter shoots at goal playing for Hull City v Bradford City, April 1988.

not work out at Bolton as Peter suffered an injury only ten seconds into his first home game for the Wanderers. After less than a fortnight and after only three appearances Peter was back at Maine Road for treatment.

This was a difficult time and demonstrated the fluctuating nature of a footballer's career. One minute Peter had been a member of a Manchester United team that seemed capable of challenging for the title; then he was in a relegation bound City side; and suddenly he's returning from Fourth Division Bolton injured: 'I've never taken anything for granted. Dad taught me that but it was difficult. I hardly had chance to prove myself at Maine Road. Sentiment had brought me back, but it couldn't keep me in the side. The Bolton set back was upsetting – I had really wanted to make a

permanent move and the injury scuppered that. A loan to Port Vale followed and then I had a spell at Brian Horton's Hull City.'

At Port Vale Peter made three League appearances during a loan spell starting in December 1987 but Mel Machin had refused permission for Vale to play him in an FA Cup tie in January, while the move to Hull City was a permanent transfer. Horton signed Peter on a free transfer with some reports suggesting the agreed deal would allow Peter to move on another free transfer at the end of the season. It was widely reported that Peter could move to the States to play for a major club.

Peter appeared in 11 League games for Hull, but as the summer of 1988 loomed it was unclear where he would move to next.

---

[1] 'Rush breaks the deadlock', *Sunday Independent*, January 18, 1987, 27.
[2] David White, *Shades of Blue* (London: Michael O'Mara Books Ltd, 2017), 119.
[3] Ibid., 130.
[4] 'Barnes in basement', *Manchester Evening News*, undated cutting in Debbie Darbyshire's collection.

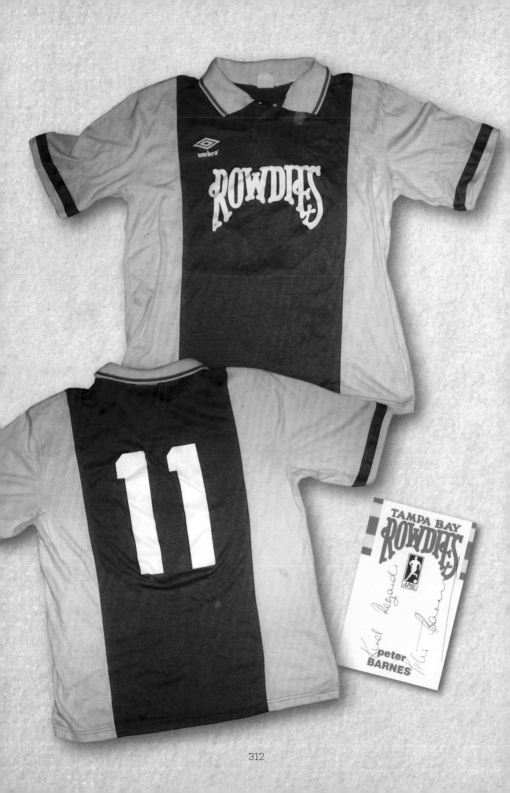

Chapter Twenty

ROWDIES AND THE REST

Former England forward Peter Barnes (33) who between 1978 and 1982 was capped 22 times, has joined yet another club. Barnes is playing in American soccer for Tampa Bay Rowdies who are based at Tampa Stadium which has a capacity of 72,000. The club is managed by another former England star Rodney Marsh (ex Queen's Park Rangers).

'It's "Bleek" for Paul', *Aberdeen Evening Express*, September 22, 1990, 7.

The period 1988 to 1990 saw Peter move to a variety of clubs with spells at Sporting Farense in Portugal, Bolton Wanderers (a second time) and Sunderland, amongst others. He simply wanted to play football for as long as he could: 'There wasn't a plan to move often but there was a strong desire to play the game as long as I could. I was only 31 when the 1988-89 season started and I felt I had more to give. I don't really count some of the clubs I played for after about 1987 because I didn't see them as permanent moves at all.'

Peter's last appearance in the Football League came on February 18, 1989 when he played for Sunderland in a 4-1 defeat at Swindon. It was his only first team game for the club, although he did play several reserve fixtures and was made welcome by manager Denis Smith who commented: 'Peter has impressed our coaches with his attitude as far as training is concerned. It looks as though he's settling in well.' [1]

'Throughout this time I worked hard to keep fit,' remembers Peter. 'I was determined to keep playing and I went from team to team. I played in Malta – flying out for games and coming back by plane straight after. I would go anywhere I could to play football and earn something as a player.

'When Danny Bergara was Stockport County manager I trained there for a while and then one day he asked me if I wanted to train the youth team. This was 1989-90. I thought about it briefly but turned him down. I didn't feel ready to give up playing for coaching. Dave Jones, an ex-team mate of mine at England youth, was eventually given that job and then fate played its part and he ended up taking over from Danny as first team manager a few years later. When that happened it caused me to think about what might have been. Maybe I should have taken the job and who knows how my post-playing career may have developed.

'I had a brief spell at Bury when Sam Ellis was there. He wanted to toughen players up by getting you to give piggybacks to other players and then running, with them on your back, up the steps of the stand. Sammy McIlroy, Jamie Hoyland and Kenny Clements were there and we used to laugh about it. I was there about a month and never managed a first team appearance.

'Sam came up to me one day and said something like: "I'm not giving you a contract Peter. Thanks for coming but I don't believe in playing with two wingers." I thought "here we go again. Another one!" As he's telling me that I can picture in my mind poor Sammy McIlroy carrying Kenny Clements on his back up the terracing and chuckling to myself! I was probably best off out of it.

'The Bury physio was Wilf McGuinness, the former United player and manager. He used to make us laugh. When Sam went out of the room Wilf would join us in laughing at his ideas. He'd be giggling: "Hey, Sammy. Can you imagine if Sir Matt had've tried to get Bestie to carry Bobby Charlton like

Barnes stocks up

By BOB RUSSELL

● FORMER England golden boy Peter Barnes completed a 13-club trek yesterday by moving to his home-town club Stockport.

● But the 31-year-old winger was held up in a traffic jam and arrived too late from Sunderland to sign on officially.

● However, Stockport secretary John Simpson said: "Due to his delay we will make an approach to the Football League to give consideration to him completing the move.

● He arrives at the Fourth Division club rocked by the sacking of player-manager Asa Hartford on Wednesday — and angry County fans are planning to boycott Monday's home game against Torquay.

● The 38-year-old Hartford was snapped up by Oldham boss Joe Royle as a midfield stop-gap.

that?" He's a great character, Wilf, and he used to have those Trebor lollypops because he was nicknamed Kojak after the bald TV detective. He used to go out to the crowd as they chanted Kojak to him and he'd be throwing these lollypops into the stands.

'So many of us had experienced life at major, trophy winning teams, with managers who were renowned throughout football for the quality of their teams but, as far as Sam Ellis was concerned, he was the expert. One day he lectured us all about the state of our boots: "If I catch anyone coming in here with muddy boots you will be fined, so I suggest you all leave your boots outside or carry them in and take them in to the boot room." He'd be doing all of that and then Wilf would be ready to throw in a one liner when Sam left the room. It was all good fun. Despite never getting a first team game this was an enjoyable spell because of Wilf and the other lads. It was one of the funniest periods of my career and I loved laughing with them all.'

While training there Peter got a call from Drogheda United and participated in three league games for them, but his major opportunity came in April 1990 when he was approached about playing in the States: 'I was in no man's land. I didn't know whether to retire from playing or what and then I had a call one day. It was Rodney Marsh and he was the manager of Tampa Bay Rowdies. He asked me to go over and join them. My daughters were still quite young and I thought "why not?" We gave it a go. We all went over and had a condominium at

Quail Oaks, Dale Mabry. It was a lovely, private area and we enjoyed living there, but it was so warm that you couldn't train in the day. We'd train in the evenings and Rodney would come out in his kit.'

Manchester born Ken Fogarty, a former Stockport County player who went on to play for a variety of clubs in the States, was Rowdies' player-coach but these were difficult days for soccer in the country. The hype of the 1970s had long since gone and this was some time before the game was boosted by the 1994 World Cup and efforts to establish a strong league structure that would last.

'We played at Tampa Stadium, where the Buccaneers were based at the time, and that held 74,000 but on a match day we'd get about three or four thousand,' recalls

Dick and Cornelia Corbett.

Peter. 'We did get over 11,000 for a game with Orlando but I suppose that was seen as a local derby. Sponsorship had fallen away and the bubble had burst. Rodney was trying to get things going again and return the sport to the position it had enjoyed in the Seventies but the time wasn't right.

'Cornelia Corbett was the owner of the team and they were now playing in the American Professional Soccer League. Her husband had been one of the owners in the Seventies and they were both passionate about the sport. I think Dick Corbett handed the club over to Cornelia completely a few years before I went over there. Cornelia used to appear in her green Rowdies tracksuit. Rodney's car had bumper stickers on including the Rowdies one "Soccer is a

New signings Peter Barnes and Ray Hudson appear on April 7, 1990 programme cover. Rowdies beat Washington 1–0; Attendance 4135.

kick in the grass" and Cornelia had similar on hers. In fact they had similar cars – I think one of them had a green XJS and the other a white XJS. Everyone loved Rodney at Tampa because of what he'd done as a footballer there.'

Peter and Rodney had, of course, been at Manchester City together when Peter made his first team debut: 'As I'd been a young player and he was one of the established stars back then we weren't close, but I think we both knew and respected each other. Rodney was a flair player and a great maverick. I remember that game in 1975 when City played Birmingham City and Rodney nutmegged Gordon Taylor (who went on to be the PFA chief). Rodney stood there with his hands on his hips waiting for Gordon to have a go again and he then nutmegged him a second time and ran around him bow-legged! It made all the headlines and was amazing to see but it must have been a bit embarrassing for Gordon. I bet Rodney struggled to get his PFA pension off Gordon though!'

For Peter the experience of being in the States was extremely positive: 'The kids loved it and the beaches were fantastic. When we played games our players' lounge was TGI Fridays. They gave us tokens for your family and friends and that was great, but so different to England. There was a lot of patriotism around games with a singer before each match singing the national anthem.'

Peter's youngest daughter Jessica remembers her father's time there: 'I was a toddler when dad was playing in England but I do remember when we lived in Florida. I watched him train at Tampa Bay and met a few people there but I didn't really think of the significance of it or anything because it was just our normal life. Mum would take us to pick him up and we'd be waiting while they finished training, but I don't remember seeing him play competitively.'

Eloise, Peter's eldest daughter, who was six when Peter first joined Tampa was old enough to remember some of the variety

of locations and experiences the family encountered during the late 1980s: 'I can remember living in Malta briefly, going to school in Portugal and having to eat seaweed soup everyday which was horrible! I also remember having my 7th Birthday in Tampa, Florida when Dad played for the Rowdies.'

For a while Neil Swift, a friend of Peter's stayed with him in Florida: 'I'd only met Peter in 1989 but we immediately became good friends. It was a bit of a whirlwind really because I remember him getting the phone call from Rodney asking him to join Tampa Bay Rowdies. It had been a difficult period for Peter because he'd been appearing for various clubs and in reserve teams and so the chance of joining Rodney came at the right time. He went over there and then I got a call one day from Peter offering to let me go and spend some time there. His family were back in England at this point. I packed my case, said goodbye to my wife and I was off!

'I stayed about a week but I ended up taking part in coaching sessions with Peter Ward, ex-Brighton, and a few other guys. It was an incredible experience. I don't think Peter gave it his heart and soul but, after some of the football experiences he had experienced in recent years, it was a great period for him. It was a chance for him to enjoy playing and I loved the fact that he'd asked me to join him for a week or so.'

Neil had a great time there and felt the whole experience was a positive one for both him and for Peter: 'I was sad to leave but, thanks to Peter, I got to meet Rodney

Marsh and many of the players. It was thoroughly enjoyable and I know it did Peter some good to be involved again in that footballing environment. Peter loves football and has always wanted to play the game, so Rodney gave him that chance to play in the States for a while. On a personal level, I was delighted that Peter had given me the chance to join him for a week or so out there. It demonstrates his nature really well that he chose to give me that chance. Peter always thinks about the wellbeing of others. His first question is always about how you're feeling and he puts everyone else above himself. He's a wonderful guy and our friendship grew strong because of that.'

The man who had taken Peter to the States was of course Rodney Marsh. He was always passionate about making soccer in the USA work but he also recognised that the players that travelled over from England wanted to experience the general way of life in Tampa Bay: 'We signed some good players, including former England internationals Peter Ward and Peter Barnes, and ex-Chelsea defender Steve Wicks… When British players came to Tampa I used to tell them that I understood they were in Florida for the summer and it was OK to have some good times because there would be plenty of days off, but football must always come first.' [2]

'The quality of football played at Tampa was good but I struggled with the heat,' recalls Peter. 'There were a few oddities with the game there at that time too. You'd see the American Football markings on the pitch which I thought was odd. Everything seemed impressive at first sight - we'd get changed in the Buccaneers dressing room

Peter takes a free-kick, against the Washington Stars at Tampa Stadium with Ray Perlee, Ken Fogarty and Michael Bates.

which was massive and our kit all laid out like new - but then you'd go out and see a few fans dotted around this vast stadium. It was a shame it didn't get more fans then.

'The day after a game I'd get hold of a newspaper to see what was said about our win. In Manchester, West Bromwich, Leeds or in Spain you'd pick up the local paper and there'd always be a report, maybe even a few pages, on a game, but in the States I'd search and search the sports pages and struggle to find the report. When I did it was usually just a small write-up. That was disappointing – I expected a full back page after a thriller!'

Mossley's close-season signing, former England winger Peter Barnes, turns on the magic and turns his marker, Fleetwood Town's Matt Hilton, inside out with another run down the left. Picture: Calvin Palmer.

Travel for away games took some getting used to: 'We were on the road for away games. They called them back-to-back and we'd be out of the state for a week or so playing say in Boston and New Jersey. We'd be travelling for a few days.'

Despite the differences this was a great experience overall for Peter: 'It was a lovely place to live but soccer wasn't quite there. We actually went out to soccer camps and did sessions for children in the area. Mostly it was girls and soccer was more their sport than boys. For me, it doesn't matter whether you're male or female, football's a great sport and it was enjoyable to see so many girls playing the game there then.'

For the Rowdies the season ended with nine wins and ten defeats and they finished second in the league. Peter's time there went mostly as planned: 'We always knew it would be six months and then that's it. It went really quickly. When I came back I knew that my age and style of football would work against me. I knew I was still powerful over ten yards but I suppose some of my pace may have gone, although I felt I still had something to offer.

'I played for a few non-league clubs when I came back, like my dad's old club Stafford Rangers. It meant something that it was my dad's old team and the lads there were great. I enjoyed it. I went to Mossley because of Eric Webster, an ex-City player and Stockport County manager. I just wanted to carry on playing. Often I was asked as a favour or I knew someone at a club. I was at Northwich Victoria, Mossley, Radcliffe Borough… I was keen just to play.'

[1] 'Owers set for big comeback', *Newcastle Evening Chronicle*, March 3, 1989, 24.
[2] Rodney Marsh, *Priceless: The Autobiography* (London: Headline, 2001), 145.

Chapter Twenty-One
FINDING A NEW ROLE

"

Former England winger Peter Barnes has taken temporary control of Runcorn following the sacking of John Carroll. Barnes, whose most recent role has been in the youth coaching set-up at Manchester City, will run team affairs.

'Barnes in the Runcorn spotlight', *Liverpool Echo*, November 28, 1995, 48.

"

Once 33 year old Peter returned from Tampa Bay he had spells at Northwich Victoria, Wrexham, Radcliffe Borough, Mossley and Cliftonville in the couple of years that followed. These were hard times as both he and his family had to adjust to life without the routine of a professional footballer engaged with a Football League team. Peter remembers this as a difficult period: 'I achieved so much early in my career – City, the League Cup, the PFA award, England… And then suddenly it's over and that's hard. When you're wrapped up in it you don't always stop and think about the great players you're playing alongside or the great clubs you're at. You live it at the time but it all happens so fast and then it's over. I had no training for a life outside of football at all. That didn't happen

back then. Fortunately, players today are encouraged to think about what will happen when their career ends.

'When I was a player I did think about moving in to management or coaching but I kept putting off making plans because I wanted to be a player for as long as possible. I loved playing and to me that's what football's about. Dad used to say to me: "Play until your legs drop off because when you finish playing you'll never have that craic in the changing rooms with the other players. You'll miss the banter; miss getting ready to go out on to the pitch; miss the crowds chanting your name…"

'He was right and I kept playing as long as I could. In fact after I stopped moving around the different clubs and leagues I played in charity games as often as I could.

I played for the City old boys – the Vets – until my hip stopped me in 2019. I just wanted to play football.'

That philosophy was similar to the great Manchester City manager Joe Mercer, who played for Arsenal until he was 39 and only stopped then because of a broken leg. Afterwards he missed playing and famously commented, when he was working as a journalist before joining Manchester City in 1965: 'Working as a journalist is a poor substitute for being a manager. And being a manager is a poor substitute for being a footballer.'

When the playing days end it can be mentally demanding but it can also be difficult in other ways too. Peter: 'Financially, it's tough as well. I had a mortgage and, of course, the family. My daughters were growing. These are stresses everyone has but it's the transformation from a player earning a decent amount to suddenly someone without a role. That's the tough part. You get used to a certain standard and then you realise you need to think about finances carefully. I came to a brick wall. That's it. I was finished as a player. What am I going to do with my life? It was not easy and it affected me quite badly. I did get a small pension thanks to the PFA but, at the time, it wasn't enough for a growing family and a large mortgage.

'Many footballers don't know what to do when they come out of the game. I speak with lots of players and they have no idea what to do. It's a difficult time. From a mental wellbeing point of view it's difficult. It's horrible how things can change. You go from being idolised to nothing. The euphoria of being idolised; having large houses; lots of money… when all that comes to an end it affects players mentally. Dad used to say that only 1% of ex-players stay in the game, so you've got to wonder what happens to the rest.'

This was an extremely difficult period and those that knew Peter felt for him. His friend Neil Swift had known him for a couple of years by this point: 'A good reason why we're such good pals today is that I didn't meet him when he was a stellar star… at his peak. I met him when he was in, I suppose, the twilight years of his career. There was his time at Tampa but other than that it was really a few days at this club and then a few at that club. Often to help a friend out or do someone a favour. That was difficult for him but, Peter being Peter, he just wanted to play football and help out his friends.'

Family remained important to Peter, especially his daughters Eloise and Jessica. Eloise, who had been born when Peter was at Real Betis, cannot remember seeing her father play football professionally but she does look back on that period of family life with great affection: 'I remember Dad getting in trouble with my Mum for leaving his kit bag in the hallway where my baby sister could get to it and we found her shaving her face with his razor! I was spoilt rotten, having every toy possible in my playroom. I had an electric Rolls Royce that stayed in the family until my cousin ran it under a car. We used to go on walks with our family dog, Heidi, who was bought as a guard dog after my Dad and Mum got burgled.'

Peter's family meant everything but, as his professional playing career ended and he was faced with the problems of trying to find a new role his marriage to Alison also came to an end. 'There was his family separation and his divorce which added to his woes,' remembers Neil. 'This happened around the same time as his football stopped and that was hard for him. He was going into a dark place and I just happened to be there. He stayed with me during some of the dark days and we became very close.

Peter with former Leeds teammate Frank Worthington.

These were really painful times for him and, I know Peter won't go into a lot of details about this, but he was extremely low. It was a terrible time. He's a very sensitive man.'

Divorce can be difficult for everyone involved and when there are children it can be particularly hard. 'There were strains on our relationships and suddenly me and Alison parted. The pressure mounts and you no longer have the role you expected. We got divorced. She was in the fashion business and moved to Italy. Our girls, Eloise and Jessica, went with her of course and that was tough for me. It was devastating actually. It affected me quite badly at the time the way my life had changed. I'd had what I saw as a wonderful playing career; we were living in a large house in Altrincham; Eloise had passed her eleven plus and was going to Grammar School; my youngest daughter Jessica was

at Prep school; everything seemed fine then within what seemed like a short period of time my playing days were over; I was getting divorced and my children were in Italy. I only got through it because I had such a close knit family with my sisters, brothers and parents. They supported me, as did Neil Swift.

'I moved out of a five bedroomed house in Bowden to live back at my mum's. I was there for about eighteen months. It was hard but, these days, I look back and think about the years of marriage I had. It was a good marriage overall. We went all over the world together and had our two lovely daughters. It was a special time and my daughters are wonderful.'

Neil felt for Peter throughout this time: 'It was really sad to see. Can you imagine what it must have been like for him to leave this footballer's house in Altrincham with

322

Peter, during this period, with a souvenir from his England days.

his belongings in a black bag and then to go to his mum's house. He had to move back into his old bedroom. No disrespect to his mum but how awful must that have been? His world had flipped on its head. It really upsets me to think about that and I know it was an extremely difficult time for Peter. He worried so much about his girls too. He stayed with me for a while and he was flitting between his mum's and my house. Eventually Peter was able to get a mortgage and move to his current home. I saw my role as one to help him get back to a position where he can take on the world. I wanted him back out there facing everything.'

Peter's eldest sister Susan was concerned for his welfare during this time: 'Peter's mood deteriorated after his wife moved to Italy with his daughters. His confidence went completely and it was a difficult time

for him. Peter made every effort he could to see his children but in terms of time, cost and everything else it was tough. Emotionally it affected him really badly of course, but then there were the financial problems. He had to sell their house and he ended up living back at mum's. Peter went really downhill but he has some good friends who helped.'

Once Alison and his daughters moved to Italy Peter struggled: 'I missed Eloise and Jessica. I used to get over to Italy as often as I could but it's not the same as living with them – or even living in the same country.'

It was inevitably difficult for his daughters. Eloise remembers: 'My parents split up when I was 11 years old and it was a tough time for all of us. We moved to Italy when I was 13. I missed him while I lived away. When he first came he used to stay in Umbria. Then he used to stay near where we lived. They got to know him at the hotel and used to give him room 7 or 11 as they were his old numbers.'

'Dad used to come over to Italy as often as he could to see me and my sister,' says Peter's youngest daughter Jessica. 'It was difficult being so far apart. Some of my Italian friends' dads knew who Peter Barnes was and they talked about him, telling me about some of his games. It was a strange part of my life because when we first went over I couldn't speak Italian but then I did my schooling and growing up there.

'When dad was leaving it was always difficult and emotional because you knew it would be several weeks, maybe a couple of months, before he would be able to get back over again. In between he'd phone us or he'd send letters – which I still treasure to this day. He even sent some faxes. I've always kept the letters and in them he'd tell me what he's been up to and he'd ask about school. They were lovely.

'I feel a bit guilty now that when I was in Italy at the age of about 17 I'd have my dad and other family members come over to see me, which was great but then you'd want to go out with your mates. Now, at my age, I realise that my dad came over to see me and there was me saying "I'm off now dad. I'll see you tomorrow" and I'd be going out with my mates. He was over for a week or ten days and I'd be going out with my friends! Now that I'm a mum I feel bad about it and realise the efforts he'd gone through to get there. He never showed any disappointment and

always said he wanted me to be happy and to see my friends but he must have been upset.'

Being so far apart was difficult for both Peter and his girls but Peter tried to make the most of the situation. He eagerly looked forward to seeing his daughters and also managed to get to catch up with another former Manchester City player from time to time in Italy: 'There was a former City player called Dennis Fidler, an ex-winger from years before me. I was sat at a United ex-players' dinner and I think it was Carlo Sartori who mentioned that Dennis lived in Italy, not too far from where my ex-wife and daughters were.

'My daughters were about twenty

10   GOALS, Monday, November 20, 1995

Where are they now?

PETER BARNES
ex-Man City and England

PASS IT OVER . . . Peter Barnes is now coaching kids

Wing ace insuring kids are all right

By VIKKI ORVICE

PETER BARNES had never planned for his future outside football.

So when he quit he took up selling insurance rather than face life on the dole.

He admitted: "When I finished playing four years ago I did not have a clue what to do. Football had always been my life.

"Most players do not plan for the future although it is such a short career.

"A few clever ones look to do something

FACT FILE

FULL NAME: Peter Simon Barnes.
BORN: June 10 1957, Manchester.
CLUBS: Man City (twice), West Brom, Leeds (twice), Real Betis (Spain), Coventry, Hull, Man Utd, Farense (Portugal), Bolton, Sunderland.
CAPS: 22 full England apps, 4 goals. 3 England Youth apps (1 goal), 9 Under-21 apps (2 goals).

been a lot of bad coaching in the last 15 to 20 years. We are creating players who are like robots who cannot think for themselves.

"Kids today do not practice with the ball enough. They are too busy stuck in their bedrooms playing with computers."

On Saturdays Barnes is back at Maine Road as a match commentator for Picadilly Radio, and last year he did a training course with Bass breweries with the aim of running his own pub.

But he admits he would still prefer soccer

there two seasons with

minutes from Florence and Dennis was about forty minutes away, so I went over. I flew into one of the Rome airports and I hired a Fiat Punto. These were the days before satnav and I had no idea where I was. I was tootling along from Rome up the country towards Florence. Dennis had told me a motorway junction to get off at and he said he'd be waiting. It seemed to take ages to get up there and then I saw the junction, but it was almost 2am and I didn't expect Dennis to be there. I turned off and, sure enough, he was stood there. I don't know how long he'd been there but I pulled over, gave him a big hug – I think I was just glad to be off that road. It was chaotic! I can laugh at it now, but it had been pretty scary. Then he drove off and I followed him.

'After that I usually flew to the small airport at Florence but there weren't many flights there, or Pisa, which wasn't far. I tended to stay with Dennis for perhaps a day or two then I'd go to a hotel close to

where my daughters lived and I'd have five or six days with them. I tried to do it three or four times a year for about eleven years. I needed to see them because I missed them terribly and I wanted them to know I was there to support them and to help them whenever they needed it. It was always a wrench leaving. It was so hard and I know they felt it too. We'd say our goodbyes and I'd get in the car and drove off to the airport. I was numb with it all at times. I'd drop the car off and sit in the airport and on the plane thinking about it all. I'd already be making plans in my head for the next visit.'

With his family in Italy and his professional playing career over Peter searched for happiness and a new direction: 'While I was going through my divorce Steve Fleet asked me to come back to Manchester City to do some coaching for community groups at the Platt Lane complex. I really enjoyed it. We coached football of course, but also hockey and other sports at night. I'm grateful to Steve for doing that because it was such a difficult time and he gave me purpose.'

Steve Fleet is a warm, compassionate man who had been goalkeeper Bert Trautmann's understudy for many, many years. A loyal man, Steve was one of the men responsible for Peter's development right at the start of his City career. By the time of Peter's separation Steve was responsible for City's Platt Lane Complex, where community initiatives occurred.

Neil Mather, one of City's community coaches at the time and a man who entered history as the founder of Manchester City Ladies, which was later relaunched as Manchester City Women, worked alongside Peter: 'It was a joy to be sharing a training pitch with Peter Barnes. We also had Neil Young, the 1969 FA Cup final goalscorer, coaching at the time. For me, a dedicated

Blue, it was a privilege to be in their company. They didn't let the fact that they'd both scored in major trophy winning finals for City get in the way. They treated us all the same and we all learned off each other. I loved that time and it was great to see them pass on their skills.'

This period working in that environment helped Peter re-adjust but, with a family in Italy, and the financial burdens that can come with divorce and setting up a new home, this was not a job that would resolve all of Peter's issues. He needed to find another role. 'I took my B and C coaching licences and I ended up becoming the Runcorn manager on a part time basis,' remembers Peter. 'A friend called Les Jones introduced me to the chairman of the club and I was offered the job. They were struggling and it was a difficult time, happening at the same time as my divorce.

'I had the former City player Mike Lester as my number two and we did okay.

I came in half way through the 1995-96 season. I loved it. We trained Tuesday and Thursday nights with me and Mike trying to play Total Football but, most importantly, to enjoy the game.

'They had big debts and the old chairman had no money. A new guy came in wanting to invest and that was that. We had a meeting at the Bowden Hotel. They gave me a cheque for four weeks' wages, we shook hands and it was all over. I left Runcorn in March 1996. I was disappointed because the next six or so games were against teams that were struggling or that we knew we could beat. We didn't get that chance of course. I felt for Mike Lester too. He was a good coach and we seemed to have begun turning things around. The atmosphere had been good and we were all enjoying ourselves but once I was sacked that was it. It left a bad taste. I always felt that I'd be able to give young players a positive view of the game and that I'd encourage them but it wasn't to be.'

A career outside of football seemed to be the way forward: 'I tried everything', admits Peter. 'I tried selling insurance. I went on a pub training course with Bass brewery thinking that I'd go down the route many footballers go down. I tried that as a relief manager, then I had the Social Club at City for about six months but it wasn't me.

'I met a lovely man called John Conway, who is still my friend today. He was a big United fan and we used to drink in the same pub, the Orange Tree, in Altrincham. He came from County Mayo in Ireland and he helped me a lot. I went working for him. We were selling 3 and 4G astroturf pitches which was interesting for me. We worked closely with Manchester City Council putting in pitches and I did that for about seven years. We stayed good friends over the years.

'I worked for a company called United Retek who cleared contaminated land with a lad called Ian Hadfield for about five years and had a variety of roles at various companies over the years.'

Neil Swift remembers Peter's desire to be busy during the years that followed the end of his playing career: 'Peter has been keen to get involved with various businesses over the years since he finished playing. He's helped a lot of people and worked with a number of people in a variety of businesses. Some have been successful and great experiences, some haven't been, but for Peter it's always been about being involved in something and helping others.'

Although Peter put considerable effort into these roles and, being the type of man he is, helped a number of people with their business ventures, none of them were as fulfilling as a football career. Like many ex-pros adjusting to a life outside of the game, he found it tough. Peter simply wanted to play football. No other occupation came close.

Chapter Twenty-Two
SCANDINAVIAN BLUES

With his daughters in Italy, his playing career over and the opportunities for a managerial career limited, the 1990s could have seen Peter's wellbeing permanently affected. Thanks to his friends, his family and his own drive, Peter continued to look for opportunities and fulfilment from other roles. 'It was still a difficult time but I had my local family behind me and some good friends and I had to carry on. I tried all sorts of things to focus on, including selling mortgages but that wasn't me. I knew as soon as I came out of the training for it I wasn't going to do that.

'It was all about finding a new niche. I kept faith and put everything I could into any opportunity I was presented with. Then one day fate played its part.

'I was walking through Manchester city centre and I saw Brian Clarke off Key 103/Piccadilly Radio. Back then Brian was the Manchester City commentator. We had a good chat and he asked me if I would have a go with him on the radio. Brian was the one who gave me that opportunity and I was grateful for that. I started to do some of the co-commentary, summarising type of work at Key 103 and I loved it. We'd be going to City games around the country and I really enjoyed that.

'I'd started the radio work before I was manager at Runcorn and so, when I was offered that role, I had to end my Key 103 work. I suggested to Brian that he should give Gary Owen a try. I knew he'd be great doing that and like me he was looking for something to get involved with. So Gary took over my job, then when I left Runcorn I started to do some commentary work for BBC Radio Manchester with Andy Buckley and Jimmy Wagg. That was great. I loved doing that and I did that for a few years. The phone-ins were always entertaining and it was all live, so that gave us a bit of excitement. There was nothing like it and they were all great people to work with.

'When games were at Maine Road I'd see all my old friends and then, whether home or away, you'd see ex-opponents like Mark Lawrenson who were also finding their feet in the media. It was a great experience and helped me a few years later when I did some media work in Malaysia.'

The Key 103 and BBC Radio Manchester roles gave Peter the opportunity to be around football on matchdays. Of course, like most former professional footballers, Peter would have preferred to have been on the pitch but the new role allowed him to experience the environment of football once more. Peter continued to fulfil this role for several years and was present in the role commentating, along with his former Manchester United team mate Arthur Albiston, on the final Manchester derby match at Maine Road in November 2002: 'That final season at Maine Road was emotional for us all. Every game was the last in some way and so we got used to all these landmark moments as the season progressed. For those of us who played there it was emotional – as it was for all fans of course. There were memories at every corner and we'd all see the ghosts of the past. I miss Maine Road but I know that everything that has happened to City since leaving wouldn't have happened had we stayed there. The move was needed but

Peter at the original Manchester City Museum in 2003.

that doesn't change how any of us felt about leaving. I particularly felt for the fans at the time.'

Peter's relationship with supporters has always been something that he has enjoyed and he has developed strong connections with many fans over the years. At Manchester City there's one group of supporters who have had a strong connection with Peter since his early playing days: 'Thanks to Morten Andersen and his visits to Maine Road when I was a young player I suppose the Norwegian fans have always meant something special to me. Their supporters club was established in the early 1970s and they have been major supporters of the club ever since.'

The Scandinavian branch of the City Supporters' Club was established in 1974 by Nils Martinsen and Peter's father Ken became their president in 1997. According to Peter the Scandinavians used to watch training at the Platt Lane training complex and then go to the Oasis bar at the complex. Ken would often be in there with other former players at the time and he would chat with the fans. Those conversations led to him being asked to become president of the club. Tor Sønsteby, a leading member of the club for decades, explains: 'We regularly teamed up several times a season when we had our branch trips to Manchester from Norway. Ken would bring along Peter whenever he was available.

'From the late nineties they both came on an annual visit to our branch in Oslo. Our branch always have a huge party after each football season is over. Traditionally we play in a five a side football tournament against other supporter teams based in Norway, then we have our yearly supporter branch meeting, followed by dinner at night

Ken Barnes with Tor Sønsteby.

where Peter and Ken were always our main guests.

'When Ken died Peter took over the post as our Branch President. Peter is still our beloved and extremely popular president to this day. It is down to his very friendly, welcoming nature and nice manners that has made him so loved amongst our branch members. He speaks to everyone… older fans, younger ones, kids… he makes them feel welcome. City should make him a club ambassador!

'Peter still comes over regularly to see us once or twice a season. He is a very popular branch president amongst our 2500 members. The camaraderie between the Barnes family and our branch members

has been nothing but phenomenal over the years. Little did I know that the young Peter Barnes who took us all by storm with his stunning wing displays for Manchester City in the 1970s would later in life become such a close personal friend. I have many memorable moments with Peter and from a playing point of view there was his goal and display at Wembley in the 2-1 win versus Newcastle in 1976 and there was his excellent England debut in the 2-0 win against Italy in 1977.

'As a 16 year old in 1977, my bedroom was covered with City's team photos from 1968 onwards, plus two big posters - one of Blondie's Deborah Harry and the other? A huge poster of Peter.

DESK ☎ ☎ ☎

Souvenir from Norway

THE Blues received a full-page tribute for their League Cup Final triumph... in one of Norway's popular local papers. The whole page, complete with pictures, has been sent to add to our Wembley souvenirs from Nils. A. Martinsen, secretary of the City Supporters' Club branch based in Fredrikstad, which was formed in 1974.

And the members of the Norwegian branch who made the special trip to Wembley were tickled pink with their week-end . . . especially when they were allowed to drink out of the League Cup at the after-match celebrations.

Says Mr. Martinsen: "It was a highly successful trip. We would specially like to thank Mr. Frank Horrocks and the City Supporters' Club on their wonderful hospitality given to us on arriving in London. Being able to attend the buffet dance after the game, and then being able to drink out of the League Cup afterwards, was a dream come true.

"That was the third time our club has been over in the past year and you can be sure we will be over another three times before the next year is over. Please express our thanks to everyone."

Only one problem . . . we haven't been able to translate the huge article. Though the pictures of jubilation tell the story what it is all about.

Drømmen gikk i oppfyllelse på Wembley

«City-fans» fra Fredrikstad fikk oppleve stor finale-fest

Enestående velkomst i Manchester-miljøet

PÅ WEMBLEY: ARNE GLOMDAHL

Best ten-pennorth in British Soccer

YOUR City match magazine has been voted the best ten-pennorth in British soccer. That is the finding from one of the first surveys conducted on 1975-76 programme

with the City match magazine taking second place. Villa were also rated the best programme priced at over 10p.

following—cover, size, team lay-out and position within the programme, contents, value for money. Special attention was given to the last section—the club's average attendance, league position

I am still sad to this day with what happened in the summer of 79 and him leaving the club.'

The branch's support of Peter and he of them over the decades has been impressive. As has the support they've given City, not simply at matches but financially too. Tor: 'It is a fact that when City had a lot less money than today our branch helped the club to finance and set up pre season games for them in Scandinavia during the 1970s to 1990s, so in that sense we have always had a very close bond with the club.'

'Throughout his time at City Peter was simply unstoppable with his speed, balance and trickery. Two games versus Spurs needs mentioning - the 5-0 against Spurs in May 1977 when he chipped Pat Jennings and the rare 3-0 away win in Feb 1979 when Peter scored one and created the other two goals!

Peter recognises the importance of the Scandinavian Branch: 'I'm always impressed by their dedication. It's one of the oldest branches of the City Supporters' Club and they stayed loyal throughout the difficult days of the 1980s and 1990s. They spend a fortune supporting City – buying

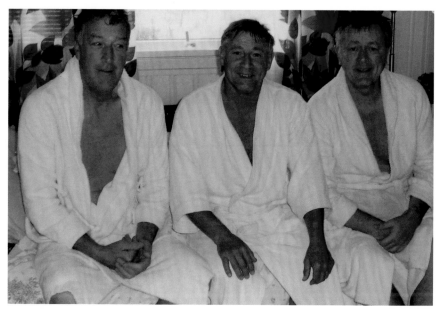

Tommy Booth, Asa Hartford and Peter in Norway.

flights, tickets, souvenirs, books… anything connected with City and they're interested.'

Typically, the Scandinavian Supporters Club branch bring between sixty and 150 members to every game. For example in 2019-20 they had 116 individual tickets sold for the game with Burnley that was eventually postponed due to Covid. That excludes those members who had their own season tickets. Similar numbers had bought tickets for the Real Madrid Champions League home leg which, when considering this was scheduled for a midweek meant that those fans travelling over would have had to take time off work and organise flights, hotels and other transport, was remarkable. Peter: 'I genuinely mean this when I say Manchester City is a much stronger club because of the dedication of supporters like the Scandinavians. This unwavering support – in good times and bad – is something I am immensely proud

of. As a player in the Seventies and Eighties I was always conscious of the effort fans made simply to attend a match and I'm sure all present day players recognise this also.

'The Norwegians have probably forgotten more about City than I'll ever know. The one thing I've learnt over the last forty years or more knowing them is that if there's a game at Halifax, Bury or Stockport County they'll come over for the City game and then try to fit in a game at a nearby ground too. They just want to make the most of their journey to England and will take in another club as part of that experience.'

During the 2020s, as Manchester City's modern day success has seen the club attract a larger volume of fans from around the globe, some Manchester based fans have been critical of those in other countries who have, in their eyes, latched on to a successful club. However, this does those non-Mancunian fans a major disservice and ignores the fact that anyone living outside of Greater Manchester who chooses City does so for reasons personal to them. As the Scandinavians have demonstrated, they are often dedicated fans who will do anything for the club they love. Peter: 'No one should ever question the loyalty of any other fan, especially not those who support the club in Scandinavia, Malaysia or anywhere else for that matter. City is a welcoming club and we should all take steps to ensure those that have chosen City are part of our family. City's been a community club all my life and that community is not one to exclude anybody.'

Peter's passion for supporters is clear. He knows that football without fans is nothing and during the 2019-20 and 2020-21 seasons he has been somewhat frustrated that fans have been unable to attend games: 'It saddens me to see major games in empty stadiums. Footballers want an audience and the football we've been seeing at City deserves to be seen in packed grounds. My old clubs Leeds and West Brom are in the Premier League and need their fans there so that they can fully enjoy the experience.'

The Covid pandemic has meant the Scandinavians have been unable to attend City matches and it has also prevented Peter from visiting fans in Norway: 'I love my trips to Norway to see Tor Sønsteby and the rest of the fans over there. They look after us well when we're there. It's an expensive country to live in - I once made the mistake of getting a round of drinks in while Asa (Hartford), Tommy (Booth) and I were over there. I'd only bought three beers and it was over twenty pounds! The cost of living is so high and when you're in a round with Tommy it can get very expensive!'

As well as regular meetings with the supporters from Scandinavia, Peter's friendship with many of the Norwegian

Peter featured in a Scandinavian United Supporters magazine.

fans has grown over the years. There are genuine, long-lasting connections there and Peter sees many of the Norwegians as an extension of his family. The first he spent some time with was, of course, Morten Andersen when both men were teenagers. For Morten work and other circumstances meant he did not make it over to Manchester for many years. In fact it was the early 2000s before he managed to meet Peter again: 'I hadn't been to City for several years and I came over with some friends of my father. After the game we met Ken and Peter Barnes. I hadn't seen Peter for around 25 years and I started to speak with him. I said: "You won't remember me." Peter replied that he did and said: "And I remember that horrible jacket you wore back then!" After that day we kept in touch and became very good friends again. Peter comes over to see us and I come to games a couple of times a year too. Thanks to Peter I also met Kevin Keegan and we are now good friends.'

Peter's friendship with Morten led to the two of them making both the front and back page of the *Manchester Evening News* in 2004. Peter: 'It was a strange time and I don't think either of us expected the media attention. Morten had been buying shares in City for many years. Every chance he could he'd buy a few shares… If he got a bonus from work that money would go into shares. This was in the eighties and nineties when, I guess, the club's shares were more likely to go down in value than up. He had an understanding family – can you imagine the discussions at home? "What, we're buying more shares in that struggling English team?"'

Morten's shareholding had grown over the years until he was the sixth largest shareholder but he still wanted to increase his holding: 'I wanted to buy some more shares but City wasn't listed on the stock exchange and so I suggested to Peter that we could meet Francis Lee and see if I could buy some off him. I wanted to get maybe 2 or 3%.'

'Me and Morten went to see Francis Lee at the Stanneylands Hotel where we had lunch together,' remembers Peter. 'Morten had known Franny since the early seventies when Morten came over to City. At our lunch he was talking with Franny about shares and it was a good chat.'

Morten: 'Francis Lee was my favourite player and I told Francis what I wanted to do. I also told him about my boss, Inge Steensland, who was a multi-millionaire. Mr. Steensland was a remarkable man and he had a good eye for investments. Franny told me that Manchester City was up for sale and he told me about the value of the club. He suggested I talk with Mr

Steensland and tell him that he could get the whole club and that I shouldn't be looking for 2% or 3% - "buy it all!" Franny has a good eye for business and I knew he was right but I didn't know what to do. I knew Mr Steensland would say no but I knew I had to mention it to him. It seemed like an opportunity. At that time buying a football club would have been like peanuts to him.'

Manchester City's major shareholders were the founders of JD Sports, John Wardle and David Makin, and they had been looking for investors. By this time even the clubs with the biggest fan bases – City were the third best supported club with an average of 46,830 (Newcastle had 51,966 and Manchester United 67,641) – could not compete financially with those clubs that had benefitted significantly from the birth of the Premier League and the development of the Champions League, such as Arsenal (a club that traditionally had a much smaller support than City). Gary Owen believes that it was the efforts of City's major shareholders that were mostly responsible for keeping City in the Premier League and at a level where they were able to survive: 'There'd have been no club had it not been for John Wardle and David Makin. No question. They kept the club afloat and poured millions into it. Without them there'd be no Manchester City and I hope everyone recognises that.'

Gary's comments are absolutely true and thanks to Wardle and Makin, together with the players and management of course, City were back in the Premier League at the time Peter was helping Morten with his quest for more shares.

'I made a presentation for Mr Steensland, telling him about the value of the club; the amount it would take to buy it and so on,' explains Morten. 'I spoke with Mr Steensland and he told me that it sounded like a good investment but he said he was too old. He was 80, almost 81, and said that most likely I was correct but it wouldn't be happening because of his age.'

That should have been the end of the matter but suddenly the story became public, much to Peter's surprise: 'We'd had a nice lunch with Franny and that was that really. Once Morten knew it couldn't progress I didn't think we'd hear any more, but then it became a bit embarrassing. I got a phone call from someone at the *Manchester Evening News*. It was quite an aggressive call: "Look Peter. We know all about it." "About what?" I replied. "Your mate from Norway who is buying Manchester City!" I was flummoxed and I said "I don't know about that. He's had shares for years but I don't think he's buying the club." I didn't know what to say. I didn't want to say anything at all.

'The call continued. "Well, we've tracked him down and we're going to call him in Norway." The *Evening News* called him and it was all embarrassing for him. His boss Inge Steensland, a self-made multi-millionaire and one of the richest men in Norway, was not happy with the publicity.'

Over in Norway Morten and his boss were suddenly faced with the media: 'Inge Steensland hated publicity and then suddenly I was on the front and back page of the *Manchester Evening News*. That day I had the whole world phone me asking me about the plans – TV, radio, newspapers… People were asking for exclusive interviews and they also contacted

Mr Steensland. It was so embarrassing, especially for my boss who really hated publicity. He came over to see me and said: "Morten, you have to learn this. When a journalist contacts you, you must say no comment and you put the phone down!" He was right.'

The *Manchester Evening News* revealed the story in its November 1, 2004 issue when it made both the front and back pages. Peter and Morten were quoted. 'Mr Steensland was not a football fan,' says Peter. 'Had he been then I think Morten may have actually been able to buy the club but, without Mr Steensland, it was never going to happen. It was a lovely story that Morten wanted to do anything to help City – and he would've helped City because he's a dedicated Blue.'

The takeover story demonstrates how, by the mid-2000s, football had moved some way off major clubs being able to challenge without significant investment and how any interest in City, no matter how great or small, would generate major coverage but also provoke the club's directors to speak with them. At the time of Morten's headline-grabbing takeover story John Wardle is alleged to have commented: 'We

Peter at an exhibition of City's history in 2002.

do need investment, so let's talk,' adding: 'I'm only too pleased to meet and discuss any investment opportunities with these gentlemen. In fact I'm looking forward to it.'[1]

Morten: 'Had Inge been younger I think he may have done it because it really was not a lot of money for him. Then he could have bought City for about £50m. His business was shipping and he used to spend about £50m on one ship. The fleet is 25 ships, so that gives you an idea of the value his business was and how much of a multi-millionaire he was. Personally, it was so embarrassing though and when I came to Manchester the next time taxi drivers and people were saying "are you the Norwegian who is buying City?" Maybe in another life, but in 2004? No.'

Ultimately, Manchester City was taken over in 2007 by Thaksin Shinawatra and then in 2008 by Sheikh Mansour. That

takeover led to the incredible level of success the club has achieved since then but at the time few could have known how everything would develop. Those who spent any time in the company of new chairman Khaldoon Al Mubarak or Chief Executive Garry Cook were left in no doubt. Peter believes he was fortunate that those leading the club in 2008 recognised the significance of history and sought to involve the former players: 'I liked Garry Cook. He took us all to Germany to watch the game with Schalke in November 2008 when Mark Hughes was the City manager. There was me, Gary Owen, Tommy Booth, Mike Summerbee, Tony Book and one or two others.

'He took us for dinner and treated us really well. We could eat what we wanted and it was a great gesture by him and the club. He then started to talk to us about the new owners – remember this was only two months after the takeover and so it

Peter at the original Manchester City Museum in 2003.

was early days when none of us really knew what to expect. He started to tell us about how they were genuine people, keen to return City to the glory days. He told us how they were going to invest, not just in the team but in the stadium and facilities. It all sounded fantastic and then he talked about strengthening the first team. He then decided to go around the table and ask us all who we'd bring in. It was wonderful stuff and you could tell then how things would change. I was so excited by it all – If only I'd been thirty years younger and could've played in the new era.'

Despite not being young enough to play for the team, Peter is of course delighted with its development: 'The way the club has been transformed is special. To me it's back to what it was when I was a young player – a major, successful club that can compete at the highest level. The level of success in recent years, particularly under Pep Guardiola, is greater and more sustained than it had been before, but it's what we all

dreamed of and felt was possible in the mid-1970s. When Allison returned in 1979 that began that process of downgrading City until we reached the lows of the late 1990s.'

As Peter implies, that period when City were unable to seriously challenge for honours in the 1980s, 1990s and early 2000s should not define the club's entire history. Manchester City was a power for most of its existence. It was the early 1970s City that Morten fell in love with and it was the dedication of fans like those in Scandinavia that kept the club going through its darkest period. Through it all Peter has appreciated the fans and they have reciprocated. Morten: 'All the Norwegians appreciate Peter's interest and involvement in them. The great thing with Peter is that you don't feel he is a footballer when you meet him because he acts like a normal person. Like you or I. He's just a normal person. He is a nice man and a great ambassador for football in Manchester.'

Peter's elder sister Susan, who has

accompanied him on occasion at events organised by Tor Sønsteby and the other Scandinavians, is well aware of the bond with Norway: 'Peter's loved by the Scandinavian City fans and he really appreciates their support and interest in him. When fans meet him and get to know him they tend to see what a nice, warm, friendly person he is.'

There is a warmth whenever Peter meets fans which his friend Neil Swift recognises: 'The thing I always say to Peter as a compliment is that it's great for him still to be loved by fans. At the Etihad Stadium he goes from box to box meeting fans… In the lounges… at supporters' events. He gets a bit bashful but it must be wonderful for him to know how much fans want to see him and talk to him. It's been years since he's kicked a ball professionally and some of the people he meets won't have seen him play but they ask him about his playing days and he enjoys telling the stories. With Peter he's remained humble whereas occasionally you'll get a former player who, perhaps, hasn't achieved as much as Peter did, who thinks they are it. Fans soon

recognise that and it's Peter they want. He's always kept his feet on the ground. He's the absolute master at making somebody feel comfortable in his presence.

'I've been with him when he's opened supporters club branches in Cyprus, Northern Ireland and elsewhere and he's great with fans. He's a great person to listen to and he comes across so well. He treats everyone the same. He cares. My own children think Peter is an uncle because of the way he's interested in them. Remember how your grandad would sneak a few pence into your hand when he visited? Well, Peter's been like that with my kids: "here's a pound, put that in your pocket." He's just a nice, humble, friendly bloke who doesn't boast about his career. You wouldn't know he played because he doesn't promote himself. He's just a lovely guy.'

[1] 'Norwegian in for Blues', *Manchester Evening News*, November 1, 2004, back page.

Chapter Twenty-Three
MALAYSIA

"
It's not just Manchester City who have been
signing world-class talent. Our FourFourTwo TV show,
hosted by Jason Dasey and Jay Menon, has swooped to pick
up ex-England internationals Tony Cottee and Peter Barnes
joining former Australia striker and in-house pundit Abbas
Saad in the Astro studios... Barnes, one of a select few to
have played for both Manchester clubs, has re-located to
Kuala Lumpur to help his family's junior football scheme.
A decade ago, his late father Ken set up the Ken Barnes
Soccer Skills Academy to develop budding
Malaysian talent.

'Who needs the octopus', *Astro Sport Press Release*, September 2010.
"

In 2000 70-year-old Ken Barnes established a football academy in Malaysia. 'Dad strove to try and give young Malaysians an opportunity. My half-sister, Karen, is out there and her and dad worked hard on establishing the soccer schools. Dad used to go over every summer and he would help and encourage young players. He'd try to bring some over for experience at City, United or Wigan.'

As Peter mentioned, Karen was living in Malaysia, running a dance school, and their dad Ken was a frequent visitor, but by 2010 his health was failing. Peter: 'Dad had fallen in Macclesfield and had broken his femur and damaged his hip. As part of his recovery him and his second wife June went over to Malaysia. Dad went to see a doctor while he was over there and they discovered that the operation in England hadn't been successful and a pin had come out of his leg, so he was in permanent pain. Within a week he'd been operated on and was recuperating.

'As I'd not seen dad for a few weeks I decided to fly over to Malaysia and see him and Karen. I'd been over there before with Denis Law to promote dad's soccer school and I liked the place.

'In Malaysia, I started to think that because I didn't have a role I could get my teeth into back home then it might be worth

Denis Law with Peter.

staying out there a while and see if I could do something on TV. Dad encouraged me to stay and thought it would be a great opportunity. Karen knew someone and I ended up getting an interview at Astro Sport TV. Astro was like the BBC of Malaysia. I had an interview with Jason Dasey, who was a presenter there. Within a few days I was offered the job, starting in August 2010. The experience of working for Key 103 and BBC Radio Manchester helped enormously.

'I hadn't actually planned to stay over there when I caught my initial flight. I was just going for a holiday and to see dad, but it all moved so quickly. I had to fly home to sort things out and then planned to come back for August. Dad also flew back to England but he passed away that July. I was in two minds about going over there once dad had died but I did. I stayed there for about three years, living with Karen, coming back and forwards.'

Peter was one of the original in-house pundits when Astro SuperSport secured the Premier League rights for Malaysia and Brunei for the 2010-11 season and he enjoyed the experience from the start. He was also popular with Astro's staff and viewers. Presenter Jason Dasey explains: 'Peter is a good mate and I really enjoyed our time together in Malaysia. It was a pleasure working with him on Astro's Premier League coverage for those three seasons and we were lucky to have him. For someone with such an impressive background, Peter was incredibly humble and brought the kind of English footballing pedigree that is hard to find in Southeast Asia.

Jason Dasey, Kay Murray, Didi Hamann and Peter in the Astro Sport Studio.

Jason Dasey and Peter, broadcasting at the 2013 FA Cup final between City and Wigan.

'He was the ultimate professional to work with, a sharp dresser who was always on time, and shared some wonderful stories about his time playing for England and at big clubs like Manchester City, Manchester United and Leeds United. He even had a stint in La Liga, which added to his credibility! The time difference meant that we would normally start work around 8pm in the evening and go through until 3 or 4 in the morning, covering game after game. Spending so much time together, we all became great mates.'

'It was a wonderful job and I love working in the media,' recalls Peter. 'We had some great times at Astro and I loved it all. It was great living in Malaysia too. I covered Champions League and Premier League football while I was at Astro and I was working that day in May 2012 when City

won the League against QPR. Our presenter Jason Dasey was a QPR fan.

'As the main presenter Jason's getting messages though his earpiece of what's happening around the grounds. He keeps directing us from the news at Sunderland to City and I'm having to comment on City losing 2-1. It's not looking good at all and I'm thinking "Typical City" as it looks like we'd blown it. Jason tells me City have equalised then he starts to speak about United's game just ending: "We're off to Sunderland now where it looks like Manchester United have won the League. Alex Ferguson is on the pitch and he's going to the players."

'I'm so fed up with City's failure. I hated that moment but, as they're showing the scenes from Sunderland, Jason leans across and says "Peter, Aguero has scored!" I jump up and Jason announces to the viewers: "We're going straight to Manchester now, where City have scored!" I can see on the screens the scenes from City with fans going crazy in the stands and the celebrations. It was superb. It was about two in the morning in Malaysia but I wanted to celebrate. Jason says: "Peter, your team has won the Premier League title 2012 and we've got a surprise for you… We want you to end the show tonight by singing Blue Moon!" I asked them to join me and I ended the show in probably the most embarrassing way by singing "Blue Moon… Yoooou saw meee standing aloooone!" I didn't have a clue what I was doing as this is going live all over Malaysia.'

Jason Dasey: 'Although Peter played for the Red Devils, he was 100 per cent a Blue. So when Manchester City won the 2011-12 title in the most dramatic of circumstances in the final seconds of the season, denying

Sir Alex and United, Peter broke into a rousing rendition of Blue Moon at the end of our show. I'll never forget this usually restrained gent singing at the top of his lungs in our studio at Petaling Jaya at 3 o'clock in the morning.'

'After the game I rushed to get the makeup off and by the time I'd come out almost all the production staff had gone,' says Peter. 'I think the people behind the scenes mostly supported United – it was like a ghost town. I jumped in a taxi and went to a bar where I'd agreed to meet a guy called Eric Kite, who was a United fan. I walked in and he had a bottle of wine waiting. He shook my hand and congratulated me on what City had achieved – I appreciated that, coming from a United fan after what had happened that day.'

Peter appeared on various in-house shows for Astro, including FourFourTwo, Football Overload, Bola@Mamak and

Kevin Keegan joins the Astro Sport team.

Stadium Unplugged. 'You put Peter on a TV network in Norway or Malaysia and he's blessed with the ability to ease into those situations and he's so worldly,' says Peter's friend Neil Swift. 'I've been with Peter in Norway, Malaysia, Portugal, Spain and so on and he's always been a warm, social, personable man. He's good on TV, radio… he's got all the positive attributes you want from a former footballer and from a man. Plus he's got that back catalogue of experience too. It baffles me why he's not on Sky TV or similar now because he knows his stuff and knows how the media works. There are not many like that on TV at the moment.

'He'd be a great asset for Manchester City or any of his other former clubs if they're trying to promote themselves in countries that Peter has a connection to – or anywhere else for that matter. He's a great role model and ambassador. He knows influential people in Malaysia for example and is so at ease in these situations.'

According to Jason having Peter as a member of their presenting team was a major boost to the channel: 'Peter always got on well with the visiting pundits that came out from the UK. It was fun to have Peter Barnes and John Barnes as pundits on the same night. John shared that Bobby Robson used to call him Peter by mistake in his early years in the England squad.

'But the highlight was when Kevin Keegan made it out to Malaysia to join our punditry team for a week. Kevin and Peter were teammates with England in the late 1970s and got on like a house on fire. I don't think King Kev would have come all the way to Southeast Asia if not for Peter's presence.

'Outside of the studio, Peter carried

The soccer school in Malaysia.

on some of the good work of his father Ken Barnes as a coach for underprivileged Malaysian kids, especially those from the Tamil Indian communities on the outskirts of Kuala Lumpur. Peter could still play himself of course! We got him out on the pitch a few times and caught a glimpse of that sweet left foot, and some of the jinks and tricks of his renowned wing play.'

Peter enjoyed his time in Malaysia: 'I'd catch him sometimes enjoying a cappuccino and a chat in the trendy Bangsar area of Kuala Lumpur,' remembers Jason. 'Peter was always very friendly and approachable and would take an interest in you.'

The life seemed to suit Peter and he tried to develop the football school while he was out there. Neil Swift visited him in Malaysia: 'He spent a lot of time out there and I think his intention was to inherit and then develop his dad's established soccer school. I think Karen had done a lot of the marketing and so on. I have this lasting memory of turning up at a field on the outskirts of Kuala Lumpur and Peter getting me to take the names of the kids that turned up for the football session. I struggled with

the names a great deal! There was a lot of opportunity to develop the soccer school but it wasn't an easy ride. There was some hard graft needed.'

Neil recognises that, despite the opportunities, Peter missed his family and Manchester. This is something that has been a feature throughout his life: 'No matter how much he enjoys the work, Peter misses his family and so Malaysia was just too far for him. He cannot be away from home for too long. That's at the heart of it.'

Malaysia was a positive, successful period of Peter's life thanks to Astro Sport and, of course, the soccer school. Sometimes eighty children would attend the sessions there. Peter: 'The kids were always polite, calling me Mr Peter. It struck me how dedicated they were. There was immense poverty there but they were always smiling and looking for the positives. It was a great experience and while I was over there I visited a group of City fans in Jakarta. I travelled as much as I could and enjoyed my time over there, but I missed my family and wanted to come home.'

Chapter Twenty-Four

FAMILY AND THE PRESENT

❝

Manchester City legends are dusting off their boots and taking to the field to help the daughter of one of their old team-mates raise thousands of pounds for charity. Former England and Blues star Peter Barnes will lead out players including Eric Nixon, Asa Hartford and Steve Redmond in support of Warrington Hospital's neo-natal unit. His daughter Eloise and her husband Jack Leighton lost their baby son Alfie when he was stillborn at the hospital in September last year.

❞

'Manchester City legends team up to back hospital',
Manchester Evening News, July 27, 2013.

Peter returned to England in 2013 but football continued to play a significant role in his day-to-day life. By this time the hospitality offering at Manchester City had increased with several former players now employed to provide a greater experience for fans. Peter had fulfilled this role off and on for several years but his return to Manchester allowed him to be a presence from 2013-14 through to the Covid pandemic in 2020.

Former team mate Gary Owen, who is the club host in the Cityzens Suite, explains: 'Peter goes around the lounges with other former players. I know he's not always the

most comfortable at introducing himself but if he's going around with Tommy Booth he doesn't need to worry. If Peter comes into the Cityzens where I am I usually do an interview with him. Once Peter gets into a conversation he's great. He's very polite. Everyone who meets him likes him – I can't say the same for myself of course!

'Peter's a great person. When the two of us were first playing for City with people talking about us having a telepathic relationship I think we clicked because we each had our strengths and it all worked well. Footballers are like ships in the night, but Barnsey and I were different. We weren't

Peter, his daughters and his grandchildren in 2021.

just footballers who played together we were friends too. When he was in Spain it was difficult to keep in touch – the days before the internet and all of that – but whenever he was in England our paths would cross. You didn't see each other often because he'd be in Leeds and I'd be at West Brom, but at the end of your careers you start to see each other more often. He was doing radio and I was doing radio; then there'd be stuff at City; then we both end up working at the Etihad on match day and so it goes on.'

The matchday work has ensured a regular pattern to Peter's week and has enabled him to stay within football. Peter loves being around the game and, as demonstrated by his time in Malaysia and on radio in Manchester, he is comfortable in this footballing environment. He has also been able to show his daughters his

world. They returned to England with their mother in 2008 and the close proximity has enabled him to see them as adults but also them to see different aspects to his life. 'I've appreciated my dad more since being back in England,' explains youngest daughter Jessica. 'It's a little surreal really. I have my dad who comes and sees me every week. He's a lovely, wonderful human being, who is kind, grounded and normal. Then I go to the Etihad Stadium and to everyone else my dad is Peter Barnes, the former City and England player.

'I then get to see what that side of his life is like and who he meets. You end up rubbing shoulders with all sorts of people. I remember being whipped off to meet Noel Gallagher and it's such a strange world but within that my dad's still the same person. He's still grounded and he'll talk to anyone.

'If I've not been to the match he'll call me to tell me what's happened and there's always a comment like 'I met Johnny Marr today' or 'I was talking to Liam Gallagher' and it is so surreal for me. He's my dad. It's lovely.

'Dad gives you time and asks you how you are. I've been with him after a game at City and we'll be leaving after the traffic's died down, but there will still be people hanging around, looking for autographs. Dad says "hello", signs the autograph and then moves on. He's still quite shy about talking in that environment and I think people can misunderstand that. He loves the way fans still treat him and talk to him, but he does still get embarrassed when asked a question.'

Having Jessica and Eloise back in England has been wonderful for Peter: 'When my daughters returned to England it was tough for them at first. I was pleased they were back in the country but they'd grown up in Italy and it's difficult going from one culture to another just like that

Peter with his daughters.

and being expected to fit straight in. I really felt for them but it was great for me that they were in England.'

Jessica explains how she felt at the time and the efforts Peter made: 'We moved to Warrington where my mum's family are from. It was hard coming back to a country at the age of 21 after leaving it when I was about 8. In the years in between you lose contact with your early friends and so it's like starting again but that's where dad really helped. He supported me on a mental level and understood how me and my sister felt. He offered to help us however we

needed. It was a hard time for us coming back to England but the main advantage has been that I've been able to see my dad every week. He's not only my dad, he's my mate now. You can confide in him and talk about anything.'

Peter felt it was important to get his family settled: 'I helped Alison, my ex-wife, get a mortgage because I knew it would be difficult to get financial affairs sorted out when returning to England. A friend of mine was able to sort out the details and she managed to get the house she wanted. It was important to me to make sure my daughters

A Barnes family celebration: Michael, Peter, Ken, Keith, Jean, Susan and Diane.

were able to have somewhere to live. We stay in touch and that's nice. I'm sure we both have regrets and wish we could turn the clock back but you can't. We have grandchildren now and the grandchildren often see their grandparents together which is nice. The important thing is to look forward and be positive, and I think we can all do that.

'My daughters are both now married to lovely guys and have their own families, but I was overjoyed that they came back to England. Family remains important and it means so much having my daughters and their families in England.'

Neil Swift recognises the significance of having Eloise and Jessica back in the north-west of England to Peter: 'He was flying over to Italy as often as he could during their childhood. He was desperate to see his kids and make sure they were okay. Family was always more important to Peter than staying late after the game to celebrate with the players. I cannot stress enough how much his family means to him – and always has.

'These last few years, the family unit is probably as strong as ever now. His daughters are back in England and their relationship is excellent.'

Sister Susan agrees: 'Peter loves his daughters and his grandchildren. He's much happier now. When they were in Italy he worried about them. He still worries a lot about every member of his family... He rings me every single day to see how I am and to make sure everything's okay. Peter's always kept close to his family and when our mum was in a care home he used to visit her every single day. He was a really good son to her and would have done anything for mum or any member of his family.

'Peter was more like mum. Our brothers Keith and Michael both resemble dad, but Peter is very much like mum. He also looks

Peter, Tommy Booth and Asa Hartford at Morten Andersen's home in Norway.

a lot like Fred, my mum's father, and he is a lot like mum's side of the family. Peter was always very shy. He was also tidy. His clothes would be all neat and put away whereas Keith's would be all over. They were totally different. I remember Peter fainting at school when he had to collect an award. It was all a bit too much for him. He's still shy and reserved now.

'Peter often talks about Mike being a better footballer than he was. I remember seeing him play for Manchester Boys and he scored a great goal from a free kick. He had a great tactical brain, like my dad, and at primary school he used to teach everyone how to play Chess.'

Peter's family always comes first, as daughter Jessica explains: 'Dad's a real family man. He always has time for his brother Mike and goes to see him every week. He's close to his sisters and has always been family orientated. He often says "You look after number one – that's your family. Family comes first." I appreciate the efforts he's made over the years. Things like the letters he used to write when I was in Italy. Think of the time and effort he put into them. I used to wait eagerly for the envelope. In it there'd be a few treats – I know it sounds silly but something as simple as an English magazine was really appreciated. It was like Christmas waiting for the letters from dad. There'd always be some memorabilia connected with City, like a match programme, and he'd talk about his week.'

Eldest daughter Eloise recognises that family remains Peter's number one priority: 'Dad visits at least once a week to come and see us and his grandchildren. He and my mum get on well these days, so we can do things together. He is an adoring grandad and moved back from Malaysia so he could be involved with his grandchildren. We have Rose (7) and Albert (2) now. He comes over every week to see them without fail and he's always asking if they need anything. He loves buying them clothes and things to do with City to wind my husband up – a Liverpool fan! Dad's teaching Rose to play chess.

'I didn't get to see him play, but I have seen him play some charity matches since we came back to England. I've shown my daughter Rose some clips of him on YouTube.'

Peter occasionally tells his grandchildren and daughters about his memories of playing football. Sometimes they come when the family least expect them. Jessica: 'Every so often dad will come in and take his shoe off saying: "My toes are hurting" and you'll see that he's got a few pains. I once asked him why he was getting so much pain and he told me all about Claudio Gentile stamping on his foot when they played against each other. He went on about the boots, the lack of protection, his blood running out of the boots and how "Gentile has given me arthritis." He definitely still suffers from that Juventus game in the 1970s!

'It's odd really. I hear people talking about Peter Barnes the footballer and what his style of play was like and then he'd be with the grandchildren just being grandad. He loves taking them out; going for walks; playing with them. My little boy is only three but it'll be nice for him as he gradually finds out more about his grandad's career.'

Thinking back to Peter's famous acceptance speech when he won the PFA Young Player of the Year award, the question has to be asked whether Peter is now more comfortable making speeches. Eloise: 'He's not so shy anymore. His speech at my wedding went well. He kept it short and sweet and he'd had a drink by then so nerves didn't get the better of him. He even had a pop at Liverpool who my husband and all his family support. He's a great networker, always meeting with people and developing contacts. He's got a good sense of humour so he's well-loved and has lots of friends. His phone is always ringing, he's very sociable. He's not your typical DIY dad, but he's got a contact for everything, so if I need any work doing he always gets someone to come and do it.'

Peter also spoke at Jessica's wedding of course: 'When I got married my dad did make a speech. It was short but very

Peter with Noel Gallagher (left) and Sergio Agüero (right) at the Etihad Stadium.

sweet and heartfelt. Although he doesn't come across as being shy I know he is, so whenever he does anything like that it really is appreciated. It probably surprises people that he is quite shy and nervous at times, yet he could go on to a football pitch in front of fifty thousand or more and be expressive.

'My son James wasn't even walking but dad was already talking about seeing whether he liked football or not. He was crawling and dad was saying "get the goalposts up". Now, of course, James is three and he's walking. Dad's often in the garden with him, kicking the ball about. James is left footed, like dad, which dad is really proud of. It would be nice if he followed his grandad but dad keeps saying that football is to be enjoyed. Dad believes it should remain fun for as long as possible and if the day comes when James is seriously interested and has the skills then we'll see. But, above all else, dad insists football must be fun.'

There has been tragedy in Peter's life over the last decade with his grandson

Alfie dying in 2012. Alfie, Eloise's son, was stillborn in September 2012. Jessica: 'I had to make the phone call to dad about Alfie. He was his first grandson and breaking the news was awful. It was a really difficult and dark time.'

This was, understandably, a difficult period for Eloise, her husband and the rest of the family. Thinking about her father Eloise remembers: 'He was great over Alfie. He came over to Warrington on the night Alfie was born, and he came to the hospital every day over the 6 days we were there - I got an infection following the emergency c-section so had to stay in. It's hard for a father to see his child in pain like that so he spent his time telling us daft stories and making us laugh. He really helped us get through the worst week of our lives, which was probably the worst of his life too.'

Although the pain of that period was severe, Peter was impressed with the staff at Warrington Hospital where Eloise was: 'He was struck by the level of care we received from the staff at Warrington Hospital and

Peter with Simon Bower, a major supporter of the City Veterans, both ready to play in a charity game.

The City Vets in Spain.

was adamant that we should do something to raise money for them. So Alfie's Match in memory of Alfie was born. City Vets played against the Warrington Hospital football team. My brother in law, Ian and I organised it to be a fun day for all the family so we found a venue with plenty of space and had market stalls, memorabilia, raffles, some rides, archery, birds of prey, guide dogs and a climbing wall.'

Eloise was pleased with the way the charity event, which was held on July 28, 2013, went: 'Dad and Derek Partridge organised the City team and got Moonbeam to turn up. City won 3-0, Jeff Whitley played out of his skin and scored two. A competition winner scored the other one, it was a dream come true for him. A hectic but great day and a really proud achievement for all of us. We raised over £8000 on the day and with other donations, we managed to purchase a state of the art wireless foetal monitor for the labour ward at the hospital. It was a fitting tribute to our son.'

Jessica remembers the efforts the family made for this special day, remembering Alfie and raising funds for the hospital: 'It

was a glorious day and a fantastic turnout. Dad is always keen to do things like this with the former players to raise money for charities that make a difference. Dad always says how lucky we are that we're healthy and he always carries that attitude with him.'

As well as Alfie's death there was also the death of Peter's mother, who was living close to him at the time of her death. Throughout Peter's life he has sought to help others and he has always tried to find an inner peace: 'I'm not a church regular but I've always wanted to make sure my mind is settled. When Gary Owen and I were first at West Brom we were taken around by a relative, Dave Sheppard. He's on the board of Bromsgrove and he took us into the jewellery quarter of Birmingham. We popped into a shop there and I bought a gold crucifix, which I've worn ever since. I don't think there's anything wrong with being a bit spiritual. You don't have to go to church every Sunday for it to matter. I've always had belief and hope. Whenever I go to a city I always try to visit a local church. I'm a frequent visitor to Chester and there's a church there, Saint Peter's, which I often visit. I like to sit in there for a few minutes and think about things. Churches are so peaceful. I think it's about having belief.

'My dad wasn't very spiritual but everybody's different. When I went to play for Real Betis I used to sit in the cathedral there at Seville. A beautiful building. These buildings make you contemplate your life and the events that you're going through at the time. When I used to go over to see my daughters in Italy I would visit the Duomo in Florence and I travelled to Assisi too. I've also been to Lourdes and I've always tried to think about spiritual wellbeing.'

Peter with his mum Jean, shortly before she passed away.

Of course, Peter's greatest spiritual wellbeing has always come from football. He's most happy when he's involved in the game and, second only to his family, it's football that drives his daily life. Until 2019, when problems with his hip meant he could no longer play, Peter was a regular for the Manchester City Veterans' team. 'Peter loved playing football and never wanted it to end,' says Susan. 'He was still playing for the City Vets until he started to have problems with his hip. He first felt it during one of their games. I think at one point Peter was the oldest playing and it used to amaze me sometimes when I saw who they were up against. Quite often it would be young lads but Peter and the others would beat them. They used to let the ball do the running for them and they'd use their skills to pass to each other and win by tactics I guess.'

Neil Swift knows how significant the Veterans team was for Peter: 'He always wants to be in the mix of football and so the City Vets team was so important to him. He loved being in the dressing room. He loved the camaraderie. I think he also kept the Vets going for his dad's sake. It wasn't an easy role to have pulling together teams of former players. People would pull out at the last minute, often without letting him know. Some didn't take it that seriously and,

for someone like Peter who believes that when you commit to something then you deliver, it was tough at times. He never likes to let anyone down and I think he remained involved because of the efforts his dad had made all those years before with it.'

'I became involved with the Vets when I was about 36,' recalls Peter. 'Frank Carrodus ran it then with support from Allan Grafton. Then me and Allan took it over with Derek Partridge getting involved later on.'

It was hard work at times but Peter enjoyed the experience of being around football in some form or another. 'I think he misses football and so he is very pleased and proud to do his matchday work at City as he is with his work with City Vets,' says Eloise. 'He loves being around the ex-players, reminiscing and talking about football and meeting the fans, particularly ones who remember him playing.'

In the late 2010s Peter began to notice a few extra aches and pains while playing. His hip had been plaguing him for some time until he had an operation in 2019. It was a difficult time as he missed the camaraderie of the dressing room and his appearances for the City Vets but, as 2020 began, he was looking forward with renewed vigour following his operation. Neil Swift: 'He had the problems with his hip, then when he had his surgery he was like a new man. We went out to Cyprus and he did a few charity events out there – he's brilliant at that. It was a new lease of life but then when we were back in England he contracted Covid-19 fairly early on.

'He was in a difficult spot and was very poorly, but he got through it.'

2020 and 2021 have been difficult years for most of us and Peter is no exception: 'It's been really hard for us all. I've missed the football. Missed meeting up with family and friends. We were stopped from doing so many of the things we loved and that was hard for us all. I know some can say football's only a game but think of all those who enjoy football because of the social life and friendships it brings. I've really missed going to games and meeting up with fans, former players and friends. It's been a difficult time for us all.'

Despite losing the routine of life and being prevented from meeting friends, family and experiencing the normality of football, Peter has tried to support his family and friends however he could. Eloise recognises that his strengths have been evident throughout this difficult period: 'He is a very positive person and likes to keep us happy and motivated, particularly good in a pandemic.'

Jessica believes that Covid has brought Peter some challenges: 'Dad is someone who can't sit down and do nothing. He likes to keep his mind active and thinking about things he can do. He sets himself goals. It's been difficult because of Covid, but before the lockdowns dad used to take James to the Etihad and show him off to everyone. Dad's been taking him into that world since he was very young.

'Dad loves being at City on matchdays or when he's doing the legends tours. It is still a really important part of his life. It's his passion. I know it's been difficult for him at times to find another role or occupation that will keep him active and interested. It's hard for footballers to be passionate about another career when they've lived a football life, and I know some do feel lost. Dad's had a number of activities he's been involved with but, if we're honest, football still means so much to dad. Once Covid struck dad really missed going to the games. He's lived and breathed it all his life and being something like a pub landlord, for example, wouldn't excite him.'

Peter does like to be out and about, meeting people. Neil Swift says: 'Some mornings Peter is on the phone to me at 6am: "Neil, the sun's out let's go for a bike ride." The two of us respond well to the sun. If it's out we're full of life and keen to make the most of the day. We can take the world on when it's a day like that. But, when it's raining or gloomy it's the opposite! We go out cycling a lot and Peter's quite handy at golf. His ball to eye co-ordination is superb and if he put his mind to it he'd be a great golfer. I enjoy my time with him and we have a lot of common interests. I could trust Peter with my life and my family.'

The last few years have brought a few challenges but Peter remains the humble family man he has always been. He loves his family; enjoys his football; and likes to contribute wherever he can. Although he is still the man who doesn't seek the spotlight, he is much more comfortable now than he was during his playing days when working in the media or meeting fans on matchday.

Thinking about the present Peter is excited by the football Manchester City have been playing in recent years: 'Today's football is fantastic and I'm so pleased that City have now gone through a decade of regular, sustained success. It reminds me of how we felt in the Seventies or how it felt at United during the opening months of the

1985-86 season. Before City's takeover in 2008 it seemed like only United, Arsenal or recently Chelsea could win the title. Since the investment in City, the game has opened up more with, of course City, Liverpool and Leicester each winning the title and others getting into a position where they could challenge. Back in the 70s any one of ten teams could win the League, then it became limited to two, possibly three. People say football's all about money and that's true to some extent but we now have more teams seriously challenging than we did in 2008.

'I'm delighted that we've had several of my former clubs in the Premier League in recent years. Obviously City and United but also Leeds and West Brom. I'd love these all to be permanent fixtures there because they've each been trophy winning giants that deserve to play at the highest level.

'It pleases me that City have invested so much money into facilities. The City Football Academy is incredible and, looking to the future, I'd like to see all clubs place an emphasis on developing good quality players and also coaches. If the investment is placed there, then our future as a strong footballing nation would be secure.

'Oh, and on a personal level, I really want to see every team bring back attack minded wingers! Let's attack and not hold back.'

A few telegrams from Peter's career including one from 'Mr and Mrs Owen and Gary'.

358

THE PETER BARNES FOOTBALL TRAINER

Throughout his football career, particularly during his international years, Peter was frequently asked to put his name to advertising, newspaper and magazine articles and products. Often he would turn down an idea or, if he did get involved, the product or story has been forgotten over time. However there is one item he put his name to that has been remembered by many, many people over the years. In fact while researching and writing this book both Peter and myself have been reminded often about that product. It was the Peter Barnes Football Trainer.

The Football Trainer was mentioned so much that we decided the cover of this book should be based on the original packaging and advertising for the product. The colouring, heading, photo spread and general wording is all based on the late 1970s advertising.

So what was the Peter Barnes Football Trainer? Well, for those who were not around at the time, it was a football training aid that was designed to improve your skills. Basically, any football obsessed youngster would hope that the Trainer would turn you from a struggling player who can't get into the school team into an international star.

How did it do this? Well, the Trainer was a ball attached to a piece of elastic that would then be clipped on to your shorts waistband. You'd kick the ball and the elastic would bring it back to you. To the average eight year old this sounded incredible. However, it didn't always work the way it ought to do. Over the last year we've heard stories of the ball being kicked so far that the elastic brought it back with a force that hit the unsuspecting child. Others talked of the elastic snapping. Occasionally, there was embarrassment when instead of bringing the ball back, the force of the kick would mean the elastic would pull the kicker's shorts down or rip them.

Peter: 'I used to get parents stopping me in the street asking for their money back. I didn't make it, I just put my name to it. I'd hear lots of stories about it. Some kids got it working really well and were happy with it, but others struggled. I was always being asked about it. It was a bit of a sensation at the time and got a lot of interest. I was even asked to go on to the BBC's Blue Peter.

'I went to the studios in London and had to demonstrate it. Somehow I did enough with it to make it work but it was so surreal. I was wearing an Adidas top and jeans and across the studio was Joan Noakes with the dop Shep. He was a bit of a Blue Peter legend. They both were.'

Peter's involvement in the product had come through a toy company called Peter Pan Playthings which made several leading toys of the era: 'I'd been approached about having my name attached to the Trainer and I went down to Peterborough to meet with them. They told me what they were planning to make and offered me a decent fee at the time and I thought it sounded good. The trouble was people thought I made it. I'd get people saying "you know your Football Trainer? Well, the elastic snapped as soon as my lad used it." If I saw someone playing with one in a park I'd turn and go the other way in case they wanted me to show them how to use it!

'I was always being asked where someone could buy one from. I remember that they sold it at Makro, a cash and carry in Eccles, and so I'd tell people about that, but they may have sold it in Woolworths too. I'm not certain how well it was distributed but a lot of people have told me they had one.'

The Peter Barnes Football Trainer gradually disappeared from shops over the years and Peter thought he'd seen the last of it many years ago but in recent years a similar product has been launched using the name of Lionel Messi. Advertising for the new product explains: 'Now you can practice doing keepie-uppies, flicks, tricks and ball control using the official Lionel Messi Pro Training Ball'

Peter: 'The Messi Training Ball has a grip handle that you hold instead of fastening to your shorts. Maybe they learned something from the Peter Pan version. There are others which have belts and all sorts of means of fastening to the child. I'm not certain whether any of them work as well… er, the same… as the one with my name though.'

If anyone reading this does still have their Peter Barnes Football Trainer then please get in touch. It would be nice to reunite Peter with one.

As well as the Football Trainer, something else Peter was involved with that has been highlighted by several people while we have been writing this book is Peter's series of articles for *Scoop* magazine. *Scoop* was produced by DC Thomson, the same company that produces the *Beano*, and Peter did a weekly column for a couple of years beginning in October 1978. The feature talked about key moments in Peter's career but, primarily, he gave his view on leading football issues of the day. He also answered readers letters. The feature was ghost written with Peter approving the content: 'I enjoyed the experience and tried to ensure I always added something personal. For example, in the first issue I talked about Maine Road but didn't just focus on the team. I talked about the groundsman Stan Gibson and how important he was. I also discussed the Junior Blues. All of these things mattered to me.

'Fans obviously want to hear about the players but I think it's so important to talk about the entire City team. The people behind the scenes and so on. I liked how, when City reached the Champions League final in May 2021, Pep spoke about the journey the club had experienced. He talked of the backroom staff and those who worked in the offices. Too often people assume it's only the players or the manager that are responsible for success but, from an early age, I understood that without the kit people, the catering staff, those promoting the club or raising funds and so on, there'd be no success.

'Also, everyone involved in football has to be aware of the importance of fans. The supporters help make the game an attractive spectacle and without their support clubs will die. Over the decades some directors at a variety of clubs have not recognised the significance of fans. They've assumed they'll turn up rain or shine, taking them for granted and not realising that they are the lifeblood of the game.

'Financially clubs may not rely on match day attendance in the same way they did when I was playing but without fans – as we've seen during the Covid pandemic – the game is not as attractive. That's true both in the stadium and for those millions watching on TV. Players thrive on support.

'I was fortunate in that fans, particularly at City, West Brom and United, supported me and encouraged me. I've also had fans show their frustrations and I totally understand that. It's football and, looking back, I've enjoyed my career. There have been some great highs and there have been some terrible lows, but overall, when looking back, I feel proud to have played for the clubs I did and with the players I appeared alongside.

'My dad used to say that football was a simple game and he was right. Like him, I was fortunate to have been able to make it my livelihood for many, many years. The aim of this book was to remind people of some great – and not so great – days at some of the country's greatest clubs and I would like to thank everyone who has bought my biography for their support and interest over the years.

'Football is a simple game but it is also a great game. Without it our lives would be so much poorer.'

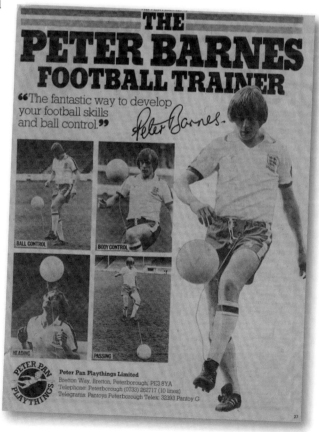

THE

PETER BARNES
FOOTBALL TRAINER

"The fantastic way to develop your football skills and ball control."

Peter Barnes.

BALL CONTROL

BODY CONTROL

HEADING

PASSING

Peter Pan Playthings Limited
Bretton Way, Bretton, Peterborough, PE3 8YA
Telephone: Peterborough (0733) 262717 (10 lines)
Telegrams: Pantoys Peterborough Telex: 32393 Pantoy G

27

Peter's grandchildren.

Subscribers

1	Peter Barnes	37	Kay-Amund	73	Per Gisle Dvergedal
2	Gary James		Almendingen	74	Yngvar Dyvi
3	Trevor Hartley	38	Jan Henning Andersen	75	Ole Morten Egedal
4	Eloise Leighton	39	Geir Andreassen	76	Svein Helge Eide
5	Jessica Barnes Pollard	40	Per Arne Andreassen	77	Brynjulv Eika
6	Susan Evans	41	Geir Andresen	78	Frank Roger Eldegard
7	Keith Barnes	42	Gorm S Andresen	79	Bent Tore Ellingsen
8	Michael Barnes	43	Stig Angelsen	80	Kåre Elserud
9	Diane Leonard	44	Ove Johan Aronsen	81	Morten Engebretsen
10	Paul James	45	John Askildt	82	Frode Schaathun
11	Gary Owen	46	Roald Arentz		Engvoldsen
12	Debbie Darbyshire	47	Anders Aune	83	Geir Engvoldsen
13	Roger Reade	48	Ketil Aune	84	Rolf Erdal
14	Neil Swift	49	Einar Barth	85	Gunnar Eriksen
15	Noel Bayley	50	Finn Erling Berg	86	Jan Harald Eriksen
16	Dave & Sue Wallace	51	Jarle Bergan	87	Sune Espersen
17	Jim Brown	52	Rune Bergan	88	Ernst Halvor Evensen
18	Colin Bottomley	53	Paal Berg Helland	89	Morten Fari
19	Pete Boyle	54	Kjetil Bergersen	90	Trond Olav Fiskå
20	Terry Christian	55	Svein R Berntsen	91	Rolf M. Flo
21	Marc Riley	56	Helge Bjerkholt	92	Gunnar Flåten
22	Morten Andersen	57	Christian Blaurock	93	Dag Roar Fordal
23	Morten Andersen	58	Roger Bollandsås	94	Ole-Jakob Friis
24	Morten Andersen	59	Erik Borse	95	Hans Petter Frøyland
25	Morten Andersen	60	Egil Botnen	96	Ole J. Fuglestad
26	Morten Andersen	61	Leiv Botnen	97	Baard Sigmund Førre
27	Scandinavian Manchester	62	Torgeir Brandtzæg	98	Halvor Gaard
	City Supporters Club	63	Leif T. Brendeland	99	Paul Tore Garvo
28	Rolf Brown	64	Wenche Bromander	100	Ingar Helge Gimle
29	KeWee	65	Reidar Bruun	101	Nils Are Golf
30	Kjetil Aanerud	66	Knut Bråten	102	Fridtjof Goyer
31	Frank Terje Aarrestad	67	Svein Ola Bråthen	103	Kjetil Gran
32	Hans Chr. Aasen	68	Raymond Chetty	104	Steinar Gravdal
33	Lars Helge Aasen	69	Morten Daae-Johansen	105	Svein Gressløs
34	Terje Aasen	70	Vegard Dahl	106	Jakob Grova
35	Steinar Aaseng	71	Erik Drilen	107	Magnar Grødeland
36	Per Arild Aasheim	72	Erik Johann Duncan	108	Per B. Grøtte

109 Jon Tore Gundhus	154 Bjørn Kaald	199 Knut E. Næss
110 Marius Andre F. Haavseth	155 Gjermund Kaldal	200 Lars Ivar Næss
111 Tom Halvorsen	156 Topias Kauhala	201 Bjørnar Oa
112 Tore Halvorsen	157 Kåre Kihle	202 Rune Oksnes
113 Steinar Hammerstad	158 Svein Magne Kjelby	203 Morten Olesen
114 Thomas A. Hansen	159 Ove K. Kjølstad	204 Andreas S. Olsen
115 Torfinn Hansen	160 Eli Klausen	205 Andreas Olsson
116 Svenn A Hanssen	161 Frode Knapstad	206 John Erik Osnes
117 Sander Harberg	162 John Arve Knippen	207 Tor Osnes
118 Magnus Hass	163 Svein Knudsen	208 Preben Pedersen
119 Espen Haugen	164 Håvard Kokkin	209 Arne Persson
120 Knut Haugen	165 Ørjan Kollsgård	210 Lars Pinderup
121 Trond Magnus Haugen	166 Jan Erik Kristoffersen	211 Kristin Omre Raknes
122 Bent A. Hay	167 Kristian Krämer	212 Erik Lohne Reiersen
123 Nina Healey	168 Tommy Kvarsvik	213 Per Arne Rennestraum
124 Ola Helstad	169 Arne Kviseth	214 Terje Rikstad
125 Knut Hermansen	170 Christian de Lange	215 Lynne Mary Rogers
126 Lasse Hirstad	171 Harald Larsen	216 Kjell Rognsås
127 Morten Piippo Hol	172 Andreas Larsson	217 Per Asle Rustad
128 Vegard Hol	173 Geir Lauritsen	218 Lars Harald Rylandsholm
129 Andreas Holø	174 Johan Berg Leonhardsen	219 Jon Rype
130 Eirik Hovland	175 Bjørn Lie	220 Jon Fredrik Rørvik
131 Paul Hughes	176 Tor Olav Lien	221 Frank Steinar Schander
132 Jan Erik Hæhre	177 Hallgeir Lillebø	222 Robert Seim
133 Halvor Hansen Høvring	178 Ove Lillestøl	223 Ola Setsaas
134 Jan Tore Håskjold	179 Sem Lima	224 Rune Setsaas
135 Morten Immerstein	180 Bjørn Tore Lindberg	225 Marius Skagseth
136 Terje Isaksen	181 Geir Henning Martinsen	226 Eivind Skjellstad
137 Svein Jakobsen	182 Nils A. Martinsen	227 Nils Skjelstad
138 Bjarne Jensen	183 Steinar Martinsen	228 Hans Petter Skjølås
139 Per Kristian Jespersen	184 Alf Magne Melkevik	229 Tor Ole Skogholt
140 Pål Jevne	185 Jon Håkon Melkevik	230 Frode Skomsøy
141 Tor Johannessen	186 Jarl Midtun	231 Jens Chr. Skrede
142 Fred Roger Johansen	187 Kurt Arild Midtun	232 Arne Solheim
143 Frode L Johansen	188 Geir Ivar Mjøen	233 Roger Solstad
144 Per Frode Johansen	189 Gerd Moan	234 Andreas S. Smith
145 Marius Johansen	190 John Helge Moe	235 Stian S. Smith
146 Vegard Johansen	191 Anne Dahle Myhre	236 Jan Sramek
147 Christer Johansson	192 Erik W. Myhre	237 Terje Stavik
148 Arne Johnsen	193 Sveinung Myhre	238 Jan Tore Stenersen
149 Bjørn T. Jonassen	194 Svein Ottar Myrvågnes	239 Mathias Stenersen
150 Ketil Jonassen	195 Terje Nansen	240 Richard Stott
151 Terje Håvardstad Jonassen	196 Ole Johan Nedrebø	241 Stein Sundsfjord
152 Espen Friis Jørgensen	197 Ove Nedrebø	242 Egil Svarstad
153 Egil Jøsendal	198 Henrik Næsje	243 Erik Svedahl

244	Knut Espen Svegaarden	267	Espen Vessang-Nielsen	290	David Blagg
245	Roar H Svendsen	268	Kai Egil Vik	291	Gary Dickson
246	Rune Inge Syversen	269	Ole Andrè Våtsveen	292	Keith Evans
247	Hans Kristian Sælen	270	Gunnar Walle	293	Michael Young
248	Tor Sønsteby	271	Geir Wingsternes	294	Nick Lowe
249	Roy Kenneth Sørdahl	272	Øystein Wolf	295	Kevin Mulvaney
250	Stein Roald Sørensen	273	Per Gunnar Østeraas	296	Graham Elliott
251	Marius Sørensen	274	Rune Østheim	297	Sid Boggle
252	Kim Kenneth Sørensen	275	Gunnar Østmoe	298	Lisa Mealing
253	Thor K Sørensen	276	Terje Åmotsbakken	299	Erika Mealing
254	Øyvind Sørheim	277	Johnny Åsen	300	Peter Wilson
255	Even Schiøll Sørlie	278	Stian Åserød	301	Francis James Cookson
256	Ronald Sørlie	279	Arne E. Åserød	302	Adam Purdue
257	Arnt Gunnar Talgø	280	Mike Jenkinson	303	Gareth Hamer
258	Marvin Taylor	281	Les Bootham	304	Steve Roberts
259	Finn Arne Thomassen	282	Alan Baxter	305	Michael Horrocks
260	Harald Thorsen	283	Mark McCarthy	306	Martin Flynn
261	Torbjørn Torgnes	284	Michael Cookson	307	Scott Corner
262	Leif Morten Trulsen	285	Ian Gregory	308	Ian Donnelly
263	Jarle Tvinnereim	286	Kevin Osborne	309	Peter McNally
264	Torbjørn Ugelvik	287	Dave Coop	310	Anthony Nolan
265	Nils J Vanebo	288	Carol Stopford	311	Ken McCarthy
266	Anne-Grethe Velde	289	John Roughton	312	Dave Masey

The City Vets present a cheque to Dr Jon Bell (Colin Bell's son), representing the Christie Hospital, in memory of former City secretary Bernard Halford in February 2020.

313 Jake Rodger	358 Paul Diggett	402 John Fern
314 Peter Dillon	359 Gary Clegg	403 Rudolph Gatt
315 Andy Conway	360 Daniel Yates	404 Michael Fidler
316 Steven Gardner	361 Joyce Darvill	405 Graeme Waite
317 Robert Thomas	362 Nigel Childs	406 Adrian Webster
318 Jonathan Meynell	363 Brian Gittins	407 Andrew Worthington
319 Mike Smith	364 Michael Baker	408 Mark Barker
320 Gordon Hyslop	365 Michael Sibbald	409 Dr Paul Ellison
321 Paul Nixon	366 Andrew Howell	410 Lance Alexander
322 Robert Harmston	367 David Connor	411 Brett Collier
323 Mark Barber	368 Tina Robertson	412 Andrew Stephenson
324 Kevin Barwise	369 Carol Beale	413 Martin Rockley
325 Nathan Rolfe	370 Paul Fowles	414 Mark Poyzer
326 Peter Foster	371 Mike Fallon	415 Toby Rose
327 David G.Hall	372 Happy 40th Birthday	416 Martin Swanson
328 Graham A.Hall	Craig Torbitt	417 Irene Henshall
329 Steve Hunt	373 Charlie Hadfield	418 Dr Richard Wild
330 Andrew Winterbotham	374 Andy Hutchison	419 Phil Banerjee
331 Paul Tuxworth	375 Nick & Mandy Bostock	420 Tina Robertson
332 Steve Rigby	376 Darren Banks	421 Steve Dale
333 Karl Lingham	377 Darren Mills	422 Karen Grayson
334 Darren Clarke	378 Andy Mills	423 Wayne Briggs
335 Andrew Wragg	379 John Baker	424 Andrew Zuill
336 Wendy & Asa	380 Bill Cronshaw	425 David and Jean Lancaster
337 Pete Tierney	381 Ian Michael Roberts	426 Allan Hackland
338 Brian Petyt	382 Roy Friend	427 Stuart Barstow
339 Ross Booth	383 Eric Heaton	428 Steve Wright
340 Steve Craven	384 Stephen White	429 Stephen Atkinson
341 Jonathan Burnell	385 Philip Goldstone	430 Rodney Stephens
342 P M Farrow	386 Roger Haigh	431 Steve Worthington
343 Martyn Hansen	387 Glen Lockett	432 Garry March
344 Mark & Janet Taylor	388 Andrew Jones	433 Stephen Hodgson
345 Mike Keegan	389 Dave Hotson	434 Ian Burns (Cases)
346 Dorothy Burgoine	390 Jeffrey McNally	435 Neil Bourton
347 Neil Mather	391 Roger Hannant	436 Darren Bourton
348 Andy Shaw	392 Tony Ford	437 George Scott
349 Steve Lea	393 Ian Humphries	438 Steven Ridley
350 Daniel Burdett	394 Mike Taylor	439 Gary Knight
351 Mark Chidgey	395 Michael Fraher	440 Stuart Hargreaves
352 Des Moloney	396 Sue Lewis	441 Savio Carrasco
353 Nigel Rothband	397 Michael McCluskey	442 Sharon Dyson
354 Helen Lee	398 Paul Richardson	443 Carole Turner
355 Lee Davies	399 Paul Barlow	444 Rob Thomas
356 Rhys Rowlands	400 Peter Croton	445 Aasif Abbasali Sufi
357 Simon Pott	401 Alistair Hay	446 Simon Robertson

447 Gary Evans
448 Steve Mackinnon
449 Guy Mowbray
450 Ray Barlow
@blackpoolbluray
451 Andrew Doherty
452 David Peers
453 Andy Hill
454 Peter Fletcher
455 Richard Donlon
456 William L Walsh
457 Mark Roberts
458 Russell Askew
459 Anthony Carroll
460 John Rowarth
461 David Roberts
462 Lee Jordan
463 Wayne "Eddie" Norris
464 Martin McNeil
465 John Hatton
466 Lynne Paigge
467 Trevor Boswell
www.citytilidie.com
468 James McMullen
469 Iain MacLean
470 Gavin Paul
471 Mark Lawson

472 Claire Robinson
473 Nathan Leonard
474 Dean Grierson
475 Marine Media Ltd.
476 Ed Stansfield
477 Alan James Whitney
478 Chris Hyde
479 Helen Drummond
480 Dave Djordjevic
481 Susan Lea
482 Steven Clarke
483 Brian Carleton
484 Rob Foreman
485 John Grimshaw
486 Wayne Reynolds
487 David Bredee
488 George Foot
489 Peter Killick
490 Howard Bootle
491 Ralph W Wilson
492 Emma Shaw
493 Steve Ashcroft
494 Paul Hayes
495 Mark Laverty
496 Richard Roberts
497 Ian Thompson
498 Andy Thompson

499 Owen Lynch
500 David Malone
501 Michael Meikleham
502 Nick Taylor
503 Richard Haddlesey
504 John Brennan
505 Mike Buckley
506 Anton Boddy
507 Nigel Swinbank
508 Lance Thomson
509 Pauline Leigh
510 David Sargent
511 Julian Yates
512 John Astbury
513 Julian Tomkinson
514 Amanda Kendal
515 Paul Slater
516 Costas Shengas
517 Steven Wilson.
518 Colin McNeillie
519 Paul Fallows
520 Dave Chalmers
Radcliffe FC
521 John Kierans
522 Donal McMullin
523 Nigel Gregory
524 Jonathan Clive Round

Gary James

Gary James is a Honorary Research Fellow at De Montfort University. He has written extensively on football since his first book was published in 1989. This is his second biography, following *Joe Mercer, OBE: Football with a Smile* which was first published in 1993. Since the 1990s, Gary has developed a reputation as a leading football historian with *The Peter Barnes Authorised Biography* being his twentieth book, following *Manchester City Women: An Oral History* and *The Emergence of Footballing Cultures: Manchester 1840-1919* (Manchester University Press), both published in 2019. He completed a PhD on the origins of football in Manchester in 2015. Much of Gary's past writing is now available at www.GJFootballArchive.com and you can follow him on twitter: @garyjameswriter or via facebook.com/garyjames4.

AUTHOR ACKNOWLEDGEMENTS

I have been working on this biography for the last couple of years. Researching, writing and, of course, interviewing Peter and others associated with his life and career. I have also returned to interviews I performed several years ago (in the early 1990s in some cases) to highlight and obtain material that has influenced the writing of this book. Over the decades I have interviewed former players, coaches, administrators, fans and others within football and have always sought to widen our knowledge of sport's history.

When Peter and I finally agreed the time was right to produce this book we spent considerable time together trying to determine how it should be written and what periods should be covered. As this is a biography, rather than a ghost written autobiography, I was keen to ensure that other voices were used to tell some of the moments of Peter's life. I have always felt that a biography offers more of an opportunity to discuss someone's career while, at the same time, ensuring that the subject is properly recorded. Peter's views have been paramount during this process and I have been keen to ensure his voice appears throughout this book.

There have been many people who have helped along the way. Of course, the main person is Peter Barnes himself. I remain absolutely delighted that we were able to work together with this book. As a young boy in 1976 I was already a regular at Maine Road when Peter achieved most children's dream of scoring in a major Wembley final. That final was a landmark moment in my support of Manchester City and it was, of course, a hugely significant moment in Peter's life. I would like to put on record my thanks for everything he achieved as a player but, more importantly, for allowing me to tell his story here. Thanks Peter.

I would also like to thank everyone interviewed, quoted or who has supported this project, and this includes Morten Andersen, Viv Anderson, Ron Atkinson, Phil Banerjee, Noel Bayley, Tony Book, Colin Bottomley, Pete Boyle, Jim Brown, Terry Christian, Steve Fleet, Ed Garvey, John Helm, Josh Langton, Rodney Marsh,

Gary James (right) with Peter Barnes in 2004.

Neil Mather, Gary Owen, Kevin Parker, Steve Rigby, Marc Riley, Tor Sønsteby, Neil Swift, Ric Turner and Dave Wallace. The wider Barnes family have also been interviewed or provided support. Thanks to you all.

As always, there will inevitably be people who I have missed or who have provided support after this page has been written. If you fall into that category then please be assured that I do value your contribution.

Particular support has come from Debbie Darbyshire, who allowed me to access and use her scrapbooks of Peter's career, and Roger Reade, who was both an interviewee and has provided support proof reading the book. Thank you both for your efforts – this book would not have reached the standard it has without you.

The aim was to capture Peter's life and career and I feel we have achieved that but I would like to stress that no publication could ever hope to capture every moment, story or influence. Peter played for a variety of clubs and it has been impossible to include every moment at every club but I hope we have managed to give you enough of a taste of Peter's life and career within this biography.

Finally, thanks for reading this book and to those who have subscribed to it. Subscribing to a book (i.e. ordering it pre-publication) helps ensure it can be published and those people who put their faith into a project like this pre-publication are a crucial part of the process. I am grateful to everyone who has supported this book in this way. Thank you so much.

Best wishes,
Dr Gary James

For more on Gary's work take a look at www.GJFootballArchive.com

Barnes in for injured Tueart

BARNES SHINES

Peter Barnes gives Revie a glimpse
of the past and hope for the future

BARNES, TUEART
CITY'S DAZZLERS

Barnes
magic
takes
award

ENGLAND YOUNGSTERS TRIUMPH

City boy gives England

Barnes a winning start

is £1½m Barnes dream debut

Italian # BARNES
target # ROCKER

Barnes nails City —City star left out again